Third Saturday in October

TENNESSEE VS. ALABAMA

Third Saturday in October

The Game-by-Game Story of the South's Most Intense Football Rivalry

SECOND EDITION

AL BROWNING

CUMBERLAND HOUSE
NASHVILLE, TENNESSEE

Published by

CUMBERLAND HOUSE PUBLISHING, INC.
431 Harding Industrial Drive
Nashville, Tennessee 37211
www.cumberlandhouse.com

Special thanks to Larry White, Sports Information Director at the University of Alabama, and
Bud Ford, Sports Information Director of the University of Tennessee, and those Vols and
Tide patriots who so generously shared of their time and memories.

Cover design by Gore Studio, Nashville, Tennessee.

Library of Congress Cataloging-in-Publication Data

    Browning, Al.
       Third Saturday in October : Tennessee versus Alabama : the game-by-game story of
    the South's most intense football rivalry / by Al Browning.—2nd ed.
       p. cm.
    ISBN 1-58182-217-0 (pbk. : alk. paper)
       1. University of Tennessee, Knoxville—Football—History. 2. Tennessee Volunteers
    (Football team)—History. 3. University of Alabama—Football—History. 4. Alabama
    Crimson Tide (Football team)—History. I. Title: Tennessee vs. Alabama. II. Title.
    GV958.T4B76 2001
    796.332'63'09761—dc21   2001042457

Printed in the United States of America

1 2 3 4 5 6 7 8 9 10—05 04 03 02 01

to the memory of Jim Goostree and Ken Donahue,
who fought gallantly for both highly respected sides in
this wonderful football series

CONTENTS

FOREWORD

ALABAMA AGAINST TENNESSEE.

Tennessee against Alabama.

It matters not which order is used when talking about those two Southeastern Conference schools. Since 1928 they have played their game (for the most part) on The Third Saturday in October.

I can say that after participating in thirty-one games on both sides of the field: more than three decades. I have participated in three games as a Tennessee player [1949–51], five as a Tennessee assistant coach [1956–60], twenty-one as an Alabama assistant coach [1964–84], and two as a Tennessee assistant coach [1985–86]. I am convinced it is the best series in the nation.

One thing is apparent: Winning the game means a lot to players from both teams. While they do not always play their best on that day, they always play their hardest. I guess it was like that in 1901, when the series got under way. I know it has been like that the last fifty years.

Nothing has changed. Tennessee has won. Alabama has won. It has been give and take for as long as I can remember.

The game has always served as a measuring stick for both teams. I played for Gen. Bob Neyland at Tennessee. He talked a lot about how the test would come against Alabama. I worked under Coach Paul "Bear" Bryant at Alabama. He talked about how we never would know what kind of team we had until we played Tennessee.

Coach Bryant thought so much of the Tennessee game that he would invite former players to practice—people like Joe Namath and Lee Roy Jordan—to tell Alabama players about the importance of winning over the Big Orange. It was always a different kind of week in Tuscaloosa before games against the Volunteers.

I have felt the same electricity in Knoxville before Tennessee plays Alabama.

The effort is always there on The Third Saturday in October.

So are the memories.

I am delighted that Al Browning, who has written columns about both programs during his twenty-nine-year career as a sports journalist, has decided to do this book. The Third Saturday in October is a golden day for many people. So will be the impact of this book that recounts the exciting and colorful story of the most glorious series in college football.

I can remember plays that could have changed the outcome of games. I can remember stories about the great coaches who have worked the games, starting with General Neyland and Wallace Wade in 1928, to John Majors and Ray Perkins. I remember the heroes. I remember the glory of winning. I remember the agony of losing.

As a Tennessee graduate, I have danced in the dressing room after Alabama victories when I coached in Tuscaloosa. As a former Alabama coach, I was ecstatic in 1985 after the Tennessee players gave me the game football after our victory in Birmingham.

There is so much to recall.

The Third Saturday in October is special. And I am honored to introduce this book by the same name.

                                                                                                    Ken Donahue

Third Saturday in October

1

Alabama and Tennessee

TEARING DOWN THE GOAL posts is an honored football tradition.

But as University of Tennessee fans celebrated victory on The Third Saturday in October in 1982, the old practice had fresh symbolism. As the goal posts fell under the weight of their jubilance, a treasured football series was lifted to its feet after a lengthy illness. The Big Orange was back. Alabama no longer had Tennessee to kick in the teeth.

Tennessee 35, Alabama 28 is what the scoreboard's neon lights glowed, and everywhere Volunteers were shouting, while ghosts of defeats past swirled in their graves, "We won! We won the game! We beat Alabama!"

That is what rang in Tennessee defensive end Mike Terry's ears as he was swarmed by orange-clad players in the end zone with seventeen seconds remaining in the game. The football was nestled in his arms after the pass interception that choked the final breath from the Crimson Tide.

It was a victory Tennessee had not enjoyed for twelve years, as Alabama had carved out an eleven-game winning streak in a series that had been known more for its wonderful stories and bitter competition that for one team dominating the other.

My, how things have changed.

Tennessee won four times in a row, including the 1982 victory. Alabama went nine years without losing on the field, with only a subsequently forfeited tie as a blemish. Tennessee enters the 2001 season with a six-game winning streak.

Also the setting has changed. Now Alabama hosts Tennessee each year on campus in Tuscaloosa, not at Legion Field in Birmingham, as the Volunteers continue to host the Crimson Tide on campus in Knoxville.

After the 2000 game, the eighty-third at the official end of a millennium, Alabama had a modest 42-34-7 advantage in a series that had its birth in 1901—and although the game is no longer always played on The Third Saturday in October, it remains an extravaganza in the minds of fans.

It is a war of fierce intensity, and many intangibles make it more colorful than the leaves that wave in cool breezes when games are played in Knoxville and more hospitable than the annual pregame gathering of fans from both programs near Denny Chimes on the quadrangle when games are played in Tuscaloosa.

There is pride, at times too much. There is respect. And, of course, there is tradition, loads of it.

Heaven knows there are superstars who live to cherish memories too valuable to toss into the wind.

The upset in 1982, which left Alabama with a 34-24-7 lead in the series, was good tonic for Deep South football tradition. It was also what S. D. "Bull" Bayer and other Tennessee faithful had been waiting for, perhaps even surviving for.

Bayer, who was born in Tennessee, was a long-time resident of Alabama. At age ninety-two, he lived in Eutaw, a West Alabama town less than an hour's drive from the Alabama campus in Tuscaloosa.

During the summer of 1982, before the upset in Knoxville, he sat in a thickly cushioned lounge chair at his house and let his alert mind run free. And, in a clear voice that hot, humid July morning, he proudly said, "How could I be anything other than a Tennessee man? Rarely are Tennessee football people converted to other teams. Tennessee people are too loyal for that, too strong at heart, especially when it comes to that intense rivalry with Alabama. Alabama has us down now, but the Big Orange is not totally out. You just wait and see; our day is coming."

A prophetic thought? Perhaps. "I told you," Bayer said in late October, after the spell was broken.

Bayer knew something about the rivalry that exists between Tennessee and Alabama. In many ways he epitomized it, having played in two such games—1913 and 1914—and having been a focal point in one of the legendary stories about the games.

"It was brutal back then, as it is now," said Bayer, who played tackle for Tennessee.

"For instance, in that 1913 game against Alabama at Tuscaloosa, I played against a tackle named W. T. "Bully" Vandegraaff. To this day, many people contend I bit off one of his ears.

"What really happened is his ear had a nasty cut at its top. It was dangling from his head a bit, bleeding a lot. He got his ear caught on the leg of my pants a play or two later, and he got so mad about it that he jumped to his feet, grabbed his ear and tried to yank it from his head. His teammates stopped him, a manager put a bandage on it, and "Bully" stayed in the game.

"Boy, was he a tough something! He wanted to throw away his ear so he could keep playing. In all my days in football, I never saw anything like that again."

The "Bull and Bully" story says a lot about this series, which began in 1901, nine years after Alabama had made its football debut. Between 1901 and 1914 the Crimson Tide took an 8-2-1 edge in the series. The rivals then took a thirteen-year break before resuming the series in 1928.

"In 1926, when Maj. Bob Neyland became coach at Tennessee, football picked up on campus," said Bayer. "His appearance, coupled with two straight Alabama trips to the Rose Bowl [for a 20-19 win over Washington in 1926 and a 7-7 tie with Stanford in 1927], really gave the series a lot of fire. When I played at Tennessee, Vanderbilt and Sewanee were our two biggest rivals, although we had our days on the field with Alabama. In 1928, however, Alabama became the team Tennessee most wanted to beat. Unless I missed something along the way, that remains the case."

The first meeting between Alabama and Tennessee set the stage for the series. It ended with two thousand fans on the field fighting. Nothing was resolved that day. The teams played to a 6-6 tie. But Birmingham hosted a red-letter event in sports history on November 28, 1901, and wounds were opened that have never been totally healed.

The *Birmingham News* described the game:

It was a game that began with every prospect of a splendid struggle, but ended up in an unpleasant controversy, with an equal score and dissatisfaction. It was anything but an enjoyable game at times, play being entirely suspended at frequent intervals until the crowds could be persuaded to leave the gridiron to the players. After almost every down, the spectators would rush across the sidelines and form a compact ring around the struggling teams, preventing beyond any possibility any further play.

The combined efforts of a squad of policemen, assisted by a number of citizens, were of little avail against the curiosity of the majority of enthusiasts, who, forgetful of everything but that the game was in progress, rushed at will upon the gridiron, forcing officials to call time until the players could secure more room. So much time was consumed in this way that even if the teams had not become involved in an argument concerning a decision in the last half, darkness would have prevented the game being completed.

The controversy and cessation of play above referred to occurred in almost the first ten minutes of the second half, and was the result of Umpire Payne granting the Tennessee team ten yards on account of an alleged offside play of the Alabamians, the decision being contested by the Tuscaloosa boys. The ball at that time was within ten yards of the Alabama goal line, and the moment play was suspended, the spectators surged over the field and crowded around the teams, yelling and gesticulating, demanding all manner of decisions of the officials.

The Alabama team refused to continue the game if the decision was granted, and as Umpire Payne refused to change his decision, the affair was hopelessly tangled. The approach of darkness found the matter still in dispute, and further operations were impossible.

Many of the football fans who attended the game left the field sorely disappointed with the turn events had taken, and expressed themselves as being anything but pleased with the apparent mismanagement of the whole affair. It was the general opinion that a few strands of wire stretched around the field would have enabled the policemen to restrain the crowd, which, with nothing to mark the lines, naturally got as close to the teams as possible. From the first play, it was evident that the game could only be played with great difficulty, and the final finish was not surprising.

Almost every football game played in Birmingham in late years had been more or less marred by the inability of the managers to handle the crowd. The game yesterday, however, was the worst of its kind ever seen here, and it is not surprising that it is looked upon as a failure from the standpoint of clean sport.

In 1901 Tennessee, coached by George Kelly, posted a 3-3-2 record, with wins over King, 8-0; Georgetown, 12-0; and Kentucky A&M, 5-0; losses to Nashville, 16-5; Kentucky, 6-0; and Vanderbilt, 22-0; and ties with Clemson, 6-6; and Alabama, 6-6.

Alabama, meanwhile, coached by M. H. Harvey, posted a 2-1-2 record, with wins over Mississippi, 41-6; and Mississippi State, 45-0; a loss to Auburn, and ties with Georgia, 0-0; and Tennessee.

Because fans were unruly during the first game, as well as after it, the two teams skipped a season, resuming the series in 1903. In 1902 Tennessee posted a 6-2 record, while Alabama had a 4-4 season.

At Birmingham on November 26, 1903, Alabama capped another 4-4 season with a 24-0 victory over Tennessee. That win over the Volunteers, who finished the season with a 4-5 record, gave the Crimson Tide an advantage in the series that it has surrendered only once (when Tennessee won in 1960, 20-7 at Knoxville, to take a 19-18-6 advantage).

Tennessee secured its first victory over Alabama in 1904, due, in part, to the strategy of its fourth coach, S. D. Crawford, who stayed at the helm only one season. The score was 5-0, and three thousand fans watched. The scoring system was quite different than today, with a touchdown counting for five points and an extra point counting for one point.

Crawford outfitted fullback Sam McAllester with a leather belt with handles sewn on each side of it. When the fullback received the football on snaps from center, he ran forward and put a foot on the back of an offensive guard. Then J. A. Caldwell and J. H. Caldwell Jr., brothers and Tennessee halfbacks, ran forward, grabbed the handles on each side of his waist, and heaved him forward. Newspaper reports say the Volunteers covered half the field with that play en route to the only touchdown of the game.

The *Knoxville Journal* reported:

The entire Tennessee team, dispatches state, played a star game. . . . McAllester was the brightest star in the galaxy. He was the man who hurdled over the Alabama line and made a touchdown. . . . The Caldwell brothers, halfbacks, aided in throwing him over the line.

"Sam" Crawford is coach. The winning of the last game of the season was due to his training. He understands the science of the game thoroughly.

Tennessee posted a 3-5-1 record in 1904, while Alabama, coached by W. B. Blount, posted a 7-3 record.

In 1905, with twenty-one hundred fans watching in Birmingham, Alabama won, 29-0, scoring 11 points in the first half and 18 points in the second. Halfback Auxford Burks and guard T. S. Sims scored two touchdowns each for the Crimson Tide. They came after a touchdown by tackle Harvey Sartain. Halfback Truman Smith kicked four extra points.

In 1906 Alabama, 5-1 and coached by J. W. H. Pollard, defeated Tennessee, 1-5-1, 51-0 at Birmingham on November 29. Nathan Stephenson Curtis scored six touchdowns for the Crimson Tide. The six touchdowns scored by Curtis is a series record.

In 1907, as has happened many times since, the kicking game was pivotal in the battle. Playing in heavy mud, Alabama defeated Tennessee, 5-0, when guard G. W. Pratt caught a deflected Big Orange punt and ran 40 yards for a touchdown.

In 1908 Pratt starred again. He kicked a 35-yard field goal with five minutes remaining in the game, lifting the Crimson Tide to a 4-0 victory in Birmingham.

In 1909, when the series made its first appearance in Knoxville, action heated and fans went into a frenzy. Derrill Pratt kicked a 37-yard field goal that November 13 afternoon to give the Crimson Tide a 10-0 victory. He missed six field goals, but the story of the day was produced off the field.

Alabama, on its way to a 5-1-2 record, escaped with a victory. Tennessee, which finished the season with a 1-6-2 record, was saddled with another heartbreaking defeat. And a game official barely got out of town with his life.

Newspaper reports say that an angry mob of Tennessee fans chased umpire R. T. Elgin to a streetcar after the game. One fan threw a rock that struck him in the head, and other fans were off target. The assault actually started during the game, when, with Alabama leading, a Tennessee halfback made a long run. Elgin overruled the play, because of a penalty, making home fans restless.

The *Knoxville Journal* reported:

For a moment, it looked as if the game might be broken up with a riot and Elgin attacked by the crowd. But the affair was temporarily quieted and the game continued.

But . . .

Unluckily for Elgin, he got aboard an open car [after the game]. The crowd collected on the south side of the street, and Elgin moved to the opposite end of the seat, but the crowd followed around. The crowd kept threatening, and the car was slow getting started. But while jeers, cat calls, and hisses were thick, no open violence was threatened until suddenly somebody hurled a missile from somewhere in the midst of the crowd and struck Elgin on the left side of the head. It was feared at first that the blow had been more serious than it proved, and the wound bled profusely. Professor Mooney and some fair-minded and peace-loving citizens collected about Elgin to shield him from the crowd, and the car moved ahead and came to the city. But the hissing crowd followed, and Elgin was not free of his pursuers until he was safely in his room at the hotel.

The man considered responsible for whipping Tennessee fans into such rowdy behavior was professor R. C. "Red" Matthews, who was billed as "the All-American cheerleader" on campus. In his book *The Big Orange,* Russ Bebb of the *Knoxville Journal* quoted Matthews as saying on the day of the game, "If Tennessee defeats Alabama today, much of the credit of the victory should be placed on the loyalty of the student body. Through thick and thin, through galling defeat after galling defeat, the fellows on the hill have this year shown that probably no other southern university has anything on Tennessee when athletic support is considered."

Alabama and Tennessee again let their respective tempers cool by not playing in 1910 and 1911. On Thanksgiving Day in 1912, November 28, the Crimson Tide, 5-3-1 and coached by D. V. Graves, used strong defense and uncanny punting to defeat Tennessee, 4-4 and coached by Z. G. Clevenger, 7-0 at Birmingham.

In 1913, as Bull Bayer remembered, fans in Tuscaloosa had to turn on automobile headlights so Alabama could complete its victory over

Tennessee. Hargrove Vandegraaff, brother of Bully and a Crimson Tide halfback, and Charles Long kicked field goals for Alabama. The game was played on the quadrangle on the Alabama campus, "exactly where Denny Chimes stands today," according to Bayer.

"As I recall," said Bayer, "we traveled to Tuscaloosa that year in a train that was late arriving. And the train had no private quarters, just a few cars. We piled in there like cows. I doubt any of us slept more than a couple of hours before the game.

"Things were done like that in those days. At Tennessee, for instance, we played games on Wait Field downtown. It was near the YMCA, and that is where we showered and had lockers. Our lockers cost twenty-five cents each, I think, and I know I rarely got my laundry done. It cost too much to smell good in those days.

"We just showed up for games less than a hour before the first kickoff and played. There was none of this stretching and loosening up like they have today before games.

"There was some trickery involved, too. We had a special pass play we used at Wait Field. In one end zone there, there was a hill. I recall our receivers standing at the base of that hill while the quarterback scrambled, then running up on it to catch passes. There was no way a defender could get high enough to knock away the ball."

More than anything else about his Tennessee career, Bayer remembered being presented "a little gold football" after the Volunteers posted a 9-0 record in 1914. That included the victory over Alabama on October 24.

"I have fonder recollections of that victory over Alabama than the game we played against them in Tuscaloosa in 1913," Bayer said. "And I still have the football they gave us in my [safety deposit] box at the local bank.

"The game in 1914 was delayed because we protested the use of an Alabama player, a quarterback who had played professional baseball. After a lot of deliberation, they decided to pull the guy out of their lineup. The controversy set the stage for a heated battle. We went right at each other, face-to-face, and it was a tough struggle, about the toughest we had that season. And there was a lot of cursing going on, more that day, it seems, than in any other game I played at Tennessee."

More than two thousand fans showed up to watch Alabama and Tennessee play in 1914. That constituted the largest crowd in school history. When the game ended, Tennessee was well on its way to a Southern Intercollegiate Athletic Conference championship. Alabama, 5-4 that season, had a lot of time to wait for a chance at revenge.

Sadly, the next game between Alabama and Tennessee did not come until 1928, when both schools were boldly proclaiming to the nation that they had arrived as feared powers, each with growing tradition and startling pride. Maj. Bob Neyland, who was in his third year as coach of the Volunteers in 1928, was responsible for the series' resumption.

"Neyland wanted Tennessee to step into the football limelight like Alabama," said Tom Siler, the retired sports editor at the *Knoxville News Sentinel.* "Alabama had been to two Rose Bowls. Neyland thought playing them could gain national attention for his Volunteers."

The events of The Third Saturday in October in 1928 proved the coach correct.

2

Wade vs. Neyland

In 1981, JUST BEFORE the University of Alabama football program resumed its successful bid to make Paul "Bear" Bryant the winningest collegiate coach in history, Wallace Wade was telephoned at his ranch outside Durham, North Carolina. The caller wanted to know what Wade, the first great Alabama coach, thought about the Crimson Tide program as it neared what has become one of its more fabled milestones.

Wade, who coached Alabama from 1923 through 1930, posting a 61-13-3 record, thus establishing himself as the "Godfather" of the program, had been involved in an accident. At age eighty-eight, he had fallen down steps at his home and had suffered a broken collarbone. His wife, who answered the telephone that August day, was told not to bother him, that his comfort was more important than the information to be obtained.

"No, let me get Wallace for you," Mrs. Wade said. "He loves to talk about Alabama. The conversation will be good therapy for him."

In a snap Wade was on the line and talking. "Yeah, I took a fall down the steps and landed on a pile of flower pots. But, hell, I had to get down those steps some way. Falling was faster than walking."

That statement tells us something about the rugged demeanor of Wade, who is most responsible for developing Alabama football tradition. A Brown graduate, he commanded the first of what are consid-

12

ered three great eras in Crimson Tide football history, years he had under coaches Wade, Frank Thomas, and Bryant.

"A lot of success Alabama has enjoyed through the years is related to tradition," Wade said before his death during the fall of 1986. "Prestige and that sort of thing make good boys want to play football at Alabama. They want to play on good teams. They want good coaching and good leadership. They want to play good opposition. They want to win championships. Tradition is a rich asset for Alabama football. To my way of thinking, there is no other school, with the possible exception of Notre Dame, with such tradition.

"I would not go so far as saying we started tradition at Alabama, but I admit we had a solid hand in it."

Not only did Alabama benefit from the teachings of Wade— "Coach Wade was a great coach, as well as a great person," Bryant said in 1982—every football program in the Deep South was rewarded by his efforts. In 1926 and 1927 the Crimson Tide made two appearances in the Rose Bowl. A 20-19 victory over Washington in the first game ripped apart a shroud of inferiority that had blanketed football in Dixie. A 7-7 tie with Stanford in the second game solidified regional pride.

After the 1986 season, Alabama made its thirty-ninth appearance in a bowl game, a national record. Its twenty-five consecutive appearances in bowl games, 1959 through 1983, is also a record. Bryant coached the Crimson Tide in twenty-four bowl games, but Wade coached in its first three.

"Not for a minute am I about to forget the man who took Alabama to its first bowl game," Bryant said before his death during the winter of 1983. "I tip my hat to Wallace Wade. Anybody who loves Alabama football should do the same thing."

It is ironic that as Alabama made national headlines under Wade, Tennessee was coming of age under the direction of its most fabled coach in history, Gen. Bob Neyland. The competitiveness of those two men, in fact, enabled the rivalry that exists between the Crimson Tide and Volunteers to become one of the finest in the nation, ranking in prestige alongside Notre Dame-Southern Cal, Texas-Oklahoma, Michigan-Ohio State, and Army-Navy.

"Back then," said Wade, "football players smelled like men. And at Alabama we had men who acted like men on the football field."

Wade said that in 1980, while in Tuscaloosa to visit Alabama for a fifty-year reunion of a 1930 Crimson Tide team that capped an undefeated season with a 24-0 victory over Washington State in the Rose Bowl.

"Football has become a sophisticated game now," Wade said, his voice clear and his mind sharp. "It has become an art. We had strategy then, too, but it was more of a war on every play, and a man not paying attention to his business paid a price for his lapse in thought.

"In those days, a win was a good win, any win, and there were no shortcuts to earning one. There were no excuses in defeat. It was bloody at times, and because we had some wonderful foot soldiers, it was usually good for Alabama."

Wade and Neyland coached against each other three times while at Alabama and Tennessee, respectively, with Neyland winning twice. It was 15-13 Tennessee in 1928, 6-0 Tennessee in 1929, and 18-6 Alabama in 1930.

"All three of those games could have gone the other way," Wade said. "They were dramatic affairs. They were damn good football games."

So, much fanfare accompanied Wade's visit to Tuscaloosa in 1980. He was greeted by a large party of admirers at the airport Friday morning. He addressed the Alabama football team on the practice field Friday afternoon. As the highlight of the reunion, he sat with Bryant, a walking cane in his hand, at a special dinner Friday night. The eighty-eight-year-old former Crimson Tide coach upstaged Coach Bryant.

Too weary to attend the game on Saturday afternoon, Wade sat in his hotel suite and listened to an Alabama win on the radio.

While he sat there, he might have enjoyed a last laugh. Incredible as it seems, Wade was forced to move from Alabama by a proud school president, Dr. George Denny, who was apparently jealous of the strong hold the coach had over the Crimson Tide faithful.

"Coach Wade and Dr. Denny never did see eye-to-eye," said John Henry Suther, an All-American halfback on an unbeaten Alabama team in 1930, the last year Wade coached the Crimson Tide. "I can recall spats they had at practice. Dr. Denny was always nosing around the practice field, playing buddy-buddy with influential members of the alumni, and many times Coach Wade would tell him to get his fanny off the field so we could get some work done. Ultimately, that kind of behavior got Coach Wade run off from Alabama. But that decision was made before his last season at Alabama. After our Rose Bowl victory at the end of the 1930 season, they begged Coach Wade to stay.

"Coach Wade was a stubborn, ruthless sort of guy. After all these years, I still shake when he comes around. We hated that man, but at the same time we loved and respected him. Even today, if he told me to leap out of a hotel window, I'd ask him what floor he wanted me on."

As a coach, Wade was a perfectionist, a trait he shared with Neyland. He drilled his teams until they were fatigued, then called on them to take another step forward.

"He was like an army officer," said Suther.

"Anything I did as a coach, I did for the good of the boys who played under me," Wade said. "I learned the value of discipline while serving in the military. We got started in football to develop boys so they can become good men later in their lives. To do that, at least in my way of thinking, you have to win some. Fortunately, we did that at Alabama.

"My years at Alabama are dear to my heart. We had some trials and tribulations, but we had some happy football afternoons. I'm satisfied with what we got accomplished at Alabama. I'm convinced that there is a bit of old Alabama in the players who are at Alabama today. I take some pride in that."

When Wade left Alabama, he was given a wrapped gift at a gala downtown gathering in Tuscaloosa. His chief rival, the school president, was present to give him a rousing farewell toward Duke.

"I never found out what was inside that box," Wade said of his gift, "because I never opened it. I was pretty bitter at that point. I have since mellowed. I'm as proud as anybody of my association with Alabama football."

In 1955 Wade became the third of ten former Alabama coaches or players to be inducted into the National Football Foundation Hall of Fame.

Alabama has not forgotten him.

TENNESSEE, MEANWHILE, has even more respect for Neyland, who in 1925—while Wade was going about the business of leading Alabama to its first bowl game—was striking a deal in Big Orange Country that would lead him to becoming coach of the Volunteers.

Tennessee had posted a 3-5 record in 1924, and it was concluded that Coach M. B. Banks, who had joined the program in 1921, was in trouble and would need help. In an effort to bolster fortunes, Dean N. W. Dougherty wrote a letter to Coach John J. McEwan at West Point, asking if he knew of a top assistant coach who needed to make a move. He received news that Capt. Bob Neyland, a former West Point football standout at end and baseball standout at pitcher, was available for duty.

Dougherty invited Neyland to Knoxville for a visit, explained the situation, and hired him as an assistant coach. In 1925 Tennessee posted a 5-2-1 record, with much credit going to the new staff member, who had reigned as heavyweight boxing champion at West Point.

For the next nine seasons, Neyland coached Tennessee to a 76-7-5 record, lifting the Volunteers into the national spotlight. That record included only two defeats in the first six seasons, which led Dougherty to say, "Hiring Robert Reese Neyland is the best move I ever made."

After serving his country in the military, Neyland returned to Tennessee as coach in 1936 and posted a 43-7-3 record over five seasons. After serving his country in the military again, when he secured the rank of general, he again became coach of the Volunteers in 1946 and posted a 54-17-4 record for seven seasons. His composite record was a stunning 173-31-12, and in battles waged against Alabama coaches Wade, Frank Thomas, and Harold "Red" Drew, he became a nemesis for the Crimson Tide.

It is interesting that Wade, not Neyland, was the first mentioned choice to replace Banks as coach at Tennessee in 1926. That is understandable, because Wade and Neyland were alike in many ways, both having been hard-nosed disciplinarians who often ruled over their players with military-like force. They were totally dedicated to the fundamentals of the game.

"Touchdowns follow blocking as night follows day," Wade said during his final season at Alabama. "And let it be known that no man deserves a pat on the back for simply winning."

Meanwhile, at Knoxville, after making his players run the same play over and over at practice one day, and having one of them say, "Major, have we not run that play before?" Neyland rebuked Dave McArthur by saying, "Goodness, McArthur, you sound like someone looking for an outhouse in the fog."

Both Neyland and Wade were searching for the same thing, a winning edge, and they went after each other with vengeance for three seasons. In the process they produced a trio of wonderful, memorable games.

Neyland started preseason practice at Tennessee in the same manner for many years. On a chalkboard, he wrote one word: Alabama.

Lindsey Nelson knew the general well. As a Tennessee student, he was hired by Neyland to tutor Big Orange players "at one dollar per hour" from 1937 through 1939. He lived and ate in the athletic dorm.

Nelson, a sportscaster now living in Knoxville, remembers how important The Third Saturday in October was to Neyland.

"The most important thing to the general, as long as I was close to him, was beating Alabama," Nelson said. "I can remember a hotshot back coming to Tennessee in the 1930s. I said he looks like something, maybe the best who ever came in here, and Major Neyland leaned back in his chair and said, 'Yeah, but you never know about a football player until he has played against Alabama.'

"That tells so much about the importance the general put on the series. He loved it. He admired it. A lot of people feel that way about Tennessee and Alabama.

"In the early years, from 1928 through the early 1940s, it was the battle each year that determined so much, with the winner often getting a major bowl game invitation. And when the general and Frank Thomas coached the teams, it was like an extension of Army and Notre Dame. Both of them brought so much of their alma maters to the Deep South with them.

"That brings to mind another story that tells how much beating Alabama meant to General Neyland.

"For thirteen years, Tennessee scheduled Chattanooga the week before it played Alabama. That was not by accident, because General Neyland, who never missed a bet, knew Frank Thomas had coached there and there was a natural carryover in style. He knew Chattanooga, under Coach Scrappy Moore, would use the Notre Dame Box offense like the Crimson Tide was using.

"So when Thomas left Alabama and was replaced [as coach] by Harold 'Red' Drew, who used the Straight-T offense, General Neyland telephoned Moore. He said, 'Scrappy, how important is our game with you?' Scrappy told him it was the key revenue game for Chattanooga.

And, General Neyland said, 'Well, Scrappy, have you given any thought to going to the Straight-T formation?'

"Well, Chattanooga made the change, which helped Tennessee prepare for Alabama, as it always had when playing Chattanooga."

But it was "Neyland Maxims" that helped the Big Orange the most. Those were his pet thoughts on winning football, which he wrote on the chalkboard before every game.

Some of his coaching secrets:

Football is composed of nothing except accidents. The great art is to profit from such accidents. This is the mark of a genius.

It follows that all plans must be made to minimize our own mistakes, then to magnify the effect of the opponents' mistakes.

In gambling, the winner's chuckle, while the losers cry, "Deal, deal, deal." In football, the winners chuckle. The losers cry, "The breaks went against us."

What are the so-called breaks? Fumbles, blocked punts, long punt or kickoff returns, intercepted passes, short punts or kickoffs.

Almost all close games are lost by the losers, not won by the winners.

Pregame harangues, as a rule, cause more harm than good. Inspiration at zero hour is a poor thing on which a coach can rely.

So Neyland spoke calmly and methodically before games, then sat on an orderly bench and directed traffic.

"I am told by several of his former players that his secret to winning was expecting to win," Nelson said about Neyland. "He thought all action was the result of thought.

"On game day, according to Bobby Dodd, General Neyland always said, 'We will win because we are better trained, better grounded, and better athletes. And they do not have the background we do.'

"Once, according to Dodd, General Neyland stayed too long visiting with the officials before a game against Vanderbilt. So, in a hurry, he merely stuck his head in the dressing room before the opening kickoff and said, 'They do not have the background.'

"Dodd laughed. The general said, 'Why are you laughing before we are to play Vanderbilt?' And Dodd chuckled and said, 'Because you said they do not have the background we do, when they have won over us ten straight times.'

"But, Tennessee won that day, so the general was right, as usual."

Neyland would be winning today, had it not been for his retirement and death, according to his first rival on The Third Saturday in October.

"Sure, he'd still win," Wade said. "I used to misjudge him. But after all these years, I realize Neyland wasn't lucky. He was simply the best coach I ever had to go against."

In 1928, they started swapping wits.

And the tradition began.

3

1928
Tennessee 15, Alabama 13

COACH BOB NEYLAND TROMPED to a corner of Denny Field in Tuscaloosa on October 20, 1928, and struggled for the proper words to say to a group of newspaper reporters. He was emotionally drained at the end of a Saturday afternoon that had seen the Alabama campus in a frenzy.

University of Tennessee football fans—and there were many of them present that day—slapped him on the back as Alabama fans, many more, staggered into the night with their heads bowed.

The first football game played between Tennessee and Alabama since 1914 was indeed exciting. "I know we won the game, but what was the score?" Major Neyland said as sportswriters scribbled notes and Tennessee fans filled the chilled air with screams of happiness.

To this day there are few serious students of Tennessee football who cannot answer that question asked by Neyland. The score was 15-13, and those numbers are firmly entrenched in the glorious history of Tennessee football. That victory over Alabama, which had achieved national acclaim with victories over Washington and Stanford in the 1926 and 1927 Rose Bowl games, proclaimed that Tennessee football had arrived.

Jeff Coleman has attended almost every Tennessee-Alabama game since 1928, when the series moved to The Third Saturday in October. He is a former business manager and athletic director at Alabama.

20

"The Tennessee victory in 1928 got the series going," Coleman said. "It brought Tennessee up to a level Alabama had achieved with its Rose Bowl victories. No longer were Vanderbilt and Sewanee our chief rivals. After that game, Tennessee became *the* rivalry from that point on.

"I have always dreaded seeing those orange jerseys.

"Much fanfare accompanied the Tennessee visit to Tuscaloosa in 1928. Southern Railroad ran special trains to campus. We had fifteen rows of bleachers on one side of Denny Field and ten rows of bleachers on the other side. Fans without seats circled the playing field. When it started getting dark late in the game and it became almost impossible to see, fans turned on the headlights of their cars so the contest could continue."

By winning, not only did the Volunteers of 1928 lend credibility to a series brought back to life, they struck another blow for Deep South football, which, with Alabama leading the way, was finally earning respect at the national level. Tennessee served notice quickly, with fullback Gene McEver returning the opening kickoff 98 yards for a touchdown.

"Was that my biggest thrill as a player?" said McEver, who until his death lived in Davidson, North Carolina. "Well, I don't know, because there were many for me when I played at Tennessee. But it was one of the best. I don't think there's any question about that game putting Tennessee football on the map."

What McEver thought in 1928, John Henry Suther, an Alabama sophomore running back in 1928, knew at the conclusion of the Tennessee victory.

Late in the first quarter, Suther attempted a punt from his end zone—"I had never punted in my life," he said—and he dropped the football on the snap from center. Harry "Hobo" Thayer retrieved it for Tennessee outside the end zone, giving the Volunteers two points for a safety. Big points they were.

"I made a costly error," said Suther. "I've thought about that fumble a lot through the years."

In the second quarter tailback Bobby Dodd, who went on to coach brilliantly at Georgia Tech, passed to McEver for a touchdown that gave Tennessee a 15-6 lead.

"We still had hope," said Suther. "If we had quit, Wade would have killed us. And, of course, it was Tennessee we were playing."

Alabama scored a touchdown and an extra point in the second quarter, adding to the hopes of fifteen thousand or so fans, then failed to score on three serious attacks on the Tennessee goal line the remainder of the game. The Crimson Tide was therefore saddled with its first home loss since a 9-2 setback at the hands of Florida in 1921.

With its "Flaming Sophomores" leading the way, Tennessee went on to post a 9-0-1 record, a scoreless tie with Kentucky the only blemish.

Alabama, which had been humbled by a 5-4-1 record in 1927, went on to post a 6-3 record.

The Flaming Sophomores of Tennessee were led by McEver, Dodd, and halfback Buddy Hackman. In their three seasons together—McEver missed the 1930 campaign because of a knee injury—the Volunteers suffered only one loss and two ties.

"That's where the Flaming Sophomores nickname came from, the performance against Alabama in 1928," said Tom Elam, longtime member of the Tennessee Athletics Board. "The nucleus of that Tennessee team was those young folks, with McEver, Dodd, Hackman, Paul Hug, and Buddy [James Quinn] Decker starring for us.

"Hackman ran back the opening kickoff for a touchdown the following week against Washington and Lee. That's where the other nickname came from, 'Hack and Mack, the Touchdown Twins.'

"Interestingly, though, Dodd played only the first half against Alabama in 1928. He went out of the game with a kidney injury. A young fellow named Charles Reineke replaced him and saved the day. He was a little guy. They said his whole uniform only weighed three pounds."

The Flaming Sophomores were the key to the victory, with McEver, Dodd, and Harry "Hobo" Thayer, another sophomore, scoring all the points for Tennessee. In addition to running back the opening kickoff for a touchdown, McEver got another touchdown on a four-yard run on fourth down. Dodd kicked the first extra point. Thayer trapped Suther in the end zone for two points.

The second Alabama touchdown was scored by fullback Tony Holm on a three-yard run in the second quarter.

The game-opening run by McEver came after Neyland attempted psychological warfare aimed at Alabama Coach Wallace Wade. In a pregame meeting moments before the fateful kickoff, the Tennessee coach suggested to the Alabama coach that the third and fourth quarters be shortened to prevent the Crimson Tide from embarrassing the Volunteers. Wade, crafty of mind himself, said he did not think his team would win that easily, but he did concede to the request "in the unlikely event we have a halftime lead that justifies such action."

Because of the heroics of McEver, time ran out on Alabama, which on that afternoon trailed Tennessee 7-0, 7-6, 9-7, 15-7 and by the final margin, 15-13. The second half was scoreless.

The McEver run to everlasting fame?

"After our guys knocked down nine of their guys, I saw two Alabama players standing in the alley in the middle of the field," McEver said. "They were on about the 50-yard line. I went right between them, split them in half, bowed my neck and let them have it. That's all I could do. Then I was clear and running for the goal line. I don't even know if anybody gave chase."

From Suther: "In one regard, McEver was like a cannonball, literally rolling over people. Then he was like a bullet, too speedy to catch."

On the fourth play after the touchdown run by McEver, Suther, playing in his first college game, ran 45 yards for a touchdown. Fred Sington missed the extra point kick, and the Volunteers led 7-6.

"I was so pumped up that I still don't recall my touchdown run very clearly," said Suther. And, by golly, that damn McEver did it to us on the first kickoff. He went right up the middle on us for almost 100 yards. His run kind of took the zing out of us and gave them a lot of enthusiasm.

"It was a wild scene that day. The return of the series was big news in both Alabama and Tennessee. I can remember being terribly excited the week of the game. And, of course, I never considered the prospects of us losing."

Col. Tom Elam was a Tennessee student in 1928. During the summer of 1986, at age seventy-seven, the self-proclaimed "shade tree lawyer" from Union City, Tennessee, served as chairman of the Tennessee Athletics Board, on which he has sat for more than three decades.

"Everybody was scared of Alabama in those days," Elam said, starting his reflections on the 1928 victory by Tennessee over the Crimson Tide. "They were bowl people. They'd had real success with Coach Wallace Wade down there. They had had so many great names in southern athletics: Johnny Mack Brown, Wu Winslett, Pooley Hubert, and folks like that.

"I went down to Tuscaloosa with some fraternity brothers in a T-Model Ford. We drove all night long—all night long—after thinking it'd be a fruitless trip. We got there just in time for the kickoff.

"Farmer Johnson was a guard on that Tennessee team, as well as a fraternity brother of mine, and I'd told him, 'Farmer, I don't think much about the idea of going down there and playing Alabama.' He'd said to me, 'Well, Tom, I don't think much about it, either, because they're so good.'

"But I'll never forget, nor will anybody else who saw it forget, the kickoff return by McEver. There are a lot of legendary stories about it. For instance, the Alabama people supposedly said they'd get more touchdowns than we got first downs. They didn't think we'd score at all.

"It's alleged that just before the opening kickoff, some Alabama guys hopped up in the stands and said, 'I've got a thousand damn dollars that say Tennessee won't score.' It took half of Knoxville to cover it, I guess, because money was thin in those days, but the wager was made. He had barely got the words out of his mouth, and some of our sharp sports from Tennessee had covered his bet, when McEver took off on the famous run.

"When McEver got to the 50-yard line, it was school out."

It was time to celebrate for all Tennessee fans who had made a tiring and eventful trip to Tuscaloosa. They included Stewart McCroskey and some of his pals from the Pi Kappa Alpha house. On the spur of the moment, he borrowed his parents' car, with them out of town.

"We ran off the road once when there was a detour but no sign," McCroskey said during the fall of 1978. "When we got to Tuscaloosa, we got instructions from the local intelligentsia and went out into the country to get a jug of white lightning.

"We got to the field just before the eventful opening kickoff."

People in Knoxville marveled, as recalled by Tom Siler, the retired sports editor at the *Knoxville News-Sentinel*.

"Pat Roddy stood in the streets of Knoxville and relayed the play-by-play from Tuscaloosa to Tennessee fans. He used a megaphone. He got his information from telegraph operator Bob Mayer. Pat told me the fans refused to believe what was happening, that they hooted him and yelled at him as if they thought he was spoofing them.

"But it was true, and ecstatic Tennessee fans turned Gay Street into a wild scene that night. The celebration continued into the morning.

"It was important to Tennessee, no doubt about that. Early in game week, Herb Brown, a reserve guard for the Volunteers, told me Neyland had the names of Alabama players written on a chalkboard. He looked every Tennessee starter in the eye and challenged him to beat his man."

Crafty recruiting on the part of Neyland and his staff made such dreams come true in Knoxville. For instance, McEver, who earned a "Wild Bull" nickname, was signed, sealed, and delivered to Wake Forest after a fantastic career at Virginia High School in Bristol.

Alabama also recruited McEver, adding to both the mystique of the series and to Crimson Tide gloom in 1928, but nobody can describe him as a giant fish that got away like Wake Forest can. He was already in school at Wake Forest, when Neyland went to work by sending assistant coach Bill Britton to Winston-Salem, North Carolina.

"I told the Wake Forest people that I figured I'd be happier at Tennessee," McEver said in 1983. "They tried to get me to stay in Winston-Salem, but my mind was already changed. When Coach Britton told me Tennessee still wanted me, even after I had turned them down for Wake Forest, well, that made me realize how important I was to them."

McEver led the nation in scoring in 1929 with 130 points. Despite a knee injury sustained during a baseball game during the spring of 1930, he was a star as a senior in 1931. He has since been awarded a spot in the National Football Foundation Hall of Fame.

Dodd, Buddy Hackman, and Paul Hug were fetched by Neyland from Nashville, where they had already signed scholarships with Vanderbilt. Dodd, too, has been enshrined into the National Football Foundation Hall of Fame, as has Neyland.

"Gene McEver was my best player at Tennessee," Neyland said.

In 1928 The Third Saturday in October became the day of reckoning for the Big Orange and the Crimson Tide.

Why was that date chosen?

"Who knows?" said Coleman. "It was just it, *the* time."

It was "the time," for sure, for Tennessee in 1928, setting the stage for a bitter struggle one year later.

4

1929
Tennessee 6, Alabama 0

As our country struggled financially in October 1929, stock was rising in a football series between the universities of Tennessee and Alabama.

Tennessee was operating at an inflationary level, for sure.

Alabama was coming back.

Consider words written by sportswriter Fuzzy Woodruff in his "Fulmirations" newspaper column:

> Probably the most spectacular game of the year will be played in Knoxville when the mighty Crimson Tide is arranged against [Buddy] Hackman and [Gene] McEver of the Volunteers.
>
> This is emphatically a grudge battle. Tennessee, so the experts say, sneaked up on Alabama last year and won. The same experts say Coach Wallace Wade and Alabama have been pointing for Tennessee this year, determined to wreak a bloody vengeance.

Was that merely hype aimed at a Tennessee homecoming game to be played October 19 at Knoxville?

Maybe, but consider words written by sportswriter Zipp Newman of the *Birmingham News*, who was in Knoxville on the eve of the game:

> There was more football conversation here to the square foot of hotel lobby space than wire grass to the square mile back in the Alabama Black Belt. In some enthusiastic Tennessee quarters, they were offering 6-to-5 [odds] on the Vols. The defunct Avondale Bank could have covered most of it.

Rarely does such advance billing fit a fight. But it did in 1929, to the delight of twenty-five thousand fans, nine thousand of which sat in temporary bleachers and watched the Crimson Tide and Volunteers in a second consecutive ruthless, thrilling show.

Tennessee won, 6-0, thanks to the heads-up defensive play of Paul Hug, Harry "Hobo" Thayer, and McEver, the offensive craftsmanship of tailback Bobby Dodd, and the powerful running of McEver.

Something also must be said about the coaching expertise of Maj. Bob Neyland, who was spotlighted in an article in the *Knoxville Journal* the morning after the contest: "Bob Neyland is the owner of Knoxville tonight, and his generalissimo, Robert L. Dodd, is his joint partner."

At that time Jeff Coleman served as business manager for athletics. He said Alabama was ready to get out of town when the game ended.

"That's the first year I can remember us having trouble with fans on the sidelines," Coleman said. "The rivalry between the two schools was heating up, and fans were becoming a little unruly. We solicited the services of an off-duty police officer in Knoxville, who not only kept order on our bench that day, but served us in that manner for many, many years afterwards.

"There was a lot of excitement surrounding the game. We discovered that after riding a train all night and arriving in Knoxville on Friday morning.

"I remember Bob Wilson, the sports editor in Knoxville, watching a few of our boys pitching pennies at cracks in the hotel and writing about our team being a bunch of gamblers. He could be vicious.

"Tennessee players were selling their tickets on downtown streets the morning of the game. There was great demand for them. Knoxville was alive and kicking, maybe because they had beaten us the year before in Tuscaloosa, and I remember how festive everything was. They even had downtown stores decorated for the game. I imagine it was more festive after the game."

Wilson might have been in error chastising Alabama players for gambling. But after watching Tennessee make three goal line stands to preserve the victory, he wrote accurately in the *News-Sentinel:*

The real story of this heroic battle is how Tennessee hurled back three assaults which carried Alabama to the Volunteers' goal. Twice in the second half they held for downs within two yards of their goal, and, another time, they repelled a Crimson Tide attack that seemed certain to produce what would have become a tying touchdown.

Hug and Thayer teamed to make the defensive play that led to the only score in the game. In the second quarter Hug blocked an Alabama punt, and Thayer recovered the football at the Crimson Tide 40-yard line. Six plays later McEver ran over guard for six yards and the decisive touchdown.

While Dodd was magnificent in directing the Tennessee offense, maintaining control of the football to protect the lead, Alabama made a spectacular bid to score a touchdown in the final seconds of the second quarter. On a fourth-down play, with the ball resting a foot from the end zone, McEver tackled Crimson Tide halfback Leon Long for no gain on a run up the middle.

Or *did* he stop the Alabama runner?

"It's sour grapes to complain after a loss, but I've never been convinced that Long didn't score on that run," said John Henry Suther, an Alabama junior halfback in 1929. "I still think we scored a touchdown.

"The crying shame, though, is what happened to us on the third-down play in that drive. We had a hotshot lawyer from Birmingham in Knoxville with us, a big supporter of our team. He was one of those excitable types, who just happened to be working on the chain gang that day. On third down, [fullback] Tony Holm ran for what looked like a touchdown, and that idiot on the chain gang started celebrating to the extent he threw down the chain and started dancing a jig. When the officials tried to measure for a possible first down, they didn't have a chain to work with, so they just called it fourth down."

Col. Tom Elam, a Tennessee student in 1929, recalls the controversy that followed the Volunteers stopping Alabama's scoring bid.

"Holm was a big fullback, by standards then, and he looked like some Jack the Ripper character, or something as tough. He was big and strong, like a character from some fantasy land, and not the best-looking guy in the world. He almost got a first down on a third-down run.

"Maybe he did.

"The punch line is this. In those days, we put a man on the chain gang and Alabama put a man on the chain gang. Our man on there was a boy named 'Poopy' Groves. He held one end of the chain and the Alabama boy held one end of the chain. Anyway, after Alabama got the ball to a critical position, 'Poopy' caught the Alabama boy off-guard and yanked forward the chain. When the official looked at the measurement, he saw that Alabama had missed the first down by a short distance, mere inches.

"We stopped them on the next play, when they could have just as easily had four plays to get into the end zone."

Suther admitted Tennessee had the best team that year. "But maybe we were better that day," he said.

Alabama was unbeaten when it went to Knoxville, having defeated Mississippi College 55-0, Mississippi 22-7, and Chattanooga 46-0, but the Crimson Tide completed its season with a 6-3 record. Tennessee, on the other hand, defeated everybody on its schedule except Kentucky, which it tied, 6-6. In the process the Volunteers extended their undefeated streak to thirty games, with a 9-0-1 record.

"There were two profound things, I think, that enabled us to go so long without a loss during my years at Tennessee," said Dodd, who now works in the Georgia Tech Alumni Office in Atlanta. "First, we were skilled when it came to playing good defense and kicking. Those are two things General Neyland insisted upon, and he was ahead of his time when it came to coaching those aspects of the game. The other thing that helped us was skillful scheduling. General Neyland never played tough opponents back-to-back. He always had a breather for us before a tough game.

"As for Alabama, well, that was always a tough game for us. The series was coming around in those years, thanks to our 15-13 victory over Alabama in 1928, and it was always a struggle. The Alabama-Tennessee game in those years featured well-coached teams that were skilled when it came to fundamentals. I'd have to rank Coach Wade right up there with General Neyland as a teacher and disciplinarian. His Alabama teams were all great, no question about that.

"In 1929, we beat Alabama by holding them on our goal line. That came a year after we barely got by them in Tuscaloosa. I'm not so sure that Alabama didn't have stronger teams than we did both of those years. In 1930, when they beat us 18-6, I'm certain the strongest team won, because we were badly crippled for that game."

Does Dodd have a special memory from his clashes with Alabama?

"The 1928 game was special, because I think it set the stage for Tennessee to take off as a football power," Dodd said. "I know it was a game we wanted to win badly, because we had heard that Alabama players were betting that we wouldn't score on them. Well, we took care of that quickly, because McEver ran the opening kickoff for a touchdown. That gave us confidence. We had a lot of outstanding sophomores on that team, and I suspect that one game, that one kick-off, gave us the idea that we could beat anybody we played.

"To this day, I don't believe I've ever seen so many talented players on a football field as I did in Tuscaloosa in 1928."

In 1929, Dodd showed uncanny intelligence as an offensive leader. He displayed his knowledge and the ability to use it quickly just after Hug, Thayer, and McEver slammed the door in the face of an Alabama bid for a touchdown that could have been decisive. His play selection, however, gave Neyland some uncomfortable moments on the sideline.

"When we stopped Alabama in the fourth quarter, we had the ball about five inches from our goal line," Dodd said. "General Neyland instructed me to kick the ball away on first down. I knew Alabama would try to block the kick, so I told McEver to run out for a pass. I figured he'd be wide open and would score on a long run. But he didn't get off the line of scrimmage, so I heaved the ball out of bounds. The Alabama players started hollering that I had intentionally grounded the ball, which I had, and they wanted the officials to call a safety. I knew the rule called for us to be penalized half the distance to the goal, so that's what the officials did. They moved the ball back about three inches. The same thing happened on the next play, except the officials could only penalize us an inch.

"General Neyland was having a fit on the sideline, so I decided I better kick the ball on third down. Fortunately, Alabama didn't block the kick, enabling us to hold on for a fine victory."

It was games like that, victories over Alabama in 1928 and 1929, that must have made Neyland smile on his ability to recruit players. It was the recruiting process, however, according to Dodd, that kept him from enjoying a special relationship with the great coach.

"General Neyland and I never did become close associates because of the way I ended up playing at Tennessee," Dodd said. "My buddy Hug and I had both been recruited by Tennessee and Vanderbilt, and we had decided Vanderbilt was the best place for us. General Neyland didn't like that, as you might suspect, and he reluctantly accepted us at Tennessee after we decided to transfer from Vanderbilt.

"Tennessee didn't pay us [Dodd, Hug, and Hackman] to transfer from Vanderbilt, as suggested by many people. I simply decided to leave Vanderbilt because my grades prohibited me from getting into school. And even after leaving Vanderbilt, I tried to get into Georgia Tech, Georgia, and Mercer, before finally deciding that my best future would be at Tennessee."

Dodd enrolled at Tennessee on a fall day at 10:00 A.M. That afternoon, he played in a freshman game for the Volunteers.

"The rules in those days said a player couldn't move to another school after playing in a game for one school," Dodd said. "General Neyland made sure a lot of us guys played in that freshman game the day we arrived in Knoxville. That kind of secured our future there."

The relationship, of course, was warm, because Dodd and his classmates produced many memorable days for Tennessee faithful.

"We had some great victories during my years at Tennessee," Dodd said, "but we never were really aware that the school was making great strides as a national power. All we really cared about in those days was going to school, having a good time, and winning football games when they came up."

Tom Elam's memory provides a most interesting finale to this hard-fought game. "I had a good friend on that Alabama team," Elam said. "His name was [C. B.] 'Foots' Clement. He was a monster. He wore something like size-15 shoes. After the game, I went up to old Alumni Gym to visit him. That's where the opposing teams dressed in those days. Ol' Foots was sweating, still huffing and puffing, when I got there. He was so tired he couldn't get his jersey off. He looked at me and said, 'Little fella, how about helping me get out of this uniform.'

"That's the way the game was played. Nobody left anything on the field."

The Volunteers won a big game in 1929.

The victory was six points—or six inches, depending on your viewpoint. And this close competition became the norm in the heated rivalry.

5

1930
Alabama 18, Tennessee 6

CHAMPIONSHIP BANNERS WAVED IN the breezes at the University of Tennessee in 1930. Winds of change were blowing hard through the Alabama football program in Tuscaloosa.

Wallace Wade, a successful coach under criticism, met force with force, even after surrendering to his critics and offering his resignation to Alabama school officials on April 30 of that year, stating in it that he was about to lead the Crimson Tide for the last time.

Alabama players, who had heard the rumors, received official word from Wade several months later, mere days before their first game of the season against Howard College. It was indeed a fiery pep talk the coach offered that day.

"Coach Wade had kept quiet about his resignation, although all of us knew he was leaving Alabama for Duke after the 1930 season," said John Henry Suther, a senior halfback on that Crimson Tide team. "But when he finally got around to telling us about his plans, well, he built a fire under us. We had a lot of talent that season, and his timing was just right. I knew that day that we'd have a helluva team.

"The wolves were howling that year. Radical members of the alumni were calling for Coach Wade's scalp. They wanted to run him out of town immediately, just because we'd won only six games the year before and only five games the year before that. They forgot about the Rose Bowl trips in 1926 and 1927. They forgot about the injuries we had during the 1928 and 1929 seasons. All they knew was that we were losing more than usual and that a new coach was needed.

"Well, Coach Wade was boiling mad about that, but he kept his mouth shut. Then he called a team meeting before our first game and gave the most emotional talk I've ever heard. He shot straight from the shoulders with us.

"Coach Wade said that it would be his last year at Alabama, that some of the radicals in the state didn't care for the way he was running things. Then he gave us a challenge.

"'Gentlemen,' Coach Wade said, 'I'm gonna win this damn Southern Intercollegiate Conference championship this season, and if you want to be a part of it, you can. If not, get out of here now and never step foot on this ground again.'

"We knew he meant what he said. Coach Wade was like a bloodthirsty army officer that day. Because of what he said, we became bloodthirsty football players."

Alabama won 10 games in 1930, finishing with an unbeaten season capped by a 24-0 victory over Washington State in the 1931 Rose Bowl. Only two teams scored a touchdown each on the Crimson Tide—Tennessee and Vanderbilt—and Alabama averaged 27.1 points per game.

Needless to say, the winds of change subsided, particularly after Alabama beat Tennessee 18-6, handing the Volunteers their first defeat since 1926. Several red-faced members of the Alabama alumni helplessly watched as Wade, with a 61-13-3 overall record, left the Crimson Tide program.

"There were days I hated Coach Wade, but I cried when he left us for Duke," Suther said. "A lot of people cried with me, including those radicals that ran him off in the first place."

In 1980 Wade returned to Alabama for a reunion of his 1930 team. He was gracious and he spoke of pride in the Crimson Tide program. He did not want to talk about his exit from Alabama, simply saying, "Some things are better left unsaid."

Wade did, however, talk about the significance of the victory over Tennessee. "Beating them was the key to our season. We had a splendid squad that year, but it proved itself in beating Tennessee. It was probably the one game that propelled us to a berth in the Rose Bowl.

"At that time, the Tennessee program was on top of the world. Under [Coach Bob] Neyland, they had beaten us two times in a row, which had people thinking, rightfully so, I guess, that Tennessee was the top team in the South. And that was not a slouch club we beat in 1930. [Fullback Gene] McEver was hurt, as I remember, and didn't play, but they had a wealth of talent at Tennessee, led by [tailback Bobby] Dodd. As I remember, Tennessee's only loss that year was to us."

When Tennessee went to Tuscaloosa to play Alabama on October 18, the Volunteers were walking into a carefully planned trap made harder to escape by a great deal of pomp and circumstance. It was Homecoming at the Capstone, and the school was celebrating its one hundredth birthday. Twenty thousand fans were at Denny Stadium that day, thanks to the construction of eight thousand extra seats, and many of them lurked along the sidelines and the back of the end zones.

"Alabama's pulse is abnormal for this visit by the mighty Volunteers," Zipp Newman wrote in his column in the *Birmingham News*.

> The stage was set just right for another all-out war with Tennessee," said Suther, who earned All-American honors that season. "The rivalry was already hot because Coach Neyland and Coach Wade were great men in their trade, and the fact Tennessee hadn't lost in so long. Tennessee had made life rough for Alabama in the previous years. We thought we had a score to settle.

Tennessee never seriously challenged Alabama that day. The Crimson Tide led 18-0 in the third quarter, but still there were boos in the stadium. Wade heard them.

"Coach Wade came up with what turned out to be a good plan for Tennessee, but our fans thought he was crazy," Suther said. "Our second team was called the Shock Troopers, and Coach Wade struck on the thought of letting those guys start the game. His logic was that we'd wear Tennessee down in the first quarter, then go after them in the second quarter.

"When the Shock Troopers went on the field for the opening kickoff, our fans took to booing something fierce. If you want to know the truth, I was booing with them. I'd been a part of two losses to Tennessee. That was my last chance to get even. I wanted to play.

"But, sure enough, the Shock Troopers took the wind out of Tennessee, and we had a pretty easy time with them the rest of the day."

Alabama scored two touchdowns in the second quarter, with half-back John Cain running 12 yards around right end for the first and Suther running 31 yards around left end for the second. Quarterback John Campbell scored another Crimson Tide touchdown on a 1-yard run in the third quarter. Halfback Buddy Hackman scored a touchdown for Tennessee on a 1-yard run in the fourth quarter.

"This Alabama team is destined for greatness," Zipp Newman wrote in the *Birmingham News* the week after the game:

> A typical Wallace Wade team, much like the 1925 and 1926 models, ended a four-year reign of terror on southern gridirons by the Black Knights of Tennessee. Spectacular blocking, fierce tackling and powerful thrusts were responsible for Alabama handing the Volunteers their first defeat in 34 games. The Crimson Tide did it without resorting to an attack through the air. They tried only one pass all afternoon.

The words were prophetic, because, after struggling in a 12-7 victory over Vanderbilt the week after the Tennessee game, the Crimson Tide defeated Kentucky, 19-0; Florida, 20-0; Louisiana State, 33-0; Georgia, 13-0; and Washington State, 24-0, in the Rose Bowl.

"Washington State was like a trout in the rapids," Maxwell Stiles wrote about the 1931 Rose Bowl game in the *Los Angeles Examiner.* "The trout knew that he was in a lot of running water, but he didn't know where it was coming from."

Suther, meanwhile, never did really figure out what was going on in the Rose Bowl, although his memories of the experience were fond.

"I grew up in Tuscaloosa cheering those Alabama Rose Bowl games from the 1925 and 1926 seasons," Suther said. "And I dreamed that someday I'd be good enough to play in a game like that.

"Once I got there, though, it was bigger and better than I had imagined. I scored a touchdown, and I never felt like my feet were on the ground. And thanks to Elmer 'The Great' Swartz, a super Washington State fullback, I left something in Pasadena to be remembered by. In the last minute of the game, I collided head-on with Swartz and lost four of my teeth. They're still out there on that field, I guess.

"Anyway, I was back at the hotel before I came to my senses. I knew I had been playing in a football game, but I wasn't the least bit sure where.

"I did know, though, that I wasn't in Tuscaloosa and I wasn't having as good a time as the other guys on our team were. I made up for a lot of lost time on the train ride back to Alabama."

At Tennessee, meanwhile, Neyland and his players recovered from the shock of a rare loss, as a 9-1 record indicates, and he began preparing them for their revenge the next season at Knoxville.

But the Volunteers were to see a new man stalking the Alabama sideline, Coach Frank Thomas, after the departure by Wade.

About the anticipated changing of the guard in the Crimson Tide camp, Newman wrote in the *Birmingham News:*

Wallace Wade has written finis to a meteoric coaching career at the University of Alabama. During his seven-year regime, the Crimson Tide has climbed football heights no other southern school has ever scaled, being the first Dixie club to win national championships and thrice playing in the national Tournament of Roses game.

Even the school president, George Denny, who did not get along with the coach, had words of praise to offer upon his departure.

"Wade has made Alabama not only a great coach, but a great leader of young men," Denny said. "We have been fortunate to have had a coach of his magnitude on our campus."

Wade left the way he would have it, with Tennessee aching after a defeat, as stated by former Volunteer tackle Herman Hickman.

"The Red Elephants swarmed that day in 1930," Hickman said. "And, that night we were standing around the tiny station, feeling glum and downhearted, waiting for the train to take us home."

6

1931
Tennessee 25, Alabama 0

FRANK THOMAS BECAME THE new University of Alabama football coach in 1931. The Notre Dame-trained leader, who had played under Coach Knute Rockne and with the Four Horsemen, arrived in Tuscaloosa to inherit a program that one year earlier had scored a memorable victory over Tennessee. That might have provided Thomas with false confidence.

Tennessee had been shorthanded for its game against the Crimson Tide in 1930. It had played without its top player, fullback Gene McEver, who was nursing a badly injured knee.

Adding to the unknowns Thomas had to face, West Point-trained Maj. Bob Neyland, a military genius, came up with a sneak attack during the fall of 1931 that remains a testimony to his greatness as a football coach. The Tennessee coach shocked the Crimson Tide with his unusual game plan that led the Volunteers to a 25-0 victory on October 17.

But former Tennessee player Breezy Wynn wonders why so many people were surprised the Volunteers came out passing against Alabama. He thinks the strategy used by Neyland in that victory was typical of his innovative ways as a coach.

"Neyland was gifted when it came to figuring out the best way to win a game," said Wynn, who was a sophomore fullback for Tennessee that season. "He spent hours planning the proper strategy for a game. He worked harder at it when we were going against Alabama. Then, as anybody who played for him will tell you, he drilled us until we had it down pat."

The Crimson Tide was left somewhat helpless when the ground-oriented Volunteers took to the air to score a resounding victory.

McEver, the "Wild Bull" who earned fame as a runner, completed six of six pass attempts for 88 yards as Tennessee confused and battered Alabama in front of twenty-five thousand fans. He earned national star of the week honors.

He also left another person perplexed, sportswriter Herbert Barrier, who watched and wrote, "In practice, Gene is likely to hit himself in the back of the head when he attempts to pass."

Al Mark, who played end for Tennessee that afternoon and wrote about the victory for the *Knoxville News-Sentinel,* explained the chain of events in a guest column the morning after the game.

> They didn't know Gene McEver was a passer. Neither did we. He was a sharpshooting fool. I guess our visitors expected him to swallow the ball. He did everything else against them.

Wynn said Neyland opted for a passing attack against the bitter rival because McEver "had a knee out of sync."

> No longer could Mac run like he had before, all over the field, breaking tackles along the way. So he learned to throw the football like Neyland wanted him to. He could still run straight ahead like a bull. But he worked so hard learning to pass for that game, as Neyland ordered, that he must have dreamed about it.
>
> As it worked out, his passing got us a great victory.

McEver scored three touchdowns. He ran for two of them, for three yards both times. He caught a two-yard touchdown pass on fourth down from [H. B.] Deke Brackett.

Brackett scored one touchdown, going fourteen yards into the end zone on a play that featured a nifty fake to McEver, who plunged toward guard.

Herman Hickman kicked an extra point.

The Volunteers dominated the Crimson Tide, getting 18 points in the second half and outgaining the rivals 298 yards to 138.

FRANK THOMAS

MOST COACHES WOULD HAVE gulped. Some might have fainted.

It was in 1931 that University of Alabama president Dr. George Denny called Frank Thomas into his office. The former Notre Dame quarterback, a roommate to George Gipp of "win one for the Gipper" fame, had just been hired to coach football for the Crimson Tide.

"Now that you have accepted our proposition," Denny said to Thomas, "I want to give you the benefit of my view, based on my years of observation. It is my conviction that material is 90 percent, coaching ability just 10 percent. I desire further to say that you will be provided the 90 percent and that you will be held in strict accounting for delivering the remaining 10 percent."

Thomas was not pleased with the statement.

"Those were the coldest words I have ever heard," Thomas said. "Do you think the propositions were correct?"

Thomas had a large enough challenge in front of him without the school president tampering with his program. He was following Wallace Wade, who produced a 61-13-3 record that included three appearances in the Rose Bowl, which meant the shoes were large.

Wade had suggested that Alabama hire Thomas, who was at the time serving as an assistant coach at Georgia. Interestingly, Denny listened to the advice of a coach who had grown tired enough of his tampering with the football program to resign and move to Duke.

"There is a young coach at the University of Georgia that could become one of the greatest coaches in the country," Wade said to Denny. "He played at Notre Dame under Knute Rockne. Rock called him one of the smartest players he ever coached."

Most people asked "Who?" when the announcement was made.

Nobody does now. Thomas was inducted into the National Football Foundation Hall of Fame in 1951.

"The sympathetic agreement was that Frank Thomas should be pitied, that he had stepped into some very large shoes, and that it was likely to be very tough for him in Tuscaloosa," said Fred Russell, the former sports editor and columnist at the *Nashville Banner*.

But Thomas was more than strong enough to face the challenge. That made The Third Saturday in October more enjoyable for Alabama fans and Tennessee fans who were learning to love the series between the two programs.

Adding much to the heated rivalry was the fact Thomas came from Notre Dame and Tennessee coach Maj. Bob Neyland came from West Point. The Fighting Irish and Army were hot adversaries during that era.

Thomas's record at Alabama from 1931 through 1946 was awesome, 141-32-8. He took the Crimson Tide to six bowl games.

Under Thomas, who in 1946 announced, "My health has become too bad for me to continue coaching Alabama," the Crimson Tide had a 7-6-2 record against Tennessee as the series became one of the better rivalries in the nation.

"Our games with Tennessee were all the same, no matter who won or who lost. Tough from the start until the finish," said Thomas, who found time during his years at Alabama to write newspaper columns for the state media. "We always knew where we stood after playing our friendly rivals from East Tennessee."

The land on which the athletic complex at Alabama is built carries the name Frank Thomas Field.

Interestingly, if not tragically in the minds of some people, Alabama never named anything on campus in honor of Wade.

"It was just too much Tennessee," said Thomas, whose first team posted a 9-1 record and was considered powerful in its own right.

The margin thrilled Mark.

"What a game!" the Volunteer end wrote in his column.

"The whole game can be summed up in three words: 'We just clicked.'"

But Tennessee, which ended its 9-0-1 season with a victory in the New York Charity Game, 13-0, over New York University, had reason to believe it would receive some criticism after the victory over Alabama.

"It's common knowledge that when the major [Coach Bob Neyland] becomes agitated, he drinks water by the quarts," Mark wrote in the *Knoxville News-Sentinel*. "He drank water by the gallons yesterday, so it won't be praise for us on Monday afternoon at practice."

Another postgame question from Mark centered around Tennessee linebacker Charley Kohlhase:

> Then there's Charley Kohlhase backing the line. He got a bad lick,
> for I had to find his car and get his money. When Charley forgets his
> money, something is wrong. But I left him talking about his girl-
> friend. That's a sure sign of sanity, as far as he is concerned.

Neyland was more pleased than Mark imagined, naturally, after his team manhandled Alabama in front of an audience that included New York Yankees star outfielder Ben Chapman, a Birmingham native.

"I'm happy as I can be with this victory," Neyland said. "The score was greater than the relative strengths of the two teams. I thought the generalship of Brackett was the outstanding thing of the game. McEver was next. The work of the linemen was next. In general, the team played well."

McEver led the Volunteers, as remembered by Col. Tom Elam. "McEver came back that season wearing a huge brace on a knee. Hellfire, it looked like an orthopedic monstrosity. We'd missed him the year before. It was good to see him out there against Alabama.

"McEver might have passed the football that year against Alabama, but that wasn't his forte, to say the least. I used to kid him about that. When he passed the football, it looked like a guy tossing a basketball or pitching a watermelon. He'd come back with, 'Well, it got the job done didn't it?' He was strong enough to push it out there.

"It's amazing anybody could throw a football back then. They were big, fat, bulky things. You either had to have huge hands or be strong, like McEver.

"The passing was one thing. But the hitting was *the* thing to me. I remember our halfback, Beattie Feathers, running head-on into an Alabama player early in the game. They bounded back and fell to the ground. As I recall, Feathers got up, while the Alabama boy stayed on the ground. Those were two studs colliding.

"I'm telling you, that Feathers was tough. They called him the 'Rambling Antelope' because of the way he ran.

"McEver had some interesting nicknames, too. 'Will Bull,' 'Black Knight,' 'Bristol Blizzard,' and so on.

"We missed McEver in 1930. We applauded him in 1931."

The Volunteer-dominated crowd at Shields-Watkins Field was joyous. As former sports editor Bob Wilson wrote in the *Knoxville News-Sentinel:* "The Tennessee band cut more capers than Mister Carter had oats."

It got better after the game, as remembered by Harold Harris, who attended that game and later became a sportswriter for forty-five years at the *News-Sentinel.*

The series was hot then. It had picked up steam after Gene McEver made the run in 1928. Tennessee fans were reaching a wild pitch during that era. They arrived in town for the 1931 game on Friday afternoon, not long after noon, and they frolicked at the Farragut Hotel.

As soon as the game ended that day, a shirttail parade erupted on Gay Street, with people weaving back and forth in the streets, wildly proclaiming Tennessee as the best team in the land.

Wilson made Tennessee sound that good with his game story in the *News-Sentinel:*

A stalwart and vicious Tennessee line, abetted by a dazzling running game and a befuddling aerial attack, featuring the incomparable Gene [Wild Bull] McEver, [John] Shack Allen and a couple of daring sophomore backs, Beattie Feathers and Deke Brackett, brought ruin to mighty red elephants from Alabama before a homecoming crowd of about 25,000.

The men of Neyland won by the surprising score of 25-to-0.

That is the kind of dominance a person like Wynn favors. The successful businessman was full of himself during his college years.

"I'm the best defensive fullback in the Deep South," Wynn said in a newspaper story that year.

Then he offered a colorful verbal résumé for the reporters: "I have no life insurance, no halitosis, endorse Ipana toothpaste, [and] Gem razor blades, never touch a drop of whiskey, wine, or beer, never smoke, have had nine autos, buy a new Ford every year, have a high forehead, love dogs, read S. S. Van Dine books, hula-hula dancers [are] my favorite show, can knock down anything from Hamilton National Bank Building to a donkey."

In his story in the *Knoxville News-Sentinel* the afternoon of the game, Bob Wilson wrote: "I know why they call the Tidemen red elephants. If you could have seen the behemoths roaming about the Whittle Springs Hotel this morning, as I did, you would agree the name fits them."

During the summer of 1986, Jeff Coleman, a longtime observer of The Third Saturday in October, indicated the Crimson Tide had a dreadful day, even worse than the scoreboard indicated.

"That was the first game we took films of the action for review by our coaches," said Coleman. "I sat in the stands with a movie camera. At halftime, after working hard to secure a quality movie, I discovered my efforts were made without my having film in the camera."

It is doubtful Thomas complained. He had seen enough of the Big Orange up close and personal.

The following year, in Birmingham the Alabama coach with the Fighting Irish background would again see a lot of orange, as well as a thrilling show staged in the rain.

7

1932
Tennessee 7, Alabama 3

THE WEATHER FURNISHED A good excuse for drinking at the game—and there was plenty of it. At first, the drinkers were somewhat timid, going to the trouble of pouring it from a fruit jar or another container into a Coca-Cola bottle. But as the game wore on and the wind and rain grew more biting, those who had it made no effort to conceal their drinking. When [Beattie] Feathers ran across for the only touchdown, one Tennessee fan dropped a quart jar he had up to his lips.

"The defeat was a great blow to the Alabama team and its fans alike. I had never before seen such confidence as the Alabama players and backers manifested before the game. Most of the betting until the rain began was on even terms, although one Knoxville man got $100 from an Alabama fan who gave the Knoxville man 12 points. However, before game time, after the rain set in and it was apparent it would not stop, Alabama supporters freely offered points or odds, calling them out in hotel lobbies.

"As the Alabama team left the Thomas Jefferson Hotel for the game, someone on the sidewalk said to one of the players, 'Well, what are you going to do?' He replied, 'Beat hell out of them.'"

Tennessee fans were celebrating after the game, staging a wild scene in downtown Birmingham. As the Tennessee Marching Band marched in the street below them, Volunteer supporters stuck their heads out of windows at the Tutwiler Hotel and dumped feathers cut from pillows onto sidewalks.

In view of the game Tennessee's Beattie Feathers played, the feathers were obviously appropriate as Tennessee loyals, well, "raised Cain."

"It was a spectacle, a helluva game, and I still remember it with fondness. It was a hot contest with kicking the highlight," Jim Dildy said recently. The former Tidesman who played that day is guilty of understatement when recalling a football game played between the University of Tennessee and Alabama on The Third Saturday in October in 1932.

That was the day that football was played in its purest sense, with kicking serving as the decisive ingredient in a 7-3 Tennessee victory at Birmingham.

Beattie Feathers of the victors and John Cain of the losers were stars of the show, as expected, and their punting duel at Legion Field that day probably will never be matched.

Tennessee won, but that is only a part of the story. The rest of it was the kicking of Feathers and Cain in front of twenty thousand fans, who braved a steady rain, cold temperatures, and gusting winds to watch. The game showed that nothing can stop Tennessee and Alabama from putting on a grand show when evenly matched.

Feathers punted 21 times for an average of 48 yards. One of his kicks went only 18 yards. The short punt was not damaging to the Volunteers because they had a rugged defense that led the team to a 9-0-1 record in 1932.

Laboring for an Alabama team that finished with an 8-2 record, Cain punted 19 times for an average of 43 yards. One of his kicks went only 11 yards, and it is remembered as the crucial play in the game.

Because they did not want to risk handling the wet football, both teams frequently punted on first down and second down. Bob Neyland, the Tennessee coach, later said, "It was the most magnificent kicking show my eyes have witnessed. Never will I see another like it."

Certainly, the statistics produced by Feathers and Cain take on added significance when the weather is considered.

"Those boys kicked the ball around like demons," said William deShazo, a longtime Alabama fan, who saw the game and counted it among his most memorable. "It was the only game I can recall attending when my shoes were filled with water. Mud was ankle deep on the playing field."

Dildy, who played tackle that day for Alabama, recalled the terrible conditions. "The weather was awful for a football game. But somehow we got through it and put on a decent show."

It should be considered:

That officials did not change footballs during the game, leaving the one Feathers and Cain kicked water-logged and coated with mud.

That the hightop shoes and cotton pants Feathers and Cain wore became soggy and heavy.

That neither Feathers nor Cain left the game, both leading their teams in rushing.

ALABAMA SCORED in the second quarter, taking a 3-0 lead on a field goal by Hillman Holley. "It was his only field goal attempt of the season," said Dildy.

Tennessee scored in the third quarter, after Feathers kicked the football dead at the Alabama 1-yard line. On first down, Cain attempted to punt the football back to the Volunteers, but after he fielded a poor snap from center, he shanked the ball out of bounds at the Crimson Tide 12-yard line.

Three plays later, Feathers took the football on a pitchout, got outside the Alabama defense, and ran around left end for a touchdown. Breezy Wynn kicked the extra point for the final margin of victory.

"When Feathers took off around end, I was chasing him," said Dildy. "And I was hollering, 'Cut back, Beattie, cut back!' I wanted Feathers to think I was one of his teammates, but he paid no attention to me. He just kept running for the end zone.

"That was it for us. It was that kind of day, miserable and wet. It was, as I said, a helluva football game anybody could have won.

"Alabama-Tennessee games have always been blood-and-gut affairs. I got hit that day by one of their guys—his name escapes me—and he knocked me all the way to a track around the playing field. Had it not been so wet and had I not slid, that guy would have broken my legs.

"All of our games with Tennessee were like that. But 1932 was the classic."

Feathers and Cain were old rivals when they started kicking for their respective teams in 1932. In the spring of that year, reported the *Birmingham Age-Herald,* they had been pitted in a special 100-yard race. The newspaper said, "Feathers was given the decision by the judges, although the spectators thought Cain had won."

A rivalry was also brewing between the coaches, Maj. Bob Neyland of Tennessee and Frank Thomas of Alabama. The day before the game, they attempted psychological ploys:

"Our preparation has been fine, but we need at least three more days to prepare for an opponent like Alabama," said Neyland.

"I'm afraid my little fellas will crumble under the weight of those giants from Tennessee," said Thomas.

Tennessee was ready enough, nobody was killed, and fans paid $1.50 each to sit in miserable weather.

The day after the game, the *Knoxville News-Sentinel* reported:

UT alumni and friends proved Saturday afternoon that they were willing to die for their dear old alma mater when for more than two hours they sat in a cold, drizzling rain to see the Volunteers fight an uphill fight against Alabama and win in the final quarter.

The game was reminiscent of the one at Lexington three years ago when Tennessee fought Kentucky to a tie during a furious snowstorm. This time it was rain instead of snow, but many in the stands hoped that the rain would turn into snow so that it would not sting their faces and drench them so completely.

The sportswriters who saw the game from the warmth and protection of the closed press box will never know just how terrible that weather was. Many of those around me said they were afraid they would get pneumonia. And after Tennessee made that touchdown, Tennessee fans did not care if they did.

"It's worth dying for," said Kyle Mynatt, one of the UT boosters.

Vendors who sold makeshift raincoats made a killing. They were caped-like affairs made of oil paper, and they sold for 50 cents and lasted about 10 minutes. Newsboys called out, "Dry papers," "rain sheet," and even "umbrellas." Many spectators covered their heads with newspapers, and some even cut holes in oil cloths to make raincoats of sorts.

The pressers uptown were also able to forget about the depression. The valet at the Thomas Jefferson Hotel refused to take the suit of one of the guests, explaining that 300 other suits were already ahead of him.

8

1933
Alabama 12, Tennessee 6

I_T WAS A YEAR_ for surprises, in organized crime and in football.

No sooner had Machine Gun Kelley been caught in a boarding house in Memphis and locked up in jail, than the University of Alabama presented Tennessee with its first defeat on Shields-Watkins Field in nine years.

"They've got me now, but keeping me is another matter," said Kelley, the notorious gangster.

The game was just as stormy, with Alabama getting two touchdowns in the second half to win.

Bob Wilson, former sports editor at the *Knoxville News-Sentinel,* was impressed with the way Alabama played on foreign turf:

> Like a storm that breaks suddenly with the wrath of destruction, the Alabama Crimson Tide, which rolled along for the first half, offering nothing more serious than an overgrown ripple, quickly turned into a roaring torrent that lashed with devastating force down through the Tennessee Valley to submerge a courageous Volunteers craft under a 12-to-6 score.

In the audience that October 21, was One-Eye Connelly, a pronounced gate-crasher who had long since earned national fame. He arrived in Knoxville three days before the game to plot strategy aimed at providing himself with "a choice seat."

"I never fail," Connelly said upon his arrival, while signing auto-graphs for a multitude of fans.

On game day, according to reports in the *News-Sentinel,* Connelly was successful. That pregame action added to the rowdiness of the twenty-two thousand fans who watched the game. The newspaper credited Connelly with contributing to the stir:

> Perhaps inspired by "One-Eye" Connelly, nearly 300 young fans crashed the gates at Shields-Watkins. Down the hill they swarmed, soon losing themselves in the crowd.
>
> All afternoon, there were incipient fights in the stands. Particularly in the second half, police had their hands full escorting from the field those who had raised their fighting spirits by drinking red liquor.

Actually, spirits were up long before then.

Tennessee had lost to Duke the previous week. The prospect of losing back-to-back games for the first time under Coach Bob Ney-land had fans on edge.

Tennessee governor Hill McAlister, a Vanderbilt graduate, even arrived early for Homecoming. He had football on his mind, not poli-tics, and he partied with the masses until the opening kickoff.

Southern Railway provided a "cent a mile" excursion ride for fans from several Tennessee cities.

A pep rally was staged on Thursday night at Eighth Street Park. "The Rose Hole, as the park was called, was rocking that night," said Harold Harris, who served forty-five years as a sportswriter for the *Knoxville News-Sentinel.*

The man who organized the pep rally for Tennessee fans that night was Col. Tom Elam, who was in law school at the time. "I made a little talk in chapel that week and urged everybody to turn out at the Rose Hole for the rally," Elam said. "I told them I wanted to see the greatest turnout, a gigantic congregation, because Coach Neyland would be there to ignite our spirits.

"We also had One-Eye Connelly on hand.

"That's the night I made my introductory statement that has stuck with me so many years: 'Friends of Tennessee, here we are.'

"Anyway, we had the damnedest bonfire you've ever seen. One-Eye added to it. He could have gotten all the tickets he wanted to the game, but he wanted to sneak in, just to prove he could con somebody.

"Spirits were high, as they were back then for all Alabama-Tennessee games, and fans flocked into town for the game. People from over my way, for instance, the good folks of West Tennessee, overcame great hardships to get to Knoxville that year. It was a 335-mile trip. People had to ferry across a couple of rivers and travel down back roads. It took most of a day for people to make a trip like that by automobile. But Tennessee people came in huge masses that year to watch."

Former sportswriter and sports editor Tom Siler covered the impromptu pep rally for the *Knoxville News-Sentinel*. He wrote, "Bar the door, Katie! Lock the windows! These Tennessee College boys and girls are on a tear."

But Alabama players and supporters were also up for the game.

"We're not afraid of the big, bad Vols," said Crimson Tide center Raymond Class.

It was a tense struggle with both teams making several goal line stands. Alabama got its touchdowns from halfback Millard "Dixie" Dowell and halfback Erskine "Bubba" Walker. Tennessee got its touchdown from halfback Beattie Feathers.

Tennessee led 6-0 at halftime. The points came when Feathers ran 12 yards for a touchdown on fourth down in the second quarter.

Walker responded with a 34-yard touchdown run in the third quarter. The score came on the famous spinner play used in the Notre Dame box formation.

Howell gave the Crimson Tide its margin of victory when he bulled over tackle for four yards on second down in the fourth quarter.

Then the Alabama defense turned back the Volunteers several more times.

"We got the ball down a bunch of times," said Elam. "We had four goes at it late in the fourth quarter from inside their five-yard line. Milton Frank missed a block on the crucial play. I never have understood why Beattie Feathers didn't run the football four straight times. I think he would've been able to get into the end zone. That was the difference."

Zipp Newman, writing in the *Birmingham News,* encapsuled the game for his readers:

Crimson Tide impounded the Cove Creek area before TVA was ready and, lashed to fury by Little Giant [Tom] Hupke, [Erskine]

Bubba Walker and Millard Howell, flooded the great Tennessee Valley with a deluge that covered Shields-Watkins Field for the first time since Kentucky defeated Tennessee back in 1924.

It was the greatest thriller of all the modern games between Alabama and Tennessee.

Tom Hupke, a 185-pound guard, towered over the field of heroic figures like a big oak above dwarfed munsho pines.

Tennessee went down like all great teams do, while fighting.

Former sportswriter and sports editor Fred Russell of the *Nashville Banner* called it "a nerve-tingling struggle."

Tennessee played the game minus several injured standouts. The Volunteers went on that season to produce a 7-3 record.

"Alabama would have never beaten us had we been healthy," said Breezy Wynn, then a senior fullback at Tennessee, who missed the game with a broken leg. "We had a lot of people sidelined."

Alabama, which posted a 7-1-1 record, wrapped up the championship in the Southeastern Conference's first season.

Defense won the game for the Crimson Tide, according to Coach Frank Thomas. "I thought the stand our boys made on the goal line in the fourth quarter was the greatest thing in the game," Thomas said. "Hupke was the greatest player on the field."

The greatness of Hupke, a defensive terror at guard, was not noticed by Tennessee fan Bobby Brandau. He had another reason for the defeat the Big Orange suffered.

"I'm convinced One-Eye Connelly is bad luck, a hoodoo, if ever there was one," Brandau said as he exited the stadium. "I'll be the first to offer a five-dollar bogus warrant to help get him deported."

That thought might not be all wrong, according to Harold "Red" Drew, who later became coach at Alabama. Before his death, he said the victory over Tennessee in 1933 was among his favorite Crimson Tide memories, "because we were so crippled that afternoon we were held together by adhesive tape."

Meanwhile, One-Eye moved on to other gates to crash, after tasting the sweetness of The Third Saturday in October.

"Sure, I remember One-Eye Connelly," said former Alabama business manager and athletic director Jeff Coleman. "Everybody had heard of him. He was infamous across the nation. He also became a Crimson Tide fan of sorts. After the 1934 season, he hoboed part of the way to California, then showed up in the press box to watch us play in the 1935 Rose Bowl game."

The successful Alabama season provided Thomas with his first victory over Neyland-coached Tennessee. Thomas was so excited, according to *Birmingham News* sports columnist and author Clyde Bolton, "that he engulfed the wrong end of his lighted cigar."

Then Thomas said, "We did it. Now I guess I can coach another year and eat for a little while longer."

Thomas got his smoking habits corrected before another victory for Alabama over Tennessee the following season.

9

1934
Alabama 13, Tennessee 6

NEYLAND TO LEAVE UT at End of Season; Ordered to Panama.

"Army Engineers Transfer Football Coach to New Post.

"To Sail Jan. 9.

"Leaves Behind a Brilliant Record of Last Eight Years."

That multidecked headline made heads spin and eyes mist in Knoxville on September 29, 1934. It appeared over the lead story in the *Knoxville News-Sentinel.*

On the opening day of his ninth season at Tennessee, with a 67-5-5 record, Maj. Bob Neyland announced intentions to leave Tennessee.

"I have not received the order as reported as yet," Neyland said, "but of course I will obey it. I have thoroughly enjoyed my service here. I shall always cherish a deep affection and a lasting loyalty."

The coach proved that later, when, like Gen. Douglas MacArthur, he returned to Knoxville in 1936.

Sadness, however, gripped the Volunteers that September. A season-opening victory over Centre, 32-0, was not enough to bring happiness.

"Are you going, Major?" former Tennessee fullback Dick Dodson asked in the dressing room after the first game, with tears coming to his eyes.

"I will always be in the army," Neyland said.

"Why, Major?" Dodson said. "You can't coach football while down there in the Canal Zone."

In Tuscaloosa, meanwhile, there was optimism as Alabama prepared to embark on an unbeaten season capped by a victory over Stanford in the Rose Bowl.

The Crimson Tide run to glory was earmarked by a 13-6 victory over Tennessee in Birmingham on October 20.

But the Volunteers, who finished with an 8-2 record, were so gallant in defeat on The Third Saturday in October that the difficult-to-please departing coach approved.

"I'm not disappointed," said Neyland, who was rarely so gracious after a loss to the Crimson Tide. "Our boys did much better than I expected. Alabama has a great team, a smart and resourceful team."

Neyland knew that about Alabama going into the game. The crafty motivational whiz pulled out all stops trying to get his team ready for the favored Crimson Tide.

During practice the week of the game, the coach noticed a rabbit on the field. "Catch it! Catch it! Run it down!" he screamed to his players.

They gave chase, thus interrupting preparations for the Notre Dame shift offense Coach Frank Thomas was using with success at Alabama.

Tennessee player Dick Dorsey stunned the rabbit by throwing his helmet at it. Teammate Howard Bailey hopped a fence and grabbed the animal, then screamed, "We're going to take this graveyard rabbit to Alabama."

They treated the dazed rabbit and fed it during the week of the game, taking it to Birmingham with them. But it did not bring success against Alabama, which left Tennessee hungry in a couple of ways.

When his players complained that they were starving on the train ride to Birmingham, Neyland attempted to bribe them. "If you beat Alabama, you can have chicken all the way home. We'll even stop in Chattanooga to replenish our supply, if needed."

Obviously, the Tennessee coach knew his team was overmatched, as did former *Knoxville News-Sentinel* sports editor Bob Wilson, who wrote, "Can ten million football experts be wrong? Just about all the boys who make a business of picking winners agree that Alabama will trample Tennessee this week."

Harold Harris, also a sportswriter for the *News-Sentinel,* remembers how the departure of Neyland at the conclusion of the 1934 season caused distress among Tennessee fans.

"Respect is the word that best describes what Tennessee players felt for Neyland," Harris said. "They hated to see him go because they knew what he taught was the way to win. The fans really grieved upon hearing the news. He was the toast of Knoxville in those years.

"The graveyard rabbit story sort of typifies how he motivated people. It wouldn't surprise me to learn that Neyland had a team manager turn loose that rabbit on the practice field, his way of firing up the boys. After all, everybody expected Alabama to romp over the Volunteers."

The Big Orange was not trampled, but it had a harder time catching Alabama halfback Millard "Dixie" Howell than it did trapping the rabbit at practice. The star of the game ran 26 times for 104 yards.

Alabama used a center as a fullback to score the first touchdown of the game. Joe Demyanovich did the honors on a seven-yard run over left guard in the second quarter.

Tennessee bounced back to tie the game at halftime, 6-6, on a one-yard run by George Craig.

The decisive touchdown came in the third quarter, when Alabama end Don Hutson, who was known more as a pass receiver, ran five yards. The end-around play used by Thomas is known as one of his more crafty moves. Riley Smith kicked the extra point.

According to Bill Lee, who played tackle for Alabama from 1932 through 1934, the Volunteers were not the only team that looked forward to the game.

"Every game we played with Tennessee was an equal to the way Alabama people feel about our series with Auburn now," Lee said at his house in Eutaw, Alabama. "That's how much tension flowed through us when we went up there or they came down here. It's a series in which nothing has come cheaply for either side. It has always been tough and spirited."

How hot was the action?

Well, an Alabama end who would eventually become more famous than the series, Paul "Bear" Bryant, was ejected from the game after Tennessee fullback Phil Dickens suffered a broken nose when punched.

Did they get the wrong man?

Wilson and one of his sportswriting peers from Alabama thought so, as he stated in his Monday column:

It was unfortunate that clean play was not one of the features of the game. I am referring to a slugging of Phil Dickens by an Alabama player.

Paul Bryant was ejected from the game by officials for allegedly having landed the blow.

"The officials did Bryant a grave injustice," said Zipp Newman, Birmingham scribe. "He was 15 yards in back of the line of scrimmage."

Tennessee players agree that it was another Alabama player, not Bryant, who knocked Dickens out.

Perhaps liking the spotlight, Bryant only halfheartedly denied being the villain during postgame reflection.

So the question of who slugged Dickens has remained for years. If it wasn't the Alabama end who forty-eight years later became the winningest college coach in history, who was it?

"I did it," Lee said in 1986, solving a mystery that existed in some parts of the nation for fifty-two years. "I'm the one the officials should have nabbed. I caught Dickens with a pretty nasty blow.

"Actually, it was an accident. I stumbled into Dickens as the play was ending. I fell on top of him and my elbow hit his nose. Honestly, I didn't mean to hurt him, not in the least.

"An Alabama player would never do something like that to a Tennessee player, at least not intentionally."

10

1935
Alabama 25, Tennessee 0

THE NOVEL WAS FINE, no doubt about that. But the real *Red Badge of Courage* should have been awarded after a different type civil war, a football game played between unfriendly Southeastern Conference rivals Alabama and Tennessee on October 19, 1935.

The recipient was Paul "Bear" Bryant, a Crimson Tide end who became a fabled Alabama coach. He played on The Third Saturday in October with a broken bone in his leg.

No fib, only a splintered fibula bone that was "healed" in mystical fashion, according to at least one news report after a 25-0 victory by the Crimson Tide in Knoxville.

On Friday Bryant was on crutches and counted out of the game. On Saturday Bryant played brilliantly as Alabama romped. On Sunday, Bryant was the subject of a column written by former sports editor Bob Wilson in the *Knoxville News-Sentinel.*

A magician must serve as physician for the Alabama football squad. Nothing less than a hokus-pokus man could have done the miracle in healing the lame, hurt and sick in such a quick time.

I almost broke down and cried out of sympathy for the cripples and Alabama coaches when I heard of the wretched condition of the visitors' star players Friday afternoon.

Bear Bryant, an end, had a broken leg. That is, as late as Saturday morning.

56

But the magician medicine man waved his wand shortly before the game. Those Tidesmen, who a few hours before had been using crutches, walking sticks and rolling chairs, suddenly became strong, husky, vicious athletes, with nary a limp to be seen.

A few days later, Ralph McGill of the *Atlanta Constitution* wrote a story that said, in part: "As far as this season is concerned, Paul Bryant has first place in the courage league. There was no bear story about Bear Bryant.

"He played football with a crack through one of his leg bones. Bryant displayed true courage and determination. Putting aside all thoughts of pain, he went on to play what is thought to be one of the best games of his career."

In the story, Bryant said he felt pain. He said, "Well, every time my weight came down on it [the leg], I knew it was there. And if I stubbed my toe or anyone hit it, well, it hurt."

A couple of years before his death in January 1983, Bryant, who had a hand in several Alabama-Tennessee battles, told how he went from sick bay to stardom:

"I'd cracked that tiny bone in my leg the week before in a loss to Mississippi State. I was on crutches. I had no idea I'd play against Tennessee. The night before the game, at the hotel in Knoxville, our team physician took off the cast. He said I'd be able to dress for the game, if nothing else.

"I asked him if there was any chance of the bone sticking out. He assured me that wouldn't happen.

"A few minutes before the game, when Coach [Frank] Thomas was making his pep talk to the squad, he asked Coach Hank Crisp if he had anything to say. Coach Hank said he did, and he got up to talk to us. He had a cigarette dangling from his mouth, and he said, 'I'll tell you gentlemen one thing. I don't know about the rest of you, you or you or you, but I know old 34 will be after them today.'

"In those days, they changed players' numbers almost every week, so Coach Hank could sell a lot of game programs. So he's up there talking about old 34. I looked down to see what my jersey number was. There it was, as plain as day, old 34.

"Cold chills were running up my spine. Coach Thomas asked me if I could play. What could I have said? I just ran on out there.

"I was as lucky as a priest, because I played the rest of that year on that broken leg. It wasn't much of a break, but it was broken, and I was fortunate to have a good game against Tennessee that afternoon."

When word of the performance spread, McGill became so skeptical that he demanded to see X-rays of the leg before writing his story for the *Atlanta Constitution*.

"I even got an ovation from fans the next week at Georgia," Bryant said. "That's the only one I can remember getting as a player."

Actually, Bryant's bit of bravery, or magic, created most of the electricity as Alabama and Tennessee clashed on sort of an off year for both programs. The Crimson Tide, fresh from the Rose Bowl, had a 6-2-1 record. The Volunteers, working without regular coach Bob Neyland, had a 5-5 record.

Alabama was dominant enough to score a touchdown in each quarter. The Crimson Tide was methodical, pounding away at the Volunteers, rarely reverting to trickery.

The "other end" opposite fabled Don Hutson caught a pass as Alabama moved to a touchdown on its first possession of the game. He caught a pass, pitched the football to a trailing Riley Smith, and blocked an opponent to pave the way to another touchdown.

Halfback/quarterback Joe Riley scored the first two touchdowns. He ran one yard on a plunge over guard in the first quarter. He ran six yards around left end on third down in the second quarter.

Quarterback Riley Smith capped the scoring for Alabama. He ran two yards on fourth down for a touchdown. He added the extra point with a kick.

Alabama showed its power throughout the game.

No wonder Tennessee fans were excited when, on the Tuesday just prior to the game, Neyland announced in New Orleans that he would be returning to Knoxville "within two years." He was expected at the Alabama game, since he was on leave from the army, but he opted to watch Southern Methodist and Rice play in his native Texas.

Wrote Wilson in the *Knoxville News-Sentinel:* "Alabama's Crimson Tide uncorked one of the most versatile and devastating attacks ever witnessed on Shields-Watkins Field as they dealt out a crushing 25-to-0 defeat to the Tennessee Vols.

"Tennessee had nothing with which to dam the roaring crowd."

According to Harold Harris, a sportswriter for forty-five years at the *Knoxville News-Sentinel,* the Volunteers did not look like Tennessee that afternoon.

"As I recall, that was the only time Tennessee wore white jerseys for a game," Harris said. "That wasn't the thing to do against Alabama.

"But Alabama was too strong for us. They had a team with guts and heart. Just look at what Bryant did. I swear, he was unbelievable, displayed amazing courage. I saw him on Friday afternoon before the game. He was on crutches, counted out of action. But at some point Saturday morning, he threw down the crutches, went out there on the field, and played quite a game.

"That was sort of typical of Bryant, I guess, because there were a lot of Tennessee people who got to where they disliked him in later years, when he coached Alabama and beat us in similarly dramatic style so many times. I was one of those people.

"But, in another way, we all adored the man, what he stood for, his ability to coach winning football. He was tough. He was smart. He knew how to win championships.

"When Tennessee finally beat Alabama in 1982, ending that long losing streak to Bryant, I had a clever tag on the front of my car commemorating that classic upset of his team at Neyland Stadium. It said: 'Majors Traps A Bear. Tennessee 35, Alabama 28.' I used to show it off and laugh about it with friends.

"Then, in 1983, I was driving in downtown Knoxville when I heard on the radio that the great 'Bear' from Alabama had died. I was shocked. I pulled into the next service station I came to and had a man take that tag off my car.

"I had respect for the man. I had it when he died. And I had it in 1935 when he threw down those crutches and helped Alabama beat us."

11

1936
Alabama 0, Tennessee 0

WHEN MAJ. BOB NEYLAND returned to the University of Tennessee in 1936, after serving our country in the Panama Canal Zone, he made a quick observation about the Volunteer football team he was to coach. This was done the day preseason practice opened in Knoxville.

"This team can win only by showing proper spirit and team cooperation," Neyland said upon surveying a small team. "We must be one for all and all for one every day this season."

That sounded like it should have come from the army man he was.

Meanwhile, Alabama coach Frank Thomas, a scholarly sort, was making public appearances during which he provided an insight into his philosophy. He talked a lot about the complicated Notre Dame box offensive formation the Crimson Tide was using with success, specifically about the importance of catching opponents by surprise with unusual alignments and trick plays.

Entering the sixth of his fifteen seasons at the Capstone, Thomas was finding it more difficult to slip up on opponents. He had won back-to-back Southeastern Conference championships in 1933 and 1934. His 1934 team had produced a 10-0 record, including a 29-13 victory over Stanford in the Rose Bowl. His 1935 team had produced a 6-2-1 record, including a 25-0 victory over Tennessee.

His 1936 team was supposed to be powerful.

It was.

Alabama produced an 8-0-1 record that season. The Crimson Tide allowed only 35 points.

Tennessee produced a 6-2-2 record that season, with two of the losses coming in the two games just prior to a visit to Birmingham for an October 17 game against "Coach Tommy" and his polished team. Almost everybody predicted The Third Saturday in October game would be a mismatch.

Former sports editor Bob Wilson of the *Knoxville News-Sentinel* seemed positive that Tennessee would not be able to master Alabama:

> Tennessee faces its most desperate fight of the season.
>
> The Max Schmeling situation before his fight with Joe Louis comes to mind this week.
>
> Not since 1932 has Tennessee been able to beat Alabama. Coach Thomas' boys have not allowed a point in three games this season. It looks bad for Tennessee. The bettors are saying three touchdowns.
>
> A win this week would be something to crow about. Tennessee fans everywhere are ready to crow.

Such grim prognostication made the 0-0 tie an accomplishment for Volunteer fans to talk about, although they chose not to crow loudly, and it produced the only blemish for Alabama that season. Wilson was enthusiastic in writing about the game:

> Displaying a magnificent brand of defensive football, replete with savage and bruising tackles, Tennessee's gallant sophomores fought Alabama's mighty Crimson Tide to a scoreless deadlock on Legion Field, scoring a mild upset as 15,000 fans looked on.

Phil Dickens and Lady Luck were the stars for Tennessee.

During the final seconds of the first half, Dickens tackled Alabama halfback Joe Riley at the Tennessee one-yard line. The timekeeper fired his gun to end the half before the Crimson Tide could run another play.

The captain at Alabama that season was James "Bubba" Nisbet. During the fall of 1986, he recalled why the Crimson Tide could not run another play after Dickens knocked Riley out of bounds.

"That was the first game played in Legion Field where they used an electric scoreboard clock," Nisbet said. "It gave them [the game officials] trouble all day. When Riley went out of bounds, I asked the official how much time we had. He said we had 25 seconds. We broke huddle. Another official came running in and called time. Coach Thomas raised sand. But the decision stood."

"Father Time saved the day," wrote Wilson.

That is true, according to a former Tennessee team manager, Richard Frank. "Among my duties at Tennessee was to keep a stopwatch at all games and check with the officials about the time left in the quarters," Frank said. "I had to keep General Neyland advised about such matters.

"Believe me when I say we had checked the time left in the half when Dickens knocked Riley out of bounds. We couldn't believe it when the official stepped in and ruled the first half was over.

"That action by the official came much to our relief and, I'm certain, much to the chagrin of Alabama players and coaches."

The quick stop to the half, whether or not warranted, cost Alabama handsomely that season.

"We were the only unbeaten major college team in the nation," said Arthur "Tarzan" White, who starred for the Crimson Tide from 1934 through 1936. "The tie with Tennessee, which was an upset victory for them, cost us a bowl game and a national championship. They played us a tough game. It was quite a battle, one of the hardest-hitting I can recall.

"We scurried around in a hurry trying to get off a play before the end of the first half. But the time was gone, the deed was done, and it proved to be most disappointing for us."

The drama produced by the scoreless tie was described by sportswriter Zipp Newman in the *Birmingham News*:

Phil Dickens saved the football game for Tennessee in the last five seconds of the first half. He shuttled across the field to bring down Joe Riley on the one-yard line. Riley had skirted out wide and was moving down the sideline. Dickens gave one final lunge, knocking Riley out of bounds. The whistle ended the half.

The next time Alabama got into scoring position was in the third quarter when it was held for downs at the Tennessee 26.

Col. Tom Elam remembers Dickens as a Tennessee standout.

"Phil Dickens was a fella with a much larger man in his upper body than his lower body," Elam said. "He was a spindly looking bird to me. He could throw a baseball harder than any man I've known.

"He had a good nickname, too, because we called him 'Phantom Phil.' He was skillful and talented. He was a phantom of sorts against Alabama in 1936."

The tackle by Dickens secured him revenge after he had his nose broken against Alabama in 1934. Judging from a story related by Ellis Dickens, his widow, nobody should have been surprised when the former Tennessee player knocked Riley out of bounds to save the game for the Volunteers.

"Phil told me about getting his nose broken," Ellis Dickens said during the summer of 1986 from her home in Spartanburg, South Carolina. "He said the trainers straightened it out with a pencil, wrapped it with tape, gave him a pain pill, and sent him back into the game.

"I guess that story sort of explains the Tennessee-Alabama rivalry, what it means, and the guts he displayed trying to help his team."

At least it shows how tough Dickens was as a player.

"Or else how crazy all of them were," Ellis Dickens said.

12

1937
Alabama 14, Tennessee 7

Madness prevailed off the football field.

The University of Alabama reigned on the field, 14-7, over Tennessee.

Such was the story that unfolded before, during, and after the Crimson Tide defeated its chief rival on October 16, 1937, in Knoxville.

Temporary seats were built at Shields-Watkins Field in Knoxville to accommodate the largest crowd ever to see a game there. Scalpers sold tickets for twenty dollars.

"A ticket for twenty dollars then would be like a ticket for one hundred dollars or more now," retired sportswriter Harold Harris of the *Knoxville News-Sentinel* said in 1986 at his house in Knoxville. "There was definitely a lot of excitement around town in 1937. The scalpers worked overtime from their makeshift offices at the Farragut Hotel. It was a mad scene throughout the downtown area.

"The hotel lobby was packed and wild the night before that game. People spilled into the streets—fans from both schools—and they whooped and hollered well into the night. They raised Cain after the game, too, and the smart bettors collected their money joyously. There were a lot of happy Alabama people in town.

"It was a hot show. Tickets to that game went at a premium."

One person anticipated as much.

"Why, I believe the game would draw thirty-five thousand or forty thousand fans, if we had room for them," said Tennessee coach Bob Neyland. "Our game with Alabama has become a classic, in total, and I look forward to the day we can enlarge the stadium to seat sixty thousand fans."

NBC-Radio dispatched a crew to Knoxville to broadcast the game on its Red and Blue networks. Paramount News dispatched a crew to make film clips to be shown in movie houses nationwide. Associated Press dispatched sports editor Alan Gould "to report on the Dixie clash that should shake the earth."

The week before, Tennessee had tied powerful Duke, 0-0, to improve its record to 2-0-1. Nobody had scored on the Volunteers.

The Crimson Tide was 3-0. Coach Frank Thomas's awesome team had outscored its opponents 126-0.

"The team I saw last week is Alabama's greatest in history," said Tennessee assistant coach W. H. Britton, who had watched the Crimson Tide take a 20-0 victory over South Carolina.

"They'll beat us four touchdowns," said Neyland, who overcame nervousness during the week of the game by reciting poetry to his assistant coaches and some of his players.

"We've got a pretty fair team, nothing exceptional," said Thomas, who appeared on a WNOX-Radio show in Knoxville the night before the game. "It'll be a close encounter."

Former sports editor Bob Wilson, writing in the *Knoxville News-Sentinel,* addressed the enthusiasm Alabama had for the game:

> Crafty Frank Thomas, boss of the Crimson outfit, is out to avenge last year's scoreless tie, the only black spot on the Tide's record. And when the astute Alabama mentor sets his cap to get revenge, he rarely misses.
>
> From all the Vol spies have to record, Tennessee is in for a beating.

Tennessee governor Gordon Browning, who was seated in the grandstand, watched Alabama win with halfback Joe Kilgrow and fullback Charlie Holm starring. George Cafego of Tennessee, then a promising tailback from West Virginia, was on the playing field making his first appearance for the Volunteers.

"We got beat," Cafego said during the summer of 1986 in Knoxville, "but it was a great game.

"I remember it fondly because it was my first action. I was chomping at the bit. I watched the first three quarters, when Alabama piled up a two-touchdown lead on us, and said, 'Damn, I'd like to be in there helping.' I wanted to get on with it. I'd heard so much about playing against Alabama. I was nervous, a whole lot, but I was anxious.

"Once I got in there, I took us down the field for a touchdown. Then we got the football back and took off again. We were about to score another touchdown when the game ended.

"That's the year things were really starting to get wild in Knoxville. Everybody was really crazy about our game with Alabama. We knew we had a chance to beat them. Just before the game started, there were hundreds of fans backed up at the top of the hill, blocked by a barricade. But as the opening kickoff drew near, they broke free and came charging into the grandstands. Everybody got fired up for Alabama when it came rolling into town, even our fans. In those days, because of the way General Neyland talked about the rivalry with the Crimson Tide, we knew how important it was to win over them.

"General Neyland told everybody the same thing. He said he wanted Tennessee to be the best in the conference and the best in the nation. He said the only way to do that was to do it against Alabama. See, that's what Alabama was in those days, the class of the conference, one of the top teams in the nation. I can even remember the general telling us during the spring and summer that we had to work hard because it wouldn't be long until we were on the field against Alabama. He got worked up for the game.

"It didn't take me long to understand what he meant. In part of a quarter, I realized Alabama was as tough as everybody said it was. It was always our roughest game, but it was always our cleanest game. There weren't a lot of cheap shots. There wasn't much jawing.

"That's one thing that makes the series so good. Another thing is the way Tennessee got in step during the 1930s. Alabama was the cream of the crop, the best in the nation, in the opinion of a lot of people, and we decided we'd get on the same level with them.

"So what we had in 1937 was two good teams playing each other. That's why our fans loved it. That's why they got all worked up for Alabama."

The game lived up to its billing, as expressed by sportswriters who watched it and wrote about it in the press box.

Ed Miles of the *Atlanta Journal* said, "Alabama players are reminiscent of those not so remote days when the Tide held sway throughout the country."

Bob Phillips of the *Birmingham News* said, "Only a brave last minute charge of a combination of players from the first and second Tennessee teams kept Frank Thomas's outfit from inflicting the most crushing defeat a Tennessee eleven coached by Bob Neyland ever suffered."

David Bloom of the Memphis *Commercial Appeal* said, "Alabama hauled Tennessee from the seat of the football mighty, depositing the Vols among the lesser lights."

Fred Russell of the *Nashville Banner* said, "More than twenty-five thousand fans, overflowing the sloping stands of Shields-Watkins Field, looked on as the red-jerseyed stalwarts crushed an unscored-on Tennessee eleven."

A lot of the action came long after the game, however, when a postgame crime wave struck the streets of Knoxville.

Said the story on the front page of the *Knoxville News-Sentinel* the next day, "A half-dozen persons reported they were victimized by pick-pockets or robbers on Gay Street."

Also, there was a story about a "free-for-all fight" breaking out at the Melody Inn hotel.

Among the people present at that game was Lindsey Nelson, who was a Tennessee student learning how to broadcast sports events, training that would later secure him a place in the national hall of fame for sportscasters.

"The thing I remember best is seeing Bob Suffridge, the great guard at Tennessee, parking cars and selling game programs," Nelson said. "He was a freshman that year, so he couldn't play, and he always seemed to find a way to make extra money.

"On the way to the stadium, I saw Suffridge parking cars at the Rose Hole on campus. He was charging a quarter per car. He jammed them in there, as many as the lot would hold, and I recall seeing cars stuck in there as late as 9 P.M. that night, because the only exit was blocked by an unoccupied car.

"Then Suffridge, an enterprising type guy, went to the stadium and sold game programs. I remember seeing him on a corner hawking them. His shirttail was out. He was perspiring like crazy. He was working hard for a buck.

"Can you imagine that? There was a freshman who would become one of the greatest players ever at Tennessee parking cars and selling game programs.

"I parked a few cars, too, during that period. See, this was before interstate highways, so nobody drove to town on the day of the game unless they lived in nearby towns. People came on Friday morning and afternoon, packing the hotels, partying, and talking. Well, some of these people didn't like driving in crowds, so they'd give me fifty cents to park their cars for them in the hotel garages. I made three or four dollars on good days.

"Another thing I remember is how people dressed for games. They wore what we folks down here call our good clothes. The women even wore high heels. It was obvious in the 1930s that football was a religion of sorts, very important to Tennessee fans and Alabama fans alike.

"It was a festive game. People got to the stadium area early. They'd ride street cars or walk, for the most part, and they'd gather in the Toddle House and other eateries on the Strip."

After all the craziness unfolded, with Alabama fans having more reason to cheer in 1937, Neyland and Thomas discussed the game with sportswriters.

The coaches had watched a typical Tennessee-Alabama game, which featured crisp hitting, with neither offense particularly imaginative.

Alabama scored its touchdowns in the second and third quarters. Tennessee made a game of it with a touchdown in the latter stages of the fourth quarter.

The first Crimson Tide touchdown was scored by quarterback Vic Bradford. The Memphis native ran three yards. Reserve quarterback Hal Hughes scored the second Alabama touchdown from two yards.

Hayward "Sandy" Sanford kicked two extra points.

Cafego passed four yards to Edwin Cheek Duncan for the lone Tennessee touchdown. Cafego kicked the extra point to fix the final margin.

The rival coaches, Neyland of Tennessee and Thomas of Alabama, reacted in the expected manner.

Said the loser, who went on to lead his team to a 6-3-1 record, "We were beaten by a better team."

Said the winner, who went on to lead his team to a 9-1 record, including a loss to California in the Rose Bowl, "I feel fine over the victory. Whew, this should be called Knocks-ville, instead of Knoxville."

They both talked about a sophomore halfback from Tennessee who starred in defeat. As read the headline in the *Knoxville News-Sentinel*, which served as praise of a gallant effort in defeat, "Watch Cafe-GO!"

It proved prophetic.

"I guess I sort of proved myself that day," said Cafego, who was personally recruited by Neyland out of West Virginia, where he had starred as a 148-pound runner for his high school team. "I'll always remember that game against Alabama as the start for me at Tennessee."

Cafego and the Volunteers were to take a more gigantic step on The Third Saturday in October the following year.

13

1938
Tennessee 13, Alabama 0

SOMETHING MORE THAN LOVE and a schoolteacher can prompt a man to recite poetry.

That became apparent on October 15, 1938, when a University of Alabama football fan, somewhat dismayed, uttered a few lines off the top of his head as he walked away from Legion Field in Birmingham.

His tragedy expressed in poetry:

> Has anyone seen Cafego?
> And which way did he go?
> All I know is he was going slow
> Which way did he take my dough?

A lot of people lost money betting on heavily favored Alabama in the 1938 game against Tennessee. The Volunteers, led by tailback George Cafego, defeated the Crimson Tide, 13-0, in a classic upset.

That is not all that was lost through wagering. Cafego and his teammates had a treat waiting for them when they returned to campus after the game.

"I'll never forget sitting in the Little Beer Garden on Cumberland Avenue the afternoon before we went to Birmingham," Cafego said. "That's where we'd go drink a few cool ones after practice.

"Everybody was talking about the game, when Bon Pollard, the owner, leaned over to me and said, 'George, you guys are going down to Birmingham tomorrow morning, right?' I told him we sure were. He said, 'Well, I guess you know those Alabama boys are gonna whip your fannies.' I said, 'Are you sure about that?'

"Bon nodded his head. I said, 'Well, Bon, you see that big beer tub over there in the corner?' He nodded. I said, 'Just fill it up. If Alabama whips our fannies, I'll buy all the beer. If we whip them, it's all ours.'

"Bon started loading it up.

"We rode the train on trips then, sitting in a private coach, and I didn't think we'd ever get back home after whipping Alabama. There was a big crowd waiting for us, a bunch of crazy fans, so I slipped off the back of the train. I was anxious to get to that cold beer and start guzzling.

"It was almost daylight on Sunday morning then. But ol' Bon was there with the beer. He knew we'd be calling on him."

The toasts were in order. It was the first victory for Tennessee over Alabama after four losses and a tie. A decked newspaper headline explained what happened before readers of the story under it learned that Cafego ran 19 times for 145 yards:

"Vols Stand Tide in 13-0 Upset"
   "They Say Elephants Never Forget—Bet They Will Try"
   "Cafego Sparks Victory with Help Of Line"
   "Bad News Spreads Sorrow over Entire State of Alabama As He Gains More Than Entire Elephant Backfield"

Under that headline displayed on the front page of the *Knoxville News-Sentinel,* sports editor Bob Wilson, who had predicted a Tennessee loss, wrote about rejuvenated enthusiasm among the Volunteers:

The great fighting spirit that started the Flamin' Sophomores of 1928 on the road to football glory, was born anew on Legion Field Saturday afternoon as 28,000 fans saw George Cafego spread bad news over the whole state of Alabama and the Tennessee Vols rout the Red Elephants, 13-0, in probably the most shocking gridiron upset of the day.
   It was Cafego, 168 pounds of TNT, who sparked the amazing Volunteers in this decisive victory over the greatest team Coach Frank Thomas has produced at Alabama.

Wilson was a bit kind in his appraisal of Alabama. The Crimson Tide posted a 7-1-1 record that year. He slighted Tennessee. The Volunteers posted an 11-0 record capped by a 17-0 victory over Oklahoma in the Orange Bowl.

The Vols allowed only 16 points while scoring 293 as they made their first major postseason appearance. Tennessee was in the midst of developing a regular season thirty-three-game unbeaten streak. The 1939 team was to shut out all ten regular season opponents.

Thomas heaped praise on the Volunteers. "We were defeated by a great football team," he said. "It was as fine a football team as I have seen since Alabama in 1934. Our players thought George Cafego was a much harder running back than Vic Bottari, California's fine ball carrier."

Tennessee coach Bob Neyland credited sound mental preparation with helping his team win. "Pregame optimism won it for us," he said in the dressing room after the game. "I'm greatly surprised. I'm overwhelmed by the decision. I'm tickled to have won like this."

Lindsey Nelson recalls long hours of labor paying dividends for the Volunteers. The famous broadcaster was a student at Tennessee in 1938. "The 1937 season had been terrible at Tennessee, by General Neyland's standards," Nelson said, "so practice for the 1938 season started on January 9. You could start early like that in those years. There weren't any rules governing practice time. And it was all directed at beating Alabama, which the Volunteers hadn't done since 1932. General Neyland had one purpose, to beat Alabama that year and every year.

"Still, Alabama had opened its season beating Southern Cal. So everybody thought they would be a great team again. And, of course, they were.

"But Tennessee had Cafego and a lot of other talented players who would later take the program to startling heights.

"Anyway, General Neyland knew the Alabama game in 1938 was the trial. He put in a new play for Cafego, who responded with a couple of particularly long runs off of it, and Tennessee won a big game.

"I recall one play starring Cafego that made the Paramount Pictures feature reel shown in theaters the following week. It showed him dragging Fred Davis, a big Alabama tackle, about 15 yards. And I remember how the announcer mispronounced his name."

Cafego, the West Virginian with family roots in Hungary, was the toast of Tennessee fans as they swarmed the streets of Birmingham in a wild celebration. More of the same was happening in Knoxville, where news of the victory spread quickly, prompting parades through downtown streets.

The "Grandstand Quarterback" was in Birmingham writing about football fever for the *News-Sentinel*:

> Your Grandstand Quarterback is writing amidst the din echoing throughout Birmingham since 5,000 victory-stunned Tennesseans came to life this afternoon after the Vols' 13-0 trampling of Alabama.
>
> This is written in the postal booth in the Thomas Jefferson Hotel lobby and such is the tumult that we cannot hear what the lady at our shoulder is saying to customers wiring the great news home.
>
> It looks more like Knoxville than Birmingham.
>
> Knoxville down here caught her breath at that early touchdown and then roared into bedlam that has prevailed since.

The "early touchdown" was scored by fullback Leonard Coffman, who scored two in the game, to go with a point after touchdown kick by Bowden Wyatt. It helped other Tennessee players to gain confidence like that possessed by guard Ed Molinski, who upon arrival in Birmingham had said, "We didn't come down here on a sightseeing trip."

Most observers thought otherwise. Pregame newspaper accounts painted a gloomy picture for Tennessee. Those press accounts started the morning after the Vols defeated Auburn the week before its game against Alabama.

"Our boys realize that they'll be meeting the No. 1 team in the nation in Birmingham," said Neyland after the victory over Auburn in Knoxville. "They know they must be ready for the greatest test of all."

Tennessee fans rallied behind that. They gave the Volunteers a rousing sendoff when the train carrying the team to Birmingham departed the South Railway Depot in Knoxville.

Sports editor Bob Wilson of the *Knoxville News-Sentinel* was present. "The big whoopee was not prearranged. The old Tennessee spirit just flared up all of a sudden. A group of sorority girls really got the rooters into action by their peppery yells."

Neyland addressed the throng: "I'm not predicting a victory. But I'll say that our boys are ready to play their hearts out."

The Volunteers were ready to do that.

Thomas must have been shocked. He spoke during a pep rally the week of the game. He said, "Alabama has been winning for so long that Alabama is not only expected to win, but Alabama is expected to look good winning. Alabama will do both against Tennessee."

The Alabama coach failed to realize that Tennessee was beginning its most stunning era in football. Not only did it become almost impossible to defeat the Volunteers, it became almost equally as difficult to score on them.

For instance, consider what Bill Rollow wrote in the *Montgomery Advertiser* after watching the Big Orange defeat Alabama:

> Duck. The Volunteers of the University of Tennessee, coached by Bob Neyland, are coming again with muskets smoking. Today, an Alabama team that was considered unbeatable was beaten. The score was 13-0. The difference in the two teams was probably greater than that.

Tennessee was at an emotional high for the game, according to Bob Woodruff, a senior defensive end on that team who served from 1963 to 1985 as athletic director for the Volunteers.

"General Neyland was going to give us a pep talk that afternoon in the dressing room before the game," Woodruff said. "He had already gone over his game maxims, a long list of things we had to do to win, when he surprised us by starting a conversation. He rarely did that.

"He got three words out of his mouth—'Are you ready?'—and we started roaring out the dressing room door. He was gonna give us a big send-off to get us ready to play. We *were* ready. We ran out of the dressing room on him before he could get going."

Woodruff is not among the more storied names from the past. But he had one play to remember against Alabama in 1938.

"We used the two-platoon system then, with the first team playing about a quarter, then the second team coming in for a while," Woodruff said. "I was on the sideline in 1938, when Alabama drove to our 46-yard line and had a fourth down with a yard to go for a first down. I had watched the films. I knew they would let quarterback Vic Bradford sneak for the yardage. I ran up to General Neyland and told him to put me in the game, that I knew what play was coming, that I could stop it.

"Sure enough, Bradford ran the ball. I charged down toward him, going straight to the hole, and he ran into me. There was no way he could have gotten through there, not with me going at full steam.

"But Bradford was a tough cookie. He liked to butt people in the mouth with his helmet. He got me a couple of times. It hurt like the devil. I sort of avoided that guy a lot of the time.

"That, too, is symbolic of the Tennessee-Alabama series. Everybody plays hard-nosed on The Third Saturday in October."

Apparently Cafego did so after another lackluster week of practice, the kind Harold Harris remembers him having all the time.

"Cafego wasn't much of a practice player," Harris said. "He'd spend a lot of time down at the Sawdust Trail, a beer joint, then go crazy on the field during games.

"Cafego was a Saturday afternoon player. If you gave him the football then, he'd cause all kinds of trouble for the opposition. He'd run with power, always with his tongue sticking out the side of his mouth, and he'd always get more fired up for games against the Crimson Tide."

One young Alabama fan noticed the Tennessee tailback was ready to play. He recalled the Cafego-Davis confrontation near the end zone.

John Forney served as the radio voice of the Crimson Tide from 1953 through 1982. One of his vivid memories of The Third Saturday in October is from the 1938 game.

"Tennessee had great players and a great team that year," Forney said. "They beat us in what was a closer game than the score indicates.

"The play I remember was Cafego trying to get into the end zone with our big tackle Fred Davis, who went on to star for the Chicago Bears, hanging onto his jersey. They had a tug-a-war that was typical of the diligent way the series was fought in those years, as now."

"That's one of the better games I played for Tennessee," Cafego said, "and that's because I knew I'd have to be at my best. Those Alabama guys were tough. We had a few casualties during my time in the series. One of their big linemen slugged Maxie Steiner and dislodged a few of his teeth. Another Alabama player hit Bowden Wyatt in the jaw and broke it.

"But we had some tough cookies, too, who wanted to win.

"It made for a helluva trip to Birmingham in 1938."

14

1939
Tennessee 21, Alabama 0

The *Wizard of Oz,* starring Judy Garland, was the movie everybody wanted to see during the fall of 1939.

But Shields-Watkins Field in Knoxville was the place to be on October 21. It was the stage on which a ballyhooed football game between the University of Tennessee and Alabama was played.

The *World Telegram* dispatched fabled sportswriter Joe Williams from its office in New York.

Life magazine dispatched fabled photographer E. E. Schaal.

Former University of Pittsburgh coach Jock Sutherland accompanied fabled sportswriter Grantland Rice.

United Press International dispatched fabled sportswriter Henry McLemore.

The *Saturday Evening Post* dispatched fabled sportswriter Francis Wallace.

The governor of Alabama, Frank Dixon, and the governor of Tennessee, Prentice Cooper, invited special guests to accompany them to *the* game.

In other words, the nation watched Tennessee defeat Alabama, 21-0, in a football game between unbeaten teams.

The only loss for the Big Orange that season came in the Rose Bowl, where Southern Cal won, 14-0, after scoring the only points registered against the mighty Volunteers in eleven games.

Alabama was not as good as thought. The Crimson Tide finished 5-3-1.

McLemore said it best in a column:

If football is important in the scheme of American things, then this one is front rank.

Down where the clay is deep and the cotton boll is rich and full, Alabama is counting on its Crimson Tide to roll again over all opposition to another of its many national championships.

Here, where the hills are high, Tennessee is calling on its Volunteers to give the state its first clear claim to national honors.

Knoxville today is a perfect example of civil lunacy. Every suburb was a wing of an asylum.

The entire front page of the *Knoxville News-Sentinel* on game day was dedicated to *the* game. Sports editor Bob Wilson wrote, "The Maginot and Siegfried Lines of football were drawn on Shields-Watkins Field."

Much was made about the matchup between coaches. Maj. Bob Neyland had posted a 101-12-8 record in thirteen seasons at Tennessee. Frank Thomas had posted a 67-8-4 record in nine seasons at Alabama.

"The boys are ready and in fine spirits," said Neyland.

"I think we will put up a good game," said Thomas.

Another headline in the *Knoxville News-Sentinel* drew attention: "Nazis Unleash Full Sea Force Against Allies." Tennessee seemed to follow suit against Alabama.

Halfback Johnny Butler led the way with a 56-yard touchdown run about which people continue to marvel. He zigged and zagged Tennessee to a lead in the second quarter, breaking what seemed like a dozen tackles in the process, running what seemed like 120 yards, and secured legendary status.

"He runs like Mercury," wrote McLemore.

"He made us look like Ned in the First Reader," said Jeff Coleman. Everybody who attempted to tackle Butler on that play seemed to arrive a split-second too late. They kept missing him by inches.

"His run made the Tennessee people have fits. All of us Alabama types were crushed. It was one of the more remarkable plays I have witnessed."

The Run will be talked about for generations.

Bob Woodruff was an assistant coach at Tennessee in 1939. He was in the press box when Butler made the memorable run to glory. "He was just twice as fast as everybody chasing him," Woodruff said with a smile during the summer of 1986.

Butler killed Alabama after most observers thought quarterback George Cafego would.

"They came to see George Cafego," wrote Wilson. "But they saw Johnny Butler. Unheralded and unsung, the swivel-hipped sophomore Butler, who runs as cunning as a fox and with the elusiveness of an eel, struck like lightning."

Other writers sang praises to Tennessee, prophetic as they were, and predicted the season would become memorable.

Wrote Williams, "Open the portals of the Rose Bowl, boys, there is a pretty fair country football team heading out that way, the Tennessee Volunteers."

Wrote Wallace, "I think Tennessee has taken the place formerly held by Pittsburgh as the dominating team of the national gridiron."

Said Sutherland to Rice, "I honestly think Tennessee would beat any team in the country. That goes for pro teams."

Tennessee looked that way dominating the Crimson Tide. The Volunteers hammered the Alabama defense with relentless fervor. The 56-yard touchdown run by Butler started the parade. It was followed by an extra point kick by Fred Newman. Bob Foxx, one of the more heralded players in Volunteer history, scored the second touchdown on a run around left end from 11 yards out of the end zone. He kicked the final two extra points.

A fake reverse resulted in the final touchdown, with Buist Warren running untouched into the end zone from 13 yards out, after Alabama had been fooled by crafty movement from the Tennessee single-wing offensive unit.

But the Volunteer defense, which was pitching the ninth of fifteen consecutive shutouts that afternoon, was more awesome than the offense. It manhandled a good Alabama offense.

The home team delighted thirty-one thousand fans by allowing Alabama only 37 yards rushing.

"It was the golden era at Tennessee, no question about that, with Neyland working his magic again," said Col. Tom Elam. "There was an air of excitement on campus when Alabama visited in 1939."

Thomas might have capped the weekend with his final printed statement about it. "I hope the war gets tougher so the government will call that fellow Neyland back to the colors. I can see I'm not going to have much fun coaching as long as he is around."

The Alabama coach must have had nightmares about Butler. At least one Crimson Tide player did.

"Johnny Butler ran all over us that day," said Holt Rast, an Alabama end from 1939 to 1941. "In fact, Fred Davis, who played tackle next to me, and I like to tell a story about that remarkable run.

"After Butler came past me twice, I hollered, 'Fred, I've had two shots at him and I haven't tackled him.' And Fred yelled, 'Don't worry about it, Holt, he'll be back around a third time.'

"It was that incredible. He must have run 150 yards to get those 56. I'll always remember that one."

Another Alabama supporter remembered "the run."

"That run looked like the crack of doom," John Forney said in Knoxville on The Third Saturday in October in 1986. "It was fabulous. So much has been written about how far he ran, but it was literally an amazing thing. He weaved all over the field. He ran at least 115 yards to get those 56 yards. He almost went from sideline to sideline. It was magnificent."

"That run by Johnny Butler was fantastic," said Ed Cifers, a former Tennessee end. "I remember getting in the way of [blocking] three Crimson Tide players on the play. Of course, he was the kind of runner who could stop on a dime, give you nine cents in change, and resume along his way to the end zone."

Woodruff is not sure Butler should have gotten as far as he did.

"Actually, I doubt he would have gained a yard had Fred Davis not tried to kill him on his first missed tackle," Woodruff said. "He tried to clothesline Butler at the line of scrimmage. Had he just reached out and grabbed him, instead of trying to take off his head, I doubt he would have gained a yard on a play that has become famous."

"That was the talk of the town on Gay Street after the victory," said former sportswriter Harold Harris of the *Knoxville News-Sentinel*. "It was Butler this and Butler that, plus Tennessee fans singing, 'We don't give a damn about the whole state of Alabama.'

"That Tennessee-Alabama game had it all. People arrived particularly early for it, dressed to kill, of course, minks and suits, and they were up bright and early on Saturday morning anticipating quite a show. Fans in those days usually hit the street at about 9:30 A.M., after a lot of partying the night before, then walked to the stadium at about 12:30 P.M. I remember them going early that day, in anticipation of a great game.

"It was a dandy, of course, and Butler made it that way. I can close my eyes right now, lean back in this chair, and see him running down the field, starting at tackle, going to end, zigging and zagging, and finally, sprinting into the end zone for the touchdown."

At that time Gus Manning was an elementary school student from Knoxville. He since has worked his way to an assistant athletic directorship in the Tennessee program. He recalls Butler frequently visiting in his house while a superstar at Knoxville High School.

"Johnny and my brother [J. T.] were good friends," Manning said. "So Johnny came to our house to eat a lot. He was like part of the family. But I was young. I idolized Johnny because of his football exploits. He was something else, an All-American, a fierce competitor. I also recall what a great billiards player he was.

"I sold concessions at the game in 1939. Cokes cost a dime, the bottled kind with twelve to a carton, which only cost a nickel in a grocery store.

"I was working my fanny off for a penny a drink when Butler made what many people consider the greatest run in the Tennessee-Alabama series. I recall the crowd going wild as he moved down the field for that touchdown.

"Interestingly, Johnny Butler made that run in a stadium located right next to the neighborhood in which he grew up. His house was located near the end zone he scored in."

According to Lindsey Nelson, the run by Butler has been seen by a lot of people. "As Bill Stern pointed out in his book, that run has been cut up into more motion pictures than any other play in history," Nelson said. "Any time there was a need for a climax, a long run, a thrilling ending to a football game, the Johnny Butler run was used.

"One such time was in *The Quarterback,* starring Wayne Morris. The character was in the Rose Bowl, but on the screen you could see that wire fence that used to run alongside Shields-Watkins Field.

"Butler filed a lawsuit over that picture. The character depicted by Wayne Morris was a drinker and a gambler. I never heard whatever happened with the lawsuit."

Nelson, who was serving as tutor for football players at Tennessee, walked to the stadium with Butler that day in 1939.

"We left the training table and stopped by the cleaners on the way," Nelson said. "Johnny picked up his suit, slung it over his shoulder, and said, 'Lindsey, I feel bad today. It's nothing serious, like a virus, but something seems out of sync.'

"Can you believe that? On the day Johnny Butler made one of the greatest runs in the history of college football, he felt bad on the way to the stadium."

15

1940
Tennessee 27, Alabama 12

THERE WAS AN ORANGE Bowl berth after the 1938 season.

There was a Rose Bowl berth after the 1939 season.

There would be a Sugar Bowl berth after the 1940 season.

That impressive run at glory was made by the University of Tennessee football program, signaling that it had replaced Alabama as the most feared name in the Deep South and ensuring that The Third Saturday in October was going to remain special.

The Crimson Tide was still winning with regularity under Notre Dame-educated coach Frank Thomas. But the headlines belonged to the Vols and their coach, Maj. Bob Neyland, who was being touted as the best in the nation. In a story written for the *New York World Telegram,* sportswriter Joe Williams said, "Major Neyland is one of the biggest sports figures in the nation. He's the most talked about coach in the east."

The "old soldier" and his team were receiving rave reviews. Games played in Knoxville were drawing people like Drummon McCunn of the Rose Bowl Committee, who told Neyland after a visit to Shields-Watkins Field in 1939, "There's something special about this atmosphere. You folks are serious about football."

None of the chatter sat smoothly with Crimson Tide fans, who in 1938 and 1939 had suffered through shutout defeats at the hands of the Volunteers. As sports editor Bob Wilson wrote in the *Knoxville*

News-Sentinel in October of 1940, during the week before the two teams played in Birmingham, "Alabama has been building up for Tennessee since spring."

That troubled Neyland, who arrived for the October 19 game more than a bit testy, although his team was ranked fifth nationally. A photographer took a picture of the coach as he rose from a sleep on the Pullman car at the Southern Railway Depot. He pointed a finger at the photographer and made him promise to destroy the negative. He tightened his tie and put on his coat before posing for a more suitable picture.

"I didn't sleep well last night," Neyland said, explaining his action.

A sportswriter rushed to his side and began asking questions. He listened without speaking, gnawing his teeth, until the sportswriter asked him who would win the game.

"Alabama, that's who," Neyland said. "Alabama will beat us. Is there anything else you want to know?"

Word of those comments spread quickly. The gossip in the streets and the newspaper story the morning of the game were good news to the Alabama fans, and joyous parties broke out among them. Not even sobering words spoken by Crimson Tide coach Frank Thomas could slow down the mobs. At a pep rally he said, "We've still got a long way to go to be ready for a resourceful team like Tennessee."

Wilson accurately reported the mood of the weekend in the *Knoxville News-Sentinel*:

> Alabama fans were worked into a frenzy.
>
> They have noticed there are a lot of cocky Tennessee fans in Birmingham. They kind of think the Vols are a little too chesty this time and that Coach Frank Thomas has stored up enough dynamite to blast them out of the stadium.
>
> They are applying a lot of psychology down here in trying to build Tennessee to the skies and lower the Crimson Tide to the basement.

It turned out that Coach Thomas's prediction was accurate. Tennessee won the game, 27-12, taking a pivotal step in a third consecutive unbeaten regular season and third consecutive Southeastern Conference championship. It was the third consecutive victory for Tennessee over Alabama.

The only blemish of that season came at its end, when Boston College defeated the Volunteers, 19-13, in the Sugar Bowl.

It was the second consecutive year that Volunteer halfback Johnny Butler electrified the crowd, rushing for 84 yards and scoring one touchdown. He set up another touchdown with a 68-yard run that featured broken tackles. Finally wrestled to the ground at the Alabama 11-yard line, he passed for the touchdown on the next play.

Wilson told the story in the *News-Sentinel:*

> Like a phantom flashing hither and yon on the gridiron, Johnny [Faster than the Wind] Butler rose to the heights of football fame on Legion Field this afternoon as he ignited a flame that carried the Tennessee Volunteers from behind to a 27-12 triumph over a great University of Alabama eleven.
>
> Some 25,000 spectators rocked and reeled in their seats as the mighty Crimson Tide surged down the gridiron behind the unerring attack of Jimmy Nelson for 48 yards to a touchdown early in the second quarter.
>
> But within two minutes these same 25,000 fans were swept out of their pews as Butler darted through the entire Alabama team for 68 yards to the Alabama 11-yard line before he was brought down. On the next play the slender Knoxville boy flipped a pass over the goal line to Al Hust, brilliant sophomore end, for a touchdown to tie the score. Fred Newman proceeded to kick the extra point and Tennessee led 7-6.
>
> But Butler was not through. A very short time later in the second period Nelson kicked to Jimmy. He caught the ball on the Alabama 48-yard line and set sail for the goal line. It was one of the spectacular weaving runs and it was pretty to behold as orange-jersied warriors mowed down the red shirts that attempted to get to Butler.

The way his players were "mowed down" angered Thomas. After the game he spewed forth bitterness, which was contradictory to his complimentary remarks about Neyland and his team the previous year. "The officials were very lax in calling clipping penalties on Tennessee, which proved costly," he said. "For the last six years they have refused to call them against Tennessee. I'm getting tired of it and I'm speaking out. I was never prouder of the way an Alabama team fought. The courage of the boys is what pleased me. It'll make us more determined for future games against the Volunteers."

Alabama showed early spark against Tennessee in 1940. Early in the second quarter halfback Jimmy Nelson ran 14 yards for the first touchdown of the game to give Alabama a 6-0 lead. Al Hust tied the game for Tennessee when he caught a 10-yard touchdown pass from Butler. Fred Newman kicked the extra point. Butler returned a punt 48 yards for the second quarter. Newman kicked the extra point.

Dave Brown returned the favor in the early stages of the third quarter, receiving a Tennessee punt and going 57 yards for a touchdown, cutting the lead to 14-12.

In the fourth quarter—with the game hanging in the balance—Tennessee quarterback Buist Warren passed to end Mike Balitsaris for two touchdowns. The first covered eight yards. Newman kicked the extra point to push the score to 21-12. The second covered 23 yards on the last play of the game.

Solidly defeating Alabama in three consecutive games provided fuel for a raging Tennessee emotional fire. Former Vol end Ed Cifers said the victories were something to be proud about.

"Beating Alabama three times in a row was an honor," Cifers said in 1986. "See, you always knew that those games would be rough, the way football should be played, that you would put on your hat knowing somebody would try to knock it off your head. Nobody had to wind up our clock for games against Alabama."

Nobody had to wind up Alabama, either.

With Tennessee leading 12-6 after Butler's 48-yard punt return for a touchdown, Crimson Tide tackle Noah Langdale collided with Big Orange fullback Max Steiner, who was delivering a block. After the play ended, Langdale said, "Come on, boy, spit out those teeth."

Steiner spat out two teeth and some blood, then said, "I'll always be happy to swap two teeth for a touchdown against Alabama."

16

1941
Alabama 9, Tennessee 2

THERE WAS A NIP in the air and all was calm.

So it was in December, when the Japanese bombed Pearl Harbor, triggering a world war.

So it was in October, when the University of Alabama and Tennessee continued their football series, adding credence to the saying that defense wins more games than offense.

How does it go? "Hold that line!"

Those words have made a tremendous impact on football. A person can hear them on sandlots and on sidelines alike. They were spoken by Alabama coach Frank Thomas at an ideal moment on October 18, 1941. He used a simple command to inspire his team as it successfully "held on" for a 9-2 victory over Tennessee on Shields-Watkins Field in Knoxville.

Stellar end Holt Rast heard the words and led a Crimson Tide goal line stand in the third quarter to lock up the first victory for Alabama over the Vols in four years. He repeatedly made important tackles during the game.

Earlier, in the first half, Alabama had staked itself to a 9-0 lead in a defensive struggle. George Hecht kicked a field goal from the 23-yard line in the first quarter. Fullback Don Salls ran one yard over left guard on third down for a touchdown in the second quarter. Tennessee did not score until end Mike Balitsaris tackled halfback Jimmy Nelson in the end zone for a safety in the third quarter.

Then, as if it was defending a naval base instead of an end zone, Alabama played ferocious defense to preserve the victory.

"I don't remember much about the goal line stand," Rast says, "but I'll never forget what Dr. George Denny, our president, said at an A-Club picnic the spring before we went to Knoxville to play Tennessee.

"Dr. Denny was making a nice little speech when, all of a sudden, he said, 'I'm sick and tired of getting beat by Tennessee.' We'd lost three times in a row to them. Nobody from Alabama liked that, especially Dr. Denny and Coach Thomas.

"I told Dr. Denny that we'd get Tennessee in 1941. He replied, 'That's what you said last year.' It was that kind of series. The school presidents got just as involved in it as did the players and the fans.

"The rivalry between Coach Thomas and Major Neyland from Tennessee was also heated. Coach Thomas would've rather beaten him than anybody else we played while I was at Alabama. He talked all the time about the boys from Knoxville, the mean Volunteers, The Third Saturday in October.

"Come to think of it, that made sense, because it might've been the top rivalry in the nation during those years."

The Alabama victory in 1941 helped it along.

Former sports editor Bob Wilson described the game for the *Knoxville News-Sentinel.* He applauded both teams.

As courageous a band of Tennessee Volunteers as ever paraded under the Orange and White banner fought the powerful and resourceful Alabama Crimson Tide to the last ditch in a bruising battle on Shields-Watkins Field, finally bowing to the enemy, 9-to-2, before a sweltering crowd of 30,000.

The Crimson Tide had rolled with great fury in the first half to gain a 9-to-0 lead. The Volunteers came back in the second half to play them off their feet, scoring a safety early in the fourth quarter and going to the Alabama four-yard line before they were finally halted in the latter stages of the same period.

With versatile Jimmy Nelson in the driver's seat and a fast, vicious charging line packed by Holt Rast, end, pouring down the gridiron, Alabama penetrated Tennessee territory several times that day.

It was a sweet victory for Coach Frank Thomas and his athletes, for it was the first time that the Crimson Tide had been able to turn the trick since 1937, 14-7, in Knoxville.

Thomas was ecstatic on the fortieth anniversary of the storied series. "I thought Jimmy Nelson played his best game for Alabama," he said. "He punted, passed, and ran well. He played better than any back we had had in years."

The victory would have been sweeter for Thomas had Neyland been his rival that afternoon. The military whiz, a nemesis for Alabama, had been recalled into service as World War II began. He turned over the reins of leadership at Tennessee to John Barnhill, who was to remain in that position through 1945, when Neyland returned to campus as a general.

But it was a welcome victory for Crimson Tide loyals. Sportswriter Harry Snyder of the *Decatur Daily* thought it was thorough. He wrote about how Alabama managed to stop the star of the game in previous years:

> Tennessee's Johnny Butler couldn't find his gun, so Alabama's Red Elephants handed the Volunteers a 9-2 lacing, although the final score did not relate the superiority the Crimson Tide held over the retiring Southeastern Conference champions.
>
> Alabama scored all of its points in the first half, besides throttling the Vols' offense completely.
>
> Butler, the Vols' 163-pound tailback, who was poison to the deep southerners the past two years, never could get going. Jimmy Nelson always kept his punts—he averaged 41 yards per boot—zooming outside his reach, or they were high enough to permit speedy tacklers to smother Butler as soon as he grabbed the ball.
>
> The Vols, in losing their first conference game since the fall of 1937, rolled up seven first downs to the invaders' nine, but they misfired on their one big opportunity, the drive ending on the Alabama four-yard line. That came in the third quarter.
>
> Tennessee threw 23 passes, completing only five, while Alabama tossed three and completed one. The Reds intercepted three passes when they seemed to mean the most.

Alabama, which had lost to Mississippi State two weeks before it arrived in Knoxville, posted a 9-2 record, including a 29-21 victory over Texas A&M in the Cotton Bowl.

Tennessee, which had lost to Duke two weeks earlier, rallied to post an 8-2 record.

While the game lacked the normal hype that had been so prevalent in recent years, it was as hotly contested as other games in the series. It also attracted two famous baseball players, Pee Wee Reese and Tom Drake of the Brooklyn Dodgers. The golden glove shortstop must have enjoyed it because the defensive star was obvious.

"Holt Rast is one of the most devastating ends that I have seen in several seasons," wrote Wilson in the *Knoxville News-Sentinel.* "The big Alabama standout was poison to the Vols all afternoon. There is only one time that I remember seeing him blocked completely out of a play and that was the time Bobby Cifers wrapped his 195 pounds of brawn around him on one of the several reverse runs. One of the wags remarked that he had kept account of the plays run at Rast, and that Tennessee had not gained an inch at his terminal. Rast is labeled a potential All-American. He gets my vote."

The performance was overlooked by most people, however, because of unsettled international relations. Those turbulent times were reflected in a headline in the *Knoxville News-Sentinel* the morning after the game: "Sub Torpedoes U.S. Destroyer 330 Miles off the Coast of Iceland."

"Football was still important, with the Alabama game stealing talk from the war, but it was slowing down some," retired sportswriter Harold Harris said in 1986. "Not until after the bombing of Pearl Harbor did we get serious about the war. But even when Tennessee and Alabama played that year, we knew it was just a matter of time before the fighting got serious."

That sobering mood carried over as Alabama went to the Cotton Bowl to defeat Texas A&M, 29-21. Although the Aggies outgained the Crimson Tide 309 yards to 75, the victors intercepted seven passes and recovered five fumbles to nail down the victory.

"The Japanese attack on Pearl Harbor came only a few days after we accepted the invitation to play Texas A&M in the Cotton Bowl," Rast said in 1977. "It distracted from the football game. The whole mood of the country was downcast. We knew we were in a war, and I was kind of anxious to get the game and my college degree behind me so I could join up and help the country.

"But I was glad to get a victory over Tennessee before I left Alabama."

17

1942
Alabama 8, Tennessee 0

THIS TIME BOTH TEAMS made it into the holiday season. That made 1942 a festive year for football programs at the University of Alabama and Tennessee. But World War II dampened an Alabama victory over Tennessee, 8-0, on October 17 in Birmingham.

The Crimson Tide went to the Orange Bowl, where it defeated Boston College, 37-21, to cap an 8-3 season. The Volunteers went to the Sugar Bowl, where they defeated Tulsa, 14-7, to cap a 9-1-1 season.

It was the seventh bowl appearance for Alabama, which had played in the Rose Bowl five times and the Sugar Bowl once. It was the fourth bowl appearance for Tennessee, which had played in the Orange Bowl, the Rose Bowl, and the Sugar Bowl.

It was the fifth consecutive year the winner in *the game* was invited to a bowl game.

But those were not happy times in our nation. The morning after the game, which was a defensive struggle highlighted by an Alabama safety, the *Knoxville News-Sentinel* ran this headline: "Drafting Of Teens Wins Fast Approval."

The normal hoopla was absent, despite Alabama and Tennessee carrying fourth and fifteenth rankings nationally, respectively, into the game.

Much of the excitement came after the game, when several Tennessee players discovered money had been stolen from their wallets by a thief who had entered their dressing room during the second half. That thievery took place at about the time Alabama began asserting itself on the playing field.

Former sports editor Bob Wilson of the *Knoxville News-Sentinel* noticed that Alabama finally displayed its potential after halftime:

> Alabama's Red Elephants, held in check in the first half, stampeded in the third and fourth quarters. When the dust kicked up by the onrushing herd had cleared away, the Tennessee Vols were found buried under Legion Field ground by an 8-0 score.
>
> If the Elephants hadn't gone on a rampage to score a touchdown in the fourth period, the defeat would be much more bitter. It would have been a 2-to-0 gift victory.

The safety came at the start of the second half, when Don Whitmire kicked off for Alabama. Bobby Cifers of Tennessee touched the football as it sailed over his head, and officials ruled it a safety when the football rolled through the end zone and came to rest against a fence.

Coach John Barnhill of Tennessee protested, without success. As he ranted and raved, chances are good he wondered about one of his pregame comments to Wilson, "That old Alabama jinx is liable to pop up again in a whale of a game."

Fullback Bobby Tom Jenkins scored a touchdown for the Crimson Tide that put the game safely out of reach, running 33 yards around left end in the fourth quarter.

With the Crimson Tide defense playing intensely, it became almost impossible for Tennessee to bounce back. That set well with John Forney, who from 1953 through 1982 served as the radio voice of the Crimson Tide. "Tennessee was enjoying a nice run on Alabama in those years," Forney said. "Alabama had won in 1941, 9-2, but the Crimson Tide people were obsessed with beating Tennessee after losing from 1938 through 1940.

"In 1942 it was Bobby Tom Jenkins who electrified Alabama fans. He ran 38 yards on a reverse for the touchdown. He was introduced by Coach Frank Thomas as the next great All-American from Alabama. Sadly for us, he left after that season and became an All-American at Navy. He would have been one of the great runners in Alabama history.

"I can still see him running around end against Tennessee. He looked like a freight train going into the end zone."

The Volunteers traveled to Birmingham on a makeshift train put together after their scheduled locomotive ran six hours behind schedule. It was crowded to the point of discomfort after Tennessee players and coaches, as well as several hundred fans, got on board. It was uncomfortably hot.

In Alabama, things were relatively cool, although Coach Frank Thomas was fretting over his pass defense. "Awful, all of it. Awful!" But he also conducted a fiery pregame pep rally.

The night before the game, he said, "The boys think they can win over Tennessee, and I think they can win. It will be a victory for the Crimson Tide, our second straight over the talented and inspired boys from Tennessee."

Those words prompted a spirited game that—because no game would be played in 1943 due to the war—provided Alabama fans with bragging rights for two years.

Sportswriter Zipp Newman of the *Birmingham News* watched the game from the press box. He wrote:

> Alabama cut loose bounding, bouncing Bobby Jenkins in the last period and the Talladega sophomore raced 38 yards for the only touchdown to give the Crimson Tide its first victory in eight years over Tennessee at Legion Field. It was one of the greatest demonstrations of line play ever seen on a southern gridiron after a scoreless first period.
>
> Still the nation's No. 1 game, that was just what it was as 25,000 Alabama and Tennessee fans watched one of the greatest games in the historic series that has decided so many Dixie championships and bowl invitations.

Sportswriter Naylor Stone, writing in the *Birmingham Post,* offered a somewhat different opinion of the game. He lauded Alabama. But he found the game somewhat uneventful.

> We believe Frank Thomas has the finest football team in all the land this year. But we are not going to make ourselves look silly-dilly by saying the Alabama-Tennessee battle was one of the greatest games of the historic series.
>
> Absent was the drama that has made this weekend so rewarding for so many people since the 1928 encounter in Tuscaloosa.

It was a grueling sort of battle, the kind that keeps you on the edge of your seat, and there was a display of brilliancy by two fine lines. Blocking, tackle and charging were vicious. But, to the average customer, it didn't give thrills, except when Bob Jenkins galloped for a touchdown.

Because so many able-bodied young men went into military service, football was suspended at Alabama and Tennessee in 1943. Georgia, Louisiana State, and Vanderbilt were the only Southeastern Conference programs able to field teams. The Big Ten Conference tried unsuccessfully to get former players to return to school for postgraduate study, so it could continue its full schedule of games.

That left Army and Navy to steal most national headlines, even in football, except when it was announced that Bronko Nagurski was returning to the National Football League at age thirty-five.

Interestingly, former Alabama player Arthur "Tarzan" White, a standout lineman from 1934 through 1936, was starring on the football field in 1942 under Neyland, who was coaching the Army All-Stars.

"Yeah, Neyland and I spent some time talking about Alabama and Tennessee games we'd participated in," White said at his house in Gaylesville, Alabama. "We both agreed it was the biggest game both programs played every year. We were both amazed by the intensity.

"I can assure you the intensity was greater when Neyland was coaching Tennessee. In 1934, when we beat them by a touchdown, those Tennessee players were fighters. In 1935, when he was away, we romped over them pretty easily. In 1936, when he returned to Knoxville to coach them, they fought us off in Birmingham and got a scoreless tie. He made a helluva difference in the way Alabama and Tennessee games were contested.

"Neyland was one of the best five coaches in history, maybe the best at the collegiate level, and I enjoyed playing three games under him.

"I've always been proud to tell people I got to play under Neyland and under Thomas, two of the great coaches in history, men who made games between Alabama and Tennessee special and fierce.

"Both coaches were in love with the series."

Because of World War II, Alabama and Tennessee fans waited patiently for the renewal of their spat, only to find that the 1944 game, a scoreless tie, left them disappointed and starving for the right to boast.

18

1944
Alabama 0, Tennessee 0

RARELY DOES A TIE impress anyone.

But Bob Woodruff, who knows a lot about football, having been a coach, player, and athletic director, was impressed. And when he considers great coaching performances, one surprising name quickly comes to his mind: John Barnhill.

This is the same John Barnhill who filled in for Maj. Bob Neyland and led the Volunteers to a tie against Alabama in 1944.

The series between Tennessee and Alabama has had more than its share of great coaches. Wallace Wade. Bob Neyland. Frank Thomas. Bowden Wyatt. Paul "Bear" Bryant. Barnhill, like many others who have taken part in The Third Saturday in October spectacle, is not as famous as those men.

"But the job he did in 1944 is as good as I can remember," Woodruff said at his office in Stokely Athletics Center in Knoxville. "He took our program after a year layoff from football and put us in the Rose Bowl. That's a strong accomplishment."

At Alabama, meanwhile, Thomas was working wonders with a "War Babies" team that secured a berth in the Sugar Bowl.

Tennessee finished its season with a 7-1-1 record.

Alabama finished its season with a 5-2-2 record.

Bob Wilson watched the action at Shields-Watkins Field in Knoxville. The former sports editor at the *Knoxville News-Sentinel* wrote:

Tennessee's Volunteers and Alabama's Crimson Tide were both right defensively. As a result, they fought to a scoreless tie in a furious battle before more than 30,000 fans.

The game was replete with scoring threats that didn't end until the final whistle. Tennessee's poor kicking and a great center, Vaughn Mancha of Alabama, spoiled the Volunteers' chances of hitting the scoring jackpot. An offside penalty also broke up a Tennessee drive.

The highly touted Harry Gilmer lived up to his advance reputation of being one of the greatest passers in Alabama history, pitching the Tidemen into several scoring positions. Gilmer was the Tide's offensive spark, but Mancha was the boy who bolted the door in Tennessee's face as he almost single-handedly broke up the Vols' off-tackle smashes and cutbacks, which have been effective against other opponents.

Buster Stephens, the Vol backfield ace, again played a brilliant game, but was never able to get into the open.

Mancha was a reason why. His defensive prowess was displayed after Johnny Mauer of the Tennessee scouting staff told the Volunteers, "That big boy is liable to give us a lot of trouble. He's strong and good."

Mancha led an Alabama defense that kept the Volunteers out of the end zone in the third quarter after they had driven to the Crimson Tide 10-yard line.

In the fourth quarter, with the outcome of the game at stake, Bill Fields of Alabama missed a field goal from the 20-yard line. He was under a heavy rush from Tennessee defense.

Meanwhile, Mancha, the Alabama defensive star, was awesome enough to receive accolades from fans of both schools, as well as from former sportswriter Zipp Newman of the *Birmingham News:*

> The spectators left the field cheering big Vaughn Mancha, who was the greatest player in the game. If he wasn't an All-American today, Dixie Howell never threw a completed pass for the Crimson Tide. Mancha made more tackles than any two players in the game.
>
> Mancha! He was a line by himself. No Alabama center ever played any more football in one game than this. They would like to put Mancha on exhibition in Knoxville as the super center.

The resumption of the Tennessee-Alabama series came as more bad news spread across the nation, some related to World War II, as expected, and some not. A headline in the *Knoxville News-Sentinel* said a lot: "MacArthur Warns Japs That United States Will Be Tough." There was a story about baseball superstar Joe DiMaggio being admitted to a hospital in California for treatment of a war injury. And, as if he had not stolen enough headlines with his performances in past Tennessee-Alabama games, an article stated that former Volunteer star tailback Johnny Butler had been fined two hundred dollars by the Pittsburgh Steelers of the National Football League for "laying down." He had joined other players in a "strike" before a game.

One Alabama fan, who read about the action taken against Butler, was overheard on Gay Street by a newspaper reporter, saying, "I wish he'd done that in 1939."

That fan is proof that people who witnessed them rarely forget flamboyant plays from the Alabama-Tennessee series. Memories from The Third Saturday in October are too golden for that to happen.

19

1945
Alabama 25, Tennessee 7

FORMER UNIVERSITY OF ALABAMA football star Harry Gilmer saw the many faces of Coach Frank Thomas while playing for the Crimson Tide.

He remembers him sitting in a corner of a dressing room in the Rose Bowl on January 1, 1946, and weeping like a child. Thomas was tired that afternoon in Pasadena, California, after Alabama had defeated Southern Cal, 34-14, to cap a 10-0 season. He also remembers Thomas smiling like a contented man on The Third Saturday in October in 1945 in a dressing room at Legion Field in Birmingham.

Thomas was happy on that October 20 afternoon after Alabama had defeated Tennessee, 25-7, in a game in which Gilmer had put on a splendid show as a running and passing quarterback. "Coach Thomas, who graduated at Notre Dame, had a lot of Knute Rockne in him," Gilmer said during a visit at his house in St. Louis. "He could fire you up with his words. He was a psychological whiz.

"That was particularly true when we played games against Tennessee. That game meant a lot to him. He was at his best then. He could scream. He could cry. He could do anything to get us ready to play the Volunteers. He did a great job in that regard in 1945."

Proof rests in the game Gilmer played against the Volunteers. He impressed former sports editor Bob Wilson of the *Knoxville News-Sentinel*, who wrote about his performance:

Hurrying Harry Gilmer, aided and abetted by a fumbling Tennessee team, practically pitched Alabama into the Rose Bowl as the Crimson Tide routed the Volunteers, 25-to-7, before a capacity crowd on Legion Field.

Thousands of Tennessee fans in the stands saw the handwriting of defeat on the wall as Gilmer started passing the Vols dizzy in the first few minutes of play. Their hopes dropped to a low ebb as the Crimson Tide went for their first touchdown in the first eight minutes of the game.

Gilmer lost no time in letting the Vols and their backers know that he was going to be the man of the day.

Gilmer and Company, and I write it that way because Gilmer was the spark that set off the touchdown fuse, had a 19-to-0 lead in the second quarter.

The Vols were without the services of two of their most valuable backs, Buster Stephens and Billy Bevis, and it was generally conceded by experts that if Stephens and Bevis were not ready for 60 minutes of rugged play that Alabama would win by a large margin.

Gilmer directed an Alabama offense that delighted fans in Legion Field. He got the scoring started early, running six yards for a touchdown in the first quarter, with Hugh Morrow kicking the ensuing extra point.

The second and third Crimson Tide touchdowns were scored by fullback Fred Grant. He ran over center from one yard for his first score and caught a 20-yard pass from Gilmer, whose quick feet sparked numerous Alabama offensive uprisings, for his second score.

Tennessee, befuddled while attempting to stop Alabama, scored in the fourth quarter. Maxwell Partin got into the end zone on a 43-yard pass from Bob Lund, a freshman who was on his way to becoming a superstar. The Volunteers' extra point was kicked by Casey Stephenson.

Alabama made it a bona fide romp in the fourth quarter, when fullback Norwood Hodges dived over left guard from one yard for the final touchdown.

"Alabama was a great team," said Bud Hubbell, who played for Tennessee that afternoon. "Gilmer was fantastic. But they had a lot of stars. We were underdogs from the outset.

"We were young. We were getting ready for better things."

The game attracted sportswriters from around the nation. The report in the *Louisville Courier-Journal* said:

In this aptly nicknamed Magic City, flying footballs bloomed into flowering bowls as Birmingham's master magician, Harry Gilmer, passed Alabama to a victory over Tennessee in a battle of unbeaten football giants.

Alabama adherents not only saw the former Woodlawn High School star help defeat Tennessee in this battle, but they saw in his magical blooming passes an almost certain bid to the Rose Bowl game in Pasadena.

Alabama, ranked fifth in the nation before the game, marched onward to a perfect record. Tennessee did not lose again, finishing with an 8-1 record.

The victory over the Volunteers came in Thomas's next-to-last confrontation with the rivals from East Tennessee. Suffering from high blood pressure, he was so sick during the 1945 season that he conducted practices from the bed of a truck. By the time the Crimson Tide arrived in Pasadena for the Rose Bowl, he was fatigued. "I don't believe I could have held up all season if my boys hadn't given me such a lift with their great performances," Thomas said as he sat in the dressing room at the Rose Bowl and wept. "I'm a worn out man. I'm glad it's over. I didn't think I'd make it this far. And I didn't think my boys had the kind of fight they displayed this entire season on my behalf."

Gilmer recalls the pep talk "Coach Tommy" gave Alabama players before the Rose Bowl game.

"He started off in a whisper with three words," Gilmer said. "He kept uttering, 'Block and tackle, block and tackle, block and tackle' until his voice grew louder. Finally, he walked to [stellar tackle] Vaughn Mancha, started screaming, 'Block and tackle,' and started pounding Mancha on his helmet. Then, he screamed, 'Let's go get them!'

"I'll never forget how we all dashed toward the door, in a wad, only to find the door had to be pulled open, not pushed. We surged back, then started again. I literally stepped on top of four or five teammates trying to get to the field.

"That's how Coach Thomas could motivate his players. Just when I thought I'd heard it all from him, he'd come up with some other way to send chills down my spine."

Gilmer recalls little about the victory over Tennessee in 1945, except the obvious: "As I remember, everything just went perfectly for us."

That was apparent. By this time the winner of The Third Saturday in October was becoming used to enjoying the spoils of victory.

In 1937 Alabama won and went to the Rose Bowl.

In 1938 Tennessee won and went to the Orange Bowl.

In 1939 Tennessee won and went to the Rose Bowl.

In 1940 Tennessee won and went to the Sugar Bowl.

In 1941 Alabama won and went to the Cotton Bowl.

In 1942 Alabama won and went to the Orange Bowl. Tennessee lost and went to the Sugar Bowl.

In 1944 Alabama and Tennessee tied, with both teams going to a bowl game, the Crimson Tide to the Sugar Bowl and the Volunteers to the Rose Bowl.

In 1945 Alabama won and went to the Rose Bowl, where it paid tribute to a great coach, who was too weary to fully relish victory.

"I'm tired, I'm sick, and I'm proud," Thomas said after his team capped a grand season with a Rose Bowl victory.

Thomas was also intelligent, according to Alf Van Hoose, current sports editor and columnist at the *Birmingham News*.

"Thomas had one of the best minds of anybody who ever coached the sport," Van Hoose observed. "He ranked right up there with Gen. Bob Neyland and Paul 'Bear' Bryant, in that regard. He was extremely intelligent.

"Never have I heard of a coach who kept up with life in general, as well as football, like Thomas did. He read magazines and newspapers all the time. He was a scholar of sorts. And, of course, he was a genius when it came to making needed adjustments during games."

"Coach Tommy" was also grand, as Gilmer can attest, when it came to motivating his Alabama players for games against Tennessee. But Tennessee had an ace in the hole, too, actually a brilliant coach who was serving his country.

World War II had taken away a great leader, Bob Neyland, who was preparing to make a triumphant return to the Big Orange in 1946.

20

1946
Tennessee 12, Alabama 0

Former fullback Walt Slater joined the University of Tennessee football program in 1941.

"I got there just after General Neyland and his teams had defeated Alabama three years in a row," Slater said at his house in St. Augustine, Florida. "I heard all the war stories.

"It was obvious to me that the Alabama game was *the* game for Tennessee. It was amazing to me how people in Knoxville got so fired up for The Third Saturday in October.

"I heard how [former Tennessee player] Maxie Steiner lost a tooth while playing against Alabama, got it knocked out, with blood spewing out of his mouth, and how he refused to come out of the game. He said something like he could get a new tooth, but he might not be able to get another win over powerful Alabama.

"That heightened my interest in what I soon found out was a dogfight game every season. Hearing about games against Alabama was entertaining. Playing in games against Alabama was fun, as well as hazardous to your health."

Because his career was interrupted by World War II, Slater played against Alabama in 1941, 1942, and 1946. The last game was the most pleasing, because on October 19 that year, Tennessee recorded a 12-0 victory on Shields-Watkins Field that remains one of the more talked-about games in the history of the Tennessee program. What happened during those sixty minutes, in which Alabama quarterback Harry Gilmer was battered by a wicked Tennessee defense, prompted Slater's memories.

Former sports editor Bob Wilson of the *Knoxville News-Sentinel* wrote:

> Displaying destructive offensive power, plus the most savage defensive play ever uncorked by any of Coach Bob Neyland's teams, Tennessee smashed to a 12-to-0 triumph over a mighty Alabama eleven. It was a battle that saw "Lighthorse Harry" Gilmer steal the show for individual brilliance by his fourth-period razzle-dazzle passing attack that made the Crimson Tide a continuous threat to score until the final whistle.
>
> After the crowd of more than 40,000 high-spirited spectators had witnessed a ding-dong combat between the gridiron giants for the first quarter, the Volunteers unleashed pent-up fury of the past four years, going for Tennessee's first touchdown in the middle of the second period.
>
> After Tennessee had dominated the third quarter (extending its lead to the final margin), Alabama came back determined that their 14-game winning streak would not be broken. And, except for the super defensive play of those gallant Tennessee forwards— Dick Huffman, the greatest lineman on the field, Denver Crawford, Ray Drost, Royal Price, Jim Myers, Bud Hubbell, Jim Powell, Norman Meseroll, Dave Stephenson, Buddy Pike, Chan Caldwell and others—they would have succeeded in their determination not to lose.
>
> Three times the great Gilmer passed the Crimson Tide within the shadow of the Tennessee goal posts in the final quarter—and three times the vicious Volunteers closed the door in their face. Twice they held the Tidemen for downs on the four-yard line. In their last desperate effort to score, the Crimson Tide saw Jack Armstrong, Vol blocking back, intercept Gilmer's pass intended for Ted Cook on the goal line.
>
> The interception sounded the doom for Alabama, and the stands roared an ovation for Gilmer as football's greatest and most spectacular passer walked with his head high toward the Alabama bench.
>
> Besides Bob Lund, with his two touchdowns, the two standout players all afternoon, everybody agreed, were Gilmer and Dick Huffman, the Tennessee tackle who was literally everywhere making savage tackles.

Lund made two small steps into the end zone for Tennessee that afternoon, but they will be recalled as leaps by Volunteer fans who watched a game in which short yardage carried a high premium.

Lund scored from six inches out in the second quarter.

Lund scored from six inches out in the third quarter.

Then, with points on the scoreboard, it was time for the Volunteers to hold on for the victory. On two occasions Tennessee stopped Alabama in four downs from the four-yard line in the fourth quarter.

And on another drive, the Vols were saved when Jack Armstrong intercepted a Crimson Tide pass at the goal line.

It was Neyland-type football at its best.

Does Slater remember? You bet.

"Harry Gilmer was magnificent," he said. "But he took a pounding from Huffman and Crawford. And he kept plugging. He got the loudest ovation a Tennessee crowd has ever given a rival player."

Among the Alabama faithful who saw Gilmer take a pounding at the hands of Crawford and Huffman was John Forney, who seven years later would become the radio voice of the Crimson Tide.

"It was unmerciful what they did to Gilmer," Forney said. "But what the Tennessee fans did at the end of the game was brilliant. They rose and gave Gilmer a heartfelt ovation.

"Huffman was so much better than anybody else on the field that day, though, like a pro playing with junior college boys. He was totally overpowering."

Gus Manning, a Tennessee assistant athletic director, was a student on campus when Huffman and Crawford manhandled Gilmer. He had returned from military service during World War II. He remembers Huffman as being too strong and too tough for the opposition.

"It was the most courageous performance I have seen by an Alabama player," Manning said about Gilmer. "Huffman beat on him every way possible. He was all over him every time he got the ball. Gilmer was totally exhausted when it was over. He played a tremendous game while taking the beating of his life from Huffman.

"Huffman was too strong for those guys. He was mean, too, because of the war experience he just had. He was a rough guy, a West Virginia native, a guy who loved to fight. I saw him aboard a ship at sea. He fought a heavyweight boxer. It took one lick. Whap! Huffman took him out. He was a barroom brawler who was put on the football field.

"Gilmer went on to play for the Washington Redskins. Huffman went on to play for the Los Angeles Rams. They played against each other in their first game as pros. Huffman got Gilmer that day, too, and said, 'Hey, my friend, I have been looking for you.' Gilmer told me that was a laugh."

Does Gilmer remember taking a beating at the hands of Tennessee?

You bet.

"After every ball I threw that day, I ended up on the ground, flat on my back," he said during the summer of 1986 at his house in St. Louis. "When we lost the ball that last time after the interception, they took me out of the game. I was glad to go.

"I was about exhausted. I remember walking toward the bench, seeing Coach Thomas coming to greet me, just to pat me on the butt, and I vaguely remember hearing an ovation from the Tennessee fans.

"I sat down. I was about to go into convulsions. My heart was pumping so hard it scared me. But more than anything, I remember the physical beating Huffman and Crawford gave me. It was a tough game."

Gilmer received a late reminder of that game when he was coaching with the Minnesota Vikings. He went to a restaurant in Minneapolis for a meeting with the coaching staff from the University of Minnesota. "When I walked in the door, I heard a booming voice scream, 'It's him! There he is, Harry Gilmer! And I'm the reason he's bald-headed today! I pulled every hair out of his head!'

"I never dreamed I'd run into Denver Crawford again."

Nor did Gilmer think he would get an opportunity to meet Neyland.

"I was in Knoxville scouting the Tennessee spring game one year, looking for pro prospects," Gilmer said, "when this large man grabbed my arm and pulled me aside. He took me over to this guy and said, 'Harry, I'm sure you've met General Neyland before.' I shook my head and looked at Neyland.

"Then, the general said, 'So, you're Gilmer.' And he reached down and gave me an affectionate hug, saying, 'Boy, I love you.'

"Never have I been so flattered as I was that day."

In the dressing room after the game, Neyland had said about Gilmer, "I doubt that football has ever seen his equal."

But the Tennessee coach, who was in 1946 resuming his coaching career after being promoted to the rank of general in the military, also had nice things to say about Huffman. "By his performance, Huffman is truly an All-American," Neyland said.

Alabama walked into a trap of sorts when it arrived in Knoxville for the 1946 game. This is how the *News-Sentinel* described the scene the day of the game:

> Jam-packed streets, horse mobs, valiant pennants—win, lose or draw—from the panorama of Knoxville today as host to some 50,000 game-goers to the great Alabama-Tennessee football tilt, including many thousands of alumni attending the largest home-coming in the history of the University of Tennessee.
>
> And no matter how pleased or disgruntled the rooters may be over the outcome of the game, they certainly have no kick coming about the weather. A light wind, clear skies and temperatures in the low 70s, making it pleasant for the spectators and not too hot for the players.

Gilmer felt some heat, however, and the entire Alabama team must have felt somewhat jinxed.

The bus in which the Crimson Tide rode to the stadium on game day experienced a broken axle, and the players completed the trip in taxi cabs and the automobiles of frenzied fans.

By contrast, at the end of the season Tennessee players enjoyed a delightful trip to the Orange Bowl, where the Volunteers concluded a Southeastern Conference championship season, during which they produced a 9-2 record, with an 8-0 loss to Rice.

The general had returned from the war, as noticed by Joe Livingston, who wrote in the *Atlanta Journal* about the Tennessee victory in 1946:

> The story of Tennessee's 12-0 victory over Alabama is the drama of a gallant, graying soldier who came home from the second war refusing to believe the things he fought for had changed. When Gen. Bob Neyland greeted a strange football squad in the summer, he was told about new trickery offenses developed during his absence.
>
> Away on the other side too long, Neyland got home too late to start over. He decided to play it close to the belt and hope for the best. The heaviest squad the general has coached punched a classy Crimson Tide team with power, the same power that stunned people a decade ago.
>
> The general didn't change, not a thing.

And, said Shirley Povich, a sportswriter for the *Washington Post:*

That old fundamentalist, Gen. Bob Neyland, gave one more demon-
stration that a football team need not be fancy if it can hit hard. Tennessee's victory over Alabama was a triumph for the rugged and
somewhat old-fashioned school of football thought.
   The dozen scouts who recorded the action must have filed
alarming reports for future opponents of the Volunteers. This is a
team that has power on both offense and defense. What they saw
was incorrectly called the single wing. Actually, it was just pure Tennessee football.

Gilmer remained the star.
   "He was rawhide and rubber," said Murray Warmath, at the time a
Tennessee assistant coach. "Our boys pulled on him from all directions, threatening to pull him apart. I thought, 'Well, there he goes for
this game. He has to be finished after that kind of treatment.' But he
was the first guy who jumped to his feet, and he never bothered to
brush off his suit."
   Huffman did his part for the Volunteers.
   "Let me tell you about Dick Huffman," said retired sportswriter
Harold Harris of the *Knoxville News-Sentinel.* "He was wicked. A
popular story back then was how he took a basketball player by the
ankles and dangled him out a dorm window at what would become
Neyland Stadium. The man was tough. The man was mean.
   "Harry Gilmer, who was admired after taking the most physical
beating I've ever seen, can tell you a lot about Dick Huffman."

21

1947
Alabama 10, Tennessee 0

COLLEGE FOOTBALL FANS FROM all parts of the nation must have been shocked after the first month of the 1947 season.

Tennessee had a 1-2 record. Alabama, which was playing its first season under Coach Harold "Red" Drew, after posting a 115-24-7 record in fifteen years under Coach Frank Thomas, had a 2-2 record.

To say something was missing on The Third Saturday in October is an understatement. Volunteer and Crimson Tide fans had grown accustomed to their teams clashing with the figurative wind at their backs. But former Alabama quarterback Harry Gilmer will tell you it never has really mattered how the two teams have fared before their annual spectacle.

"You know, when I got out of [Birmingham] Woodlawn High School and reported to Alabama for my freshman season in 1944, I had no idea what playing college football meant," Gilmer said at his house in St. Louis. "The only college football I had seen was when I stopped on my way home from school to watch Howard College practice.

"So you can imagine how shocked I was when I went onto the field the first time to play Tennessee. I learned a lot in that baptism. I learned that the two teams always fight it out like crazy. It was like that in 1944. It was like that in 1947."

Gilmer got the last laugh on the Volunteers on October 18, when he led Alabama to a 10-0 victory at Legion Field in Birmingham. It was a clutch play by Gilmer that got Alabama rolling toward a victory in a game that seemed destined to end in a tie. It took a courageous call on the part of Drew to set it up.

Alabama had driven to the Tennessee 10-yard line in the third quarter. It was fourth down. Zeros were on the scoreboard. Instead of instructing Bob Morrow to kick a field goal, Drew opted for a play that sprung Gilmer for a run into the end zone. The quarterback faked one of his patented jump passes, tucked away the football and ran for a touchdown. As Tennessee players shook their heads in both dismay and disgust, Morrow kicked the extra point to make the score 7-0.

In the third quarter, after Gilmer led another march up the field, Morrow kicked a field goal from the 17-yard line to establish the final margin.

The Crimson Tide caught fire after that victory, finishing with an 8-3 record, which included a 27-7 loss to Texas in the Sugar Bowl.

Tennessee never recovered. The Big Orange posted a 5-5 record, which heightened criticism of Gen. Bob Neyland for continuing to coach the single wing offensive formation, instead of the more popular T formation.

"I doubt I played a better game at Alabama than the one I did against Tennessee in 1947," Gilmer said. "It was one of those afternoons when everything clicked for me and our team."

Apparently former *Knoxville News-Sentinel* sports editor Bob Wilson agreed with that self-analysis. He wrote the morning after the game:

> Sharp-shooting Harry Gilmer put on one of the greatest and most spectacular passing exhibitions of his illustrious career at Alabama in the short span of five minutes as he pitched the Crimson Tide to a 10-to-0 triumph over the unlucky Tennessee Vols.
>
> A sweltering shirt-sleeved crowd of 31,670 almost forgot that the great passing wizard was in the ball game in the first half, when he attempted only one pass and the Volunteers dominated play, muffing several chances to score.
>
> But Gilmer became the whole show as the third quarter got under way, completing five consecutive passes as the Crimson Tide rolled 49 yards to their touchdown. The fireworks started after Gilmer took one of Hal Littleford's punts and returned it 10 yards.
>
> The Volunteers fought valiantly as the Crimson Tide continued to roll furiously, managing to thwart a scoring threat by stalling the

Tidemen on the one-yard line. They battled gamely to check the Tide on the seven-yard line early in the fourth quarter. Coach Red Drew rushed Hugh Morrow into the game to try for a field goal. His kick covered their money.

Neyland, who was coaching Tennessee for the second season since returning from service in World War II, saw reason for optimism after the defeat. "Gilmer is leaving," he said, "and we should be happy about it."

The happiest man in the stadium, however, had to be Drew. He had been under criticism since replacing Thomas as coach. Alabama fans did not appreciate his conservative style.

"Alabama conceivably could have a disastrous season, despite its veteran senior team," Bill Waddell wrote in the *Birmingham Post* after the Crimson Tide lost at Vanderbilt to drop to 1-2.

According to Ray Richeson, an Alabama guard that season, the Crimson Tide turned around its season "with rededication." He added that "beating Tennessee helped it along nicely."

But the season ended with Alabama being soundly whipped by Texas in New Orleans. And, sadly, Gilmer finished his career with a miserable game, five yards rushing and three pass completions in 11 attempts.

"You've always got to remember the bad along with the good," said Gilmer. "But I'll always have fonder memories of my last game against Tennessee than my last game at Alabama."

The thrill of The Third Saturday in October remains for Gilmer now that his glitter has faded.

It has always been that way with Alabama and Tennessee, as stated excitedly the day before *the* game in 1947 by Naylor Stone, a sportswriter for the *Birmingham Post:*

> Old Bamas will take down their hair tonight. They will turn back the calendar a lot of years and throw robust verbal blocks at one another. What we are getting around to is telling you the Alabama alumni will frolic. After all, doesn't the Crimson Tide roll against the whiskered enemy from Tennessee tomorrow afternoon?
>
> These Old Bamas will exercise their tonsils. They'll bring back old yells. They'll yell "Yeah, Alabama" and enjoy themselves.
>
> Do you know the meaning of tradition? Mr. Webster, that smart cookie, says it is an old custom so well established it is almost as effective as law. It's definitely like that when Alabama and Tennessee play.

These battles give you thrills. They make butterflies flutter in your stomach. They make goosebumps pop out on your spine. We've never left one of these battles feeling shortchanged.

These rivals give their finest performances when they go at each other. That's why we know the skirmish this week will be one of those thrillerdillers with a lot of extra frills tossed in.

The game in 1947 was just that, a thriller-diller with a surprise or two. A more startling surprise was in waiting, however, and it came in 1948 in the form of a midget who became a giant.

22

1948
Tennessee 21, Alabama 6

Sometimes the best surprises come in small packages.

The University of Tennessee football team discovered that in 1948, when on October 16, a tiny running back named Hal Littleford led the Volunteers to a 21-6 victory over Alabama. His performance, which came on Shields-Watkins Field in Knoxville in front of a disbelieving audience, was one of few encouraging signs for the Vols that season in which Tennessee posted an uncharacteristic 4-4-2 record.

Alabama did not have a great season, either, finishing 6-4-1, including a 55-0 victory over Auburn in the resumption of that heated intrastate rivalry that had been suspended since 1907, when a death occurred following a postgame fight.

The victory over the Crimson Tide, said Gen. Bob Neyland, "was the best performance for Tennessee since 1946."

Alabama coach Harold "Red" Drew said, "Tennessee looked good, particularly that little running back Hal Littleford."

"Who was that guy?" was the sentiment of Crimson Tide fans after the game in which Littleford subbed for injured star J. B. Proctor. "That guy" was a five-foot-ten-inch, 155-pound running back.

"I couldn't make the training table today," Littleford said during a visit at his house in Johnson City, Tennessee. "I was lucky to have even made the squad in 1948.

"To have played an instrumental role in the victory over Alabama, whether or not it was substantial, was a thrill for me. That rivalry always separates the men from the boys. It's *the* game for a Tennessee player.

"The 1948 game was like all the others. We got in our licks. They got in their licks. Then everybody parted as friends. It's a rivalry based on rough play and mutual respect. And, for sure, that victory was one of the rare bright spots we had that season. Beating Alabama salvaged the season for us."

The effort by Littleford spawned hope among Tennessee fans. That thought was captured the morning after the game by Bob Wilson of the *Knoxville News-Sentinel.* He wrote:

> Hurrying Hal Littleford was a ball of fire as Tennessee's Volunteers regained their prestige of being a powerful running and devastating blocking team in crushing Alabama's Crimson Tide, 21-6, before a howling throng of 45,000 homecoming spectators at Shields-Watkins Field.
>
> With J. B. Proctor, Tennessee passing star, sidelined with an injured knee, Coach Bob Neyland tossed a heavy offensive load on Littleford's shoulders. The pressure was on him and he knew it. But the ex-Bristol [High School] Blizzard soon convinced the largest crowd to witness a sporting event in the state that he can go when the chips are down. In no time, he became the Vols' vaulter to victory and he carried his burden as if it were a sack of feathers.
>
> Although he didn't score any of Tennessee's three touchdowns, Littleford's dashes kept the Tidemen on the run and played an important part in putting the Vols in scoring position.
>
> Statistics disclose that Hurrying Hal amassed a total of 105 yards in carrying the ball 17 times. And, my friends, that is an attractive afternoon of work for any player.

Tennessee broke open the game in the fourth quarter with a pair of touchdowns. The Vols led 7-0 at halftime, after Bob Lund caught a 22-yard touchdown pass from W. C. Cooper and Jim Powell kicked the extra point.

The Crimson Tide bounced back with a touchdown in the third quarter. Charley Davis ran four yards at left guard on fourth down, but Alabama muffed the extra point attempt that could have tied the game.

HAROLD "RED" DREW

DOOMSAYERS WERE BACK IN full force in 1947 after Frank Thomas had resigned as University of Alabama football coach. When Harold "Red" Drew was named as his replacement, the standard by which he was judged was very demanding, to say the least.

Consider this poetry written by famous sportswriter Grantland Rice:

The winds from Tuscaloosa now face a
    mournful ride.
For Tommy isn't back to lead the Crimson Tide.
Though Red Drew is a winning coach who'll
    keep the winning spell.
There's still a sigh of sorrow deep in Alabama's
    dell.
The winds from Tuscaloosa have carried old
    refrains.
Of victory through Southern suns and
    Autumn's driving rains.
From bowl to bowl the Crimson Tide has fought
    its way to fame.
But Tommy's on the sidelines now, and nothing
    seems the same.

Drew fooled a lot of folks. His record from 1947 through 1954 was 54-28-7, which was not exactly as good as Wallace Wade or Frank Thomas, but it was good enough to keep people's attention at Alabama. He took the Crimson Tide to three bowl games, two of which have historical significance.

Alabama defeated Syracuse, 61-6, in the 1953 Orange Bowl. That is the most points scored by a winning team in a bowl game.

The Crimson Tide played and lost to Rice in the 1954 Cotton Bowl. That is the game in which Alabama player Tommy Lewis ran from the sideline without his helmet on his head and tackled Dickie Moegel as he advanced toward what appeared to be a sure touchdown for the Owls.

Drew did not have much luck with Tennessee. His record against the Volunteers was 2-4-2. He opened as a winner, 10-0, in 1948 and closed as a winner, 27-0, in 1954. They tied in 1949 and 1953.

Drew was educated at Bates. While he brought an Ivy League intellect to the Southeastern Conference, his warm personality led some people to believe he was not tough enough as a coach.

A rival, however, loved him.

"Red Drew was a classy guy," says Gus Manning, an assistant athletic director at Tennessee. "I loved being around him at various meetings. He was a big Irishman who told stories with a Yankee accent. He was a delight to talk to.

"Because Drew had a great sense of humor, which showed all the time, a lot of people thought he was a soft coach. I never saw that. Look at his record. He was great with strategy.

"Mostly, though, people remember Drew because of his personality, the tremendous person he was, not for his many victories at Alabama.

"I remember Drew for the classy manner he conducted himself in the Tennessee-Alabama series. He epitomized the respect that has always been a highlight in the series. He got along with everybody. He was respected by General Neyland and everybody else from Tennessee."

Drew coached some of the top names in Crimson Tide football history. One of them, Paul "Bear" Bryant, cried at the cemetery in Tuscaloosa when Drew was buried in 1979.

"I loved him like a daddy," Bryant said about Drew that afternoon at the cemetery. "Coach Drew was my personal coach when I was trying to play some at Alabama. He was one of the greatest people I ever knew. He was a class person. He meant a lot to Alabama. He meant a lot to me."

The first Tennessee touchdown of the fourth quarter was scored by George Balitsaris, who ran seven yards over right guard. The second touchdown of the fourth quarter was scored by Cooper, who ran three yards over right tackle on fourth down. Powell kicked both extra points.

Littleford handled all kicking chores for Tennessee, too; and he made numerous key plays on defense.

Does he recall it as his best game at Tennessee?

"I might have had better games," Littleford said, "but I don't think there's another one that's so memorable.

"One thing that adds a lot to it was hearing that I'd start for injured J. B. Proctor. I'd always thought a second-team or third-team player was just as important to the team, because I'd been in military service and was taught that type of philosophy, but I was excited going out there first against Alabama.

"I'll never forget how the old '10' play worked so well that day—three steps to the right, a spin, and a dash over tackle. It was a Tennessee tradition back then.

"And, with regrets, I'll remember not being able to get into the end zone. That was sort of the story of my career. It seems like I'd always got pooped when I got near the goal line."

The Tennessee-Alabama game in 1948 prompted memories of another impressive victory. In 1928 the Big Orange upset Florida, 13-12, then heard accusations from the Gators that the grounds crew had wet down the field before the game, trying to slow down the rivals.

On the Friday afternoon before the 1948 game, Drew noticed that Shields-Watkins Field was unusually damp. "So they do wet down the turf in Knoxville?" he said with a smile.

They did. But by the time of the opening kickoff it was dry enough for Littleford to have a fast track.

The question the following year was who would be allowed to run. Coming up was a season for ineligible players.

23

1949
Tennessee 7, Alabama 7

SOUTHEASTERN CONFERENCE COMMISSIONER BERNIE Moore was not a popular man when he walked into Legion Field on October 18, 1949. He was in Birmingham to watch the University of Alabama and Tennessee play a football game that ended in a deadlock, 7-7.

"I guess I'm just about a one-man wrecking crew," Moore said to former sports editor Tom Siler of the *Knoxville News-Sentinel*. They were visiting before the Crimson Tide and Volunteers went to war, each without a star player because of ineligibility rulings.

Earlier, Moore had ruled ineligible Alabama center and team captain Doug Lockridge and Tennessee fullback and co-captain Ralph Chancey. They had used up all of their years of eligibility, because both played in 1942, just before football was suspended for a season due to World War II.

"What a week I've had with this," Moore said about his rulings that wiped out the final seasons for several other players, too.

Interestingly, both coaches, Harold "Red" Drew of Alabama and Gen. Bob Neyland of Tennessee, pleaded ignorance because they were not leading their programs in 1942.

Neither team had done all that well before they clashed, with Alabama having been beaten twice and Tennessee losing once. So it would seem the tied game was appropriate.

Bob Davis, an administrative assistant in the Tennessee Athletic Department, tells how hard-fought a game it was.

"I was a sophomore center that season," Davis said, "and I'll never forget how I got hit by an Alabama defensive lineman named Mike Mizerany. He was a huge all-SEC player. On one punt during the game, the ball, Mizerany, and I got to our kicker at the same time.

"That's the day the general got on me so badly. He said, 'Well, Davis, I noticed you learned a new way to block. You get knocked on your back, turned completely over, and kick at your man as he runs past you.' He had noticed how Mizerany handled me.

"But on a more pleasant note, I recall something else about Mizerany. He never failed to tell me I was doing a good job when I managed to block him. That's how it was all the time when Tennessee played Alabama.

"When you played in that game, you didn't have any hand-shaking or back-slapping afterwards. If you got whipped by your opponent, you just left the field after the game, got to the dressing room as quickly as you could, and got your nose fixed.

"It's true what the general said about our games with Alabama. He always said you don't know how good you are until you play against Alabama. He said you beat Alabama with your heart. It's true. It's been like that most years for Tennessee."

Former *Knoxville News-Sentinel* sports editor Bob Wilson also noticed how tough the contest was. In his column the morning following the fray, he wrote:

> In one of the most savagely fought and thrill-packed battles of their long series, Tennessee and Alabama, the hot rivals, settled for a 7-7 dogfight before 41,000 dampened fans.
>
> The Orangemen from the hills of East Tennessee and the Red Elephants from The Capstone packed all of the scoring in the first half and spent the second half keeping the customers on edge by making daring threats to score. Both, however, lacked the punch.
>
> Pat O'Sullivan, Alabama's great linebacker, who played with the Tide as the Elephants defeated the Volunteers, 10-0, two years ago, again was the outstanding factor in holding Tennessee to a tie. His recovery of fumbles and interception of passes wrecked numerous invasions of Alabama territory.
>
> Both the Vols and the Elephants muffed what appeared to be good scoring chances in the second half.

Lindsey Nelson recalls Neyland disdaining a field goal opportunity late in the game. The sportscaster thinks that was the result of the general recalling an experience he had in losing to Boston College, 19-13, in the 1940 Sugar Bowl.

"I've been told General Neyland wiped thoughts of a field goal out of his mind after the loss to Boston College," Nelson said. "In the Sugar Bowl, Tennessee had a field goal that hit the crossbar and bounced back. Boston College took the football and drove for the winning touchdown.

"As I'm told, the Tennessee-Alabama game ended in a 7-7 tie in 1949 because General Neyland passed up an almost cinch field goal in the fourth quarter that could have been the difference."

Neyland passed up the field goal opportunity just after the fourth quarter opened. Tennessee had blocked an Alabama punt and recovered the football at the Crimson Tide 10-yard line. Three plays netted nothing.

The Volunteers came up empty on a fourth-down gamble.

That was the most dramatic moment in a game that saw both teams score touchdowns in the first half.

In the first quarter, Bernie Sizemore ran one yard for a touchdown on fourth down, a score that, coupled with a Bert Rechichar extra point kick, gave Tennessee a 7-0 lead.

In the second quarter, James "Bimbo" Melton of Alabama ran two yards for a touchdown over right tackle. Ed Salem kicked the extra point that ended the scoring in a game that had several more threats.

Ralph Chancey remembers both teams having good chances to win. A former Tennessee assistant coach under four coaches—Neyland, Harvey Robinson, Bowden Wyatt, and Jim McDonald—he now is a special administrative assistant at Tennessee. He has always regretted not being able to play in 1949 against the Crimson Tide.

"I didn't know anything about the ineligibility thing until it happened," Chancey said about the ruling that ended his career during what he thought was his senior season. "It disappointed me for a couple of reasons. First, I was a team co-captain, which proved unsettling to the squad, and, second, it happened the week before we played Alabama.

"The Alabama-Tennessee game has always been number one with me. I'd rather beat Alabama than anybody else we play because I've always considered them as one of the best teams in the nation.

"I've disliked several teams more than Alabama, but I've always wanted to beat Alabama because of the respect involved in the rivalry. It was always a pleasure playing against them, almost an honor, definitely a thrill.

"For instance, in 1947, I had an appendectomy two weeks before the Alabama game. But I was on the field when the opening kickoff came. A Tennessee man could heal quickly for the big ones. I could get ready to play in a hurry against Alabama."

The tie in 1949 settled nothing. But it said a lot about The Third Saturday in October.

"What did I tell you?" said Neyland after the game. "I told you yesterday it would be a hard struggle, a tough game, a typical Tennessee-Alabama battle. These two teams never show up lazy on this weekend.

Both teams played inexperienced people in preparation for strong seasons in 1950, when they clashed with something meaningful at stake.

"I could look at our squad during practices in 1949, then at the way we did against Alabama in October, and I knew something good was about to happen at Tennessee," said Hal Littleford, a former Tennessee running back who co-captained the team with Chancey. "It was obvious to everybody that the horses were there."

As Chancey said, "I thought all through that season, especially after becoming an unpaid assistant coach after my eligibility expired, that Tennessee was moving toward great things. There were times that I shook my head in disbelief when looking at our talent during practice and games. I knew we were headed toward a few glorious seasons."

24

1950
Tennessee 14, Alabama 9

Rarely has a football game received such a glowing stamp of approval. "This was one of the greatest contests I have ever seen," Gen. Bob Neyland said in the University of Tennessee dressing room on October 21, 1950. "I expected a typical battle from Alabama, tough to the finish, and that was what I saw on the field this afternoon."

Neyland, who coached the Volunteers to victory at Shields-Watkins Field in Knoxville, was not overstating a thing.

Alabama coach Harold "Red" Drew agreed with his every word. "We played our best game of the year, but it was not good enough, not against such a classy Tennessee team that found a way to defeat us."

The Tennessee way was dramatic, to the delight of a home crowd, and it prompted glittery writing from Bob Wilson, former sports editor of the *Knoxville News-Sentinel*:

> Tennessee's Volunteers lived up to all the fighting traditions of the hulking Mountaineer riflemen for whom they are named in waging a fierce and courageous fourth quarter comeback to defeat mighty Alabama, 14 to 9, Saturday afternoon.
>
> Trailing 9 to 7 with time running out fast in the final period, the Volunteers tore a page from a movie script as they roared over land for 76 yards to score the clinching touchdown with only one minute to play.
>
> Credit for the hard-earned, but well-deserved Tennessee triumph belongs to the whole Vol team. But the magnificent running of

three backs played a highly important role in the conquest of the Crimson Tide.

It was fullback Andy Kozar's bazooka-like charges through the massive Tide line that led to the first Vol touchdown.

And, in the waning minutes of the bitter struggle, it was the flashy and spectacular jaunts of sophomore wingback Ed Morgan and tailback Harold [Herky] Payne that sent the Vols well on the road to victory. Both runs were more than 20 yards each.

With only five minutes and 35 seconds remaining in the game, the Volunteers apparently realized it was now or never for them if they were to emerge victorious. And from there they went like infuriated cavemen for the score that won the game.

Kozar scored the touchdown, his second of the afternoon, on a one-yard run at the end of a time-consuming drive.

The Volunteers, who had lost the second game of an 11-1 season to Mississippi State, 7-0, were not to be denied as they marched against Alabama and on into the Cotton Bowl, where they defeated Texas, 20-14.

Alabama went on to post a 9-2 record, but the Tide did not get an invitation to a bowl game. Tennessee obviously profited by winning.

Kozar recalls the drama. Now an executive vice president at Tennessee, he reflected upon the 1950 game. "It was my first chance to play against Alabama," said Kozar, who had started the previous spring as the sixth-ranking fullback on the team. "That's the main reason it's such a special game to me. Alabama was our bell game, when we found out how good we were. We knew if we were able to defeat Alabama, we'd be able to compete with anybody else on our schedule."

The former fullback, who at 230 pounds was the largest member of the Tennessee offense, speaks matter-of-factly about the stirring drive to victory the Volunteers made in the final minutes.

"There wasn't really that much concern when we took possession of the football at our 24-yard line," Kozar said. "It was business as usual, really, because the general had instilled in all of us that it wasn't over until we thought it was over.

"Besides, we'd practiced that situation a bunch of times. The general always drilled us on certain situations during practice. He'd say we were this far from the end zone with this much time to get there. So we were used to the pressure.

"I didn't even react with elation when I scored the game-deciding touchdown. There wasn't any of that hotdog stuff in those days. I knew if I showed any emotion, the general would take me aside and say, 'Why are you so excited? That's why we practice. To score is the mission.'

"It's not too exciting to talk about. But that's how it was."

Tennessee fans who were present in 1950 would beg to differ with the star of the hour. According to Bob Davis, a center on that victorious team, the playing field was covered with debris seconds after the game ended.

"That's the last time I remember there ever being a card display at a Tennessee game," said Davis. "Our fans threw them from the stands in jubilation after our comeback victory. I can remember wading through them on my way to the dressing room.

"As for driving 76 yards for the winning touchdown, well, we remembered how Alabama had stopped us on the four-yard line earlier in the game. We had the kind of team that'd answer a challenge, particularly after we'd been denied a scoring opportunity."

On The Third Saturday in October in 1986, Col. Tom Elam sat in a hotel room in Knoxville and recalled the Volunteers' victory in 1950. He was seventy-seven years old at the time and serving as chairman of the Tennessee Athletics Board.

"I remember our student body using the card section display," Elam said. "That might have been the day they quit using it because of the wild celebration after the game. The cards were all over the playing field at the end of the game, after Kozar dived into the end zone to cap the winning touchdown drive."

Interestingly, Jim Goostree, a student trainer at Tennessee in 1950, became a member of the Alabama football family after his graduation. He was trainer there from 1957 through 1984. "The game in 1950 was one of the more exciting in the Alabama-Tennessee series," Goostree said in 1986, "because the Volunteers won it when it looked like the Crimson Tide had matters in hand.

"Also, it is interesting that General Neyland used two whimsical plays on the final touchdown drive to win the game. The general rarely resorted to such trickery in his attack."

Goostree knew about the plays, a fake pass and a naked reverse, because Neyland allowed him to sit in on skull sessions with the

Tennessee quarterbacks. Both runs were made by halfback Ed Morgan. Tailback Hank Lauricella faked a run the first time and a pass the second. The two plays covered 23 yards and 28 yards respectively, and they kept alive the memorable scoring drive.

"Thinking about those plays and that drive still gives me goose-bumps," Goostree said. "It was now or never for Tennessee. That team had enough to it to do it when it had to."

Remembering makes Kozar wonder what happened to the Alabama defense.

"We didn't disguise those trick plays very well," Kozar said. "I've always thought somebody from Alabama went to sleep."

Goostree, meanwhile, thinks that Neyland's knowing when to use The "hip" play and the fake-pass play is a testimony to his greatness. "I think that drive is a lasting tribute to the general," Goostree said. "He was a great coach, one of the best in history—ranking alongside Paul "Bear" Bryant of Alabama—and that victory proves it.

"The general—you will notice I always refer to him as that because of the respect I have for him—knew he had to find an edge to defeat Alabama that season. The team worked on those whimsical plays over and over during practice, as was his way, and they were run to perfection in the game.

"After that victory, the general added to his stature, which was already overwhelming. His presence was unbelievable, even as he stood and watched practice, and his militaristic principles were unyielding. The man was awesome. And we can thank him, in part, for the wonderful Alabama-Tennessee series we watch today."

The thriller of 1950 drew rave reviews from sportswriters. From Zipp Newman of the *Birmingham News:*

> Valiant Alabama all but tore down the stadium and uprooted Tennessee with a brutal ground attack. But the Crimson Tide couldn't down the Vols. Two breaks were the difference in a spine-tingler.
>
> Alabama's loss to Tennessee will go down in history of the Vol-Tide series as one of the most cruel. There was fierce tackling, terrific blocking, hard running and good strategy. It had all the thrills fans could stand. There couldn't have been a dry thread left in the colorful stands.

From Raymond Johnson of the Nashville *Tennessean:*

> It was the type game that a stalemate would have been more in keeping with the way it was played.

From Ed Danforth of the *Atlanta Journal*:

> It was a game on the pattern of the long series between the two keen rivals, rocking and rolling from start to finish.

Alabama scored first when Harold "Red" Lutz kicked a field goal from the 19-yard line in the first quarter, overcoming a difficult angle. The Crimson Tide had to settle for three points after the Tennessee defense stiffened at the end of what appeared to be a march toward the end zone. Kozar scored in the second quarter on a two-yard run over left guard. Abe Shires kicked the extra point.

In the third quarter a hush fell over the stadium when Alabama halfback Bobby Marlow broke over left guard and ran 43 yards into the end zone, giving the Crimson Tide the lead. The extra point attempt was missed.

Then the defenses controlled the game until the Vols took over the ball on the 24-yard line, their backs to the wall, the clock their enemy.

Seventy-six yards to glory was the theme that started a decisive march toward the end zone.

As Tom Siler, former sports editor of the *Knoxville News-Sentinel*, said, "With ten minutes remaining, Tennessee's chances were worth no more than a Confederate bankroll at Fort Knox."

But Tennessee survived in triumphant fashion, taking a victory that sent the Volunteers winging toward a memorable national championship in 1951. Frank Lauricella was a junior for the Vols in 1950.

"That 76-yard drive and victory over Alabama just set us on our way," said Lauricella, who was to star against the Crimson Tide in 1951. "It gave us all kinds of confidence, especially since Alabama was such a powerful team that year. To me, it was a major step toward our national championship."

"After we moved for the winning touchdown against Alabama, which was the toughest team we played that season, we felt like we could gain three yards against the Russians in Moscow," said Bob Davis. "That game, more than any other one, got us started toward a national championship."

The crown came in 1951.

25

1951
Tennessee 27, Alabama 13

ONE OF THE MORE important attributes of a successful politician is a keen sense of timing. Tennessee governor Gordon Browning displayed his political skills during the fall of 1951 when, two days before The Third Saturday in October, he continued his ways as a betting man.

"After winning the Brazos River in Texas with a bet before the Cotton Bowl last season, I'm willing to put up anything in the state of Tennessee on a bet with Alabama governor Gorden Persons," Browning said before the University of Tennessee and Alabama played football at Legion Field in Birmingham. "Governor Persons can name it. I'll put it up."

The Tennessee governor had reason to feel confident. The Volunteers were heavy favorites when they arrived in Birmingham to play Alabama. The 14-point choice of the oddsmakers did not disappoint their fans, covering the line on the nose with a 27-13 victory. In the process they took a giant step toward the only national championship Tennessee has claimed. Not until it was defeated by Maryland, 27-13, in the Sugar Bowl did the Vols stumble that glorious season, during which it posted a 10-0 record.

With tailback Hank Lauricella leading the way, Tennessee exploded in the second half to defeat a struggling Alabama team that posted a 5-6 record, the first losing season for the Crimson Tide in five decades.

As sportswriter Zipp Newman wrote in the *Birmingham News,* Tennessee dominated the game, although the Crimson Tide fought hard to hold off its talented rival of so many years:

Hank Lauricella, the All-American tailback with the superb supporting cast, put Tennessee one step closer to a New Year's Day game with a rousing 27-13 victory over lion-hearted Alabama.

The script was the typical Alabama-Tennessee one, written in 1928, and this game could have been the most spectacular game for fierce play, crisp blocking and never giving up in the history of a series dating to 1901.

Those who came to see Tennessee work over Alabama stayed to see Alabama make Tennessee cut loose with a game that parallels Tennessee's great victory over Texas in the Cotton Bowl last season.

It was either team's game going into the third quarter, when Alabama had a fumble that cost it a first down at the Tennessee 13-yard line and Lauricella's 76-yard quick kick to the Alabama four-yard line changed the Crimson fortune.

Tennessee was quick to go out to a lead, scoring twice in the fourth period.

Lauricella was the difference in the two teams. He had that kind of day. He was the nearest thing to Beattie Feathers the series has seen. He threw one 20-yard touchdown pass in the second quarter and he streaked 35 yards for a touchdown behind great blocking in the fourth quarter.

The performance enabled Lauricella to place his name among the more storied figures who have starred on The Third Saturday in October. That comparison was made by sportswriter Guy Tiller in the *Atlanta Journal:*

Gene McEver, Harry Gilmer, Dixie Howell and George Cafego moved over to make room for another immortal in the traditional Tennessee-Alabama football rivalry after Hank Lauricella personally broke the back of a highly keen Alabama team.

Mighty Tennessee, ranked second in the nation, was fought off its feet in the first quarter when Alabama scored a stunning touchdown.

A crowd of 45,000 spectators could barely believe their eyes when Alabama came back from the brink of football destruction, three straight defeats, to manhandle the Vols.

Lauricella, on the bench for a brief rest, rushed into the game in the second quarter. He pitched a perfect strike to wingback Bert Rechichar for a touchdown. Lauricella came through in the clutch again before the half ended when he skipped 27 yards down the sideline to get his teammates out of a hole deep in their territory.

Then, early in the fourth quarter, Lauricella dashed 35 yards for a touchdown on the most spectacular run of the game. The third Tennessee touchdown broke Alabama's back.

There were more than a few anxious fans in the stands at Birmingham when halftime came with the teams playing to a 7-7 tie. Halfback Bobby Marlow had run one yard in the first quarter for a Crimson Tide touchdown, with Harold "Red" Lutz kicking the extra point. Tennessee countered when Lauricella passed 20 yards in the second quarter for a touchdown to Rechichar, who added the extra point.

Tennessee grabbed the lead for keeps in the third quarter, when fullback Dick Ernsberger ran two yards for a touchdown, with Rechichar kicking the extra point.

Tennessee made it 21-7 early in the fourth quarter, when Lauricella ran 35 yards for a touchdown and Rechichar kicked the extra point.

Alabama tried to bounce back, with Marlow scoring a touchdown on a one-yard run over right guard to cut the lead to 21-13.

But Tennessee's Vince Kaseta caught an 11-yard touchdown pass from Harold "Herky" Payne to fix the final margin.

"I remember the general pointing at his heart and saying, 'Here is where you beat Alabama,'" said Jim Haslam, a member of the national championship team.

That was how the Vols did it in 1951. Lauricella displayed a heart as large as any of the others that have been on the field in the series.

"Whew!" Gen. Bob Neyland sighed in the dressing room, after pulling off his sportcoat and hanging it on the back of a chair following the game. "Man, those Alabama boys were tough, just like I'd expected. I'm relieved to get this one behind us. It's always a tough test for us in Birmingham."

Lauricella, who rushed for 108 yards on 15 attempts and passed for 113 yards on 16 attempts, remembers the bruising battle. At his house in New Orleans, he recalled having a hand in 221 of the 391 yards Tennessee gained against the Crimson Tide. "It was clearly my best game at Tennessee," Lauricella said. "And, it provided me with an unusual break that changed my life. Because of that performance, I was able to secure some honors that helped launch my career after graduation.

"Joe Williams, a sportswriter for the New York World Telegram and a syndicated columnist, was covering the North-South Golf Tournament in North Carolina the week we played Alabama. Somebody got his attention, talked him into coming to our game. He was part of the old school. He understood and loved the Big Orange-Crimson Tide tradition.

"He was there to see me play pretty well. He wrote a strong article about me, mentioning that I deserved Heisman Trophy consideration, and it was sort of the making of Hank Lauricella at the national level."

The undoing of Lauricella could have come during the game when, on intuition, he called and made the important quick-kick from deep in Tennessee territory.

"Alabama had driven almost to our goal line," Lauricella said. "We stopped them. Andy Kozar, our fullback, gained 11 yards on first down. I decided to make a quick-kick on the next play.

"The quick-kick broke open the game. We got field position and exploded on Alabama. The general approved. That was his philosophy. He believed in gaining yardage on changes of possession, defense, and kicking, then waiting for a break that would lead to a touchdown. He always said he would take position on the field instead of possession of the ball. I wonder what he would have thought about me had I shanked the quick-kick.

"Why did I quick-kick? Who knows? It just seemed like the thing to do at the time. It was done on a whim, I guess, and it worked out beautifully. See, nobody had to tell us about what it meant to beat Alabama. Those stories were told every year by Tennessee fans."

Lauricella impressed two of his teammates, fullback Andy Kozar and center Bob Davis, with his performance. Said Kozar, "Hank was intelligent. He was a leader. He ran the game plan beautifully against Alabama. He surprised them with his passing."

Said Davis, "The thing that made him superb was his confidence. Hank was good, too, evidenced by the fact he was personally recruited out of New Orleans by the general."

Tennessee's 1951 team had awesome talent, as recalled by Jimmy Wade, a freshman reserve defensive halfback who went on to become a splendid tailback.

"I was in awe of my teammates all season," Wade said. "I spent most of my time just following those guys around, wondering what I was doing riding the same bus with them to practices and games. Basically, I spent my freshman season on cloud nine, just floating around as a member of a championship team."

A vital member of that national championship team was a terror named Doug Atkins, who went on to secure hall of fame status in the National Football League as a defensive end. He received a rude greeting in his first game against Alabama in 1950. He got even the next two seasons.

"I'd have to say our games against Alabama were the hardest-hitting I played in while at Tennessee," Atkins said at his house in Knoxville. "That's because I got hit harder in the 1950 game than I've ever been hit. I got the hell knocked out of me by a dandy little halfback named Bobby Marlow.

"I intercepted a pass about twelve yards beyond the line of scrimmage. There wasn't anything between me and the goal line, so I thought I was about to make a run to glory.

"But just after I caught the football, that little guy collided with me. He stuck his head just above my eye, sort of under those little ol' helmets we wore, and it knocked me dizzy. Both my arms flopped out. The football fell to the ground like an apple falling out of a tree. I just wilted. I saw two of everything the rest of the day."

Jim Goostree, a Tennessee student trainer in 1951, who now serves as an assistant athletic director at Alabama, notes something that indicates the tough demeanor Atkins had as a player.

"I recall one thing about the 1951 game," Goostree said, "that being what Doug Atkins did to Bimbo Melton. At some point early in the game, Atkins clotheslined Melton and sent him to the sideline. It was a brutal lick that got the attention of everybody."

Such is The Third Saturday in October way—take your licks like a man and get even when you can.

Atkins played on Tennessee teams that never lost to Alabama, which is somewhat of a rarity. "It's obvious why that happened," Atkins said. "We had a lot of good boys on those teams, good talent, and we had a great coach who always managed to do it right, putting the round ones in the round holes and the square ones in the square holes."

Neyland was particularly sharp in 1951, but not as sharp as he was when he went to New Orleans and successfully recruited Lauricella.

26

1952
Tennessee 20, Alabama 0

Tom Siler, former sports editor of the *Knoxville News-Sentinel*, coined a term after the University of Tennessee had played three unceremonious games at the start of the 1952 football season: "Tailback Blues." That is what the Volunteers seemed to have after the offense had three false starts in two victories and one defeat.

That changed on October 18 on Shields-Watkins Field in Knoxville, where Tennessee defeated previously undefeated Alabama, 20-0, in an upset that helped the Volunteers secure their third consecutive major bowl game invitation.

The Vols, which had an 8-2-1 record, lost to Texas, 16-0, in the Cotton Bowl that season.

Alabama, which had an 10-2 record, defeated Syracuse, 61-6, in the Orange Bowl that season.

The day after Tennessee shut out Alabama, Siler wrote:

The "Tailback Blues," a ditty recently popular in these parts, is no longer on the Hit Parade [East Tennessee version].

A star was born on Shields-Watkins Field—Jimmy Wade, a sophomore engineering student from Lynchburg, Virginia.

His debut was unprecedented in the annals of [Gen. Bob] Neyland football at Tennessee. This blond, 170-pounder, a substitute on the defensive platoon last year, had never before run a play from scrimmage, had never thrown a pass, had never called a signal for the varsity.

Jimmy sat out Tennessee's first three games, sidelined by a wrenched right knee. No one could know for certain how he might react in the pressure-packed renewal with Alabama. Until he came along, the opposition feared [fullback] Andy Kozar, with good reason, but no one else.

Now, November opponents will see Wade and Kozar, Kozar and Wade, and the combination figures to become as famous as ham and eggs, or country ham and red gravy. Wade is the tailback that makes the Volunteers go, a wispy outside runner who not only will torment all rivals, but the outside running will make Kozar's power running doubly effective.

Wade's emergence as a star, along with the established Kozar, enabled Gen. Bob Neyland to cap his career against Alabama in grand fashion. He retired at the end of the 1952 season, compiling a 12-5-2 record against Alabama.

After trying to stop the newly found combination, the "W and K Duo," in 1952, Alabama could have offered a strong witness on behalf of Tennessee power on offense. Wade and Kozar combined for 277 yards, with the former getting 153 in 18 carries, as Tennessee won for the third consecutive time.

Kozar broke the ice with a three-yard run in the first quarter. The touchdown came after Mack Franklin blocked an Alabama punt and recovered it on the Crimson Tide 20-yard line.

Not until the fourth quarter, when Wade went to work, did Tennessee score again. The little halfback ran around left end for four yards and a touchdown on a fourth-down play. Vic Kolenik kicked the extra point for a 13-0 lead.

The final touchdown came on a 10-yard pass with only five seconds remaining in the game. Pat Shires threw the football to Frank Alexander. Kolenik kicked the extra point as fans erupted in celebration.

"Hey, who in the hell was that guy?" an Alabama player said about Wade after the game, repeating a similar question presented about unheralded Tennessee tailback Hal Littleford who starred in the 1948 game. "We knew about Kozar, but nobody told us about the little guy."

Said Alabama coach Harold "Red" Drew, "That's the most powerful one-two running punch I've seen in years."

Wade would agree with that statement.

"That was a good year and good game for me," Wade said during the summer of 1986 at his house in Tulsa, Oklahoma. "I guess I was a little tougher than people thought I was.

"I recall being like a one-story walkup looking at skyscrapers during our games against Alabama. But somehow, maybe because we had a fine team blessed with an abundance of talent, I was able to do fine against them in 1952 and 1953."

As Tennessee romped to a national championship in 1951, including a 27-13 victory over Alabama, Wade played as a reserve defensive back. He got his feet wet, "or my nose reddened," against the Crimson Tide.

"General Neyland was counting on Pat Shires and me at tailback in 1952," said Wade, who also performed as a shot put and discus ace for the Tennessee track team. "But both of us were hurt. That's why our offense struggled early that season.

"I guess everybody was surprised when our offense exploded against Alabama. It's sort of surprising that I played that game.

"Our trainer was Mickey O'Brien. He wrapped my knee with a tight bandage. General Neyland looked at it during practice that week and asked Mickey how I'd be able to play wrapped up like that. Mickey told him, 'Well, he's not gonna be able to play without it.' As it worked out, that was one of my better games.

"I remember it being tough, too, as were all of our games against Alabama. That was the game we aimed at. It was the rivalry that mattered the most to a Tennessee player."

How did it feel to play the last season under Neyland?

"Well, to tell you the truth, the general had been aloof for a while," Wade said. "He didn't have all that much contact with players during that stage of his career. That's how he wanted it, how he thought it had to be. When Coach Robinson took over, it wasn't that different.

"But it's obvious the general was a great coach. He was fantastic at organizing and measuring up personnel, then using it as it should be.

"I'll never forget a couple of his pet lines before games. He'd either say, 'It's a day for ponies,' or, 'It's a day for mudders.' And, amazingly, he always got it right."

In 1952, Tennessee had both, a darting tailback and a powerful fullback.

"Jimmy Wade was small," Kozar said, "but he was tough. Having him in the backfield was a blessing. You always have it a little easier pounding between the tackles when you have an outside threat in the backfield with you. Our opponents had trouble figuring out who to key on."

"I saw a picture that's among my favorites," Kozar said. "It shows me shaking hands with the Alabama quarterback, Clell Hobson, after the game. A Crimson Tide linebacker, who was leaning on Hobson with his head bowed, cried as the quarterback and I talked. I think that picture says a lot about the rivalry."

Any portrait of Neyland would have to communicate something about The Third Saturday in October. He was a part of it for so long. Columnist Alf Van Hoose of the *Birmingham News* remembers him as the finest strategist the sport has known.

"If you put a gun on me and forced me to choose a guy who'd win a game for you, it'd be Neyland," Van Hoose said during the summer of 1986 in Birmingham. "He was a master coach. He was brilliant in many ways on the field and off the field.

"Neyland used military philosophy as a coach, more specifically than anybody in history, and his pearls of wisdom, in that regard, are longlasting. For instance, he'd often say defeat has a thousand faces, which is military-like terminology. He talked about games being lost through mistakes, not won through outstanding plays.

"Neyland was an engineer at West Point. That means he was considered one of the more intelligent cadets. I'll never forget how he showed his intelligence playing bridge. He could have been a life master if he'd concentrated on it.

"Neyland left his mark on football, no doubt about it, and he left his mark on the series contested on The Third Saturday in October."

Bill Lumpkin, sports editor and columnist at the *Birmingham Post-Herald*, recalls a humorous incident that explains how much winning over Alabama meant to Neyland.

"During a SEC Meeting in the 1940s, after Tennessee had lost to Boston College, 19-13, in the 1941 Sugar Bowl game, somebody convinced Neyland that Thomas had helped the opposition with its scouting report. Frank Leahy, who had played with Thomas at Notre Dame, was coaching Boston College. Well, Neyland was irate. He charged up to Thomas's hotel room, ran through the door, found the Alabama coach in the shower, and started swinging wildly at him.

"Thomas dodged every punch, people who saw it said, but he got out of that shower understanding more about how much importance Neyland placed on Tennessee winning over Alabama."

Col. Tom Elam of Union City, Tennessee, knew Neyland as well as anybody who has been associated with Tennessee. During the fall of 1986, he recalled how the general and he had discussed how the 1952 season would be the last on The Hill for the coach. "Neyland didn't feel good at the start of the 1952 season. He had acquired a physical problem of some sort during military service," Elam said. "And, of course, he was never dedicated to taking care of himself. For example, he was a pretty good size drinker.

"By 1952 Neyland wasn't like he was when we first met. He was sick. He'd gotten extremely large. I'd remembered him as a tall, stately and strong man who could've whipped everybody on his team. By that time, he'd developed such a huge stomach that he wore slipper-like shoes because he couldn't bend over and tie his shoes without difficulty.

"He'd told me early in the season that 1952 would probably be his last as coach at Tennessee. This concerned me a great deal. I had fears that our program would never be the same, that we'd sort of go down the drain when he left the command post, that it'd never be the same as it was under the general. I knew there'd never be another one like him.

"It was a difficult time at Tennessee. But Neyland knew he was approaching the end of the line."

27

1953
Tennessee 0, Alabama 0

OOPS.

NBC-TV goofed.

After bragging that three million people would be watching the University of Alabama and Tennessee play football at Legion Field in Birmingham on October 17, 1953, the network must have wondered if anyone still had a television set turned on when the game ended.

Rarely does a scoreless tie prompt much interest, not even when a couple of famous graduates from the colleges, Mel Allen from Alabama and Lindsey Nelson from Tennessee, are teamed as commentators.

"When they started working on the schedule that year, Mel and I got together and decided to make a pitch for Alabama and Tennessee on television," Nelson said. "We got it done, convinced the folks at NBC to televise it. Well, you can imagine how they felt after it was over. The folks in New York were livid. My goodness, nothing-to-nothing, a scoreless tie. That was not exactly what you want on television."

Allen did play-by-play that afternoon. Nelson handled color. They announced at the start of the telecast that they were Alabama and Tennessee graduates, respectively, and then they did their work.

"Our alma maters were not mentioned again until it came time to sign off the air," Nelson said. "Then, Mel said, 'So, we have seen a nothing-to-nothing tie and Lindsey and I can still be friends.' I thought that was a classic departure for us."

Actually, upon reflection Tennessee fans had reason to feel good. Alabama was a 13-point favorite, and the Vols celebrated in their dressing room. The tie did not make Coach Harvey Robinson happy.

"Men," said Robinson to his players in the dressing room, "we're never going to celebrate a tie. But I want you to know that you played well. I'm proud of the way you fought Alabama until the finish

Moments earlier, Robinson had been summoned by a NBC-TV official for a postgame interview.

"Please smile big for us," the official said before the Tennessee coach went on camera.

"Never," said Robinson. "Only when we win."

Tennessee thought it might have won on the final play of the game. With the football at the eleven-yard line, Alabama quarterback Bart Starr retreated to pass in desperation. He was grabbed at the five-yard line by Tennessee defensive end Tommy Hensley, who knocked him backward to the goal line, picked him up and dumped him in the back of the end zone.

"I jumped up and down, pleading with the official to call it a safety," Hensley said during the summer of 1986. "But he wouldn't buy it. I wasn't trying to con him. I was trying to sell him a safety on behalf of good ol' Tennessee when we needed two points to win."

Albert Elmore was a sophomore quarterback on that Alabama team. He admits he felt relieved when the game official Hensley pleaded with ruled Starr down outside the end zone.

"I remember that play well," Elmore said at his office in Birmingham. "I thought they had Bart trapped for a safety. I remember watching the film of that game with assistant coach Hank Crisp. He jumped up and said, 'Gosh, that's how close we came to losing.' It looked close to me, too."

Alabama also missed a golden chance.

While attempting to kick on the third down, Tennessee punter Bobby Brengle fumbled a snap from center in his end zone. He was rushed by five Alabama players, but he managed to run the football to the one-yard line. Dave Griffith was sent into the game to punt. He, too, bobbled the snap from center but managed to kick the football to the 36-yard line.

The 1953 edition of The Third Saturday in October did not create much fanfare. Alabama finished with a 6-3-3 record, including a loss to Rice in the Cotton Bowl. Tennessee finished with a 6-4-1 record, playing its first season after Gen. Bob Neyland's retirement.

The Volunteers were not the same as they were under Neyland, who had turned over the reins of leadership to former assistant coach Robinson. Col. Tom Elam talks about the unsettling transition. "Harvey Robinson was as fine a person as anybody I remember. He had no bad habits that I can remember. But I'm not sure he had the personality and powerful thrust of leadership to bring a transition from Neyland to somebody else. I'm not sure anybody did.

"Robinson deserved the opportunity, though, as Neyland had expressed to me. It just didn't work out for him or Tennessee. The end for Robinson came after our loss to Georgia Tech in Atlanta in 1954. I was walking from the hotel to the stadium with Neyland. Even before that game, he mentioned that a change was coming. I think he or his representatives were already talking to Bowden Wyatt by then."

Bob Wilson, former sports editor of the *Knoxville News-Sentinel,* noticed the lack of fire on the eve of the Tennessee-Alabama game. He wrote:

> My, my, how times have changed. It used to be on the eve and day of Alabama-Tennessee games this metropolis of Birmingham was as wild and woolly as a frontier town when the West was young. But not any more. You would hardly realize that the two old rivals of the gridiron were clashing for the 36th time this afternoon.
>
> There were but very few supporters of the Crimson Tide and Volunteers whooping it up around the hotels and on the streets last night.
>
> The fact that the Vol-Tide melee was the game of the day on NBC's nationwide TV hookup, undoubtedly resulted in hundreds of the supporters of the two teams from all parts of Tennessee and Alabama not showing up.
>
> I can't remember before when a Vol-Tide game wasn't a sellout. But this one isn't.

Nor did the game develop as Naylor Stone, former sports editor of the *Birmingham Post-Herald,* predicted it would. The week of the game he wrote, "The Crimson Tide will stack the Vols like cafeteria trays."

"I really don't recall there being a great deal of fanfare among players about being on television that year," Jimmy Wade reports. "All we knew was that we were playing another game against Alabama.

"Actually, I thought it was pretty exciting. Maybe that's because I thought I was going all the way for a touchdown with an intercepted pass until somebody headed me off.

"But my brother watched the game on television up in Virginia, and I remember what he told me about it. He said, 'Television, gee whiz, nothing to nothing, so what?'

"I guess it was boring for people at home. But it was exciting enough for players on the field that afternoon."

NBC-TV executives, however, were so upset about the lack of action on the playing field, they telephoned the press box during the fourth quarter to express their disgust to Nelson and Allen, who would later become hall of fame sportscasters.

"It was as boring a game as I can remember," said Alf Van Hoose, sports editor and columnist at the *Birmingham News*. "It was dull beyond belief. My gosh. It was a scoreless tie."

AN OCCASIONAL tie notwithstanding, The Third Saturday in October brings out the excitement for all Tennessee and Alabama graduates. Nelson found that to be true when he and Allen teamed for a later telecast.

"Mel has a brother named Larry Allen, who also went to Alabama," Nelson said. "He served as a spotter for Mel during games. He had been indoctrinated to SEC football.

"Mel and I were at the Yale Bowl to do a Yale-Cornell game. It was the Friday afternoon before Tennessee and Alabama were to play on Saturday afternoon. Larry walked over to me in the stadium, looked at his watch, and said, 'Well, Lindsey, I guess they're down at Legion Field in Birmingham and they're coming out for their final pregame practice just about now.'

"No doubt about it, Tennessee-Alabama games create interest for their fans no matter where they are."

Further proof of that rests in the reflections of a retired broadcaster who was just getting started in 1953.

"It was exciting just watching Tennessee warm up in those years," said John Forney, who from 1953 through 1982 served as the radio voice of the Crimson Tide. "They ran that splendid single wing offense. The tailback stood there waiting for the snap from center and looked so stately and proud. Alabama, on the other hand, worked out of that Notre Dame Box offensive formation.

"The scene was marvelous, no matter the score, as usual on The Third Saturday in October."

28

1954
Alabama 27, Tennessee 0

ALABAMA'S DREADFUL LOSING STREAK came to an end.

A coach whom many people thought was unfairly criticized got a last laugh on a bitter rival.

Those were the recollections thirty-two years later.

As a smile came to his face, he shook his head and leaned back in his chair. Then retired Tennessee athletic director Bob Woodruff said something astute about The Third Saturday in October. "It's uncanny, really, but you can forget what the oddsmakers and experts think about an Alabama-Tennessee game. I've been amazed through the years by how things can change so quickly in the series.

"Just when you think you've got the upper hand, when you know Saturday afternoon belongs to you, you're faced with a sad Sunday morning. There's no such thing as a comfort zone in the rivalry."

Woodruff was talking about other football wars. But he could have been explaining specifically what happened on October 16, in 1954, on Shields-Watkins Field in Knoxville.

Although Alabama went into a tailspin in following weeks, it looked like the picture of health that afternoon in defeating Tennessee, 27-0. It had been six seasons since the Crimson Tide had tasted victory over their bitter rival. And to the surprise of everybody who watched it, the Crimson Tide claimed the triumph under the field leadership of reserve quarterback Albert Elmore.

Sports editor Jesse Outlar of the *Atlanta Constitution* who attended the game described the action in a column:

> Albert Elmore, a 192-pound reserve, is the greatest Alabama quarterback in history—on Shields-Watkins Field.
>
> Elmore stepped into ailing Bart Starr's shoes and fired the Tide to a 27-0 victory over dazed Tennessee, the most lopsided defeat ever administered the Vols here by their ancient rivals from Tuscaloosa.
>
> A crowd of 40,800 amazed fans saw something they'd never seen before. The lean junior riddled Tennessee's supposedly tight pass defense with three touchdown heaves, rushed for 107 yards and called a near-flawless game.
>
> Halfback Corky Tharp, who romped 96 yards for a Tide touchdown, halfback Bobby Luna and the entire Alabama line were great. But it was Elmore, the unheralded substitute, who turned what was rated a tossup into a romp.
>
> You have to flip the pages of this bitter rivalry back to 1906, the day Alabama won, 51-0, to uncover the last time the Tide won by such a large margin. It was the first Alabama triumph over the Vols here [in Knoxville] since 1942, the first Coach Red Drew's men have won over the Vols since 1947. . . .
>
> Alabama tore a page out of Tennessee's book of fundamentals to achieve one of its brightest victories in its long and storied football history. The Tide troops intercepted four passes, recovered two Vol fumbles and partially blocked a kick.

Alabama seized control of the game early, as the pro-Tennessee fans looked on in horror. It was obvious Elmore had come to play.

Elmore passed 11 yards to Luna in the second quarter for the first touchdown. Luna kicked the extra point.

Two touchdowns in the third quarter took away all semblance of drama. Elmore passed 7 yards to Tharp and 25 yards to Nick Germanos. Luna added both extra points.

The thrill of the game, for all practical purposes, came in the fourth quarter. Tharp intercepted a Brengle pass and ran 96 yards for the final touchdown, weaving among blockers and defenders along the way.

Sportswriter Raymond Johnson said it quickly when talking about Elmore:

> Albert Elmore did a better pinch-hitting job for Alabama than Dusty Rhodes did for the New York Giants in the recent World Series.

He broke up a scoreless tie late in the second quarter when he ignited an 85-yard touchdown drive.

It's easy to see what this Alabama boy did for the Crimson Tide against Tennessee was more impressive than what Rhodes did for the Giants.

"As I recall, Rhodes was an Alabama boy, too," Elmore said recently at his office in Birmingham.

"That was my best game at Alabama, one in which we were hot, one in which everything we tried seemed to work. I honestly think playing in Knoxville helped us. They had a big crowd there, as usual, but we managed to take them out of the game by dominating Tennessee.

"Of course, every game we played against Tennessee was important. It was *the* game every season. Because the Alabama series with Auburn was dormant, it served as a measuring stick for the team.

"When we left Knoxville that afternoon, we thought we had one of the better teams in the nation, because they had been so strong."

Elmore and his teammates did a lot for Drew, a troubled coach, when they defeated Tennessee. Drew produced an acceptable record leading the Crimson Tide, 55-29-7, but he had the misfortune of following legends Wallace Wade and Frank Thomas. So the 1954 game against Tennessee was his last in the rivalry, which means winning must have been sweet for him.

"Drew was solid as coach," said Alf Van Hoose. "But football was never life or death for him. Frankly, Drew suffered because of his place in a lineup of great coaches at Alabama. There was Wallace Wade. There was Frank Thomas. There was Harold "Red" Drew. He was like a baseball player in a lineup that featured Willie Mays, Ted Williams, and Hank Aaron. He was good. But he never stood as tall as he could have because of the coaches who came before him."

Drew was happy with the win over Tennessee during his last season, but his last team did not win another game after defeating the Vols. Alabama finished with a 4-5-2 record, spelling doom for him.

"I have no idea why the wheels came off after we beat Tennessee," said Elmore, who had the distinction of having been a better college quarterback than Starr, who is in the National Football League Hall of Fame following a stellar career with the Green Bay Packers. "But a victory over Tennessee was the highlight of every season for an Alabama player in those days. It certainly was for us in 1954.

"I can still remember the excitement that prevailed the week before that game. The scout team wore orange jerseys at practice. You could see the intensity on the faces of our coaches. It was a tense week."

Meanwhile, Tennessee also struggled, finishing with a 4-6 record. The loss to Alabama was particularly troublesome.

"I sat in the stands that day with a bum knee," said Wade, the star Tennessee tailback in previous seasons. "It was embarrassing listening to what our fans said about our team. By the time Alabama whipped us so soundly, it was obvious we were in for a long year."

An aspiring sophomore tailback from Tennessee, John Majors, who now coaches the Big Orange, was pressed into action against the Crimson Tide. He made his first start in that game.

"I threw three pass interceptions against Alabama that day," Majors said during the summer of 1986 at his office in Stokely Athletics Center in Knoxville. "It was a terrible debut.

"I was the understudy for Jimmy Wade. I had expected to be red-shirted that season, had welcomed it, and I had to play before I was ready. It was a disappointing day.

"We used a new umbrella defense against Alabama. Albert Elmore tore it up. He had a good day of football. Our offense was complicated, but Alabama solved it.

"That game was typical of our season. We were on our way headed downhill. The loss to Alabama was the beginning of the end for the [coach] Harvey Robinson regime at Tennessee. He was a great gentleman. He had a fine football mind. He was a good strategist. But his timing was unfortunate because he had to follow a living legend like Gen. Bob Neyland."

With Alabama completely dominating the Volunteers in all aspects of play, some of the more memorable highlights from The Third Saturday in October took place off the playing field.

The 1914 Tennessee team, the first to win any kind of championship, was holding its reunion that weekend. They spent much time rehashing their 17-7 victory over Alabama that year. "We should have blanked them," Farmer Kelly, the Tennessee captain in 1914, told Tom Siler, then a columnist for the *Knoxville News-Sentinel*. "A favorite play was the tackle around. I took the ball from Bill May, our quarterback, and hit the line. Somebody unjointed me, and the ball popped up in the air. Bully Vandegraaff grabbed the ball and ran 35 or 40 yards for a touchdown. The boys didn't let me forget that one, because getting a shutout against Alabama was important to us."

Getting a shutout over Tennessee was just as important to Alabama in 1954, although the "spy" found on the Hill during game week, a student from Tuscaloosa, did not contribute to the Crimson Tide's triumph. "I made a bet with some boys back home that I could get into a UT class," Alabama sophomore Buddy Morrison told Tennessee officials who accused him of being on campus to spy on Volunteer practices. "And I did it.

"By the way," he said, "I want all of you folks from Tennessee to know you've got some friendly students up here."

29

1955
Tennessee 20, Alabama 0

BOWDEN WYATT WAS THE new University of Tennessee football coach.

John Majors was the new star on the scene.

The Volunteers marched on October 15, 1955, to the beat of a loud drummer, took Alabama in hand, and solidly defeated the Crimson Tide, 20-0, at Legion Field in Birmingham.

Meanwhile, Alabama was starting an ebb in football under new coach J. B. "Ears" Whitworth. The decline in stature would become so severe a couple of years later that some members of the alumni attempted to organize a players strike against the leader.

The real beginning of the Majors era in Tennessee football, which in 1986 was still in bloom with John Majors coaching Tennessee, was pleasing to a multitude of Volunteers who attended The Third Saturday in October gathering.

Consider what former sports editor Bob Wilson wrote the day after the game in 1955 for the *Knoxville News-Sentinel*:

> John [Drum] Majors came of age as a Tennessee tailback as he ran, passed and kicked the Volunteers to a surprising 20-0 victory over Alabama's Crimson Tide this afternoon.
>
> After a slow start, Majors broke through as bright as the sun that showered down on the 33,000 spectators.
>
> Running with the driving power of a 200-pounder, instead of the lightweight 165-pounder he is, Majors slashed Alabama's eight-

144

man line, sweeping the ends time after time for gains that sparked the Vols to victory.

After leading the attack that carried the ball to Alabama's eight-yard line in the second period, Majors hit end Roger Urbano with a touchdown pass and Tommy Priest converted.

In the fourth period, the hurryin' Huntland lad again directed a march that carried to the Crimson Tide two-yard line. He then raced around right end to score and Priest converted.

Tennessee's final touchdown came late in the fourth period with reserve tailback Bobby Gordon doing a fine job of running. With the ball on the one-yard line, fullback Lon Herzbrun hit left guard for the tally.

Majors made it look easy.

But he remembered the game as being tougher than it appeared to be for the victorious Volunteers.

"It was a beautifully played game, from our standpoint, although I shanked two punts against Alabama that year," Majors said. "I also remember it being the game that sent us on our way under Coach Bowden Wyatt, who came in that season and turned around our program.

"I guess I did okay that day. I know it was a special victory for all of us because we were face-to-face with Alabama.

"Alabama wasn't winning then, starting a bad slump, but we had great respect for them. At Tennessee, you don't forget what somebody does to you as a sophomore, not when they killed you like they did us in 1954. Instead, you're glad you've got them on the schedule the next year.

"Actually, that Alabama team was sort of beaten up, ragged looking. My brother, Joe Majors, was recruited by Alabama. He told me one time that the years under [coach] J. B. Whitworth were brutal at practice.

"The Alabama players had tape on their pants and all over them. My brother told me they used to beat each other up like tomatoes during practice, that they'd scrimmage against each other and pile on the piles. Those Alabama guys were beat up before they played games, or appeared to be, but they still got after us.

"Even when they didn't have a good team at Alabama, I was terribly excited about playing them. I was especially excited knowing I was a part of the rivalry I'd heard so much about.

"We knew about the series, most of us guys from this area, and I don't recall anybody having to strongly urge our people to have respect for Alabama. You just took it for granted, as a Tennessee player, that Alabama wouldn't ever be an easy touch."

Another valuable member of the Tennessee team in 1955 was end Buddy Cruze. He teamed with Majors on several key pass plays during their careers. He recalls the former tailback as being more intelligent than ultratalented.

"John Majors was raised to be a tailback, if ever anybody was, because he was schooled to be one as a kid," Cruze said. "Shirley Majors, his father, was a great coach in high school and at Sewanee. He taught all of his sons how to play the position.

"There were larger people than John Majors. There were better passers and punters than John Majors. There were better runners than John Majors. But nobody knew the position better than John Majors, understood how the tailback was supposed to perform, and could do all of the things a tailback was supposed to do with a nice degree of expertise."

The tailback was brilliant in the victory over Alabama that added spark to a Tennessee team that had stumbled early in the season. The Volunteers went on to post a 6-3-1 record.

"At the time, Alabama was starting its worst period of football in history," said Bobby Gordon, a sophomore tailback at Tennessee in 1955 who lives in Knoxville. "But nobody knew that. So beating them that year was important to all of us who had grown up with such respect for the series. It was, after all, the first team of consequence we beat that year. We had two losses in our first two games. Beating Alabama got us rolling."

The loss to Tennessee was one of many for Alabama, which fumbled frequently all season and posted a 0-10 season, the first winless campaign in history for the Crimson Tide.

Rival faces mirrored that situation after the game.

Wyatt was smiling. He predicted "even brighter days for Tennessee starting next season."

Whitworth was near tears. He said, "We had the same chances Tennessee did today, but we couldn't go and they could. I'll tell you this Tennessee looked better today than we thought they'd be. My old buddy, Bowden Wyatt, is doing a great job. I hope he wins a lot more.

BOWDEN WYATT

Bob Neyland called him "perhaps the finest captain a University of Tennessee football team has had."

John Majors called him "one of the greatest coaches in the history of the game."

Paul "Bear" Bryant called him "a great football strategist."

His famous coach loved him.

His famous player loved him.

His famous adversary loved him.

A lot of sports personalities felt that way about Bowden Wyatt, who played football at Tennessee from 1936 through 1938 and coached the Volunteers from 1955 through 1962.

"Bowden Wyatt was justly famous as a football coach," said Tom Siler, the retired sports editor and columnist at the Knoxville News-Sentinel. "But he also had a great talent for friendship.

"People who knew Bowden never forgot him. For years, the Tennessee faithful flocked around him at the annual conventions, looking to him as the titular head of the Vol-trained coaches.

"Bowden was the same as a coach as he was as a player. He loved hard-hitting enthusiasm and possessed around-the-clock energy. His favorite expressing was, 'Hitch up your guts and go.' It said a lot about him."

Siler, a longtime observer of Tennessee football, thinks Wyatt reached the zenith of his coaching career in November of 1956. His Volunteers defeated Georgia Tech, 6-0, in Atlanta while en route to a 10-0 regular season.

John Majors was a star on that team. "Bowden Wyatt is considered a great coach by anybody who knows football," he said. "He might be overlooked in some circles, like outside of this part of the country, but he will forever be remembered as something special to me."

Alabama partisans, including Bryant, have reason to consider Wyatt as a dreaded nemesis. He definitely left a mark on The Third Saturday in October.

As a player, Wyatt had an even record against Alabama, 1-1-1. There was a 0-0 tie in 1936, a 14-7 Crimson Tide victory in 1937, and a 13-0 Volunteers victory in 1938.

Wyatt, who once suffered a broken jaw against Alabama but stayed in the game, played when Tennessee allowed the Crimson Tide few points. There was a definite carryover. The first three Tennessee teams he coached, after arriving on campus from Wyoming, shut out Alabama. The scores were 20-0, 24-0, and 14-0. His next three teams allowed Alabama only seven points in each game. The scores were 14-7, 7-7, and 20-7.

"Bowden believed in defense and kicking," Bryant said during the 1980 season, the week before Alabama played Tennessee, barely more than two years before his death in 1983. "He got that from the general [Neyland]. I stole a lot from both of them."

Bryant put Wyatt's tricks of the trade to good use when coaching against Wyatt in 1961 and 1962. The Crimson Tide won 34-3 and 27-7, respectively, and those losses had a lot to do with Tennessee looking for a new coach in 1963.

Wyatt left Tennessee with a bitter taste in his mouth.

But he left fond memories in the minds of Tennessee fans who remember him today as a great player and a great coach.

Wyatt was recruited to Tennessee by assistant coach Hugh Faust. When Faust's recruiter arrived in Kingston, Wyatt was fishing a long way from his house, thinking nothing about football. But when Wyatt heard who was waiting for him, he got interested. He told people, he took off "running all the way home because Tennessee wanted to talk to me about playing football there."

Also, I hope he treats us as good up there next year as we treated him down here this year."

According to Wilson, Tennessee fans visiting Birmingham were looking for a place to party before and after the game.

His column said: "Visitors from Knoxville and other towns who remained overnight and wanted to do a little dancing had to go outside the Magic City to do their waltzing and foxtrotting. Birmingham has some kind of an ordinance prohibiting dancing where hard drinks are served. Hence, the lack of night spots inside the city."

It appeared from the outset of his career that Majors was born to be a tailback in the single wing offense employed by Tennessee.

"I guess I had a good chance of being raised to be a tailback because my dad was a tailback," Majors said. "My father was a great coach, a builder of winning teams everywhere he worked, in high school and at Sewanee, and he taught me how to play the game.

"Also, my dad was a great athlete. He was one of the quickest human beings God ever put on the face of the earth. He was probably the greatest quail shot known to man. He had great hand-to-eye coordination. He had quick hands, quick feet, and quick eyes. He was super turning double-plays as a shortstop in baseball. He punted, passed, and ran in football. He played the pivot in basketball. It's quite possible I got a lot of that from him."

Regardless, Alabama fans saw Majors and had fits. He added to the agony of the Crimson Tide program, which went through a very frustrating season in 1955.

"It was a time of demoralization on campus," said Jeff Coleman, now in retirement in Tuscaloosa after serving as Alabama business manager and athletic director. "Those were not happy days, to say the least. The 1955 season was one we all wanted to forget as soon as it ended."

Meanwhile, the arrival of Wyatt as coach of the Volunteers provided a boost for the program. He brought stability and success, as noticed by Col. Tom Elam. "Bowden was at that time the epitome of what a coach should have been," Elam said. "Had it not been for some personal problems, he might have been coach at Tennessee for a long time.

"He had great success against Alabama. Of course, the rivals from down there had hit bottom by then. It was a low ebb for the Crimson Tide.

"It might be a fair statement to say Alabama had become just another game during their brief period under Ears Whitworth. It seemed to me that Georgia Tech was the more formidable foe at that time."

Regardless of how bad Alabama had become, Cruze is more than happy to remember the victory in 1955 over the Crimson Tide. Also, he is heavy in praise of his coach, as are most of his players at Tennessee.

"During the spring of 1955, his first after inheriting a program that was somewhat in disarray, Coach Bowden Wyatt immediately proved himself to all of us," Cruze said. "His message from the outset was clear—'Everybody will have a chance to prove himself'—and I'm proof he meant it. I was not even on the eighth team when practice started that spring, because of an injury I'd had in 1954, but I made it to the first team in two or three weeks.

"Coach Wyatt did something else that got our attention. We had a fullback named Tom Tracy, who might be the best athlete who ever stepped on campus. One day at practice, he loafed after Coach Wyatt called for a fullback. Coach Wyatt kicked a football about twenty-five yards down the field and said, 'Get me another fullback in here. We don't have time to wait for him.'

"That's when we all knew that Coach Wyatt would be fair with everybody.

"Also, he was honest. Before the 1955 season, he told us there were better players than us and he'd be going against better coaches. 'But,' he quickly added, 'none of them are gonna outwork Tennessee.' He said we'd work three times as hard as our opponents every day, and that's why we'd end up beating most of them.

"Coach Wyatt did a wonderful job with us in 1955. He took good players, not great ones, and won games. He used that season to prepare us for even better things in 1956.

"At the Alabama game there were unusual pregame activities on Legion Field. A few minutes after noon, with only a handful of spectators in the stands, a hefty guy about the size of Chief Sanooke ambled on the field. He was attired in complete Indian regalia, including head feathers. For all I know he may have been an Indian. He emptied a bag containing two footballs and a bicycle pump. Then he pumped the footballs tighter. After he had tried to kick a couple of goals from about the 25-yard line, a smartly dressed man walked on the field and escorted the chief to the sideline."

Alabama would have favored Majors joining the chief-turned-place-kicker on the sideline. The crafty junior was too much for the Crimson Tide.

"All told," wrote Ed Miles in the *Atlanta Constitution*, "the dirt-packing dodger from Huntland, Tennessee, lugged the ball 30 times for a net gain of 117 yards, after subtracting 23 yards in losses he had while trying to pass.

"Drum Majors plainly reflected the craftsmanship of a new coach, Bowden Wyatt, as he dazzled thirty-three thousand fans drawn to the Dixie classic more by its ancient tradition than by the expectations of the fireworks the Vols produced.

30

1956
Tennessee 24, Alabama 0

ALABAMA WAS STAGGERING AND ready to be finished off by a University of Tennessee football team that won the Southeastern Conference championship in 1956 and had a tailback who finished second in balloting for the Heisman Trophy.

Sportswriter Norman Bassett of the *Tuscaloosa News* attended the 24-0 victory by Tennessee over the Crimson Tide on October 20 at Shields-Watkins Field in Knoxville. Said Bassett:

> They say they brew a potent variety of white lightning in these Tennessee hills, and Alabama got three good shots of it losing to the Vols before 27,500 fans.
>
> Although John Majors, senior tailback, came off the injured list to score once against Alabama, it was his sub, Al Carter, who did the real damage, getting two of Tennessee's scores.
>
> The Vols' touchdowns were definitely of the lightning variety. Carter's 44-yard burst behind typical sync-like downfield blocking gave the Vols their second score. Majors got his on a 43-yard scoot in the third period. The other two Vols scores were short hauls into the end zone. One came at the climax of a 73-yard march. The other came at the end of a 37-yard push.
>
> For Bama, it was another of those games when it looked good, except in the scoring department. The Tide outgained the Vols on the ground, 181 to 165, and picked up 98 yards passing to 70. The

Tide lost the ball on a fumble only once, but had four passes picked
out of the air by Tennessee.

It was the seventeenth consecutive loss for Alabama, which was
coached by J. B. "Ears" Whitworth. The Crimson Tide did not quit,
according to a column written by former sports editor Tom Siler of the
Knoxville News-Sentinel. His story told about an interesting verbal
exchange during the game between two Tennessee players, guard Bill
Johnson and end Murray Armstrong.

"Take care of yourself out there, Murray, because they're still
cracking," Johnson said as he left the field in the fourth quarter for a
rest on the Tennessee bench.

"You got it," Armstrong answered as he entered the game.

A few plays later, Armstrong came out of the game with his right
hand cupped across his mouth. He was minus a tooth.

That might have prompted the postgame reflection offered by Tennessee coach Bowden Wyatt, who said, "It may sound strange to say
about a team that isn't winning, but this Alabama team is playing good
football. I mean they hit hard—they were working hard to score to the
very end—and that speaks well for their morale."

But the Crimson Tide did not score against the Volunteers for the
second consecutive season, although it took a fiery pep talk from Tennessee tackle John Gordy during a time-out to help preserve the shutout.

When Alabama secured a first down at the Volunteers' six-yard line
late in the second quarter, Gordy addressed a defense that had been
labeled weak because both Duke and Chattanooga had scored 20
points on it the two previous weeks. "Let's find out now if we've got a
defense," Gordy yelled to his teammates, who responded by allowing
the Crimson Tide three yards on the ensuing four plays.

"All that stuff about us not having a defense sort of got under my
skin," said Gordy, who now lives in Santa Ana, California. "I really got
a kick out of stopping them on the goal line."

Another Tennessee player who took part in that goal line stand
was end Buddy Cruze. He recalls the importance of keeping Alabama
out of the end zone. "We played platoon football," Cruze said, "and
the second team was on the field when Alabama got to our six-yard
line. During a time-out, we talked Coach Wyatt into letting us go into
the game. The shutout meant a lot to us.

"Having been a Knoxvillian, born and raised, the series with Alabama meant a lot to me. Unfortunately, Alabama had slipped a little at that time, leaving Georgia Tech as our most heated rival. But keeping the Crimson Tide from scoring was still important, just the same.

"We put it to them pretty good that afternoon."

That is what Clettus Atkinson thought. The sportswriter stated it simply enough in the *Birmingham Post-Herald:* "Tennessee—too tricky, too tough, too talented, the story as the Vols ran through, around, and over Alabama."

On the flipside, Whitworth watched helplessly as Majors and Carter ran through his defense. The former, who finished second to Paul Hornung of Notre Dame in the race for the Heisman Trophy, had 59 yards. The latter had 54 yards. Fullback Tommy Bronson had 44 yards.

So frustrated was Whitworth after the game, he said, "I wish I'd had a shotgun. I would have shot Majors and Carter. But it would've had to have been a 10-gauge. I couldn't have hit that pair with anything smaller."

Majors recovered quickly from an injury to produce havoc for the Crimson Tide. "I got ready for Alabama on Wednesday or Thursday, after sitting out with a separated shoulder," Majors said. "I really wanted to play against them, particularly since I was a senior."

It was important for Majors to play because of his quest for the Heisman Trophy, although Cruze thinks his teammate was at a disadvantage in such balloting. "Nobody from this part of the country really had a chance of winning such a media thing as that," he said. "And, of course, you have to remember who was in that famous senior class of 1956: Hornung, Majors, Tommy McDonald, Jimmy Brown, John Brodie, and a lot of other standouts."

Bobby Gordon, a junior tailback in 1956, was more outspoken about the Heisman Trophy balloting. "It was a fluke. It showed the weight Notre Dame has. We all thought John Majors should have won it. We were disappointed. We considered him losing the Heisman Trophy to Hornung a team loss."

What does Majors think after all these years?

"It'd be extremely egotistical for me to say I deserved the Heisman Trophy that season," Majors said. "I was just a viable candidate, I guess, and I don't say that to be diplomatic. I'd say there were some pretty good candidates that year."

The Volunteers were good that season, too, as evidenced by the unbeaten record they took into the Sugar Bowl. Baylor defeated the Volunteers, 13-7, in one of the more memorable New Orleans classics, and Tennessee lost the national championship to Oklahoma.

"That was a fluke, too," said Gordon, "because we beat a lot of teams better than the ones Oklahoma beat. At that time the Big Eight Conference was nothing more than Oklahoma and the Seven Dwarfs."

Alabama, which ended its dreadful losing streak by beating Mississippi State, 13-12, the week following their loss to Tennessee, posted a 2-7-1 record made more bitter by a 40-0 loss to intrastate rival Auburn in the last game of the season.

"I'm proud of my boys for trying hard," Whitworth said during the week before the losing streak ended. "They haven't had anything good happen to them this season, nothing to encourage them, but they're still playing like demons. They're not the terrible losers so many people think they are."

Majors, meanwhile, graduated from Tennessee as a winner who did not receive his due honor.

"John Majors was one of the more competitive players I've seen as a sports journalist," said Alf Van Hoose, sports editor and columnist at the *Birmingham News*. "He was one of the top players in the Tennessee-Alabama series that I've seen since watching my first of those games in 1942.

"Majors could do it all, anything it took to win. He was one of those guys who'd always do better than expected in crucial situations, whether it meant running, passing, or kicking. He was a splendid all-round performer, among the best in the nation.

"Both Tennessee and Majors were close to being the best team and best player, respectively, in the nation that year."

31

1957
Tennessee 14, Alabama 0

THE LUMPS ON THE field were painful.

"You knew you'd be playing for sixty minutes every time you faced Alabama," said Joe Schaffer, a University of Tennessee fullback who captained the Volunteers in 1959. "That's definitely how it was in 1957, no matter how bad the situation seemed to be getting down their way."

The editorials in newspapers were stinging.

J. B. "Ears" Whitworth was a man in trouble as he went about the business of coaching the Alabama football team in 1957. His team had an 0-2-1 record as it prepared to host rival Tennessee, a record that had become far too common in the minds of Crimson Tide supporters; and his critics were already searching for his replacement.

"I have a three-year contract," Whitworth said. "This is my third year. I have nothing more to say."

The man was in a precarious situation. Tennessee made it a lethal one.

The Vols, coached by Bowden Wyatt, went to Legion Field on October 19 and shut out the Crimson Tide for the third consecutive season, 14-0. Everybody watching was convinced Alabama would be playing under a new coach the following season.

Wyatt was on top of the world. He had coached against the bitter rival on The Third Saturday in October three times and had escaped unscathed. In fact, his Tennessee teams had dominated Alabama, not merely defeated them.

Whitworth was in a precarious situation. Some of the Alabama alumni attempted to organize a players strike. So the Alabama program was in dire straits, as noticed by Jim Goostree, the former Tennessee student trainer and graduate, who was in his first year of almost three decades of service as Crimson Tide trainer.

"As enthusiastic as I was, I didn't realize the personnel within the Alabama program, as well as the attitude of the squad, was as bad as it was," Goostree said during the summer of 1986, when he served as an assistant athletic director at Alabama. "As I found out quickly, there wasn't enough raw talent present. And there weren't enough demands being made.

"I've heard that players from other programs, including Tennessee, developed an uncomplimentary attitude about players from Alabama. I've heard they considered them regular students attempting to play football."

THE CRIMSON Tide posted a 2-7-1 record in 1957. Tennessee, fresh from the Sugar Bowl and on its way to the Gator Bowl, where it defeated Paul "Bear" Bryant-coached Texas A&M, 3-0, posted an impressive 8-3 record.

In keeping with the tradition, Alabama gave one of its finer performances of the 1957 season against the Volunteers. Wyatt and his players had to work up a sweat, as Tom Siler noted in the *News-Sentinel:*

> The Tennessee Volunteers play football these days as if the script had been prepared by Alfred Hitchcock.
>
> No one gets killed, but the suspense is terrific, and the cash customers are afraid to leave until "the last man is out."
>
> This puzzling Tennessee team held to the same routine again in whipping an Alabama team that was frothing at the mouth with desire. As against Mississippi State, the Vols scored all 14 points in the last quarter.
>
> Bowden Wyatt, who seems to be bearing up pretty well under this strain, summed up the game by saying, "It's always great to beat Alabama. I'm glad it's over."
>
> And, certainly, Tennessee didn't hurt the Crimson Tide for three quarters. It seemed that Alabama and its bristling eight-man line would slap the Vols the rest of the day.

Without Bobby Gordon on this day, Alabama would have probably held Tennessee, an 11-point favorite, to a scoreless tie.

Gordon dazzled thirty-two thousand fans with his passes on the run in the fourth quarter. He passed to end Tommy Potts for the first touchdown. He tucked away the football and ran five yards for the other.

"It would have meant more to me had Alabama not been so pitiful," said Gordon, who lives in Knoxville. "Besides, I think our defense won the game. It was a determined outfit."

Former sportswriter Zipp Newman of the *Birmingham News* noticed that Gordon was as determined as anybody on the playing field. He wrote:

Clutch-man Bobby Gordon broke open the Alabama-Tennessee football game at Legion Field, leading the Vols to a 14-0 victory after they were outplayed in the first half.

Early in the fourth quarter, the Vols needed three yards on fourth down at Alabama's 25. Instead of trying to buck the ball, Gordon, old flash incognito, drew back his flipper on second down and tossed to Tommy Potts, who ran into the end zone for a crucial score.

From that point, it was Tennessee's game.

But Alabama challenged the goal line frequently during the game. In the first quarter, at the end of a 74-yard drive, the Crimson Tide fumbled the football at the Tennessee 6-yard line. In the fourth quarter, Tennessee produced a classic goal line stand. Though Alabama had first down at the two-yard line, the Volunteers took possession of the football at their 13-yard line.

"When I was a freshman, Alabama tore us up," said David Emory, a senior halfback at Tennessee in 1957. "That made us better, I think, intensified our determination. We shut them out the rest of my career. I think one reason is the way our enthusiasm picked up the week we played them."

The beleaguered Alabama coach noticed that.

"They were just too much for us when it mattered the most," Whitworth said before boarding his last plane after a game against Tennessee.

Alf Van Hoose, sports editor and columnist at the *Birmingham News,* recalls Whitworth as being a tad unlucky on The Third Saturday in October in 1957.

"Whitworth told me once that he was a bit unfortunate against Tennessee in 1957," Van Hoose said. "He said Tennessee had a guard named Bill Johnson who tipped off every play they ran by the position of his feet before the snap. He said the Alabama scouts had noticed that and that they knew exactly what Tennessee was going to do before every snap. There was no way Alabama could lose the game. But, as fate would have it, two days before the game Johnson sprained an ankle and was sidelined.

"After the game, Whitworth said, 'Well, that's the way it goes.'

"That statement said a lot about Whitworth. I always thought that was sort of typical of his approach to coaching football. It was an awful time for Alabama and for Whitworth. The team was losing, and the coach had the alumni yelping at his heels."

Whitworth's contract ran through December 1, 1957. Alabama had a new coach, as well as fresh life, two days later.

32

1958
Tennessee 14, Alabama 7

MAMA CALLED" AT A proper moment.

About ten months before the University of Tennessee evened its long football rivalry with Alabama, 18-18-5, with a 14-7 victory on October 18, 1958, the Crimson Tide sent out a plea for help to Paul "Bear" Bryant. He became coach at his alma mater on December 3, 1957.

"The reason—the only reason—I'm going back to Alabama is because Mama called me," Bryant said while announcing he was leaving Texas A&M to attempt to restore football fortunes at Alabama. Then, in character, the coach started talking about the Crimson Tide again becoming a winner.

"It's the players who make the coaches, my friend, and the mothers and fathers who make the players," Bryant said upon his arrival in Tuscaloosa. "In a situation such as the one at Alabama, the thing is getting the material and teaching kids to forget a losing complex. I have to teach them to win.

"If a man is a quitter, I want him to quit in practice, not in a game. There has been enough of that at Alabama. I demand all they've got. We've got to know during practice whether we can get that in games."

With those words, after a tough rebuilding process at the Capstone, The Third Saturday in October again became a date worthy of reverence.

A casual observer could tell The Third Saturday in October would again become a date worth remembering. Even though Bryant-coached

Alabama lost to Tennessee in his debut as a mentor in the series, the outclassed Crimson Tide fought hard.

"Alabama is a much better team now than it has been," said Tennessee coach Bowden Wyatt, who won his fourth game over the Crimson Tide in as many tries. "Bryant has some good football players. I feel relieved that we were just good enough to win."

The new coach in the series was not content with that.

"I'm not satisfied with anything," Bryant said after his team experienced a rash of penalties. "We've allowed a golden opportunity to slip away from us."

Then, as a parting shot, Bryant surveyed Shields-Watkins Field in Knoxville and said, "Well, we'll be back up here in two years. I'm not saying we'll have a great team. But I'll bet we play Tennessee a helluva lot stronger game than we did today.

"I'm looking forward to our players competing like Tennessee players do against us. They knock you down, then get up, and they knock you down again. I'm confident we're making progress toward doing that."

Fred Sington Jr., a junior on that Alabama team, remembers the progress being rudimentary at the beginning. "We had to learn how to win again," Sington said in his office in Gadsden, Alabama. "We had forgotten how.

"That loss to Tennessee in 1958 helped us a lot. We knew we should have won. We fumbled three times inside their 10-yard line. We left that game with a lot of confidence. We were coming back strong."

Tennessee was already strong, with one family in particular providing stars for the series. It was tailback John Majors who led the Volunteers to victories over Alabama in 1955 and 1956. It was sophomore tailback Bill Majors, his brother, who paced the Volunteers to their conquest of the Crimson Tide in 1958.

Sportswriter Frank "Red" Bailes of the *Knoxville News-Sentinel* explained it thus:

Sophomore Bill Majors showed his heels to 34,200 sun-bathed fans and Alabama's Crimson Tide to lead the Vols to a 14-7 victory.

The 170-pound tailback from Huntland, Tennessee, sparked touchdown marches in the second and third quarters, scored both

PAUL "BEAR" BRYANT

HE WAS CHEERED IN November 1981. He had become the winningest college football coach in history when his team defeated Auburn.

He was touted in many circles as the finest coach in history when he retired in December 1982.

He was dead in January 1983.

People contend Paul "Bear" Bryant of the University of Alabama, by way of backwoods Arkansas, could not live without coaching football.

That is debatable.

What is not questionable is his greatness in his chosen profession, his ability to teach trade secrets of life to his players, and his penchant for winning at a staggering pace.

And, in these years after his death, there is reason to wonder what The Third Saturday in October would have been without this man who played on that day for three years (1933–35) as a Crimson Tide end and coached on it twenty-five years (1958–82).

He loved the rivalry. By his own admission, he got so wrapped up in it that he sometimes became sick at his stomach the week of *the* game. "Sometimes I stopped on the side of the highway on the way to work and puked," he said. It was on Thursday afternoon before Tennessee was to be played on Saturday afternoon that he always concluded his post-practice press conference with two words: "Be Brave."

Lindsey Nelson recalls a time with Bryant that points out how much defeating Tennessee meant to him. Incredibly, this was while he was still coaching at Texas A&M, before he returned to Alabama in his hounds-tooth hat.

"I was in College Station [Texas] prior to the Texas-Texas A&M game one season," Nelson said. "I had accompanied Coach Bryant and four Texas A&M supporters to a party in Houston, and we were driving back to College Station.

"One of the Texas A&M supporters turned to me as we were riding down the highway. He said, 'Lindsey, is this not the greatest rivalry in the nation? Texas A&M and Texas. Wow!'

"I told him that rivalries, I guess, were the product of where you come from. I told him down our way nothing was more important, or better, than the Alabama-Tennessee game.

"It was then that Coach Bryant jumped to attention, turned to face us, and said, 'Yeah, Alabama and Tennessee, the greatest rivalry in college football. The best game going. The top of the line.'

"Those Aggies just sat there stunned. They looked at each other in disbelief. Here was their coach on the eve of their game talking about the greatness of the Alabama-Tennessee rivalry."

Bryant left quite a mark on The Third Saturday in October, as well as a lot of other weekends, because he posted a 16-7-2 record coaching the Crimson Tide against the Volunteers. Incredibly, that final tally came after he dipped to 5-6-2 in the series before winning 11 games in a row.

His overall record, from 1945 at Maryland through 1982 at Alabama, was 323-85-17. He got better with age, with his teams from the 1970s establishing a national record for games won. He won 232 times at Alabama.

"You found out what kind of person you were, player you were and winner you were when you played against Tennessee," Bryant said. "That game was a time of reckoning for us all."

His grade: Winner.

Jim Goostree knows why. The Tennessee graduate served as trainer at Alabama from 1957 through 1983. He remembers Bryant well.

"I think the strongest virtue of Coach Bryant was his willingness to dedicate his whole life to football," Goostree said. "The game consumed

continued on next page

almost all of his time. I think he thought about football many hours when other people—competitors—were thinking about other things.

"Also, I think Coach Bryant had success because he truly loved his athletes. He cared for them in ways people will never really understand or appreciate. Not only was he concerned with the way they conducted their lives in the university setting, but he genuinely wanted the training they received in a football environment to be reflected by success later in their lives. Stories continue to surface about how he helped individuals in quiet ways, former players and others, and I doubt all of his good deeds will ever be known or appreciated.

"Coach Bryant won because he could work with young men. He could instill confidence and pride in them, then could get the most of them physically and mentally. Also, he could change with the times. He was so dedicated to the game that it never had a chance to pass him by.

"Coach Bryant was gifted when it came to establishing goals, then reworking them. In 1958 he recruited a class of football players at Alabama and said that the goal of that group of freshmen was to win a national championship in 1961. That happened. After the third national championship in 1965, the morning after the announcement, at 3:00 A.M., he put a sign on the bulletin board in the athletic dorm: 'We can make it four.' The 1966 team responded with an unbeaten and untied season. He always thought it should have been the national champion. The next one came in 1973.

"We should all be thankful that we had him as long as we did. And we should be thankful for the standards he established at Alabama."

That brings to mind poems Bryant discussed less than a month before his death. Few people realized he was so inclined.

But he had one poem—"What Have I Traded For What God Has Given Me Today?"—that he read almost every morning. Bryant interpreted the poem to mean, "Every minute should be spent on a purpose, and that purpose should be good, not bad. We should try to win within the rules of society, competing fairly and treating others as we want them to treat us."

Then, he added, "If only I had found this poem many years ago, then my life would have been better, more rewarding."

That sounds impossible to most people.

It brings to mind another poem he contemplated—"The Old Man and the Bridge"—and his reaction to it.

The poem deals with an elderly man who came face to face with a river. He crossed it, wading the water, and returned to the other side to start building a bridge. Upon seeing this, several younger men ran to his side and asked, "Why, Old Man, are you building this bridge when you know you will never pass this way again?" The Old Man looked at them, smiled and said, "Because, my friends, other people must pass this way behind me."

As much as any man, Paul "Bear" Bryant prepared the way for many who have participated in The Third Saturday in October.

touchdowns and kept the Vols in the game with damaging punts and quick-kicks.

Alabama stayed in the battle until the last, however, throwing a late aerial attack against the No. 1 pass defense team in the country in a vain stab at their first Southeastern Conference win of the season.

Bryant, who had never coached a victory over Tennessee in Knoxville, after trying with Kentucky, wasted little time going to work upon his arrival in Tuscaloosa. "There is an air of mystery," wrote former sports columnist Benny Marshall in the *Birmingham News,* "and there is an air of determination."

After the Volunteers' victory over the Crimson Tide, Marshall said:

Alabama fought the good fight, slashing at Tennessee with a defiance that demanded more. But, in the end, out in the hot of this blue-skied autumn afternoon, Alabama's own sins did them in. Paul "Bear" Bryant's troops won most of the statistics. Tennessee won the football game.

Alabama, aiming for a knockout, moved to mid-field late in the fourth quarter. But, Tennessee, scrambling for its life, halted the threat on its 40-yard line with barely more than a minute to play.

Alabama's fourth straight loss to Tennessee was in the books.

According to Col. Tom Elam, the longtime chairman of the Tennessee Athletics Board, the arrival of Bryant as coach at Alabama did not strike fear in the hearts of Volunteers. They had remembered, he said, good success against Kentucky teams coached by the Bear.

"There wasn't a feeling that we had a monster on our hands," Elam said. "His Kentucky teams had gone scoreless for three seasons against us under him, even with great talent. But I did notice how he'd been successful with those Texas A&M Aggies.

"I never dreamed he'd later run off a long streak of wins against Tennessee. Once he got us, he got us good during the 1960s and even more during the 1970s. It didn't take long for me to realize they were getting better down in Alabama. Even his first team in 1958 got after us pretty good."

One person from Tennessee who knew Alabama was going to be strong under Bryant is Gus Manning, who was sports information director in 1958.

"I'd heard for a couple of years that Bryant was going to leave Texas A&M to return to Alabama," said Manning, who developed a long and warm friendship with the former Crimson Tide coach. "I'd heard that the only reason he'd left Kentucky was to position himself for a move to his alma mater.

"It didn't take Bryant long to have an impact on SEC football. His first team was a good one. He'd reminded Alabama players how important it is to play hard all the time. He knew the importance of getting them ready to fight against Tennessee on The Third Saturday in October.

"But I'll remember Bryant for his off-the-field antics as much as for all his victories. He was a delight to be around at meetings. He'd set the pace when it came to having a good time.

"I'll never forget what happened at the SEC spring meeting in 1958. A lifeguard came up to me at the pool and said, 'Sir, we need your help in quieting down a commotion on the beach. I'm having a problem. Your coach, Bowden Wyatt, and the Alabama coach, Paul Bryant, are down there kicking sand on all the pretty girls.' This was early one morning. Bryant and Wyatt were having a good time together, as usual. When I told them [Bryant and Wyatt] about that, they just laughed.

"Bryant was like that. He got along well with Tennessee people, even told me once that he'd learned how to coach winning football from General Neyland, but he'd show up ready to battle us every October."

A lot of people noticed renewed intensity at Alabama after Bryant returned to his alma mater. One observer was former columnist Naylor Stone of the *Birmingham Post-Herald*. He wrote:

> We always shrink inward like a winter apple just before an Alabama-Tennessee game. It has been that way a lot of years. It has become that way once again.

Tennessee, ebbing a bit itself, posted a 4-6 record. Alabama, working hard to regain its lost glitter, posted a 5-4-1 record.

"I don't recall Alabama being any tougher in 1958 than they were in 1957," said Joe Schaffer, a former Tennessee guard who now lives in Cincinnati. "Of course, I don't remember them ever playing what you'd call soft football against us.

"I'd heard stories about Tennessee-Alabama games long before I arrived in Knoxville. I haven't seen or heard anything to indicate there has ever been a lag in intensity. It's a classic rivalry watched nationwide."

Among the Alabama players who labored that first season under Bryant is Billy Richardson. He lives in Birmingham, where he has become a successful businessman.

"It was rough," Richardson said about his first year on campus. "Practices were something like none of us had gone through. Most of the stories people tell about the early Bryant days are true.

"I wasn't there for the first spring training under Bryant, but I remember how aware the news media were of what was happening in Tuscaloosa. They showed films of practice almost every day. I remember watching them and getting scared just thinking about showing up for fall practice.

"The varsity had already been practicing for a week when we got there. I remember looking out on the practice field and noticing only 30 players were left, because a lot of returnees had quit and gone home.

"I went out there for my first practice scared to death. We had a scrimmage and a bunch of people got hurt. I guess everybody out there felt like walking off at one time or another."

Richardson said "it wasn't uncommon" for him to lose "14 or 15 pounds" during a normal Bryant-directed practice, down from his paltry 170.

Jim Goostree was in his second season as trainer at Alabama when Bryant returned to Tuscaloosa. He recalls the strenuous routine the new coach prescribed. "Coach Bryant went to the whip immediately," Goostree said. "And that's stating it mildly.

"Recruiting was over quickly, because he sold prospects on the idea that Alabama could again become a champion, and the work started.

"And from the outset, Coach Bryant talked a lot about Tennessee, how things were done in that program, and for several years he got extremely uptight before games against the Volunteers.

"Coach Bryant carried a fondness for the Alabama-Tennessee rivalry with him to his grave. The importance he placed on The Third Saturday in October boggles the mind."

33

1959
Tennessee 7, Alabama 7

So CLOSE, YET SO far away.

That was the afterthought for Alabama fans following the University of Alabama and Tennessee's fight to a 7-7 tie in a dramatic football game on October 17, 1959.

Fred Sington Jr., has thought about that Third Saturday in October many times since—for good reason.

The Crimson Tide place-kicker had the chance to become a hero that afternoon at Legion Field in Birmingham. But with his hometown audience looking on, he missed a 31-yard field goal on the next to last play of the game to deprive Alabama of what would have been its first victory over the Volunteers since 1954.

"I stood there and wished the ground would open up," Sington said, at his office in Gadsden, Alabama, while remembering his missed field goal attempt. "I wanted to disappear. I thought how the club had played good enough to win, and I had deprived us of the opportunity to do it.

"And I immediately thought about Coach Paul Bryant, how much beating Tennessee meant to him. I felt terrible from that standpoint.

"No excuses. I just missed it."

Interestingly, as Sington points out, he is "the only man in the history of this great series who could have won two games with a field goal." He played in 1953, a scoreless tie, before joining military service. He missed from a more difficult 48 yards in the fourth quarter that year.

But neither field goal attempt was easy. The miss in 1959 came with the football sitting on the left hashmark. Because of unusual substitution rules, Sington had to play at flanker the three previous plays or else not get back into the game unless a time-out was called.

"The funny thing, if you think of it as being humorous, was me running pass patterns against Bill Majors for those three plays in 1959," Sington said. "On the third play, after it was obvious Pat Trammell was not going to throw the ball to me, I was wide open in the end zone. Maybe I should be glad the ball never came my way. It would have been more terrible missing a touchdown pass than it was missing the field goal."

The muffed opportunity came at a time when Alabama thought it had a chance to end a long drought against Tennessee. The afternoon before the game, Crimson Tide coach Paul "Bear" Bryant was a cautious optimist when he said, "I think we've got a bona fide chance to win this time. It's up to us. I'm almost sure we'll be there at the end."

Alabama had its chance at the end of an afternoon that featured keen anticipation in the Crimson Tide camp.

Alabama beat the clock to give Sington the chance to become a hero. The Crimson Tide started at its 47-yard line with 3:34 remaining in the game. Six plays netted two first downs and moved the football to the Tennessee 27. Bryant sent Sington into the game as a decoy flanker. Quarterback Pat Trammell passed over the middle to Duff Morrison for 19 yards.

Sington had his kicking tee brought onto the field with 13 seconds remaining. He missed the field goal attempt by three feet to the left.

THE VOLUNTEERS had scored on their second possession. Bill Majors ran two yards from his tailback position, and Cotton Letner kicked the extra point.

The Tennessee defense turned back Alabama several times in the third and fourth quarters.

Alabama gained 186 yards in the game. Tennessee managed only 88.

Benny Marshall, former sports editor and columnist for the *Birmingham News*, was in the Alabama dressing room before the game. He recorded the moments in waiting this way:

Back of the door, the Crimson Tide waited. It was quiet at 1 o'clock underneath Legion Field where the men who play football for Alabama and Coach Paul Bryant pulled on the shoes, and the pads, and the red shirts and thought about Tennessee.

Quiet is best. Yells don't win football games.

Bryant shut the door behind them and his face was serious. He had lighted a cigarette and thrown it away in the gravel, and his eyes were on the clouds overhead that all but hid Birmingham downtown.

"Is it going to rain?" he asked a visitor who didn't know. The clouds weren't talking.

The crowd came slowly in the last hour before Alabama and Tennessee were to play again. The crowd watched the clouds, too.

Bryant grinned, turned to speak with Jerry Claiborne, his No. 1 assistant, and Pat James, who coaches masterful defense.

Bryant, talking with [assistant coach] Carney Laslie, said, "I think we can win. I think we can beat them. If we don't give something away, we'll make it. We'll get after them, I know."

Alabama did that. But the Crimson Tide did not win.

Wrote former sports editor Tom Siler in the *Knoxville News-Sentinel:*

The scoreboard lights glistened in the gathering gloom of Legion Field: Tennessee 7, Alabama 7.

Alabama partisans quickly translated this into an Alabama victory, and Tennessee fans glumly accepted it as a defeat.

Actually, the Crimson Tide badly outplayed the Volunteers for three quarters, the last three. Tennessee rushed quickly to what appeared to be an easy touchdown in the first quarter; as it turned out, that was to be the last easy mark of the day.

Tennessee, for instance, gained 60 yards by rushing in the first quarter. When the day was done the Vols had a net rushing total of 49 yards, which gives you the general idea. Thereafter, Tennessee was cornered and fighting off an enraged Alabama that came to the quick realization that the Vols could be had.

So Bowden Wyatt was feeling relief when he met with the press after the game. It was the first time in five tries that he had failed to defeat Alabama. "Nobody likes a tie," he said, "but it's better than getting beat.

"This was a typical Alabama-Tennessee game, rough and tough. I never have seen one to the contrary."

Interestingly, it was the third tie between the two teams in the most recent twelve years. There was only one Alabama victory during that time. Tennessee had been in control of the series.

That made the missed field goal more important.

"Man, was I glad to see it," said Wyatt, whose team posted a 5-4-1 record, losing its final three games.

"Nobody misses one on purpose," said Bryant, who lauded his team and on the following Monday morning had a chat with Sington.

"Coach Jerry Claiborne was the first person to confront me after I missed the field goal," Sington said. "He told me to forget about it, that I should remember the kicks I had that helped us win games, that those things happen, that I was not the only person put in that position. Then, on Monday morning, Coach Bryant talked to me. He told me I should forget the miss, that if I kept dwelling on it, I would never be able to kick another field goal."

Bryant also praised the remainder of his team, which posted a 7-2-2 record, including a 7-0 loss to Penn State in the Liberty Bowl.

"I'm as proud of this team as I would've been had we won," Bryant said. "They put it on the line for four quarters. They got behind in the first quarter. It's easy to make excuses and quit at a time like that. But they fought back. We played five times better today than we have all season. I guess that's because we were on the field with those orange shirts. Nobody has ever seen a bunch of youngsters put more into anything. Our players were good enough to win, from an effort standpoint, and I'm pleased because of it."

Joe Schaffer, a Tennessee senior and team captain in 1959, now lives in Cincinnati. He sympathizes with Sington more now than he did that fateful afternoon in Birmingham.

"I remember him trying and missing that field goal," Schaffer said. "I remember turning around after rushing the kick and realizing he'd missed it. I remember being happy he did.

"You have to understand. We were fighting for our lives when Fred Sington tried to beat us with the kick. I remember saying, 'Thank God,' and then smiling from ear to ear.

"I sort of feel for him now, after all these years, but I wasn't sorry at all that day. It's terrible to say, I guess, but when you're playing for Tennessee against Alabama, it doesn't matter how you get a win, or a tie in this case, as long as you do it."

Alf Van Hoose covered *the* game in 1959. He recalls with a chuckle what Bryant told him privately after Sington missed the field goal that would have lifted the Crimson Tide to victory. "I remember Bryant talking about that fat tackle, Sington, that he had been feeding for several years, missing the chance to win the game," Van Hoose said. "He laughed when he said it. But it was clear how much not winning that game had upset him."

For Bryant, close was not good enough.

For Sington, it was far from it.

34

1960
Tennessee 20, Alabama 7

IT WAS QUICKLY OBVIOUS to everybody that the war was under way.

Bunny and Buddy proved as much.

The fire was back, totally, when the University of Tennessee and Alabama gathered in Knoxville on October 15, 1960, to continue their football rivalry.

Jim Goostree said that was apparent on the opening kickoff. "Bunny Orr of Tennessee received the opening kickoff, and Buddy Wesley of Alabama tackled him," Goostree said. "He really belted him. They collided and bounced back from each other. Wesley, in turn, collided with Jim Cartwright of Tennessee. The collision knocked out Wesley. He was unconscious when I got to him, which was quickly, and I thought he was dead.

"Blood was pouring from under his helmet. They had to hold up the game for a while so we could treat him. It took an edge off our team, for sure, because it looked mighty bad.

"The reason it happened is interesting. Wesley had taken the rubber padding out from the top of his helmet because his teammates had been kidding him about going bald. He thought the rubber pad was causing it. All Wesley had to soften the blow was the thick cords that held the rubber pad in place.

"The way those two guys collided—boom—he needed that pad. It was the type of collision you'd expect in Alabama-Tennessee games."

The opening day set the tone for the ensuing struggle. The game is recalled as one of the most vicious in the history of the series, as noticed by Tom Siler in the *Knoxville News-Sentinel*. Siler wrote:

> Tennessee 20, Alabama 7 is the best news we've had since Khrushchev went home. And talk about hitting, these Volunteers and Crimson Tiders could teach the Yankees and Pirates a thing or two.

Tennessee won the game, 20-7, after exploding offensively with three touchdowns in the first two quarters. Alabama, fighting back, had the upper hand the remainder of the afternoon, although it was not enough.

Alabama scored its touchdown in the second quarter on a 13-yard pass from Laurien Stapp to Leon Fuller. That was not the only Crimson Tide offense in the game. Alabama outgained the Volunteers 211 yards to 106. That unrewarded dominance left Alabama people moaning. But there was another reason the loss was painful to Bryant. Wrote Siler:

> This Volunteers victory reminded you of the Yankees' 10-0 World Series slaughter of Pittsburgh a week ago, in which the Yanks scored six runs in the first inning. Like the Bucs, Alabama was whipped before the invaders had worked up a good sweat.
>
> Tennessee scored more points [20] in 18 minutes than any Paul Bryant coached team had yielded since 1956, when the Texas A&M Aggies [coached by Bryant] whipped Texas, 35-21.
>
> Coach Bryant, after the third Tennessee touchdown, yelled, "Come on, let's have some fun. The next three quarters are ours."
>
> Later, Bryant yelled, "Get some backs up here [near his dispatch station on the sideline]. Isn't there anyone who wants to play?"
>
> Paul Bryant, football professional if there ever was one, was just having his little joke.
>
> You could close your eyes and just listen to the leather crack. And, if you are as old as I am, you could see Gene McEver and Bobby Dodd, Fred Sington and Dixie Howell, Bob Suffidge and George Cafego, Harry Gilmer and Holt Rast, Hank Lauricella and Ted Daffer, Bobby Marlow and Albert Elmore out there as foes of old.
>
> And that collision between Buddy Wesley, Bunny Orr and Jim Cartwright will be remembered about as long as Mike LaSorsa's 41-yard touchdown dash. Orr took a sideline kickoff. Seeing he was hemmed in, he lowered his head like Bolivar The Bull and smashed

into linebacker Wesley, a nimble little man who weighs about 180, who in turn, collided with Cartwright.

Cartwright limped off. Orr was dazed, but finally got to his wobbly feet. Wesley was carted off on a stretcher. Subsequent examination revealed only superficial injuries that included a nasty three-inch gash across the top of his head.

What it was was football—football of the most aggressive, grim, demanding sort.

Billy Neighbors was a junior tackle at Alabama in 1960. Now living in Huntsville, Alabama, he recalls the loss to Tennessee as being hard to swallow.

"That's the worst game we played during my three years with the Crimson Tide," Neighbors said. "We were better than them, but we lost it because we made too many mistakes.

"Actually, I think we lost the game during preparation for it. On Wednesday afternoon, assistant coach Pat James gave us a wild and woolly pep talk in Tuscaloosa. He talked about his mother almost dying and his brother getting killed in the war. Somehow, he related all of that to us playing Tennessee in the football game. It got us riled up, to say the least, and we peaked too soon. We left our game on the practice field.

"To show you how fired up we were, a couple of us got in a fight during pregame warmups. By the time the opening kickoff arrived, we were finished.

"Then Wesley got hurt on the opening kickoff. God, we thought he had a fractured skull. The blood looked like it was coming out of his ears.

"Anyway, I'll never forget what happened when we got back to Tuscaloosa that night. They locked all the doors at the athletic dorm and told us to stay inside, that they didn't want us to see our friends because we'd embarrassed the university.

"And they told us one of our teammates, Wesley, was dying in the Knoxville hospital.

"That'll tell you how important the game was."

Bill Battle was a sophomore end at Alabama in 1960. He became coach at Tennessee in 1970, resigning under fire in 1976 with a 59-22-2 record. He is now a successful businessman in Atlanta.

"My baptism in the Tennessee-Alabama series was a wild one," Battle said at his sports licensing office in Atlanta. "The one thing that was most apparent to me was how uptight Coach Bryant got before games with them. It was obvious from the outset of my career how important it was to him.

"Another thing I recall was how tough it was playing defense against their single wing offense. I had to take on two blockers, one with my hip and one with my shoulder, and those weren't normal people they had. I had a miserable day, an awful time, a tough beginning against them.

"It was wild from the start, when Buddy Wesley collided with Bunny Orr, with Jim Cartwright in there somewhere.

"Wesley was laying face down. His hands were trembling. He was bleeding out of his head. I was standing right there. I thought, 'Oh, my God, he's dead.' It wasn't a pretty sight. And of course, I'd been scared out of my mind before I saw that.

"When Orr got up, all the Tennessee players started cheering. That made it more intimidating.

"I'll never forget how Coach Bryant was at halftime, after they did all that scoring on us, making it 20-7. He was calm. We thought he would be screaming, throwing people around. We'd made a lot of mistakes that led to their touchdowns. Instead, he was telling us how we'd played well. He was building confidence. I learned a lot from that.

"But it was bad the next week. Coach Bryant went on his Sunday afternoon television show. We were watching it at the athletic dorm. He said I know we have a lot of guys sitting around this afternoon looking at their watches, wearing that sweet after-shave lotion, wanting to get out on campus and mingle with the girls on sorority row. Then, he said, 'But this week, we're gonna run off all the riff-raff at Alabama.' You talk about scared people.

"And Coach Bryant did what he said he'd do. Gosh, what a bad week that was at practice."

Battle recalls, with a chuckle, Pat James making his famous and stirring talk to Alabama players at the Wednesday night meeting before the game. He said Crimson Tide players did not know whether to cry or laugh. He said he knew after that address how important it was to get ready to play against the rival from East Tennessee.

"Pat told us his brother was one of the first people killed at Pearl Harbor," Battle said. "He hadn't wanted the war to end, not after that, that he'd wanted to keep punching, punishing, and killing the enemy. He said that's how Alabama players had to fight against Tennessee.

"And he told us about running fourteen miles to get a doctor who saved his mother after she had a heart attack. He said that was how he had a part in saving her life. He said that's how Alabama players had to feel in a game against Tennessee in Knoxville. He said we had to play that game like we were fighting for our mothers' lives.

"Pat was quivering and crying. We were stunned. We just sat there and looked at him in disbelief."

So Alabama fought hard. But the Tennessee defense triggered the victory, forcing Alabama into early mistakes, as recalled by Lee Roy Jordan, a Crimson Tide sophomore linebacker that season who later became an All-National Football League player at that position with the Dallas Cowboys.

"We had several crucial mistakes early in the game—fumbles and interceptions—and they put us in a hole," Jordan said at his ranch near Dallas. "We felt we had a chance to win. Afterwards, we felt we should have won. But it was Tennessee that did win.

"I'll never forget how they knocked us around up in Knoxville that day. That's how it was with their single-wing offense. I don't know if I was ever hit like that again, from all sides, because as soon as a Tennessee lineman got finished trying to block me, there'd be a back following him through the hole. It was a punishing game from the start."

Former sportswriter Frank "Red" Bailes wrote about the game in the *Knoxville News-Sentinel:*

Tennessee's defensive giants struck Alabama two damaging blows in the first quarter and came back with the knockout punch in the second to take some of the Crimson out of Bear Bryant's Tide.

Halfback Ray Abruzzese fumbled on Alabama's first play. Jim Cartwright, linebacker, recovered for the Vols at the Alabama 18-yard line to set up the crucial victory.

Tennessee turned this and another first-quarter fumble into touchdowns, then marched 57 yards in 10 plays in the second period for another score.

The Vols' touchdowns came on a magnificent catch by Charley Wyrick of an eight-yard pass in the end zone from Bill Majors; Mike

LaSorsa's 41-yard spring with a recovered fumble and a three-yard smash by tailback Glenn Glass.

Alabama marched 77 yards for its only score in the second quarter, fighting gamely to rally. But sensational punting by Majors and Gene Etter and gritty, hard-hitting defensive play kept the Tide from building up momentum in the second half.

The victory by Tennessee enabled the Volunteers to claim its only lead in The Third Saturday in October series. They were on top, 19-18-6, for the first time since the initial tie in 1901.

"It was not exactly an Alabama suicide," wrote Alf Van Hoose in the *Birmingham News,* "but close to it. Eight times a red-shirted team wanting so badly to do a mighty job dropped the football on a field shaking with oldtime Alabama-Tennessee jostling. Five times a warrior in orange got it. This, more than a thousand pictures, tells a bitter story. Alabama gave. Victory died."

For Bryant, who was making good things happen in Tuscaloosa, it was another painful defeat in Knoxville. His record against Tennessee, including his years at Kentucky and Texas A&M, dipped to an astounding 1-8-3.

He spoke with respect about Wyatt, who had an unbeaten record against the Crimson Tide. "I thought I was dedicated, but when that Wyatt starts to grit his teeth, he just frightens me to death," Bryant said about his coaching rival.

But that was to change in 1961, in stunning fashion, when a powerful Alabama team made up of the first recruiting class wooed by Bryant became the talk of the nation.

Sports Illustrated saw the Crimson Tide coming of age. In 1960 the magazine dispatched a writer to Tuscaloosa to do a preseason story about Alabama and the grizzly coach.

In part, it said:

As the season opens, Alabama is bear-ly strong. Bear Bryant, the Alabama football coach, is a disciplinarian, a perfectionist and a recruiter without peer. Also, a moaner. He can moan so loudly, he has been called the pretender to the throne of pessimism.

The king is Wally Butts of Georgia, who once talked a sports editor into picking Furman over Georgia in a game that Georgia wound up winning, 70-7.

Southerners say that when it starts to rain, Butts and Bryant think about building arks.

However, Bryant was better gathering future stars on the recruiting trail, and as the song goes, they fell on Alabama in 1961. And the coach was training them his way, punishing the defeated.

"They didn't feed us after the loss to Tennessee," Battle said. "We hadn't eaten since our pregame meal, and we were already back at the Birmingham airport. We were starving. We all made a run on the candy counter there.

"Then, when we got to the dorm, Pat James called us together for another meeting. He said he'd seen all of us standing around that candy counter. He called us worthless people. He vowed we'd have a gut check. "We had one the next week at practice."

The labor provided Alabama with hefty dividends the following season.

35

1961
Alabama 34, Tennessee 3

THE BIRMINGHAM PARKS AND Recreation Board worked harder than the University of Alabama football team did on The Third Saturday in October in 1961. As dawn broke about Legion Field with the opening kickoff in a game against Tennessee only hours away, workmen frantically labored building temporary seats in the stadium.

The previous night, as normal pregame madness gripped the city, it was announced that eighty-five hundred seats in the upper deck were unsafe for occupancy. That meant fans who held tickets in that part of the stadium either had to accept refunds or sit on hastily constructed planks.

The five thousand who chose the latter option sat among forty-eight thousand fans who watched a Crimson Tide team, marching toward a national championship, defeat Tennessee, 34-3, with an impressive show of force.

By the time darkness fell on the Magic City, with Alabama fans celebrating their first victory over Tennessee since 1954, it was apparent Paul "Bear" Bryant's rebuilding job had been completed.

The reconstruction crew was rewarded.

"Coach Bryant walked onto the team bus at the stadium after the game and told us we had a great team," Billy Neighbors, a tackle on the 1961 Alabama team, said during the summer of 1986 at his house in Huntsville, Alabama. "That was a big deal to us because he'd been telling us how lousy we were.

"Then Coach Bryant announced that he was gonna give us all a personal gift, a ring, because we'd beaten Tennessee. I've still got it, as do a lot of the other guys, a red stone with an *A* inscribed in it. And as a lasting memento of the man who bought it and gave it to me, it has 'Paul Bryant' inscribed on it. It's one of my more prized possessions.

"The rivalry with Tennessee was something. Hell, it was unreal. The tradition counted for something. It got you to play. The talk and hype might have pushed the annual game out of proportion, but all of us got caught up in the mystique of it, started viewing it as a battle for our lives.

"That's how Coach Bryant looked at it. He'd tell us to be brave, to fight hard, to show class. He'd get so up for the game himself that it'd rub off on all of us.

"It's a good thing, too, because when we played Tennessee, it was like cats and dogs fighting."

Lee Roy Jordan agrees with Neighbors. "That was a special game, as those rings Coach Bryant gave us were special gifts," Jordan said at his ranch near Dallas. "Mine [his ring] is sitting in a jewelry box beside two Super Bowl runnerup rings and an Alabama national championship ring. It was given to us, I think, as a tribute from Coach Bryant to the men who helped him reestablish Alabama football as a winner. To me, it's *the* ring from my years with the Crimson Tide."

Jordan and his teammates earned those rings with a magnificent display that hinted a national championship was drawing near. Alabama dominated the Volunteers, for sure, piling up 342 yards as it gave the scoreboard a workout.

Place-kicker Tim Davis, who kicked four extra points and field goals, was busier than usual. Mike Fracchia, the leaping fullback, scored the first touchdown on a five-yard run. Quarterback Pat Trammell passed nine yards to halfback Butch Wilson for the second touchdown. Halfback Billy Richardson ran eight yards for the third touchdown. Trammell ran one yard for the last touchdown.

Alabama had balance as well. Fracchia gained 44 yards rushing. Wilson had 42. Richardson had 37. Trammell completed 13 of 19 passes for 156 yards.

It was 20-3 at halftime.

The victory by Alabama over the Volunteers was a longlasting memory for Col. Tom Elam, longtime chairman of the Tennessee

Athletics Board. "I went down to the Alabama dressing room after the game, as I usually did after our games against them when they played under Bryant. I said, 'Bear, you really fixed our clock today.' He looked at me with those penetrating eyes, which were one of his trademarks, and said, 'You didn't like it a damn bit, Tom, and you know it.' Those were his words. He was right.

"That was the beginning, I thought, of the real Bryant dynasty down in Tuscaloosa."

Before his death in 1983, Bryant remembered that Alabama team that produced an 11-0 record, including a climactic 10-3 victory over Arkansas in the Sugar Bowl.

"I could name so many favorite players on that team," Bryant said. "Mike Fracchia, Billy Neighbors, Pat Trammell, Lee Roy Jordan, Jimmy Sharpe, Richard Williamson, Billy Richardson, Ray Abbruzzese, Bill Rice, Bill Battle, Charley Pell, Darwin Holt, Tommy Brooker, Cotton Clark—they played like it was a sin to give up a point.

"We had sixteen or seventeen players, the nut of the team, and all sixteen or seventeen were leaders. Trammell, the quarterback, was the bell cow of the whole outfit. He was my favorite person of my entire life. I never had another leader like him. The players rallied around him like puppies. He could make them jump out a window to win."

Trammell died in 1968 from cancer, but his teammates remember him.

"Pat was an outstanding person and a brilliant guy," said Richardson, now a successful businessman in Birmingham. "Coach Bryant thought so much of him that he had the authority actually to send people off the field during a game. He was rough. He like to scrap. He was some kind of leader.

"Coach Bryant and Trammell spent so much time together that their thoughts paralleled. Coach Bryant would be thinking of a play on the sideline, and Pat would be calling it in the huddle."

Neighbors said Trammell sometimes vetoed plays sent in from the bench. "Pat was the only guy I've ever seen who'd argue with the coaches, cuss at them, tell them they were wrong. He was the leader. He never took any bull off anybody, even Coach Bryant."

The coach-quarterback combination worked like a charm on October 21, 1961, with a national television audience watching. Alabama was impressive as it defeated the Volunteers.

"It was one of the hardest-hitting encounters I ever took part in," said Buddy Fisher, a Tennessee end in 1961. "Coach Paul 'Bear' Bryant is the all-time best. He always has been. Just about everybody in football loves to play a great team, which Alabama had back then, and we got ready for it because we wanted to beat the best."

The best team was too much for the Volunteers in 1961, as noticed by Tom Siler in the *Knoxville News-Sentinel.* He wrote:

"We want 40! We want 40!"

This point-thirsty goal was denied jubilant Alabama students on this cool and sunny afternoon at Legion Field.

But this was the only thing denied the partisans of Alabama on a day that will be long remembered. They got everything else: four touchdowns, four perfect conversions, two field goals, Tennessee fumbles and a tremendously satisfying triumph.

Coach Paul (Bear) Bryant laid to rest for all time the notion that he breaks out in a cold sweat at the mention of the Tennessee Volunteers. Never again can Tennesseans place any stock in the jinx, the hex, the psychological monkey on his back.

The "hex" ended before the opening kickoff, according to Howard Schnellenberger, who was an assistant coach at Alabama in 1961 and was head coach at Louisville during the summer of 1986. Bryant had put him in charge of the game plan for Tennessee.

"I think by the end of the week the players thought they could win over Tennessee," said Schnellenberger, who was credited by Bryant with coming up "with a masterful game plan."

Bill Battle, a junior end at Alabama in 1961, agreed. "The arrival of Howard Schnellenberger was important to Alabama in the series with Tennessee," Battle said. "That was apparent when Coach Bryant introduced him to the squad. He said this is the man who has been in charge of scouting Tennessee for Kentucky for several years. He said he would be responsible for scouting them for us.

"That was a confidence builder. It was amazing the air of confidence Howard Schnellenberger could exert, even then, as he does now as coach at Louisville. His arrival at Alabama pointed out again how important it was to Coach Bryant to beat the Big Orange."

One of the highlights of the game plan designed by Schnellenberger was the Utah pass. As former sportswriter Marvin West wrote in the *Knoxville News-Sentinel*, "Trammel! showed the outclassed Vols a soft, basketball-type pass play and made it perform like a brand-new invention." The pass is one of the shuttle variety made by a retreating quarterback to a halfback running toward center and guard. It is used by many teams today.

Trickery did not have as much to do with the resounding Alabama victory as did recruiting. When Bryant courted his first class of freshmen in 1957, he told them they would be national champions in 1961.

"We were in the basement of our athletic dorm," Neighbors said while remembering the first address Bryant gave his freshmen. "Coach Bryant told us we'd be national champions if we worked hard, dedicated ourselves, and paid the full price. None of us knew what he meant by paying the full price, but all of us bought what he said. We pointed toward the national championship from that night on."

Interestingly, Tennessee claimed a 3-0 lead over Alabama in 1961, before the Crimson Tide went to work. Sophomore George Shuford kicked a 53-yard field goal, the longest for a collegian in twenty years.

"That bothered us," Neighbors said, "because we were scared to death of Tennessee before that game."

The field goal must have delighted the television audience, which saw Tennessee lose for the fifth time in six video showings. Tennessee, beginning an ebb in its stature, posted a 6-4 record for the year.

"We never got anything done," said coach Bowden Wyatt, who lost to Alabama for the first time.

"It was our greatest game ever," said Bryant, who after the game turned down an invitation to play in the National Trophy Bowl in Washington, D.C., with hopes of winning the national championship elsewhere.

"When Coach Bryant came back to Alabama for spring practice in 1958, there were 126 people at practice the first day, only 46 people on the last day," said Fred Sington Jr., who was among them. "We lost 60 people the first five days. It was survival of the fittest, or either survival of those dumb enough to think we could make it, and we felt like an elite group.

"It had to be that way."

The plan included something seemingly devious.

"That's the year we started a new class on campus, Advanced Sports Techniques," Battle said with a chuckle. "It started in the winter, in January, and met three days a week. We had an hour in the classroom on both Monday and Wednesday. We had two hours in pads on Friday as a lab.

"I was an arts and sciences major. I had to audit the darn class, in pads, without getting credit for it.

"But there were a lot of football players in there. By the time we got to spring training, we all knew our offense. Heck, we'd been practicing two months. We were ready to get on with the scrimmaging as soon as we went onto the field in April."

Was that legal?

"I'm sure it was," Battle said. "But it was outlawed after the 1962 season.

"See, as all of us knew, you could always count on Coach Bryant being on the leading edge when it came to securing those kinds of advantages."

The Crimson Tide was starting a roll, which became more apparent on The Third Saturday in October the following year.

36

1962
Alabama 27, Tennessee 7

Paul "Bear" Bryant the football coach turned into Paul "Bear" Bryant the con man after a noteworthy victory on October 20, 1962.

"It's good to win anywhere," Bryant said after his University of Alabama team defeated Tennessee, 27-7, on Shields-Watkins Field in Knoxville in the dedication game for Neyland Stadium. "This isn't any more special to me than winning a game in Birmingham, Tuscaloosa, or anywhere else."

Nobody believed him. After all, Shields-Watkins Field had become a nightmarish scene of sorts for a coach who had not tasted victory there, not in four tries with Kentucky and two with the Crimson Tide.

"There's no doubt about that being a monumental victory for Coach Bryant," Jim Goostree said about the conquest in 1962. "He'd get uptight about games against Tennessee, sometimes too much so, so it's apparent he considered that one something extra."

Goostree confirmed Bryant once talked about getting so aroused before games against the Volunteers that he would pull off the side of the road en route to work and relieve an upset stomach.

So it stands to reason the Alabama coach was the man of the hour as his team dominated Tennessee for the second consecutive season.

Tom Siler thought so. Reporting for the *Knoxville News-Sentinel,* he wrote:

Neyland Stadium was dedicated yesterday afternoon before 44,698 spectators, and no one enjoyed it more than Paul (Bear) Bryant.

October 20 will be long remembered as the day thousands paid homage to General Robert R. Neyland and as the day Coach Bryant won his first game in Knoxville.

In words of one syllable, Alabama had a superb pass attack and Tennessee had almost none.

Or, if you prefer, Alabama's pass defense was like a radar net; Tennessee's was like a fish net.

This battle, first in the arena which shall forevermore honor the name of the late Gen. Neyland, was fought in the air.

It had to be. Tennessee's line was magnificent, by far the finest performance of the season. So was Alabama's. The Crimson Tide gave up 187 yards to Tennessee on the ground, a line that had yielded only 75 yards previously in four games. But it was obvious that the Vols were not going to whip Alabama on the ground.

So it was the air, or nothing.

Alabama was ready. Tennessee was not.

Alabama, which went on to post a 10-1 record, including a 17-0 victory over Oklahoma in the Orange Bowl, had soon-to-be-famous Joe Namath as its sophomore quarterback. Tennessee, which posted a 4-6 record, did not have anybody like him.

Namath completed 9 of 13 passes for 148 yards. One of them went for a touchdown to halfback Benny Nelson, who caught another touchdown pass from quarterback Jack Hurlbut.

Alabama got its offense on track after Tim Davis kicked field goals from 27 yards and 23 yards to give the Crimson Tide a 6-0 lead. Namath and Nelson teamed on their touchdown pass of 35 yards to make it 12-0 at halftime.

Tennessee, which had a 254-yard offensive day, scored its lone touchdown on a six-yard pass from Bobby Morton to Jerry Ensley. The extra point was kicked by George Shuford.

The Volunteers, down 12-7, dominated the third quarter. But the fourth quarter belonged to the Crimson Tide.

Cotton Clark ran three yards for a touchdown, with Davis kicking the extra point, to give Alabama a 19-7 lead. The icing on the cake for the Crimson Tide came when Nelson scored a touchdown on a 20-yard pass from Hurlbut, who ran for a two-point conversion.

The deed was done.

Alf Van Hoose, then a sportswriter with the *Birmingham News,* was impressed by the Alabama passing attack. He wrote:

Joe Namath and Jack Hurlbut pitched. Benny Nelson and Richard Williamson caught. Alabama shattered an old Tennessee jinx with a go-stop-go performance and triumph.

Loosey goosey Namath was as poised as Ralph Terry of the Yankees.

Said Goostree, "With Namath in the game, on the field anywhere, we came to expect happy afternoons like the one we had at Tennessee in 1962."

Dr. Gaylon McCollough was a sophomore center at Alabama in 1962. Obviously, he spent a lot of time with the star quarterback.

"Joe Namath was the best athlete I've ever seen," McCollough said at his office in Birmingham. "He was a leader who exuded confidence in an unusual way, not with cockiness but with force. And he was a super team player.

"I've wondered many times what he would've accomplished had he not suffered all those knee injuries. He had the first one when he was at Alabama.

"I'm amazed how he responded. I'm talking about a six-foot-one-inch guy who could dunk a basketball behind his head. What an athlete he was.

"Just imagine the car that won the Indy 500 trying to get around the track on three wheels. That's how it was with Joe. But he still won, became a star, one of the all-time greats.

"His ability is reflected by what Coach Bryant did when Joe arrived on campus at Alabama. He changed the offensive scheme to suit him, so Joe could sprint out and pass, jump and pass, and it worked wonders for us in games against Tennessee and everybody else."

Harold Harris was a sportswriter at the *Knoxville News-Sentinel* when Namath starred for Alabama. Now in his retirement, he remembers how the future "Broadway Joe" operated against Tennessee.

"I hated Namath, even after he turned pro, because of the way he played against Tennessee," Harris said. "All Tennessee people despised him.

"But that fellow could hum that tater. There wasn't a defense that could stop him. You knew he'd hit his target. You knew it was a matter of time until he would eat you up."

Maybe that is why Kirk McNair, publisher of *Bama Inside the Crimson Tide* magazine, recalled Namath this way:

"When those white shoes trotted out onto the field, it was like a bolt of lightning went through the stadium," McNair said at his house in Tuscaloosa. "Joe Namath had both talent and charisma."

The Alabama defense, which was gritty all afternoon against Tennessee in 1962, was led by linebacker Lee Roy Jordan. He went on to star at that position for the Dallas Cowboys of the National Football League.

"We never had an easy time with Tennessee," Jordan said. "We might have gotten them good on the scoreboard my junior and senior seasons, but that's not all of the story. The games were hard fought from start to finish.

"The one in 1962 was like all the others. But it was special in that Coach Bryant had never won in Knoxville. I remember feeling proud to have been a part of that victory."

Bill Battle was a senior end at Alabama in 1962. He was playing for the Crimson Tide the last time in a stadium in which he would coach Tennessee from 1970 through 1976. At his sports licensing office in Atlanta, he recalled the loud crowd that greeted the visitors.

"Tennessee crowds were always the same when we went there," Battle said, "vocal and one-sided. But they were never nasty. It's how you want your crowd to be when you're at home. It's not all that much fun, hostile more than anything, when you're playing the Big Orange in Knoxville.

"It's sort of interesting, I suppose, since I later learned to love the roar of the Tennessee crowd. But I hated those people in 1962. I knew Coach Bryant felt that way about them.

"Winning there is a happy memory for an Alabama player. It's more significant because Coach Bryant wanted to win there so much."

There was some gloom at Alabama that week. No sooner had the Crimson Tide defeated Tennessee, pushing its unbeaten streak to twenty-three games, than the *Saturday Evening Post* published a strong article criticizing Bryant's coaching tactics. It was titled "College Football Is Going Beserk." It was written by Furman Bisher, sports editor and columnist at the *Atlanta Journal*. It accused the mentor of teaching brutality to his players.

Through his lawyers, Bryant asked the magazine for a retraction after the article first appeared in an issue dated the day after the resounding victory over the Volunteers.

Bill Lumpkin, sports editor and columnist at the *Birmingham Post-Herald*, defended Bryant in print:

> It's getting to the point where a person can't pick up a national publication without reading how college football is deteriorating into a class of degenerates.
>
> Football's crime, it appears, is winning.
>
> How silly can one get?
>
> That's like criticizing the selling techniques of an insurance agent who has peddled millions of dollars worth of policies.
>
> This ridiculous approach is somewhat puzzling since unemployment is highest among losing coaches.
>
> Bryant's coaching tactics, the hell for leather teachings, have drawn the fire of literary pens.
>
> Someone said when Bryant came back into the conference, it resulted in other coaches shoving the volleyballs and dusting off the pads. The truth of the matter is Bryant's return startled a few people, in that they had to get off the seats of their trousers and begin earning their pay.
>
> Hard work is the Alabama coach's successful formula. He believes in winning, and he instills winning in his players.
>
> Tackling or pursuit football has been used as an example of his so-called modern trend of hard-nosed football. These are merely new words for old terms. The game always has been hard-nosed.
>
> That's the winning way.

That was the way it had always been on The Third Saturday in October. Tennessee had to swallow more of the same the following year.

37

1963
Alabama 35, Tennessee 0

WHAT DO YOU GET when you mix the passing of Joe Namath with six fumbles by a struggling Tennessee team?

You get a forgettable football game, such as the one played in Birmingham on October 19, 1963. The scoreboard said enough: Alabama 35, Tennessee 0. But nobody seems to remember much about the game.

"I'm sure a lot of good things happened to us that day," said Dr. Gaylon McCollough, who was a junior center for the Crimson Tide in 1963. "But it seems like a pretty uneventful game today.

"All I remember is we won with ease, which wasn't all that surprising. In those days, we didn't go into games wondering if we'd win, even battles with Tennessee. We wondered how we'd do it."

Interestingly, Alabama hosted Tennessee one week after experiencing a rare defeat, 10-6, to Florida, and the Crimson Tide appeared to be looking for somebody on which to dump its wrath.

The romp over the Vols was complete, as it was described by Tom Siler in the *Knoxville News-Sentinel:* "This was the agony of agonies and the Tennessee players seemed almost as shocked by the Alabama flood of points as were the disgruntled partisans in the stands."

Wrote sportswriter Marvin West in the *News-Sentinel:*

Almost-perfect Alabama stuffed Tennessee into the hamburger machine today at Legion Field. Coach Paul Bryant let Joe Namath turn the crank and ground out a 35-0 victory over the Vols.

The loss was the worst ever by a Tennessee team since the South-eastern Conference was formed in 1933. A capacity crowd of 54,000 saw the rout, boosted along by six Vol fumbles. Three Alabama touchdowns came as direct results of the bobbles.

Namath, as expected, was the worst troublemaker. He passed for 141 yards and three touchdowns and capped his performance by falling through guard for another six points.

Tennessee threatened seriously but once, getting the opportunity after an Alabama fumble. The Vols got as far as the nine-yard line, but four passes fell incomplete.

Alabama led 14-0 after the first quarter, 21-0 at halftime, and 35-0 after the third quarter. Winning coach Paul "Bear" Bryant instructed his team to quit passing at that point.

Alabama was methodical putting together its convincing victory over the beleaguered Volunteers. The Crimson Tide had 335 yards in offense. Tennessee had 148.

Benny Nelson ran 36 yards for the first touchdown, and Tim Davis kicked three extra points.

Namath's touchdown passes were for twenty-six yards to split end Jimmy Dill, three yards to end Charles Stephens, and five yards to halfback Hudson Harris. Namath passed to Nelson for a two-point conversion after running for the final touchdown from one yard out of the end zone.

"The Alabama coach called off the dogs, as the saying goes," said Siler, who got Bryant to admit as much.

It is safe to say that Bryant had more trouble with the *Saturday Evening Post* in 1963 than he had with Tennessee, which was playing its first and only season under Coach Jim McDonald. On March 16 the magazine, which a year earlier had accused the coach of teaching brutal football, struck again and harder with an article about something more scandalous. "The Story of a College Football Fix" shocked the nation.

The article detailed how Bryant and former Georgia coach Wally Butts supposedly had conspired by telephone to "fix" a game in 1962. It alleged that Butts gave Bryant information about the game plan Georgia was to use in that 35-0 victory by Alabama. Both men filed lawsuits. The FBI conducted a probe, and both coaches passed polygraph tests. Both men won huge monetary settlements.

Bryant was irked. He charged that the *Saturday Evening Post* "was renewing its effort to slander and to discredit southern football." He made a dramatic speech to the people of Alabama during a hastily arranged television appearance.

Benny Marshall, former sports editor and columnist for the *Birmingham News,* observed the denial address Bryant made to the public. Marshall wrote:

> At 4:15 the red light was on. The face of Paul Bryant faced the people of Alabama. "This is Paul Bryant of the University of Alabama," he said. And, then he hit. He hit again. Halfway through he came to the clinching argument, the new bombshell aimed at the rumors he had bet. The story was full of strangeness that branded him and Wallace Butts as fixers, riggers. The voice was angry, for Bryant was angry, and the eyes signaled a willingness to fight back in defense of honor and integrity in Alabama football.
>
> Defense? It was offense Sunday afternoon. The life and career of Paul "Bear" Bryant were face-to-face with the greatest crisis of Paul "Bear" Bryant's life.
>
> But Paul Bryant always was a big-game man. Sunday afternoon, he was winning again.

Almost seven months later to the day, Bryant and Alabama were winning again over a Tennessee team that posted a dismal 5-5 record. Siler described the scene, as well as the mood, in the *Knoxville News-Sentinel* the morning of the game:

> The air of tenseness and apprehension in this steel center cannot be traced this time to well-known strife between races. Alabama partisans, in the wake of a 10-6 loss to Florida, are wondering if the Crimson Tide is ebbing. Tennessee fans are wondering if in 1963 they must settle for supremacy over Tulane and Vanderbilt.
>
> This year, the chamber of commerce is trying to show visitors that blighted Birmingham is not a jungle town. On every downtown street corner a blue and white sign says, "Welcome, We're Glad To Have You In Birmingham." This sweet spirit of hospitality is not necessarily shared by the noted Alabamian by adoption, Paul "Bear" Bryant.
>
> By his standards, the spirit of hospitality was carried entirely too far last week when Florida won a game of pattycake from Alabama that had lost but once in the last 32 games.

"It was Alabama," said Bobby Gratz, a Tennessee guard in 1963, "and there was 'Bear' Bryant. We were trained to believe it was a bigger game because of those things. There was no love from the very start."

Tennessee end Buddy Fisher remembered Bryant as "all-time best coach. We loved to play against his team. Alabama was always great."

The Volunteers, meanwhile were floundering in 1963. Bowden Wyatt had retired as coach a year earlier, and Jim McDonald was the interim coach. Doug Dickey would become coach a year later.

McDonald lasted only one year as coach at Tennessee. The program was searching for a new leader as he worked.

"That's an interesting thing," said Col. Tom Elam. "I'd picked up the *Knoxville News-Sentinel* after a board meeting. The headline said, 'McDonald Is the New Volunteer Coach.' I wondered how that could be the case when no official action had been taken. It turned out that the team had taken a straw vote to usher him in as coach.

"It didn't work. There was some monkeyshine going on. The loss to Alabama down in Birmingham didn't get him. It was a culmination of a lot of things."

So The Third Saturday in October that season became a massacre of sorts staged amid a mess.

"I remember that game as a total disaster," said McDonald, who lives in Knoxville. "Everything went wrong for Tennessee that day. Alabama got the football five times within our 15-yard line after fumbles. It was ridiculous."

It was a sign of the times in Knoxville.

Wyatt had been forced to resign after he refused to abandon the single wing offense. The 4-6 record in 1962 was the decisive factor. McDonald had been elevated to interim coach. The former Ohio State star athlete inherited a program in disarray.

So Tennessee looked outside its immediate family for its next coach. Dickey became the first non-Tennessee figure since Bob Neyland to become the Volunteers' leader.

Dickey rolled up his sleeves and went to work. The fruits of the labor showed quickly.

38

1964
Alabama 19, Tennessee 8

THE THIRD SATURDAY IN October began yet another change in 1964.

Dr. Gaylon McCollough, a star on the Alabama team that year, remembers how the Tennessee football program sported a fresh look that season in a couple of ways. First, there was a new coach. Doug Dickey, a former Florida quarterback, who talked a lot about defense in an effort to add spark to a floundering program.

Second, while the middle guard, Steve DeLong, was the same person who had played for the Volunteers in previous years, McCollough recalls that he, too, seemed different.

McCollough, an Alabama center who labored against Tennessee and DeLong that October 17, said both the Tennessee program and the Vols' middle guard were vastly improved. Those changes produced a bittersweet afternoon for the Crimson Tide star.

"I've got memories of personal experiences from The Third Saturday in October that year," McCollough said at his office in Birmingham. "We won, which is good, because that's the object of the game. But it's the only time I remember being manhandled on the football field during my three years at Alabama."

The Crimson Tide won, 19-8, claiming its fourth consecutive victory over the Volunteers. And McCollough scored the only touchdown of his career.

"Wayne Cook blocked a punt and the ball bounced into my arms," McCollough said about the second Alabama scoring play in the game. "I lugged it 22 yards into the end zone. That was in the fourth quarter, as I remember, and it sort of iced the game for us."

That he mentioned ice is appropriate. Players treat bumps and bruises with the cold stuff. There were a lot of bruises in both dressing rooms after the game.

"I'd played against Steve DeLong the two previous years," McCollough said, "and I'd had a relatively easy time blocking him. I'd graded well in both games. When I saw he was going to be playing on me in 1964, I sort of relaxed, felt confident about going to Knoxville.

"Well, he'd changed a lot. He was into weights. He'd gotten larger and stronger. He'd changed his style, moving off the line of scrimmage about three yards, much like a linebacker, and he gave me fits.

"We ran 55 plays that day. Not once did I get a clean block on Steve DeLong. He ate me alive.

"At halftime, after it became apparent I couldn't handle my man, assistant coach Pat James came up with a plan to help. Tank Mitchell, a small guard, and I were going to switch back and forth on the middle guard, depending on the play. That didn't help.

"On the first play, Tank tried to block DeLong, who literally tossed him aside and made the tackle for a two-yard loss. In the huddle, Tank said, 'No more, Gaylon, that's your guy to block the rest of the game. I'm not tangling with him any more.'

"I tried the rest of the day, but I never did block him.

"I think that tells you something about the Alabama-Tennessee series, how the team that's on the bottom fights hard to improve enough to get back on top. It's always tough when the Crimson Tide and Volunteers play each other. Doug Dickey was getting the program back on solid footing in 1964. There's no doubt about that."

The arrival of Dickey as coach definitely helped the Tennessee cause. The rivalry was fading, with Alabama dominating the Vols under Coach Paul "Bear" Bryant, until Tennessee hired a man who would made the series competitive again.

"We went out there thinking we could whip them," said DeLong. "I still think we could have."

"I wish we had another chance," said Hal Wantland, a junior tailback from Tennessee.

Tennessee won the second half.

"It was 16-0 Alabama in the first half and 8-3 Tennessee in the second half," said Tom Siler. "It was two games for the price of one.

"There were enough mistakes for a season. Tennessee lost the football on fumbles three times, had two passes intercepted, and had two punts blocked. Alabama fumbled away the football twice, had three pass interceptions, and had a punt blocked. It was not a cleanly played game, to say the least."

Alabama got three points in the first quarter on a 31-yard field goal by David Ray. The Crimson Tide got 13 points in the second quarter, when Steve Sloan ran one yard for a touchdown, Ray kicked an extra point, and McCollough made his surprising run for a touchdown.

Tennessee cut the lead to 16-8 in the third quarter. Wantland ran seven yards for a touchdown, then for the two-point conversion. Ray fixed the final margin with a 23-yard field goal in the fourth quarter.

The Crimson Tide took an important step toward its second national championship under Bryant in 1964, posting a 10-1 record, with the lone blemish coming in a 21-17 loss to Texas in the Orange Bowl.

The loss in the Orange Bowl involved a controversial decision involving Namath. The Alabama quarterback claimed he scored on a sneak play in the fourth quarter at the Longhorns' goal line.

"I'll always know I got into the end zone to win that game for us," said Namath, who the next morning in Miami signed a New York Jets contract that made him the highest-priced rookie in pro football history.

Tennessee posted a 4-5-1 record in 1964, but the Volunteers showed spunk against the Crimson Tide.

"This was the kind of defeat that can do us a lot of good in the long run," Dickey said after his team forced Alabama to play its regulars the entire way for the first time since 1960. "We played hard."

Bryant, who was not one to frown on victories, no matter how sloppy the one over Tennessee was in 1964, had little to say after the game. He stayed in the dressing room a long time before greeting the news media.

"This was a big one for us," Bryant said. "We must have played hard, or else we wouldn't have won in Knoxville, and I'm proud of that. Tennessee showed its old toughness this afternoon."

Dickey noticed Bryant wearing the houndstooth hat.

"To me, the first thing getting into the series meant was playing against Bear Bryant," said Dickey, who was starting a six-year campaign in Knoxville that would culminate in two Southeastern Conference championships. "Not being from Tennessee—rather from Florida—the rivalry itself was not significant to me at the time. And, you must remember, I was a young coach who hadn't experienced the series.

"But going against Bear Bryant and the national champions from 1961 meant something to me. It was somewhat of a personal challenge to me to be coaching against Bear Bryant. I'd played against teams he coached as a collegian. It was obviously a big thing to me and a lot of other people.

"We didn't have that good a team. We had a good defense that'd fight. We had an offense that couldn't do anything at all.

"That reminds me of what Bear Bryant said to me that first day we competed as coaches. He said, 'Doug, I wish you all the bad luck in the world.' I thought, 'Well, that's a heckuva thing for a guy to say to me. But if that's the way he wants to play, okay, let's get on with it.' He had all the players, then wanted me to have all the bad luck, too. Geez.

"And I recall Ron Widby, a great punter who was leading the nation, shanked a kick early in the game. I said, 'My gosh, Bryant does have control of something out there.'

"But we were in the game in the fourth quarter. I was pleasantly surprised we played that well. It was an encouraging loss for Tennessee.

"To tell the truth, the intensity of the rivalry didn't set in with me during that first game. They were so good. We were so bad. But that changed the following year, when we went to Birmingham. I'd never been there. The first thing that struck me was, 'Hey, this isn't too bad a place to play.' We had our people there, about ten thousand of them, as always, and that made the atmosphere good.

"I realized the importance that year. I was very intense. I didn't sleep well. I was more uptight about it. I realized how much Alabama respects Tennessee. I learned that there's no such thing as up and down in the series, that both teams always come ready to play, highly motivated. There's never a flat moment when the Big Orange and Crimson Tide play. I developed an appreciation for that."

The Tennessee student body flashed appropriate signs during the Alabama victory in 1964. They said: "Damn the Tide!"

Tennessee fandom felt that way. The new Vols coach was figuring out a way to do that.

39

1965
Alabama 7, Tennessee 7

THE DRESSING ROOM DOOR at Legion Field was locked. So Paul "Bear" Bryant, who had just discovered something worse than kissing a sister can come from a tie, knocked it down.

A Birmingham Police Department officer heard the noise as the door fell to the concrete. He rushed inside the University of Alabama football dressing room. He was angry.

"Who knocked down that door?" the police officer said to Bryant.

"I did," Bryant said after yanking a cigarette from his mouth.

"Well, okay, Coach Bryant," the police officer said before hurrying toward the dressing room exit.

"Actually," said Jerry Duncan, a junior tackle at Alabama that season, "Coach Bryant knocked down the door, just took it off its hinges, after requesting that [Alabama state trooper] Capt. Joe Smelley shoot the lock off of it with his gun. He found the door locked, cussed a bit, and said, 'Joe, shoot the damn thing open.' Captain Smelley said, 'Coach, I might kill three or four people if I do that.' Then, to the surprise of everybody, Coach Bryant said, 'Well, get your fat fanny out of my way.' And then he just knocked the damn thing down. We walked over it going into the dressing room."

In the grandstands, thousands of fans were talking about the bizarre finish to the game they had witnessed, with Tennessee loyals laughing more than those who favored the Crimson Tide. The game produced one of the weirdest finishes in the storied history of The Third Saturday in October.

The overriding emotion? "It was clear," said Kirk McNair, the publisher of *Bama Inside the Crimson Tide* magazine, who in 1965 covered the game as a sportswriter for the *Maryville-Alcoa Times* in Tennessee. "It was as if Alabama had lost and Tennessee had won."

The reason is obvious.

Alabama muffed what appeared to be a cinch field goal opportunity that would have won the game.

The football was on the Tennessee 18-yard line with 34 seconds remaining. After taking possession at its 25-yard line, the Crimson Tide, behind the brilliant passing of quarterback Ken Stabler, moved it to a first down just inside the Tennessee 10-yard line. Fullback Steve Bowman gained 2 yards. On second down, an errant pitchout resulted in a 10-yard loss.

So on third down, with no way to make a first down, Stabler scrambled on a pass play and ran 14 yards to the four-yard line.

Then with the clock ticking and with Alabama place-kicker David Ray hurrying onto the field with his tee in his hand, Stabler lined up the offense, called 99 Quick as the play, took the snap from center, and threw the football out of bounds to stop the clock.

Stabler, known as "the Snake" by Alabama fans, had looked to the sideline while lying on the ground after being tackled. He had noticed that the yard-marker an official was holding was behind him. He mistook it for the first down marker, jumped to his feet, and hurried toward a rendezvous with embarrassment.

With Ray standing helplessly behind him, trying to stop the foolish play, Stabler threw the football safely out of the reach of everybody.

The clock stopped. Six seconds remained.

But Alabama had run out of downs, and Tennessee took over the ball.

"I've never had a worse feeling in football than that," Duncan said at his office in Birmingham. "We'd run up and down the field on Tennessee all afternoon, but we'd been unable to get the ball in the end zone more than once. In essence, we'd won the war but had tied the game.

"I could've killed Kenny Stabler that afternoon, but I understood how it happened like it did. He was only a sophomore. The crowd was going crazy. There was confusion on the bench. We were in a hurry. I didn't know it was fourth down, either, so I couldn't say a thing to the Snake.

"I can tell you tying that game was worse than getting beat. We'd been picked as the favorite for the national championship, which we later won, and we'd kicked Tennessee all over the place that day.

Ken Donahue was in the press box that afternoon. He was in his second season as an Alabama assistant coach, after playing for Tennessee in 1949 and 1950, and he was as shocked as anybody.

"To be honest with you," Donahue said during the summer of 1986, when he was defensive coordinator at Tennessee, "that play unfolded so quickly it was hard to understand what was going on. I remember thinking, 'My gosh, what is this?' I knew it was 99 Quick we were running. I just sat there as stunned as everybody else was.

"I agree with most Alabama folks. We gave that one away."

John Forney, who served as radio voice for the Crimson Tide from 1953 through 1982, remembers trying to keep Stabler from making one of the more memorable blunders from The Third Saturday in October.

"Stabler raised up to throw the pass out of bounds," Forney said during the fall of 1986, "I stood up in the press box and screamed into the microphone, 'Wait!' I knew what he was gonna do. There was no way to stop him.

"They had a '4' on the down marker. But the scoreboard said third down. I knew Stabler was confused.

"Stabler threw the pass. I screamed, 'It's too late!' I knew it was over."

So did a devoted Tennessee supporter seated in the stadium. "I couldn't believe what I saw," said Col. Tom Elam. "But what I remember is how I was madder than hell when Alabama scored its only touchdown that day. I thought the timekeepers were a little lax in the performance of their duties. I remember Alabama running two plays in what seemed like four seconds.

"It wasn't much of day for me. I'd just come out of the hospital after a kidney operation. Kathleen and I had to use three seats for two people because I had a cane and couldn't move around much. I didn't need anybody to poke me in the side.

"Some Alabama bird, one of their fans, kept hopping up and down in front of me. I couldn't see, couldn't keep up. Finally, I said,

DOUG DICKEY

His FACE WAS ALIVE with pleasant thoughts. Then it was laced with an almost sickening frown.

Doug Dickey was sitting in his office at Stokely Athletics Center in Knoxville and remembering the good and the bad from the 1965 University of Tennessee football season.

The euphoria came on a Saturday afternoon. The sadness came on a Monday morning. Those hours, which came less than two full days apart, were the making of Dickey as a great figure in the folklore of Big Orange football.

On The Third Saturday in October in 1965, at Legion Field in Birmingham, Tennessee tied Alabama, 7-7, in a strange game that signaled the end of Crimson Tide dominance in the series.

On the next Monday morning before dawn, three Tennessee assistant coaches were killed when their automobile was struck by a train at a crossing in Knoxville. They were Bill Majors, Bobby Jones, and Charlie Rash, who were on their way to work. All three left wives and young children.

Dickey, who a year earlier had become a head coach for the first time, was not experienced when it came to handling such a tragedy. But he managed to do that in 1965 in a manner that earned him almost instant respect.

One person who noticed that is Haywood Harris, who during the fall of 1986 was serving for the twenty-sixth season as Tennessee sports information director. "Coach Dickey was young," Harris said. "He was just starting his career with his first head coaching job.

"Even though he shared our helpless feeling, knowing nothing he could do could undo the tragedy, he spent the entire next week comforting members of the coaches' families in their darkest hours.

"I was impressed. So were a lot of other people.

"I am convinced the sharing of grief by all concerned brought together in a remarkable way our coaches and athletes, as well as the remainder of the university community. More than twenty years later, it saddens me greatly.

"In that regard, one of the more pleasant memories in the Tennessee-Alabama series was followed by one of the more tragic events I can remember.

"I can just imagine the buoyant conversation among those coaches as they traveled toward the office that fateful morning. The banter among great friends might have contributed to the accident at the railroad crossing. They had to be happy about the game the Volunteers had played two days earlier.

"All three were great young men and talented young coaches. I imagine all of them would have become head coaches. They worked hard. They had worked harder than usual in preparation for our game against Alabama.

"To me, the most significant thing that has happened in the series occurred in Birmingham in 1965, when we tied Alabama. Even if we had lost a close game, it would have been a landmark advance for our program. The tie was satisfying because of the dominance Alabama enjoyed in the series at that time."

Col. Tom Elam also recalled the manner in which Dickey handled the tragedy.

"He was marvelous," Elam said. "He didn't panic. He didn't moan or shout. He was a gentleman about it. He did what he could. He didn't let it tear up his football team. He talked a lot about the contributions those young men had made to the program. He talked about the impact they'd had.

"It was an emotional time at Tennessee. It had a unifying effect on the entire program, on all of us, as we grieved over the loss of three fine gentlemen. It was like war, like a bomb dropping. But nobody quit. Dickey produced a textbook display of how a

continued on next page

man should react to a terrible situation like that. The team carried right on after it happened."

The man leading the Volunteers back was Dickey, who in 1964 saw good things in his debut game against the Crimson Tide, a 19-8 Alabama victory. It took him until 1967 to end a six-year winless streak for the Volunteers against The Third Saturday in October rival, but he made it three wins in a row before he departed for Florida after the 1969 season.

Alabama coach Paul "Bear" Bryant had a 2-3-1 record against Dickey-coached Tennessee.

Enough said.

"In 1964, when Coach Dickey arrived, it was obvious he was an outstanding coach and Tennessee would regain the luster of its past," Harris said. "We had gone through six mediocre years. He showed everybody that brighter days were at hand for a proud program."

Dickey had a 46-15-4 record at Tennessee. The three wins over Alabama stand out in his memory.

"When I was at Tennessee as coach, the Tennessee-Alabama game again became the biggest of the year in this part of the nation," said Dickey, who in 1985 returned to Tennessee as athletic director. "When *Sports Illustrated* came in on Tuesday to cover a game to be played on Saturday, I knew we had something special working in the series.

"I can tell you it was great being a part of the competition that existed then and exists now between the two programs. To win made it memorable for a lifetime.

"Alabama normally brought out the best in us. Our players thought they would play at their best every time out. And, of course, there was no substitute for having Coach Bryant in a game."

Dickey, a former Florida quarterback, said he "acquired a great feel for the tradition at Tennessee. It was meaningful to me. It still is. I had not known it before becoming coach, but I saw it and I studied it.

"In those early years, that Tennessee tradition challenged me."

Dickey passed test after test.

A person who noticed is Marvin West, the former sportswriter and sports editor and columnist at the *Knoxville News-Sentinel*, now sports editor for Scripps Howard News Service in Washington, D.C.

"It was no accident that Doug Dickey won at Tennessee," West said. "He was a winner from the outset. He had intensity. He was brilliantly organized. He had some great players, too, and tradition to work with."

Dickey added to that tradition in commendable fashion. Tennessee fans remember that. So do Alabama fans.

'Brother, I'm just out of the hospital. I'm not in much shape to do anything about you jumping up and down and blocking my view. But this place is full of Tennessee people, so I imagine I could get enough of them to help me keep you in your seat.' He looked at that stick [the cane] and sat down.

"He was sort of down in another way when the game ended."

A visitor to both dressing rooms would have told the story. One was happy. The other was sad.

Jim Goostree was in the Alabama quarters. A Tennessee graduate, he was trainer for the Crimson Tide from 1957 through 1983. During the summer of 1986, he sat at Indian Hills Country Club and remembered a vow he made on a memorable Third Saturday in October in 1965.

"Our dressing room was a picture of confusion that afternoon," Goostree said, "as happened a lot in those days. I remember David Ray running onto the field to attempt the field goal. I remember how my heart sank when Kenny Stabler got under center to take the snap on fourth down.

"I declared that day that I would never let something like that happen again, that I would run out onto the field screaming and hollering if I had to, that I would do anything to make the officials stop a play like that before it got under way. I might have been able to save a victory had I done that in the Tennessee game that year.

"We were stunned. Tennessee was happy. I remember their players shaking hands with Kenny Stabler and thanking him.

"Alabama whipped Tennessee that day. But Alabama tied Tennessee."

The spoils went to the favorite, as wrote Tom Siler in the *Knoxville News-Sentinel:*

> Alabama sent a messenger to the Tennessee dressing room minutes after the fiery 7-7 tie.
>
> He wanted the game ball. Terry Bird, offensive tackle, had the ball.
>
> "Who gets the ball on a tie?" asked Coach Doug Dickey.
>
> He thought for a minute, obviously rankled at the Alabama request. Then, he said, "Vince [assistant coach Gibson], get the ball and give it to them. Yeah, give it to them."
>
> "Yeah, okay," said one of the Tennessee players. "Give them the ball. They won a moral victory."
>
> Paul Bryant once said that a tie was like kissing your sister. The only kissing going on was Orange and Red, leather against leather, heart against heart, gut against gut. And when it was over, Tennessee was the victor, Alabama the loser.
>
> This was the football battle Tennessee fans had been waiting for, and they had been waiting for eight years. This was the battle that turns the Tennessee-Alabama game from a one-sided thing into the vibrant, fiery, lively series of long ago.
>
> Tennessee turned the football corner on this tie.

Dickey was both pleased and thankful. "We were lucky to get the tie, just plain lucky," he said before going on to lead the Volunteers to an impressive 8-1-2 record and a berth in the Bluebonnet Bowl.

Bryant was apologetic. "You would have won without me," he said to his players who were waiting for a guard to unlock the dressing room door he knocked down. "I lost the game, pure and simple, because a coach is supposed to be more organized than I was today."

Then Bryant issued a warning, praising the long-time rival. "Tennessee is getting better," he said. "They are gonna be tough in the future."

As the coach talked, his players sat with their heads bowed in the dressing room, asking why for what seemed like a thousand times.

"Everybody was trying to determine what had happened," said Charley Thornton, who was serving as sports information director at Alabama. "It was like a tomb in there. Every person had defeat in his eyes."

Postgame comments reflected that in the form of slips of the tongue, one from Dickey and one from Bryant.

"Our punter had a lot to do with the win," said Dickey.

"I take responsibility for the loss," said Bryant.

During the summer of 1986, when he was serving as principal fundraiser for the Alabama Alumni Association, Thornton was asked if he remembered how Stabler reacted to his mistake that locked "the tie."

"Nothing much bothered Ken Stabler," Thornton said. "He was so poised. He had what it takes to be great. He was great, you will recall, as a pro quarterback. And you might remember, he bounced back strongly enough in 1965 to lead us to an Orange Bowl victory over Nebraska and a national championship that season. Then he became one of the finer quarterbacks in National Football League history while leading the Oakland Raiders to many championships.

"'The Snake' made a mistake. But he made up for it like a champion."

During the summer of 1986, Dickey said he is thankful for the goof that enabled his Volunteers to tie the Crimson Tide. "We were fortunate," he said. "It looked like we were gonna lose the game for sure.

"Our kids fought hard. They understood how crucial it was for a program that hadn't beaten Alabama since 1960. The press was starting to write about them dominating us. It was time for Tennessee to do better.

"When Stabler threw the ball out of bounds, I thought that was unbelievable. It was obvious they'd gotten confused.

"It certainly felt like we won. We thought we were going to lose. It was a much better feeling tying than losing to them again. We tied them, no question about that, and that meant we were playing nose-to-nose with a program that had won a national championship the year before and was still up there headed toward another one.

"It was a crucial game for Tennessee. We had a bunch of sophomores who got a lot of confidence out of that. It was a pivotal decision that helped us move on to better things. That laid the groundwork for our Southeastern Conference championship in 1967.

"Of course, we went from a high point of exhilaration associated with tying a national champion to a low point of sadness when, on the following Monday morning, we had three coaches killed in an automobile accident. It was a devastating thing. It wiped everybody out for a long time. There were three wives left without husbands and seven young boys left without fathers. It was a tragic thing.

"To me, that game will be remembered two ways, for its extreme happiness and for its utter sadness."

Does Dickey remember the argument over the game football?

"Yeah, I recall that," he said with a hearty laugh. "First, you've got to realize we didn't win. But to have '7-7 in 1965' written on it would've meant something to us. It didn't mean a thing to them, because it was a setback, as far as they were concerned, like a loss.

"To Tennessee, though, it was gain in our program at that time. People say ties aren't worth anything. That one was to us. From that point on, we knew we could play with them."

The closeness that prevailed on The Third Saturday in October the following year hammered home that point.

40

1966
Alabama 11, Tennessee 10

Two decades later he could laugh. But he had felt like both hiding and crying on an earlier rainy day.

Gary Wright was handling the memory like a man—with a chuckle—and he acted as if dubious fame is not so bad.

"Don't feel badly about asking me about it," he said. "I've heard about it every day since 1966."

The former University of Tennessee place-kicker, who became a pharmacist in Heflin, Alabama, chuckled again. "I've wondered several times if I'd be remembered so easily if I'd made that field goal."

On The Third Saturday in October in 1966, under a heavy sky that had produced rain most of the football game, Wright missed a 20-yard field goal that allowed Alabama to escape Neyland Stadium with a dramatic 11-10 victory over Tennessee.

Hundreds of stories were born that afternoon.

"I was standing in a chute in the south end zone waiting to go to our dressing room," said former Alabama trainer and Tennessee graduate Jim Goostree. "I thought no way Gary Wright was gonna miss that field goal. He was a great kicker. I thought the game was lost. Then, to my surprise, as well as to my joy, I watched the official call it no good.

"It was close, mere inches, and I recall the Tennessee fans reacting both ways. First, they cheered wildly. Then, they got quiet.

"I still have a picture of me in the dressing room after that game. I was dancing on an equipment trunk, a towel around my waist, doing my variation of 'The Tennessee Waltz.'"

There are a lot of Tennessee fans who thought Wright was successful on his field goal attempt. Among them is Col. Tom Elam. "I was in the press box," Elam said. "I saw it. I couldn't believe it. I would've sworn in court on the strength of salvation that the kick was good. I still say so. But I have to take into consideration the angle that exists between the press box and the goal post."

The frustration of Elam was similar to the fatigue of John Forney, who was handling play-by-play duties for the Alabama Radio Network. "That game took more out of me as a broadcaster than any I recall," Forney said. "I was shaking when it was over. I was wrung out. I was almost disoriented.

"We got the field goal to go ahead 11-10. Then Dewey Warren, who was as gutty a quarterback as I have seen, took Tennessee down the field for the field goal attempt by Gary Wright. It was back and forth through the fourth quarter.

"I remember seeing a Tennessee team manager standing behind the goal post in an orange rainsuit as Wright lined up for the kick. I kept my eyes on that guy. He sank to the ground and grabbed his head. Before the officials signaled the kick no good, I screamed, 'It's no good. It's no good.' The reaction of that team manager told me that.

"It was a fantastic ending for Alabama at the end of a rainy day. It started raining and never stopped. It was a miserable mess.

"That reminds me how surprised I was when we won the coin toss and chose to receive the opening kickoff. And, of course, we fumbled to help them to a quick touchdown. Once they got that 10-0 lead in that quagmire, I never thought we had a chance to win.

"From that point on, it was emotional give-and-take. We got the lead. It was total relief with a minute to go. Bam! They came back. It was truly one of the greatest games I can recall. The drama of it all really took a toll on me."

Wright was forced into the situation after Alabama rallied from a 10-0 deficit behind quarterback Ken Stabler.

End Austin Denney had caught a four-yard touchdown pass from quarterback Dewey Warren, with Wright adding the extra point kick,

to give Tennessee a 7-0 lead. Wright had kicked a 40-yard field goal
to make it 10-0.

Stabler had run one yard for an Alabama touchdown in the fourth
quarter. The quarterback had passed to end Wayne Cook for the two-
point conversion to cut the Volunteers' advantage to 10-8.

It was time for theatrics. Alabama made a surge to a 17-yard field
goal by Steve Davis that gave the Crimson Tide what appeared to be
an insurmountable lead.

But Tennessee fought back. The Vols drove up the field in a flash.
With another down at its disposal, with Bob Mauriello ready to run
into the end zone, the Volunteers called their final time-out to set up
the field goal attempt.

"I don't know who called time-out," Warren said. "I didn't."

Nobody ever admitted doing so.

A nickname was coined after the loss.

"One of the managers at Tennessee noticed that W is my middle
initial," Wright said. "After that kick, he said, 'Hey, Gary, does that
stand for wide?' From that day forward I was called Wide Wright.

"It's an appropriate nickname. I missed three field goals kicking
for Tennessee. They were all about the same, short and with a tough
angle, all easy enough to make.

"The one against Alabama was the toughest, by far, because the
game was so important to me. I'm from Alabama. I'd chosen to go to
Tennessee as a walk-on. Alabama had sent me a letter while I was in
high school, asking if I'd be interested in joining that program if
recruited, and I'd written 'No' on it and sent it back."

So devoted to Tennessee is Wright, he has refused to attend Alabama games played at Legion Field—not far from his home—and he
attends almost every Big Orange home game in Knoxville.

"That's one thing that makes living with the miss easier to handle,"
Wright said. "I played at Tennessee. Not many people had an opportunity to be where I was in 1966."

That was small consolation, however, at the time.

"When I looked up from the kicking tee, the football was soaring
over an upright, drifting badly to the right," Wright said. "I looked at
the official. When he called it no good, I wanted to hide. My heart
sank. I wanted to crawl under a tarp on the side of the playing field.

"I'd kicked all my life. I'd made a kick like that in my mind a million times. That one, I missed, no matter what a lot of people still think. I always thought all you had to do to make a kick in Neyland Stadium while playing for the Big Orange was land the football in the stands.

"I was crushed.

"That night I went to a concert in Knoxville. I was so heartbroken I didn't remember a song the group played. But I do remember that somebody from Tennessee went looking for me. They thought I was off somewhere attempting suicide. I was just trying to forget."

The missed field goal allowed Alabama to complete an 11-0 season, which included a resounding victory over Nebraska in the Orange Bowl.

Was it good fortune? That depends on who you want to believe.

"I didn't think Gary Wright had a prayer of making that field goal," said Kirk McNair, who was covering the game as a sportswriter for the *Maryville-Alcoa Times* in Tennessee. "The weather conditions were terrible. So was the angle."

Ken Donahue recalled the drama. "It was a hurry-up type field goal attempt," he said, "and the angle wasn't good. It wasn't ideal, not with the weather like it was, but I felt lucky when he missed it. You're bound to feel fortunate in a situation like that."

Alabama Coach Paul "Bear" Bryant was relieved, obviously, but he offered another reason why people should not have gotten so upset about the miss. "If I were on Tennessee's side, I'd say Alabama was lucky. Call it fate, good fortune, or just plain luck, we're grateful for the win. But I don't think their kicker should feel so bad. We would've blocked it if he'd kicked it straight."

"That's not true," Wright said. "That might've been better for me, because I could've blamed it on somebody else, but that's just not true. It's mine to live with. A miss is a miss, even against Alabama, which makes it more of a miss."

Tennessee, which posted an 8-3 record that season, with the losses coming by seven points and *the* point, went on to defeat Syracuse in the Gator Bowl. The Volunteers had not defeated Alabama since 1960.

In the *Knoxville News-Sentinel,* Tom Siler described the bad fate that befell Tennessee. He wrote:

The clock showed 16 seconds to go in a dying football game, one of the great rain-soaked battles of Shields-Watkins history.

All that had gone before was as nothing as 56,368 spectators sat in horrible fascination as if transfixed by a rattlesnake about to strike.

Bob Johnson made a fine snap to Dewey Warren. Dewey set the ball down just so. Gary Wright, head down, swung the leg through, and off sailed the ball.

That awful sound, the agonizing hush, and then referee Charles W. Brown signaled no good, off to the right.

Alabama's mighty roar was all but drowned by the groans from Tennessee partisans. Alabama players frolicked on the sidelines. One Tennessee coach tossed his jacket in the air, another fell prostrate on the ground, and it slowly sank in that a mighty cause was lost.

Was the field goal really good? Quarterback Warren said it went through the uprights and then curled right. Wright, cleaning off a tear-stained face, said, "It was curling off badly by the time I looked up."

Pictures taken of end zone faces were revealing. Faces looking directly at those uprights were caught in wonderment, puzzlement. This would indicate that the kick was awfully close, good or bad, but hairline.

So be it, and leave the alibis to others. The score was 11-10, movies are no help at all in judging the validity of field goals, and even in the heartbreak of the dressing room the Tennessee boys, twice defeated by a total of four points, proved themselves as one of the top teams in the nation.

Later, Bryant would term that Alabama team, which rebounded from a 10-0 deficit to win over Tennessee, with quarterback Ken Stabler leading the rally, "The most productive we've had in my years coaching in the program."

Twenty years later, Wright made an interesting counterproposal, by saying, "We had the best 8-3 team in the nation."

The reflections are numerous.

Jerry Duncan, a senior tackle on that Alabama team, recalled that the Crimson Tide had arrived in Knoxville on a mission. Bryant had on his game face after the tie in 1965.

"When we arrived at the Knoxville airport, the chamber of commerce had representatives there to greet us, including the president," Duncan said. "They gave us all big envelopes with little items in them, such as a map of Knoxville, a key chain with Neyland Stadium on it, and coupons for free sandwiches. The president tried to hand one to Coach Bryant, who grabbed it from him, tore it open, saw the map, and said, 'Hell, we didn't come up to go on some damn tour.'

"Then, to our amazement, Coach Bryant wadded up the map and threw down the envelope. He wasn't impressed, to say the least, and we couldn't believe how rudely he acted. But that sure did get us ready to play.

"The game was a typical Alabama-Tennessee game. We all put it on the line, swapped our licks, and went home. That's how it was. I always got hit harder against Tennessee than anybody else we played. Why, playing Auburn back then was just a piece of cake, compared to playing the Big Orange.

"Actually, I never considered us losing to Tennessee in that game, not even when Gary Wright lined up to attempt that field goal. We didn't think we'd lose to anybody. I do remember, however, being stunned when they rolled down the field to set up the field goal after we'd taken the lead for the first time. But, as for the kick, the conditions were bad and the angle wasn't the best in the world. I sort of thought we'd block it.

"It was a helluva deal, without question."

Austin Denney, a Tennessee end in 1966, almost got away for a touchdown on a pass play that set up the missed field goal. "I wish I'd taken it on in," he said. "It would've saved Gary Wright a lot of heartbreak."

Coach Doug Dickey was left to soothe Wright's disappointment.

"On either Sunday afternoon or Monday afternoon, Coach Dickey took me aside for a talk," Wright said. "He told me I'd get the chance to kick another field goal like that, that I needed to put that one behind me, or else run the risk of not making the next one. That helped my feelings a whole lot."

Dickey remembered attempting to do that and talked about the roller-coaster ride a college football player must make.

"I'm sure I visited with Gary at some point after the game," Dickey said. "That's only natural. It wasn't the end of the world. He needed to know that. It can get pretty emotional for young men in a colorful series like that one. You've always got those type situations to deal with. After all, they're only kids, eighteen or nineteen years old, with emotional reactions."

It was not totally unemotional for the losing coach. "We had it won," Dickey said. "Then we didn't win.

"The thing that hurts the most, after all these years, is remembering how we came back on them to put ourselves in a position to win. Maybe it'd been better if we'd just fumbled away the game on our drive toward the field goal attempt that failed."

Maybe Alf Van Hoose, sports editor and columnist at the *Birmingham News*, said it best:

> You gotta have heart.
> Alabama had it.
> You gotta have luck.
> Alabama had it.

So on that cloudy and damp October 15, 1966, Dickey walked to Bryant at midfield, shook his hand, and said, "I know exactly how you felt last year."

41

1967
Tennessee 24–Alabama 13

IT WAS SUITABLE FOR framing.

So a lot of University of Tennessee football fans still have copies of the cover of *Sports Illustrated* the week after The Third Saturday in October in 1967, when the Volunteers showed they had grown weary of losing to rival Alabama. The cover shows a Tennessee defensive back, Mike Jones, plowing into an Alabama pass receiver, Dennis Homan, to break up a pass. Accompanying it were the words *Tennessee Overwhelms Alabama*. They might not have been strong enough.

The score was 24-13 at Legion Field in Birmingham, in what can be remembered as the game marking a resurgence in *the* series.

Wrote John Underwood in *Sports Illustrated*:

All right, you long-sufferers. You have been looking for the way to beat Alabama. Here's how you do it. Very simple.

First hand, you get two top quarterbacks, one who passes like a professional and runs like he would rather not. Call him "Swamp Rat" Warren, just for fun. And, one who is a terrific natural athlete. Call him Charlie Fulton, who also doubles as a tailback and frightens people no matter what he chooses to play.

Are you getting this down?

Then, you make a raid into Alabama and grab a prospect from under the nose of "Bear" Bryant. That's the hard part. Better do that at night. Call this prospect Richmond Flowers Jr., of the Montgomery Flowers. Flowers can catch and he can run with what he has caught.

Then, you go down to Tampa, Florida, and get a couple more quarterbacks and shove them onto the defensive team. They will love it.

Now, pay attention. This is where it gets tricky. You allow both Warren and Fulton to get hurt before the game. Knock them right out of action, see, and you bring up a quarterback with a name nobody can pronounce, Bubba Wyche.

Does it rhyme with tyke, rich, psyche, rice or swish? His father says with "ich." Bubba is a fellow who has been hanging around for four years, serving time on a meatball squad and aching to get his chance to earn his laundry money.

So, on this lovely, clear day in late October, you put the baby-faced, blue-eyed, turned-up-nose and nice-as-you-can-be Bubba Wyche on the painted turf of Legion Field in Birmingham before the largest crowd, 72,000, to ever see an Alabama-Tennessee football game. Then, you add expatriate Flowers, who once got a wire from Alabama that said, "The Bear will make you regret your unfortunate decision," and those two former quarterbacks from Tampa, defensive halfback Albert Dorsey and linebacker Steve Kiner.

You tell Wyche to throw passes, Flowers to catch them, Dorsey to intercept when [quarterback] Ken "The Snake" Stabler throws and Kiner to intercept Alabama's runners.

And, there you have in capsule how Tennessee beat Alabama last weekend by a score of 24-13.

With this victory, up went Tennessee to the top of the Southeastern Conference, which is called the real Big Ten with justification. Down went Alabama's 25-game unbeaten streak. Up went Coach Douglas Adair Dickey's first victory over Paul "Bear" Bryant.

This story will serve to explain how an inspiring young coach just four years into the race and with a name like Douglas Adair can beat a famous older coach named Bear.

Incredibly, that article captured just part of the emotion.

"This is the greatest victory of my life, for certain, defeating Alabama in Birmingham," said Dickey.

"We've waited a long time for this one," said Bob Johnson, a Tennessee center and team captain in 1967. "But I can already tell it was well worth the waiting."

"Now I can go back home, to Montgomery, and go to parties again,' said Flowers.

But they were upstaged.

"It's my birthday! It's my birthday! Boy, what a birthday present. We beat Alabama, and I scored my first touchdown. Boy, what a birthday!" The young man talking was twenty-two-year-old Albert Dorsey, who intercepted three passes and ran into the end zone with one of them.

Tennessee intercepted five passes.

"It's the most exciting thing that happened to me as a player," Dorsey said during the summer of 1986 at his house near Nashville. "And it's memorable in a different way now than it was then.

"I made All-American that season. I'm a one-game All-American. If I hadn't done that against Alabama, I would've never gotten such an honor. That's how it was playing against them, important every time, and that's why intercepting three passes against them changed my life.

"Other than that, the main thing I recall about winning over Alabama in 1967 is how bad I felt. I had the flu. I had a fever of 102 degrees. I was miserable because it was so hot on the field."

Tennessee broke open the struggle with 10 points in the third quarter to take a 17-7 lead. The outburst came after Walter Chadwick had run one yard for a Big Orange touchdown, with Karl Kremser kicking the extra point, and Ken Stabler had run eight yards for a Crimson Tide touchdown, with Steve Davis kicking the extra point.

Chadwick passed 11 yards to Ken DeLong for the second Tennessee touchdown, covering 11 yards, with Kremser kicking the extra point. Kremser gave the Big Orange a 10-point lead after three quarters with a 47-yard field goal.

Alabama fought back into contention with Ed Morgan running one yard for a touchdown early in the fourth quarter. Then it was time for Tennessee to hang on for dear life, with Dorsey starring, as the Big Orange labored for a victory that turned the tables in the rivalry.

Suddenly the Volunteers and the Crimson Tide seemed as even as the final statistics in 1967 indicated. Tennessee gained 234 yards; Alabama gained 242 yards.

Dorsey was the man who nailed down the victory for Tennessee with heroics on three consecutive series in the fourth quarter, with the Volunteers leading, 17-13, and Alabama trying to rally for a victory.

"And," Dorsey said, "it should be pointed out that I'd played a lousy game up until that point. It was as if I wasn't even out there."

Interception one: "Alabama was a two-man team, basically, with quarterback Ken Stabler throwing to flanker Dennis Homan," Dorsey said. "They'd been trying to pass on [Tennessee defensive halfback] Jimmy Weatherford all of the game, with no success, so they started throwing the football to my side of the field. I was playing a zone defense, lying back and waiting for the football, and it started coming. The first one was tipped. I got it breaking on the ball, after thinking, 'Oh, no, it's the fourth quarter and here comes Alabama to beat us again.'"

Interception two: "It was another tipped ball, by Jimmy Glover, I think, and I caught it standing behind him," Dorsey said.

Interception three—and glory: "It was a simple down-and-out pass route," Dorsey said. "I cut in front of the receiver, picked the football out of the air and ran into the end zone for the touchdown. To me, that was the ultimate, scoring the knockout against Alabama.

"See, that's a great series, Alabama and Tennessee, and the games are always good, hard-fought, and clean. Of all of our opponents, that's the one we wanted to beat the most.

"I'll never forget what happened the week after the game. The Tennessee fans were great, of course, but I received more letters from Alabama fans, who wanted to congratulate me. I'll never forget that mail as long as I live. It was like, 'Okay, you beat us, so enjoy it.' That's why Tennessee players love to go to Birmingham for games. Those are real football fans down that way."

Dickey remembers that the Volunteers went to Legion Field to work.

"We had a job to do," he said, "and we got it done in nice fashion. I thought an important factor in that game, other than us being better than they were, was our new pass defense. We had a man covering Alabama pass receivers short and a man covering Alabama pass receivers deep. It was a combination man-to-man defense and zone defense. It was something new on the scene. We were experimenting with it.

"Weatherford was brilliant playing man-to-man pass defense.

"Dorsey was great playing zone pass defense. Stabler threw three passes that hit him in the head in the fourth quarter. All he was doing was backing up and playing like a center fielder in baseball. The ball came right to him. Finally, on the last one, he caught the ball and ran into the end zone for a touchdown that iced the game.

"It was another typical Tennessee-Alabama thing. There was the tie in 1965. There was their one-point win in 1966. Then, there we were in 1967, with them trying to rally for a winning touchdown, down 17-13, until Dorsey intercepted that last pass and turned it into a score for us."

While writing a column in the *Knoxville News-Sentinel* the morning after the game, Tom Siler captured the essence of the moment, then errored when predicting the future for the Alabama coach. He wrote:

Paul (Bear) Bryant lost more than a football game Saturday afternoon on Legion Field. No more is he the Big Daddy of Dixie football.

Throw away the jokes about walking on water. Sweep out the good-luck charms. Junk that old blue sweater which he always said brings good fortune. That's all passé, cleaned out, and no more.

Some will say it was only a football game—this 24-13 smasher Tennessee scored on Alabama before 71,849 cash customers.

But it may have been a lot more than that. Bryant and Alabama are stripped of the cloak of invincibility. The myth grew a year ago when Tennessee, the superior team on that October day in Knoxville, blew a field goal from the Tide 3. At that time, Bryant himself said, "If the kick had been true, we would have blocked it."

Now, Bryant faces the sunset of a great and brilliant career in the field of coaching, having won championships at Kentucky, Texas A&M and Alabama. And he isn't likely to get another streak going, not at his age.

History tells us those days were just on hold, that Bryant was not finished. But as a sign of the times, a telephoner asked an interesting question of the *Knoxville News-Sentinel* Sports Department the night after the thrilling Tennessee victory over Alabama in 1967.

He said, "A bunch of us fellows were wondering about Coach Dickey's return from Birmingham. Does he intend to come up on the plane with the team, or will he just walk up the river?"

The Volunteers flew home, and Tennessee fans were waiting when they returned to Knoxville. John Ward recalled the celebration at the airport. "I was doing the Doug Dickey television show at that time," Ward said. "We did it the night after we returned from road games, and I was in a hurry to get the film processed when we returned to Knoxville.

"We landed at the old terminal on a chartered plane. There was no security whatsoever. There was no need in those days.

"I was always the first man off the plane because I was always nervous about getting the film processed. They opened the door and I saw fans right up against the plane. It was a throng. They had come through the fence. It was a mass, several thousand, people as far as you could see.

"Then it dawned on me: 'What am I doing getting off the plane first.' I told Coach Dickey to go on down first. He told me to come with him.

"The thing I remember most was the first person we saw standing beside the plane. It was Dr. Andy Holt, the school president, who was three years from retiring. He was not in great health. He was jammed in there. It was a moving time, seeing him there, seeing the fans there.

"Nobody got hurt, but a mass of people were there, an excited crowd. It showed how the hunger and the excitement are always there for the Tennessee-Alabama game. It always will be."

42

1968
Tennessee 10, Alabama 9

Jimmy Weatherford was "the man of the [vicious and dramatic] hour" when the University of Tennessee and Alabama stole the hearts of the nation on The Third Saturday in October in 1968.

He put himself in that glorious position by thinking about "the dreadful hour" the Big Orange suffered through in 1966.

"I kept thinking about that 11-10 thing," Weatherford said while reflecting on his heroics in the final seconds of a 10-9 victory over the Crimson Tide at Neyland Stadium on October 19. "I could see it happening, a field goal winning the game for them, after we had failed."

In 1966 Gary Wright of Tennessee missed a field goal attempt at the end of the game that allowed Alabama to win. In 1968 Weatherford, a physically unimpressive defensive halfback who played better than he looked, blocked an Alabama field goal attempt with five seconds remaining to preserve a Tennessee victory.

He used his brain as much as he used his hands.

As Tom Siler of the *Knoxville News-Sentinel*, wrote after the game:

Just make it Coach Weatherford, if you please.
   The Neyland Stadium clock read "00.05." Alabama had the ball on Tennessee's 19.
   A crowd of 63,392 was in an uproar, some shouting orange-flavored encouragement, others screaming of a reddish hue.

Mike Dean of Alabama was standing at the 26, a mere mortal cast in a hero's role, a moment he would remember the rest of his life, field goal or no field goal. Oh, yes, the score was Tennessee 10, Alabama 9.

Jimmy Weatherford spoke to [rover back] Nick Showalter. "You take my place and let me play up here."

Showalter trotted back to sideback. Weatherford lined up, as he put it, "just a little too wide for the end man on the line to touch me." At the snap, Jimmy darted across the line, untouched by a foreign hand, and raced to that imaginary line where he thought the ball would have to travel.

He leaped. A hand struck the ball. It popped up in the air 15 feet or so, settled down into the arms of Mike Jones, who picked up two blockers and ran it 35 yards or so after the time had run out.

"No, nobody told me to change places with Nick," said Jimmy. "We just did it. I thought it was a good idea."

The entire Tennessee team was sharp. The Big Orange posted a 9-2 record, which included an SEC championship and a dramatic loss to Oklahoma (on a missed field goal) in the Orange Bowl.

Alabama was gutsy. The Crimson Tide tried to rally, only to lose because of Weatherford. The record that season was 8-3, including a resounding loss to Missouri in the Gator Bowl.

In the first quarter the Volunteers got a 7-3 lead when Richmond Flowers ran one yard for a touchdown and Karl Kremser kicked the extra point. The touchdown drive covered 63 yards. That was followed by a 28-yard field goal by Mike Dean of Alabama.

Kremser kicked the lead to 10-3 with a 54-yard field goal with a shade less than eight minutes remaining in the game.

Undaunted, Alabama drove 80 yards for a touchdown with 1:12 remaining. Donnie Sutton caught a four-yard pass from Scott Hunter in the end zone. Then trying to win the game in the final two minutes, Hunter passed incomplete on a two-point conversion attempt that Crimson Tide coach Paul "Bear" Bryant deemed "a stupid idea."

That left the Crimson Tide with one option.

Alabama got the onside kickoff it needed. But Dorsey saved the game for Tennessee by blocking Dean's field goal attempt.

"I was stupid, percentage-wise, for asking my players to go for two points after our touchdown," said Bryant. "We could have just as easily gotten the onside kick after tying the game."

Perhaps. . . . But nothing came cheaply in that game, as is usually the case when the bitter rivals clash. And *if* is a huge word in football.

"Both teams just knocked the stew out of each other," said LSU assistant coach David McCarty, who attended the game as a scout. "What licks they passed!"

A Tennessee linebacker from that season agrees. Jack "Hacksaw" Reynolds was a junior. Later he became a Super Bowl champion with the San Francisco 49ers in the National Football League.

"Alabama played good, tough, hard-nosed football all the time," Reynolds said during the summer of 1986. "I liked their style because that's exactly the way we played it back then at Tennessee."

Alf Van Hoose noticed the same thing. He wrote about the game for the *Birmingham News:*

> The stage was all set to make it one of football's all-time classics. The scene was fitting. Perfect. Storied old Neyland Stadium on a golden October Saturday. All it took was a 36-yard field goal by little Mike Dean.
>
> But in these cruel times, there sometimes is a jagged ending.
>
> Old prince and pauper tales may have been replaced. Life is harsh.

The fright lingered for the star, who during the summer of 1986 at his house in Macon, Georgia, recalled the drama.

"I felt like I could block a lot of field goals, all of them, not just that one," Weatherford said. "So I suggested to Showalter that we try something different. It was just a chance, one of those oddities that worked, like throwing the dice and winning.

"What did we have to lose? They were gonna win if we didn't block the field goal. It was that simple. So I went after it. They took the bait, gave me just enough of an opening to get to the ball quickly, and I got my hand on it.

"Then I laid on the ground and worried. I was afraid to look up. I didn't know if I'd gotten enough of it. I knew a lot of footballs had wobbled through the uprights. I can't tell you how happy I was when I turned around and realized we'd won the game."

Almost twenty years later, while working as a candy salesman, Weatherford recalls with more pride "a supreme compliment" he received at the end of the 1968 season.

"I was playing in the All-American Bowl in Tampa, Florida," he said. "Coach Bryant was coach of our team. When I arrived at the hotel at the start of that week, he was the second or third person to greet me. He said, 'Son, I'm glad you're playing for me this week. I've gotten sick of seeing you on the other side of the field.'

"That's a wonderful compliment for anybody. It also tells you something about the way the Tennessee-Alabama series is conducted. Alabama has always had a reputation for being at the top of the heap, hard-nosed and tough. Tennessee has always had the same reputation. That's why the series is so great. That's the spark of it."

Tennessee made it come alive again with a victory in 1967, a blocked field goal in 1968, and a romp in 1969.

"But," said Weatherford, "I think the 11-10 loss in 1966 set the stage for us. We knew Alabama would be challenging us at all times, as always, even though we were the better team.

"You have to understand, people like Steve Kiner and Jack Reynolds, plus a lot of other guys, weren't all that impressed with what Alabama had done. Most of us were more interested in what Tennessee would do. And, of course, Tennessee always gave Alabama its best shot."

According to Tim Priest, a Tennessee sophomore defensive halfback in 1970, Weatherford was tougher than he looked. "Jimmy was my roommate in 1968, and I was so scared of him that I didn't say a word to him until halfway through the season. I did congratulate him after the win over Alabama, however, because it's clear he saved our butts that afternoon."

Dickey thinks the 1968 game "epitomizes the series in a lot of ways, good defense, good effort, and important kicking." He made that observation during the summer of 1986 at his office in Stokely Athletics Center in Knoxville. "Goodness, it's almost always nip-and-tuck in those games! That was the fourth in a row like that.

"And the Weatherford swap with Showalter, which led to us blocking that last field goal attempt, tells you something else about the Tennessee-Alabama series. The players come to get after it. It's important to them. They're ready every time out. Coaches get plans organized. Players win the games."

Col. Tom Elam, the longtime chairman of the Tennessee Athletics Board, recalls a meeting with Bryant after the Volunteers' victory in

1968. "Bryant told me after that game, 'had you rascals beat. Then I screwed it up.'"

But it was Hunter who learned the most valuable lesson on The Third Saturday in October in 1968.

"We were warming up before the game and one of their cheerleaders kept letting Smokey, their mascot, come over close to us and bark," Hunter said. "I got tired of it and took a kick at that old hound. When we were walking to the dressing room, Coach Bryant walked up beside me and said, 'Scott, we've got enough trouble up here without you trying to kick their dog.'"

Weatherford must have seen it.

43

1969
Tennessee 41, Alabama 14

Pᴀᴜʟ "Bᴇᴀʀ" Bʀʏᴀɴᴛ ᴅɪᴅ not sound like a coach who forty-eight hours earlier had watched one of the University of Alabama football teams wrap up a national championship in the Sugar Bowl.

A mark of greatness, it is said, is remembering more humble times. So on this morning not long after the 1980 Sugar Bowl, in which the Crimson Tide capped an unbeaten season with a victory over Arkansas, Bryant was talking about more painful encounters.

"There's no place for contentment in this business," Bryant said. "I'm not talking about learning that now. I'm talking about how I learned it long ago, in the late 1960s, the hard way.

"We'd had a lot of success, national championships in 1964 and 1965, a more deserving unbeaten team in 1966, and I was fatheaded. I'd come to expect us winning, all the time.

"But that changed in 1968 and 1969, when everybody was shooting at us and hitting the target.

"For instance, I'll never forget as long as I live how Tennessee humiliated us in Birmingham in 1969. They beat us 41-to-something, could have been nothing, had us down 34-zip, crushed us, embarrassed us, dog-whipped us—you name it.

"That one got me to thinking I'd lost my touch, that it was time to move over, give somebody else a chance.

"We were outclassed so badly I didn't want to show my face. I remember how miserable I was doing my TV show the next day.

"It was all orange. It was sickening. I wanted to puke."

On that television show, which was carried throughout the state of Alabama, Bryant indicated he was not about to throw in the towel. He said, "I guess we'll lose the faint-hearted now. Well, we can do without you. All of you letter-writers, to hell with you. I don't even have time to sort through them, much less read them. I know I'm old and fat, but I'm not ready to give up. I hope our players aren't."

It looked bad for Alabama that October 18 in 1969.

At least Doug Dickey thought so. He was in his final season as Tennessee coach, putting the touches on a second straight Southeastern Conference championship, plus his fourth consecutive win over Alabama.

"That's the only time I ever thought we physically dominated that game," Dickey said. "That's unusual for that series.

"It was so convincing that our second offense drove 80 yards for a touchdown against them early in the fourth quarter. That's practically unheard of on The Third Saturday in October. But we had a fine team, of course, and their defense might have been down a little during that time."

Former sportswriter Marvin West recorded the debacle in the *Knoxville News-Sentinel.* He wrote:

> It was never-never day at beautiful Legion Field, an afternoon of happy history as Tennessee's very Big Orange simply stampeded Alabama, 41-14.
>
> Never before had Bear Bryant's Tide lost three years in a row to anybody. He has lost three straight to Tennessee.
>
> Never before had Bear lost two weeks in a row. He has now.
>
> And never had a Bryant defense been bombed for so many points. He once went a season and gave up less.

There is another never-never to this happy Tennessee story. Never before, or since, have Alabama players taken such a tongue-lashing from an opposing player as they did that afternoon from Big Orange senior linebacker Steve Kiner.

His mouth got him in trouble later that season when he said something about quarterback Archie Manning and some "mules" from Mississippi. The Rebels won, 38-0, to blemish what would become a 9-2 record for Tennessee. The Big Orange capped the season with a loss to Florida in the Gator Bowl.

Kiner was particularly tough on the Crimson Tide on The Third Saturday in October, knocking down opponents, then lecturing them.

"I was on the Tennessee sideline standing beside Coach Doug Dickey," said Bob Davis, now an administrative assistant in the Tennessee Athletic Department. "They had a play that ended right in front of us. Kiner was in on the tackle. The score was 34-0. Coach Dickey was taking the first defense out of the game.

"Before he came to the bench, Kiner screamed at the Alabama players. He pointed at Coach Bryant and said, 'Look over there at that poor old man. He looks pitiful. Can you see him? You sorry sons-of-a-bitch have let him down. You should be ashamed of yourselves.'

"Kiner loved Tennessee. And he respected the Bear."

When the game ended, Bryant put his arm around Kiner, walked a ways with him toward the dressing room, and shared a few words with him.

In the dressing room, Kiner told a sportswriter, "I'm tickled to beat Alabama for the third consecutive year. But, I swear, I'm a little sad, too. I can remember when there was some pride associated with wearing those red jerseys."

Charles Thornton was sports information director at Alabama in 1969. He saw Bryant almost daily. During the summer of 1986, at his office in Tuscaloosa, he remembered how the Crimson Tide coach reacted to those remarks.

"Actually, Coach Bryant hated hearing that, especially that part about pride in the red jerseys," Thornton said. "But he respected the way Kiner played football and Tennessee in general.

"Coach Bryant knew Kiner had hit the nail on the head. On his television show the Sunday afternoon after the game, after he had read the quotes, he agreed with Kiner.

"I don't remember seeing Coach Bryant more disappointed than he was that afternoon. And you've got to remember he'd get pretty downcast after Alabama lost to either Tennessee or Auburn, by any margin, especially 41-14."

The romp got under way quickly. Fans were barely settled in their seats when Gary Kreis caught a five-yard touchdown pass from Bobby

Scott. Bobby Majors shocked them with a 71-yard punt return moments later. Then Jackie Walker intercepted a pass and ran it 27 yards for the third touchdown of the first quarter. George Hunt kicked three extra points in the first fifteen minutes and added a 22-yard field goal in the second quarter.

A 31-yard field goal by Hunt gave the Big Orange a 27-0 lead in the third quarter.

Scott ran two yards for a touchdown, with Hunt adding the extra point, to make it 34-0 early in the fourth quarter.

Alabama was reeling worse than any Bryant-coached team had. Some consolation for the Crimson Tide was gained when Johnny Musso ran one yard for a touchdown in the fourth quarter, with Neb Hayden running for a two-point conversion. That cut the Tennessee lead to 34-8.

Tennessee answered with a six-yard touchdown run by Richard Callaway, with Hunt kicking the extra point, making the score 41-8. A six-yard touchdown run by Musso only made the embarrassment less severe.

Alabama managed only 20 yards rushing. Curt Watson had 116 yards rushing for the Volunteers.

What was happening to the Crimson Tide?

Ken Donahue knows. He was an assistant coach at Alabama from 1964 through 1984. During the summer of 1986, while serving as defensive coordinator for the Big Orange, he discussed the situation Bryant faced.

"The talent level at Alabama had fallen off drastically," Donahue said. "Recruiters from other places were telling prospects we had so much talent in stock, because we'd won so much, that there was no way they could play for the Crimson Tide. So they went elsewhere.

"It's obvious Tennessee had a far superior team to Alabama in 1969. That wasn't a contest. They drilled us. And, of course, Doug Dickey was doing a heckuva job."

Alabama finished with a 6-5 record, which included a loss to Colorado in the Liberty Bowl. It never recovered from the battering Tennessee gave it on its home field.

Kirk McNair, who was assistant sports information director at Alabama, said, "Tennessee beat us like a drum, then kicked us in the teeth."

Jim Goostree agrees. He was Alabama trainer from 1957 through 1984, and now is an assistant athletic director for the Crimson Tide.

"It'd become apparent after the 1969 game that the scales had tipped the other way completely in the great series," Goostree said. "Tennessee was rolling. For something like that to happen at that stage in the history of Alabama football, well, it was tremendously embarrassing."

One Alabama man saw the whipping taking shape.

"I knew we were in trouble during warmups in 1969," said John Forney, who served as the radio voice for the Crimson Tide from 1953 through 1982. "Tennessee players looked super. They were crisp. They were impressive just looking at them. I remember thinking, 'Wow, we are in trouble today.'

"The teams were far apart at that point. Tennessee had momentum. They had people who bordered on greatness. That is a tribute to what Dickey did when he took over as coach in 1964. We were short on talent in some areas.

"It was an utter humiliation. They were flogging us in front of our people in Birmingham. It was about as bad as any game I can remember.

"I can remember saying something on the radio about a jet coming over the stadium. I got a letter from a Tennessee fan who said, 'You son-of-a-bitch, there was no way you would tell anybody how bad the Big Orange was whipping the Crimson Tide. You had to talk about airplanes.'"

Tennessee fans and players loved it.

"We were all together," said Kiner. "It was the closest teamwork we'd had at Tennessee. It was a fantastic effort by our defense. It was the best I'd ever seen us have.

"Beating Alabama three times in a row gave me the greatest feeling in the world. I can't explain how happy it made me."

It was dynamite for everybody associated with Tennessee.

"It was a good one," Dickey said about the victory in 1969, "but it wasn't quite as satisfying to me as the win in 1967.

"I can't think of a more important win for me or the Tennessee program while I was there than the one over Alabama in 1967. That was it for me. It was a turning point in our program. Without a doubt, it made a statement that we were doing okay, after a bad lull."

Dickey chose to leave Tennessee while he was ahead, 3-2-1 in face-to-face battles with Bryant and with a second Southeastern Conference championship in three seasons safely tucked away. He left the Volunteers to coach at Florida, his alma mater.

"It was like our father was leaving us," said Tim Priest, a junior defensive halfback on that Tennessee team. "He'd taught us how to win, especially over Alabama, and it hurt us when he left for Florida."

"The upper hand we had on Alabama had nothing to do with me leaving for Florida," Dickey said. "But I did take into account that we were playing about as well as we could at Tennessee. There wasn't much left to do except to keep on keeping on. There were other opportunities in front of me.

"I felt I'd done all I could do. I'd turned around the program. Florida called and asked if I wanted to come back. I hadn't left anything undone at Tennessee. My alma mater was calling."

44

1970
Tennessee 24, Alabama 0

CHARLES THORNTON REMEMBERS FORMER University of Tennessee coach Bill Battle being as active as a cat on a hot tin roof the night before his football team played Alabama on October 17, 1970.

"Bill was nervous, no question about that," said Thornton, who at the time served as sports information director for the Crimson Tide. "They had a little smoker the night before the game, and he kept moving around the room, never stopping in one place very long, maybe for fear that the sportswriters present would try to hem him up for interviews.

"And because our quarterback, Scott Hunter, had his arm in a sling at practice the day before the game, Bill thought the old master, Coach Paul 'Bear' Bryant, was trying to pull a fast one on the young whipper-snapper." Maybe "the old master" was trying to fool one of his former players from Alabama, who, at age twenty-eight, was the youngest head coach in the nation.

If so, he failed.

Intercepting eight passes, five thrown by Hunter, Tennessee humiliated Alabama, 24-0, at Neyland Stadium in Knoxville as Battle made his debut against his alma mater.

Battle remembers being calmer than Thornton thought before the game. He lives in Atlanta where he is a successful businessman. He had been forced to resign at Tennessee after the 1976 season, with a glowing 59-22-2 record, which included five losses to Alabama.

"For whatever reasons, and I'm not sure to this day what they were, I was about as calm as I've ever been before a game," Battle said at his office in Atlanta. "I was quite composed, as I recall.

"Maybe it was confidence. Tennessee had beaten Alabama three straight years. I felt like we could win again, that we should win again because we had the better team.

"I went to that smoker the night before the game and wasn't nervous at all. I'd dealt with the press before.

"But I do recall Coach Bryant trying to psych me out a little. He put his arm around me when a newspaper person took our picture and said, 'Bill, I know you're gonna sleep like a baby tonight.' I told him I thought I would. And, I did, soundly and confidently.

"I might have been a little more nervous the morning before that game than the others because I was coaching against Coach Bryant. But I really don't think I was as nervous as I was in 1966, my first year as an assistant coach at Tennessee, because that was the first time against Alabama for me.

"I do recall being a bit uptight just before the opening kickoff. I'd watched films in my room at the Holiday Inn by the airport the night before, studying their passing game. I felt good up until the time our players started dressing. Time passes slowly then.

"I opened the dressing room door and walked into the breezeway. I did that a few times, just to get out of that tense dressing room. On my last time out, I looked out at the field, where the Alabama quarterbacks were warming up, and I saw Scott Hunter throwing the football. He was throwing it on a rope. I said, 'By golly, that old sucker, Coach Bryant is pulling a fast one on us.'

"But we were prepared for all of their quarterbacks. I sort of knew Coach Bryant would have Scott Hunter ready for us. We were fortunate enough to intercept eight passes and shut them out. It was one of those days when good things happened to us. It's a nice memory for me, even to this day."

John Ward, the voice of the Big Orange on radio and television, recalls the meeting Battle and Bryant had the night before the game in 1970.

"They had a reception at the Faculty Club. I arrived at about the same time Battle did, or went with him, and I remember how he was aware Bryant would be there.

"When Bryant came in, I remember the expression on both faces when they shook hands and wished each other well, so to speak. I assume Bryant had a good sense of humor because he was straining to say something nice. Battle was torn between seeing Bryant as both a coach and a competitor.

"I think they were both uncomfortable, maybe uncertain. Really, they shook hands and stayed away from each other."

The victory—the fourth straight by the Big Orange over Alabama—left little doubt that the Volunteers were dominating The Third Saturday in October.

Sportswriter Marvin West wrote in the *Knoxville News-Sentinel* the morning after the massacre:

> The too-good-to-be-real fairy story at Neyland Stadium yesterday must have been 'Alabama and the 40 Thieves.'
>
> Tennessee's unbelievable ball-hawks, led by Captain Tim Priest, robbed the Tide of eight passes [a school record] as the very Big Orange defense administered a streak-breaking 24-0 shutout on Bear Bryant's Alabama.
>
> Never has the Crimson Tide passing game been treated so rudely. Priest got three interceptions, Jackie Walker two and Bobby Majors, Jamie Rotella and Conrad Graham one each.
>
> Holding Alabama scoreless was a landmark occasion for the Volunteers. The Tide had produced points in 115 consecutive games, dating back to the 1959 Liberty Bowl. One team in collegiate history, Oklahoma, has had a longer streak.
>
> This sunny, nippy Saturday will be unforgettable for other reasons. It was Bill Battle's first time out against his former coach. The show attracted a Neyland record crowd of 64,947. Alabama people will have trouble forgetting the wreckage of their attack. Never had the Tide lost more than five passes one afternoon.
>
> And, never before has a Bryant-coached team bowed four years in a row to any school.
>
> It must be getting a mite uncomfortable.

It was uncomfortable for Alabama, but at least one Crimson Tide player from that year has maintained his sense of humor. Split end David Bailey recalls going into the offensive huddle, looking at Hunter, and saying, "Scott, this time try to throw the ball to them and

BILL BATTLE

HIS HAIR SHOWED SOME gray. That happens when a man reaches forty-four years of age. But it was a youthful Bill Battle who talked about The Third Saturday in October on a hot summer afternoon in 1986.

Battle leaped from his chair to show how, as an Alabama defensive end, he had trouble fighting off blockers in a Tennessee single wing offense in 1960 on Shields-Watkins Field in Knoxville.

"It was as tough a game as I can remember playing," he said.

Battle came out of his seat again, laughing as he moved, to show how a Big Orange defensive halfback grabbed a football off the back of a Crimson Tide end in 1961 in Birmingham.

"We beat the Big Orange pretty good that afternoon," he said.

There were more somber memories of his years as a Tennessee coach. He was an assistant coach in 1966, head coach from 1970 through 1976.

"I'll never forget the first game we had at Tennessee against Alabama," Battle said. "I'm talking about 1966, when I was an assistant coach under Doug Dickey, the game in which they beat us 11-10 when we missed a chip-shot field goal on the last play.

"I was in the press box with some of the other assistant coaches. When we missed the field goal, I dropped my head onto the table in front of me, wanted to cry, did cry some, and stayed there an hour. Eugenia [his wife] and the rest of my family waited downstairs for me. Finally, they gave up and went home.

"I've thought about that a lot since then, particularly when I've considered how some Tennessee people doubted my loyalty. It was a game I wanted to win badly. It didn't take me long to realize which side of the bread my butter was on. I cashed my checks in Knoxville."

Battle is a familiar name in the series that exists between Alabama and Tennessee. He was a star Crimson Tide player from 1960 through 1962 under Paul

"Bear" Bryant. He coached the Big Orange against his alma mater.

His record as a player in the series was 2-1.

His record as a head coach on The Third Saturday in October was 1-6.

"The biggest thing that caused problems for me at Tennessee was not being able to beat Alabama and Auburn regularly," Battle said.

"That contributed, at least I heard comments about it," said Col. Tom Elam, longtime chairman of the Tennessee Athletics Board. "But I think he might have just lacked the maturity he needed at that time. He was young. He was put into a position before he was ready.

"Bill Battle is a fine person. He has good looks and a great personality, no bad traits that I know of, and a good family. But he seemed overwhelmed by the task at hand when he got started at Tennessee.

"I think he was a victim of circumstances, in a couple of ways. He moved into that job before he was adequately prepared for it, like Terry Brennan had at Notre Dame. And Alabama was such a critical point to us, as it remains, and not beating them but one time contributed to his demise."

It got so bad in Knoxville that some Tennessee fans sent a moving van to his house when his wife was pregnant.

"That's life," Battle said about his reign as Tennessee coach after he earned a national championship ring at Alabama in 1961. "I'd never let what a few sick people did to us—the ones who sent the moving van to our house, the ones who constantly moaned and groaned about our teams—destroy my many pleasant memories of coaching at Tennessee.

"We've forgotten most of the bad times."

That stands to reason. Since resigning in Knoxville, Battle has become very successful in the business world, which includes his presidency of an Atlanta-based sports licensing business that boasts Tennessee among its more lucrative clients.

see if I can intercept it." He did well enough, catching twelve passes, a school record.

Priest, a lawyer in Knoxville, chuckles upon hearing what Bailey said to Hunter. "That's interesting because I remember a pass late in the game when Bailey jumped over me and caught it. I thought interception number nine was falling into my arms, when, jumping higher than I thought anybody could, he took it away from me.

"But, more than anything, I'll always remember what it was like shutting out Alabama and winning by such a large margin.

"At Tennessee, the Alabama game is the biggest of the season. They had 'Bear' Bryant back then, which made the game more special for us, sort of like an honor to be out there with him coaching on the other side of the field.

"It's just an intense rivalry, no matter who plays or coaches, one based on hard play and clean play. The hitting in that game was crisper and harder than usual. The week of the Alabama game was always different. That game took precedence over everything else. Sophomores were told they didn't earn their letters until they played against the Crimson Tide. There were no doubts at Tennessee that week, as well as no studying, just let the books slide to prepare for the game.

"In 1970, we were up, playing good, while Alabama was down a bit, struggling along. We just clicked all afternoon. A major reason why was the game plan designed by our defensive coordinator, Larry Jones, who scouted Alabama with assistant coach George Cafego.

"We knew everything they'd do running the football, because they tipped us off with certain shifts and movements, and they became terribly frustrated. Late in the game, their players were even talking about how we knew where they'd try to run.

"Consequently, they had to pass a lot. We'd be there waiting for every pass, which is how I got three interceptions, and their quarterbacks had a bad afternoon, throwing high almost all the time.

"That was a great afternoon for Tennessee—a shutout against Alabama."

Tennessee led 7-0 at halftime and 14-0 after three quarters. A touchdown run of one yard by Bobby Scott had opened the scoring, with George Hunt kicking the extra point, and a touchdown run of four yards by Don McLeary padded the Big Orange lead in the third quarter, with Hunt kicking the extra point.

A 35-yard field goal by Hunt early in the fourth quarter put the game out of reach. A 22-yard pass interception return for a touchdown by Jackie Walker in the fourth quarter, with Hunt kicking the extra point, capped the afternoon for Tennessee.

The arrival of Battle, which came on the heels of a somewhat hasty exit by former Tennessee coach Doug Dickey to his alma mater, Florida, prompted mixed reaction in Knoxville. Many Big Orange fans knew he was a bright coach with glowing references. But many more knew him as a former Alabama end.

The new coach helped his cause when he told Big Orange fans the day before the game that it was not a family feud. "It's Tennessee against Alabama. It isn't Bill Battle against Paul 'Bear' Bryant."

The doubting legion must have been pleased to read the remarks of W. R. Battle, father of the coach, in the *Knoxville News-Sentinel* the morning after the game. Said the elder Battle, who lived in Birmingham, "I never thought I'd see anybody hold Alabama to less than two touchdowns. I didn't think it could be done. I personally saw Alabama's game with Southern Cal and have watched TV films of their other games. They have an explosive offense.

"But I'm very happy over the outcome."

So was Battle, who led Tennessee to an 11-1 record that season, including a victory over Air Force in the Sugar Bowl. It did not matter to him that his team defeated an Alabama team that would struggle to a 6-5-1 record, including a tie with Oklahoma in the Bluebonnet Bowl.

"It doesn't matter how strong Tennessee and Alabama teams are when they play," Battle said. "It's still the biggest thing going.

"For instance, I'll never forget how the World Series was always being played The Third Saturday in October. That's one of the great events in sports. But I don't even remember who was playing in it when I was coaching Tennessee against Alabama. The World Series doesn't mean a thing to Tennessee and Alabama people, not when *the* football game is that week."

Battle had some help in 1970. Entertainer Tennessee Ernie Ford was among the Big Orange loyals. "If you bring us luck like that, we want you around here all the time," Battle said to Ford in the Tennessee dressing room.

"That was my first victory over Bear Bryant," Ford said while wearing an orange jacket. "And they put me in charge of pass interceptions.

It was more fun than smoking cornsilks out behind the barn." He delivered that remark in country style, reminiscent of the way Bryant talked about football games. But the coach was not in a jovial mood after the drubbing.

"I'm real proud of Bill," Bryant said about his former player who was the toast of Knoxville on that day. "But I'm not very happy for him. This was a big win for him, I'm sure, but a terrible loss for us."

Battle was so emotional after the game that he did not remember what he said to Bryant when they met at midfield and shook hands.

"I was on the sideline, all wrapped up in the action, then the game ended," Battle said. "My players overwhelmed me like a wave, yanked me from my feet, put me on their shoulders, and rushed me to the middle of the field. I don't recall what Coach Bryant said once I got out there to shake his hand. There wasn't any serious conversation. He just congratulated me on a great victory and went on. I'm sure he was most gracious."

Priest recalls Battle being smooth before the game, "on an even keel all week," but the former Tennessee player said he realized how important the game was to the former Crimson Tide end.

"Not once did Coach Battle say anything about us playing Alabama, like that's my alma mater, that's my old coach, that's my this or that's my that. All he said was, 'Folks, this is Alabama,' and we knew what he meant when he said that."

Battle remembers it that way.

"I just told them regular Tennessee-Alabama stuff," Battle said. "That was enough for them. They knew the significance."

But Ward still wonders if perhaps defeating Florida in 1970 was more important for Tennessee than defeating Alabama. He has no doubts that the Big Orange was awesome that season.

"There was a major promotion under way against Doug Dickey in Knoxville," Ward said. "People wrote songs about him for the radio. People were pointing toward the Florida game, not toward Alabama, which was an exception.

"People took Dickey leaving personally. Alabama was in a down cycle. It made the Florida game *the* game that season.

"It was a great season, either way, because that was a superb Tennessee team. Defensively, it was a group of unknowns who came together to produce thirty-six interceptions and a lot of touchdowns.

That defense went against a lot of great quarterbacks, one at SMU, one at Florida, one at Auburn, one at Army, one at Georgia Tech, and as always, one at Alabama. It passed the test almost every week against great names.

"Everything came together defensively. The defense set the tone. It was a confident group. Those types of things have to come naturally. They did in 1970. Tennessee fans loved that team."

An Alabama fan feared it.

John Forney remembers finding false security in the *Knoxville News-Sentinel* the morning before Tennessee romped past the Crimson Tide. Then he handled play-by-play duties on the Alabama Radio Network.

"I remember the *News-Sentinel* running pictures of several of our players with a caption that said, 'Still Mean, Lean, And Hungry Alabama.' I was hoping the newspaper was right. I feared they were wrong. They were.

"Tennessee just whipped us."

The Big Orange gave Battle a happy start against his alma mater. While he received the game football, he now says with a chuckle, "I don't know where it is now. It's not in a trophy case, or anywhere like that, unless it's by accident. My kids were at the age then that they probably kicked it around in the yard. It's probably scuffed up in a box somewhere."

Interestingly, Battle almost escaped the series with a 1-0 record against Bryant. The fabled Alabama coach came close to leaving Tuscaloosa that year.

Alabama was in a struggle for its pride in 1970. The humiliation at the hands of Tennessee heightened conjecture that Bryant had become too old to continue coaching. The Miami Dolphins' owner Joe Robbie thought otherwise, as remembered by Logan Young, who was a close personal friend to the Crimson Tide leader.

"Joe Robbie had Coach Bryant hired for the Dolphins," Young said. "They were paying him much more money than he was making at Alabama, plus a ton more than they gave Don Shula when they hired him. They had given him a set-up like a king. I know. I saw a copy of the contract. He had a penthouse at the Palm Bay Club. He had 10 percent of the team.

"Coach Bryant told the Alabama Board of Trustees that he was leaving for the pros. They talked him out of it. At the Senior Bowl in

Mobile, Coach Bryant told Joe Robbie, 'Joe, they want me to stay. I thought they'd be happy that I wanted to leave. I've got to stay with my school.'

"Robbie told me it was the worst news he had ever heard. He said, 'I wanted Bear Bryant, nobody else. He broke my heart when he turned me down.'

"I can tell you now that Coach Bryant was gone. Then he decided to stay. He sort of rededicated himself to restoring Alabama to what it once was."

Forney remembers "a recommitment."

"I was at a meeting of Alabama boosters at the Stafford Hotel in Tuscaloosa," Forney said. "Bryant showed up late and walked to the dais. He made the damnedest talk about winning football that I had heard, or have heard. I can remember Doug Layton leaning over to me and saying, 'John, I don't have any idea how good he can coach now. I suspect he's still the greatest. Regardless, I want him on my side.'

"We all left knowing Alabama was coming back."

The next news Forney and his broadcast partner, Layton, received from Bryant was that Alabama was going to the wishbone offense.

45

1971
Alabama 32, Tennessee 15

DURING THE SUMMER OF 1971, Crimson Tide coach Paul "Bear" Bryant conducted secretive meetings that were to lead to the winningest decade in the history of the sport. It was during June and July that Alabama coaches met with Texas coaches to study the mechanics of the wishbone offensive formation.

"We'd decided to sink or swim with it," Bryant said after a 1971 season that produced an 11-1 record, including a 32-15 victory over Tennessee and a 38-6 loss to Nebraska in the Orange Bowl game that determined the national champion.

After back-to-back miserable seasons, both resulting in five losses, Bryant changed from a pro-like passing attack to a military-like running attack. He did that after his team was tied, 24-24, by a wishbone-running Oklahoma in the 1970 Bluebonnet Bowl.

Kirk McNair, who during the summer of 1986 was editor of *Bama Inside the Crimson Tide* magazine in Tuscaloosa, recalled seeing Bryant doing something unusual on the flight home from the Bluebonnet Bowl.

"No sooner had we gotten on the plane did Coach Bryant start doodling on a legal pad," said McNair, who was at that time assistant sports information director at Alabama. "I walked past his seat to see what he was doing. It was then that I saw him scribbling the wishbone formation on the paper. He worked on it all the way home.

"I had no idea at the time, but he was laying the groundwork for a new era in Alabama football, an amazing run to two more national championships."

The wishbone era at Alabama started in stunning fashion. In a season-opening game in Los Angeles, the Crimson Tide defeated Southern Cal, 17-10. The Trojans were the preseason favorite for the national championship. That victory came after much secrecy prevailed in Tuscaloosa.

"Southern Cal had no idea we were going to run the wishbone," McNair said. "Few people did, outside of the coaches and players, because Coach Bryant told people not to tell anybody about it. I was told to ask visiting sportswriters at practice not to write anything about formations. They agreed because most of them had no idea there was anything new going on.

"The entire plan almost went up in smoke when the Southeastern Conference Skywriters visited Tuscaloosa. One of the sportswriters from Florida had talked to one of our players from his city. During a press conference, the sportswriter asked Coach Bryant, 'I understand you have been working solely on the wishbone offense this summer?' Coach Bryant was coy. He said something like, 'Ah, we always work on power formations to be used down around the goal line. This is nothing new. Besides, we do it the simple way, not like Texas and Oklahoma, who do this and do that.' Coach Bryant started drawing plays on the chalkboard, obviously knowing a lot about the wishbone, and I thought, 'Oh, no, I wish he would shut up.'

"But nobody figured it out."

So secretive was Alabama that the Crimson Tide did not show the wishbone formation during pregame warmups in Los Angeles. And as the ultimate precaution, Bryant told Alabama Radio Network announcers John Forney and Doug Layton to refrain from talking about the new offense until after the opening kickoff, as if a West Coast station was broadcasting the game.

Southern Cal was befuddled.

So was everybody else—except Nebraska—with Tennessee doing the most commendable job stopping the Alabama wishbone during the regular season.

On October 16 at Legion Field in Birmingham, Alabama had to score twice in the last minute to pad its margin of victory over the aroused Volunteers. The Crimson Tide piled up 325 yards in offense, with stellar senior halfback Johnny Musso running for 115 yards on 22 attempts. But most of the damage was done late in the game.

It was hot in Birmingham on The Third Saturday in October. So was the action.

Alabama passed 20 yards for its first touchdown, surprisingly, with David Bailey catching the football thrown by Terry Davis.

Tennessee took a 7-6 lead in the first quarter when Curt Watson ran four yards for a touchdown and George Hunt kicked the extra point.

The Crimson Tide got nine points in the second quarter to take a 15-7 lead at halftime. Bill Davis kicked a 22-yard field goal; Terry Davis ran six yards for a touchdown.

The lead jumped to 22-7, seemingly out of the reach of Tennessee, in the third quarter. Terry Davis and Bailey teamed on a 16-yard touchdown pass; Bill Davis kicked the extra point.

Fighting back early in the fourth quarter, the Big Orange got a nine-yard touchdown run from Watson and a two-point conversion run from Walter Chadwick, cutting the lead to 22-15.

But Bill Davis kicked a 39-yard field goal and Musso ran five yards for a touchdown, with Bill Davis kicking the extra point, to make the final margin 17 points.

Marvin West, the former sportswriter for the *Knoxville News-Sentinel,* noticed that Tennessee, which would complete the season with a 10-2 record, played admirably against the powerful Crimson Tide. West wrote:

> Aggressive Alabama, bigger than the town bully and maybe meaner, chased Tennessee all around Legion Field, but didn't really rip the Volunteers until it was almost time to go home.
>
> The unbeaten Tide triumphed, 32-15, before a record gathering of 73,828, but it was still a ball game with just one minute remaining. Seven points then separated the foes in what has become one of the great Southern classics.
>
> But the knockout was waiting. It started with a field goal. Then came Tennessee's eighth turnover, a fumble five yards from the Tennessee goal. And then came Johnny Musso. It should be Mr. Johnny Musso. He stuffed the ball into the end zone on one big blast and what would have been a good game to replay tomorrow turned into a rout.

Paul (Bear) Bryant's football team is 6-0, fourth-ranked and rising in the national polls, perhaps headed for dizzy heights. And, yet, Alabama did not look overwhelming.

Bryant was relieved, as usual, and he praised his defense that allowed Tennessee only 161 yards, just 53 on the ground.

Big Orange coach Bill Battle was surprised. He said, "I felt like we were going to beat Alabama, and I think every man on our squad felt that way. Our defense did a great job. Alabama has a well-balanced team. Johnny Musso is great. You think you've got him tackled, and he'll jump and buck and get five more yards. In summary, we played well at times, then very, very, very sorry at times against an outstanding team."

Tennessee fought until near the end, when it came up inches short on a fourth-down try for a first down at its 29-yard line, the questionable ruling by the official opening the flood gates that led to Alabama scoring 10 points in the final minute.

The Crimson Tide was methodical. But it was also a bit fortunate.

"It just kills me that Alabama got all those points in the last minute," said Curt Watson, a Tennessee fullback in 1971, who now flies with the Navy's Blue Angels. "It looks like they drilled us. I swear we got rooked out of the ball at the 30 [on the fourth-down gamble with about three minutes remaining in the game].

"Our defense really hung in there, particularly after we had a lot of turnovers early in the game, when it would have been easy for us to get run out of the stadium."

It was Musso who led the charge. He finished fifth in Heisman Trophy balloting that season.

It was the Secret that led to the glory.

Now a businessman in Birmingham, during the summer of 1971, Jeff Rutledge was a redshirt quarterback at Alabama.

"I'll never forget the day Coach Bryant told us we were going to the wishbone offense," Rutledge said. "We were shocked. I couldn't believe we were going to revamp our offense three weeks before we played a national power like Southern Cal.

"But we had quick-footed Terry Davis at quarterback, a perfect guy for the wishbone offense, and, of course, we had Johnny Musso. I guess what we had was more apparent to Coach Bryant than to the rest of us. Besides, we'd been down in 1969 and 1970. It was time for a change of some kind.

"It's amazing how secretive something like that could be. But that's how it was with Coach Bryant. He told us to keep our mouths shut about the change to the wishbone offense. That's what we did."

Battle was surprised, like everybody else, when Alabama opened the season in the wishbone. Early in the season he knew he would have to defend against it on The Third Saturday in October, but, he said, "Hell, there wasn't any time to spend on extra preparations for that offense. We had other people to play in previous weeks.

"We studied it on Thursday and Friday the week previous, after we got the hay in the barn for our game against Georgia Tech, which was our normal way of beginning our mental gymnastics.

"But our major problem wasn't the wishbone. Our problem was injured quarterbacks. We went through four before we got to Alabama.

"That considered, we played them pretty well. The defense hung in there. The offense tried hard to move the football, with heavy restrictions, and did on occasion. The game turned around in a big way in the fourth quarter, as I recall, when they punched in a couple of touchdowns to pad the margin."

Battle laughed heartily at the mention of the controversial fourth-and-one play his team failed to convert late in the game, in the process opening the door for the Crimson Tide.

"What do you say?" Battle said. "Good gosh! The chain stretches. We don't make it. Maybe the lines were crooked.

"But that wasn't all that strange a thing. I can remember three or four calls by the officials in our games against Alabama and Auburn that had great impact on the outcomes. Maybe it was a subconscious fear, but it seemed like Coach Bryant and Coach Ralph 'Shug' Jordan of Auburn got a few charitable calls from the zebras against us. Maybe that's because they were established and famous, while I was young. It seemed like Alabama got one that day.

"We were playing to win. It doesn't matter how much you get beat, seven points or twenty. The object with me was to win. I got a lot of notes and telephone calls from gamblers who didn't appreciate that approach."

The victory over Tennessee helped spark Alabama to 103 victories during the decade, which is more stunning considering only six came in 1970. The Crimson Tide, which was starting an eleven-game winning streak over the Volunteers, won national championships in 1978 and 1979.

Jim Goostree, a Tennessee graduate, now an assistant athletic director for the Crimson Tide, recalls the birth of the wishbone in Tuscaloosa.

"No question, the offensive formation had a lot to do with our success in 1971 and throughout the 1970s," Goostree said. "But still, it was the personnel and Coach Bryant's motivation that led to that period of excellence in Alabama football.

"During the summer of 1971, when the new beginning was taking place, Coach Bryant and his assistant coaches did a great job selling our players on the merits of the wishbone offense. And there was an unbelievable sense of rededication in the program after the bad seasons in 1969 and 1970.

"I think you also have to remember how well our defense, led by assistant coach Ken Donahue, played during that period. It was as if Alabama went back to the basics, sound kicking and hammering defense, at the same time we adopted the wishbone offense.

"It was more of a people thing than a gimmick thing, good players winning. Johnny Musso sort of typified that with his game against Tennessee in 1971. What can you say new about him? He just chewed up opponents, wanted to kill them off, with his running and blocking. He always gave total effort, which makes him one of my favorite former players, and he did that without regard to the punishment he was taking.

"He got after Tennessee because he knew the importance of the rivalry. But he got after everybody else, too, because he liked to compete and he loved the Crimson Tide."

46

1972
Alabama 17, Tennessee 10

THE UNIVERSITY OF TENNESSEE football fan was wearing orange overalls and an orange hat. He approached Alabama coach Paul "Bear" Bryant as the Crimson Tide leader was walking to a team bus parked outside Neyland Stadium on The Third Saturday in October in 1972.

The Miracle was complete by then—a 17-10 Alabama victory over the Volunteers—and the Tennessee fan was angry.

"You're the luckiest son-of-a-bitch in the world," the Big Orange fan said to Bryant, after jumping in front of the coach, who was being escorted by two Alabama State Troopers.

"Thank you very much," Bryant said, tipping his famous houndstooth hat.

Nary a serious student of *the* series has forgotten what transpired on October 22, 1972, in Knoxville. And you can be sure Colin Hart, a sportswriter for the *London Sun,* who was present at the game, told his friends in England that he saw an unbelievable football show.

As Hart said after the game, "With five minutes to go, I would have given Alabama as much chance of winning as Mark Spitz has of drowning in his bath.

"I think what distinguishes all great teams is their faith in themselves. Alabama obviously has this. They are not ranked third in the nation for nothing.

"Tennessee has what I take to be a great defense. I thought it cracked some when Alabama really put on the pressure. For the whole

245

day, Tennessee seemed to be the better team. Alabama pulling it out was unexpected, to say the least. But such endings help make sports the fascinating thing it is."

Fascinating?

That is an understatement.

Alabama scored two touchdowns and two extra points in the span of thirty-six seconds late in the fourth quarter to win.

Marvin West, writing for the *Knoxville News-Sentinel,* watched in disbelief. His shock showed in his writing after the game:

> Amazing Alabama, undefeated and untied, is still rolling along atop the Southeastern Conference today.
>
> You gotta be kidding.
>
> The Tide's vaunted wishbone attack rammed in two fourth-quarter touchdowns for a thrilling 17-10 triumph over Tennessee.
>
> Unbelievable. The wishbone was bent double.
>
> An inspired Volunteer defense, the best it has been in recent years, had a record crowd of 72,049 open-armed to receive a juicy upset. But the defense broke down near the finish, permitting 14 points in a shocking span of just 36 seconds.
>
> Pinch me. Perhaps it wasn't real.

But it was.

With 2:39 remaining, Alabama trailed 10-3 and had the football 48 yards from the Tennessee end zone. Quarterback Terry Davis passed to split end Wayne Wheeler for 20 yards. A run by fullback Steve Bisceglia, off a crisp block by guard John Hannah, gained 26 yards, after a lot of tackles were broken along the way. Halfback Wilbur Jackson scored the first touchdown on the next play, diving over the goal line.

Then came the first stunning development of the afternoon.

Bryant send place-kicker Bill Davis into the game to attempt an extra point that tied the game.

Tennessee fans booed his decision not to try for a two-point conversion.

So did John Forney, from 1953 through 1982 the radio voice of the Crimson Tide. "I was stunned first when we did not go for two points on the conversion attempt after the first touchdown," Forney said. "I am sure the inflection of my voice told the audience that. It was unbelievable. I still wonder if I approve of it."

The coach got the last laugh.

After the ensuing kickoff, which was mishandled, with Tennessee facing a third down at its 12-yard line, quarterback Condredge Holloway ran a draw play. He was hit by Alabama defensive end Mike Dubose, fumbled the football, and watched Crimson Tide defensive end John Mitchell recover it at the Big Orange 21-yard line.

Enter the wishbone offensive unit.

On the first play after the turnover, Davis faked a handoff at guard, looked at a trailing halfback at right end, tucked the football under his arm, and ran into the end zone.

Hardly a sound was heard when Davis kicked his second extra point. Crimson Tide supporters in attendance were as stunned as Tennessee supporters.

Several Tennessee and Alabama fans listened to the closing excitement on radios. They had left the game early in an effort to beat the traffic. As Crimson Tide loyals danced, several Big Orange supporters tossed their radios into the Tennessee River that runs alongside Neyland Drive beside the stadium.

Remembering is pleasing for Alabama players.

"It was an exciting finish that pointed out what can happen when you keep hammering and keep hammering and keep hammering," Dubose said during the summer of 1986, when he served as an assistant coach at Alabama. "That win proved to us what Coach Bryant told us a thousand times. He always said you have to hang tough in the fourth quarter, keep working, play good defense, and keep from beating yourself. That sort of summarizes how we beat Tennessee in 1972 in Knoxville.

"We had played good defense all afternoon. And you have to remember, we had the type team that year that never thought it was beat until there was no time left and the scoreboard said so. I doubt any of us thought we would lose, not even when they led us, 10-3, but I doubt any of us knew exactly how we would win.

"It just happened beautifully.

"No, I never questioned Coach Bryant when he kicked the extra point to tie the game, 10-10, because I knew there was enough time remaining. I recall how his decision sort of fired up our defense and gave us confidence. It was like he knew we had enough to us to stop them, to do our part to win the game, to set up our offense.

"On the fumble by Condredge Holloway, I just happened to be in the right place, at middle linebacker, protected by our big tackles, Mike Raines and Skip Kubelius. I never got touched. I happened to get one of those once-in-a-lifetime hits on Condredge, squarely on the football and the fumble occurred. The next thing I saw was John Mitchell getting up with the football.

"Yeah, there was happiness, and relief, but there was more work to be done. We still had to get in the end zone. Of course, Terry Davis took care of that in quick fashion. Boy, was he something as a quarterback."

That is what Forney thought. "We were lucky. Terry Davis made a brilliant solo effort. He was great.

"It was a tough day of football. There was an antagonism present that I had never seen on The Third Saturday in October.

"I had some friends who rode a boat to the stadium. I told them as they left to get back onboard for the trip home that they better make sure they knew where the life preservers were. There were a lot of upset Tennessee supporters on the dock that afternoon."

The memory remains painful for Tennessee players.

"We were two minutes from the finest victory our team could have," said Jamie Rotella, a Tennessee linebacker and captain in 1971. "I felt we had whipped them good. Everybody was playing above his ability, which was what we had to do against such a good team. We just made some mistakes at the end.

"But Alabama made some great plays. I never saw a more determined run than the one Steve Bisceglia made to set up their first touchdown. He came through there like a wild man."

Tim Townes, a Tennessee fullback, termed the defeat "an awful dream."

But John Ward, the radio voice of the Big Orange, said during the fall of 1986 that he had a feeling Alabama would rally. "I never thought the game was won. The reason was because of Paul Bryant. He always controlled the pace of the game. That was almost always the case against Tennessee, with the definite exception being 1970, when he was soundly whipped, with the only possible exception being in 1982, when Alabama was not like usual but was still charging at the end.

"It seemed like Bryant never played his last card. He always seemed to have something left at his disposal. Even when he walked off the field, I always thought there was something else he had ready, if needed.

"When Tennessee made runs at Alabama, his team always seemed to be in control of the tempo, which, I think, was a reflection of him. So, in 1972, I never felt the Big Orange had control of it.

"I was upset and disheartened as a fan, of course, because it was an empty feeling after Tennessee had shut down the wishbone.

"But we never got the cork in the bottle. I felt it was about to pop out. That was the way I always felt when Tennessee played against Bryant, not just that year, because he always seemed in control.

"If we needed to be one way on offense, we were always another for his sake. If we needed to be one way on defense, we were always another for his sake.

"Bryant had control of the tempo."

Still, everybody thought they were dreaming when Bryant chose to attempt a tying extra point after the first touchdown.

"But they won," said Bill Battle, who was coaching Tennessee that day. "Coach Bryant must have known something."

Actually, Bryant was persuaded to "go for one" by Alabama assistant coach Pat Dye, now head coach at Auburn. According to Ken Donahue, who in 1972 was defensive coordinator for the Crimson Tide, the decision was made hastily.

"We talked about it in the press box," said Donahue. "We figured we should put the monkey back on their back, go for the tie, and make them gamble on offense to win the game. We figured our defense could get the ball for us one more time in the final minute.

"Coach Bryant already had a two-point conversion play called. He had told us before the game that, if that situation came up and there was enough time for our defense to regain possession of the football, we would tie the game and go for a late rally. But he was about to go for two points and the win.

"Pat Dye ran up to him on the sideline. He told him he had a feeling we could hold them, get the football back, and win with a field goal. Coach Bryant made a snap decision to listen to the advice.

"Yeah, I felt mighty lucky that day.

"It was just another tough game against Tennessee, with the normal hitting going on, and Alabama managed to squeeze by at the end."

Jim Goostree recalls "a lot of whoopin' and hollerin' in the dressing room" after the game. "Carney Laslie and I had hid several boxes of cigars and cigarettes in our dressing room, just in case we had reason to celebrate, and I recall Coach Bryant distributing them himself that day. He hated cigars, really despised them, but he even stuck one in his mouth in 1972."

Kirk McNair, now editor of *Bama Inside the Crimson Tide* magazine, was assistant sports information director at Alabama in 1972. He got on the press box elevator at Neyland Stadium just after the Crimson Tide had scored the first touchdown.

"George Smith from the *Anniston Star* was with me," McNair said. "I remember saying, 'Well, George, when we get down to the field, we will have either won 11-10 or lost 10-9.' I couldn't believe it when I looked at the scoreboard and saw 10-10 up there.

"I figured we'd gotten a penalty that made us go for one [on the extra point attempt] instead of two. When I heard we'd kicked the extra point to tie the game, well, I was sort of ashamed.

"But, as was the way with Coach Bryant, it worked out in the end."

Battle, who now lives in Atlanta, grimmaced while reflecting on his team's loss in 1972.

"I had the feeling we were the best team and ought to have won that day," Battle said. "That game, plus a 10-9 loss to Auburn in 1971, was one I thought we had won and should have won. I can wake up in the middle of the night sweating while thinking about the loss to Alabama that year. I get heartburn talking about it now.

"We really played super. Defensively, we were as good as we could have been. Offensively, we moved it up and down the field.

"We had the game in good shape. In reflection, as it worked out, maybe we were too conservative. But it was our game until late.

"On both of their touchdowns, we had a breakdown on defense, in part because they had some different offensive schemes for us. Basically, we had a stunting linebacker that got hung up and couldn't commit to either the fullback or the quarterback.

"What killed me was them going for a tie on the first extra point. I couldn't believe it. I knew they weren't gonna kick it. I knew Coach Bryant wasn't gonna go for a tie in Knoxville. That was instilled in me. That was the Alabama way. I told our guys to watch for a fake.

"Swoosh—he kicked that sucker right through there. Tied the game.

"I still believe to this day that Coach Bryant was playing for a tie. He knew Alabama played one more conference game than everybody else, that a tie wouldn't kill their chances for the conference championship. I know damn well that's what he was thinking, not that they'd get the football back with a chance to beat us later.

"Then, after they tied the game, I told everybody to watch for an onside kickoff. I've got my best back deep and everybody else up there waiting for the short kick.

"Boom—he kicks off deep.

"Goodness gracious.

"It wouldn't happen again in a million years, but Haskell Stanback, our best halfback, a pro five or six years, mishandled the kickoff and we took possession at the 12-yard line.

"Then, we were gonna try to win. We didn't want to do anything foolish, but we weren't playing for a tie.

"I thought we might get Condredge Holloway loose on a little quarterback draw. I figured that little rascal, who was shifty and quick, might run a long time once he got into the secondary. He got there, but their linebacker Mike Dubose met him.

"It's amazing, all that happened. It's incredible that we lost."

47

1973
Alabama 42, Tennessee 21

THE GREAT PLAY WAS going into its closing act with the setting perfect on The Third Saturday in October in 1973. Alabama 21, Tennessee 21.

The game was in the fourth quarter, with a national television audience watching. Veteran observers of the fierce rivalry were talking in terms of "best ever" in the press box high above Legion Field in Birmingham. It was college football at its best.

Then, to the amazement of everybody, a baseball player got involved.

Robin Cary, a second baseman on the Crimson Tide baseball team, was inserted in the game by Alabama coach Paul "Bear" Bryant. Cary, who was sent into the game to catch a Tennessee punt, not necessarily to run it back, scooted 64 yards for a touchdown that opened floodgates.

In rolled the Crimson Tide with force, 42-21, winning the fourth quarter and its third consecutive victory over Tennessee.

"That run by Robin Cary busted it open, no doubt about that, and then we put it on Tennessee," said Gary Rutledge, an Alabama junior quarterback and a star on The Third Saturday in October in 1973. "At that time, the game was in doubt. It was going back and forth. But we took that touchdown and built on it. We sort of exploded."

That eruption by Alabama changed some of the reviews written by sportswriters after the game. For instance, Marvin West, a former sportswriter for the *Knoxville News-Sentinel*, saw a party being crashed.

Alabama takes all the fun out of football.

Underdog Tennessee was out in the sunshine at crowded Legion Field, playing the powerful Tide nose-to-nose. It was a real battle, crammed with big plays and jolting tackles. The score was tied and there was talk of a monumental upset.

And then the fourth quarter started. Before the Vols could get Alabama stopped, the Tide had run off with a 42-21 romp. It was no contest, unless you were among the 72,226 here or in the giant TV audience.

"We felt we could win the fourth quarter," said Tennessee Coach Bill Battle. "We talked about it—today, all week, since August. We weren't afraid, we weren't awed. Alabama sure does have a lot of people."

One of those unheralded reserves became the hero, breaking the struggle with a 64-yard punt return. Robin Cary took a Neil Clabo kick at his 36, broke a tackle, and was surrounded by Redmen. Robin made one good move and went on unmolested.

In the next five minutes, Wilbur Jackson sprinted 80 yards to score with a pitchout, Cary recovered a fumble on a kickoff, and Paul Spivey rammed in another touchdown.

It was an avalanche.

The run by Cary surprised the crowd. "That little guy couldn't outrun his sister," said Robert Fraley, an Alabama sophomore quarterback in 1973, now a lawyer in Orlando, Florida. "But he sure outran a bunch of Volunteers in Birmingham."

"It took Robin two days to get to the end zone," said Mike Dubose, a Crimson Tide junior defensive end in 1973. "That was pretty good for him. It normally took him a day and a half to run 40 yards."

Battle was stunned, as were most people associated with Tennessee, but the coach offered credit where it was due.

"Alabama won like you're supposed to win, in the fourth quarter," Battle said after his alma mater had defeated his team. "I felt like we could do that ourselves. It takes pride and guts to do it. I know we have that, too.

"I think this Alabama team is better than the national championship team I played on [as a Crimson Tide end] in 1961. Coach Bryant has more good players now than he did then.

"Also, Alabama uses a lot of players. They do a fine job of having those fresh men ready to throw at you."

Bryant did have a bevy of stars at his disposal. He used sixty-three players on an unseasonably warm afternoon. He grinned broadly in the aftermath.

"I've been in a lot of big games, and they've come out both ways," Bryant said. "I've been in games where I was much prouder to win or I wanted to win more. But I've never been in a game with a gang I'd swap for these guys."

His "guys" from Alabama went on to post an 11-1 record, which included a monumental loss to Notre Dame, 24-23, in a Sugar Bowl game played for the national championship.

Tennessee, which carried a 5-0 record into the game against Alabama, had an up-and-down ride to an 8-4 record, which included a loss to Texas Tech in the Gator Bowl.

Battle remembers taking "a skeleton crew" to Birmingham. He thought his "badly injured" team got tired. He wonders about rumors he has heard about Alabama players confusing his players on the pivotal punt return by Cary.

"At the end, our guys looked like they were running in glue," Battle said. "They had fought a good battle. They were tired. In the fourth quarter, it was like men and boys out there. It was like race cars and puddle-hoppers. Obviously, they were better and deeper than us in the fourth quarter.

"Hell, that run by Wilbur Jackson can tell you that. He was twice as big as one of our defensive halfbacks, but he ran off and left everybody, including our fastest guys.

"And then there was that punt return.

"Our people overran a short kick. Then, our players told me after the game that the Alabama guys were hollering, 'Fair catch! Fair catch!' I don't know if it made our guys relax, nor am I sure it really happened, but it's interesting to think about now.

"The thing about that punt return that I remember is a clip that wasn't called. One of their guys clipped Bill Rudder, a fabulous defensive player, who in turn fell into two of our other guys who got hung up in the crash. That sprung their punt return man, who wasn't even their best one, on his way to the end zone.

"It might sound like sour grapes, but the clip made a difference. We didn't get a call on an important play."

It was a game of big plays, for sure, from the beginning, as recalled by Rutledge. He passed 80 yards to split end Wayne Wheeler for a touchdown on the opening play, setting the stage for fireworks.

"I think that play caught them by surprise," Rutledge said. "We'd been running the wishbone since 1971, mostly the same way, with the fullback running on the first play so we could see how each of our opponents would try to stop us. We opened it up in 1973. It was planned all week. We worked hard on it.

"But I had no idea we'd score so easily. Wayne Wheeler was so open on that play, at least 15 yards behind everybody, that I was sort of scared to throw the football. I aimed it like a dart. He caught it, ran a few steps, and walked into the end zone."

Alabama used more trickery that afternoon. For the first time in the wishbone era, Rutledge recalls, the Crimson Tide put a halfback in a slot behind the tight end.

"That was because it was Tennessee we were playing," Rutledge said. "Everybody knew Tennessee played reckless defense, ran people all over the place, got after us like wild men. So we did that to make Tennessee adjust to us, not us to them. It was a smart move by Coach Bryant and his staff. They prepared us well for that game."

The preparation included fiery talks during the week from assistant coach Ken Donahue, a Tennessee graduate who was at that time serving as defensive coordinator, and from trainer Jim Goostree, a Tennessee graduate.

"Coach Donahue and Coach Goostree always got us fired up for the games against Tennessee," Rutledge said. "It was obvious it meant a lot to them, as it did to Coach Bryant, and they let us know that every week.

"I particularly recall what Coach Goostree said. He'd go on and on about cocky Tennessee players and talkative Tennessee fans. He'd tell us about the history of the series, what it'd meant for so long to so many people, and he'd suggest we play at our best if we hoped to win.

"It usually took that against Tennessee and everybody else, especially during that era, when everybody seemed so riled up to play Alabama."

Rutledge seemed pumped up after his first pass that afternoon. "He was the most excited player I'd seen," said Kirk McNair, an Alabama assistant sports information director in 1973 and editor of *Bama*

Inside the Crimson Tide magazine. "I guess I was," Rutledge said. "It was a dream come true."

It was more. It made his brother look like a prophet.

Jeff Rutledge, who would later lead Alabama to a national championship as a quarterback, was a high school student in 1973. He was at the game, sitting in the upper deck at Legion Field.

"Just after the opening kickoff, I told the people seated around me that I thought Alabama would go for the bomb on the first play," he said. "Gary had told me about the first play the night before the game. You should have seen those folks after he passed that football to Wayne Wheeler. They thought I was a genius. I never did tell them who I was. I just let them leave thinking about my prediction."

The first pass was entertaining, as was most of the play performed on a stage of sorts covered with artificial turf. The final scene left the audience in shock.

48

1974
Alabama 28, Tennessee 6

JIM GOOSTREE HAS BEEN presented the game football three times after the University of Alabama has defeated Tennessee, his alma mater. The one he received on October 19, 1974, ranks as his most memorable.

The former Crimson Tide trainer had a major role in the 28-6 victory claimed by Alabama at Neyland Stadium in Knoxville.

"I was so happy after that victory that I did the 'Tennessee Waltz' in the dressing room and remembered listening to the song on *Dixieland Down South* as a kid," recalled Goostree, a native of Clarksville, Tennessee. "I could close my eyes after that victory and see Roy Acuff and the Smoky Mountain Boys performing. I could close my eyes and recall round-dancing and square-dancing at Dunbar Cave in the good old days.

"Now, more than anything, I can remember how Robert Fraley, a hardluck quarterback from [Winchester] Tennessee, contributed mightily to us beating Tennessee in 1974. His shoulders were banged up, even that afternoon, but he did quite a job in Knoxville.

"I remember how Coach Bryant was so pleased with Fraley playing so well in his home state."

Alabama was much stronger than Tennessee that year. That is obvious. The Crimson Tide resembled the Red Cross when it went into the game, with a multitude of injured players. But it solidly whipped the Big Orange.

"I look down this roster and see a lot of crippled people," Goostree said during the summer of 1986 while holding an Alabama press guide from 1974 that listed two dozen players listed as doubtful for the game. "Somehow we got the job done against great odds."

The long odds included playing with the top two quarterbacks, Gary Rutledge and Richard Todd, out of the game; the starting quarterback, Jack O'Rear, hobbled by a bad leg; and the only other available quarterback, Fraley, nursing a badly bruised toe.

Also, Alabama was playing on the heels of an 8-7 victory over a Florida State team that had lost nineteen consecutive games when it visited Tuscaloosa. No wonder Bryant passed out victory cigars to his players after the Crimson Tide used a deadly defense and an opportunistic offense to secure its fourth consecutive win over Tennessee.

A time of reckoning had passed.

"The team got together for a team meeting the Monday night before the game," said Mike Dubose, a senior end for Alabama in 1974. "We hadn't shown a lot of enthusiasm in recent weeks. You could've heard a pin drop during that team chat. The whole atmosphere changed with that gathering. A lot of people had doubts in the back of their minds about how well they'd play. That meeting turned things around for us."

Alabama went on to post an 11-1 record, losing its chance for a national championship with a 13-11 loss to Notre Dame in the Orange Bowl. It was a handsome turnaround.

Tennessee, meanwhile, rebounded to win five of its remaining six games, which included a 21-21 tie with Vanderbilt, to post a 7-3-2 record. The Volunteers defeated Maryland, 7-3, in the Liberty Bowl.

The happiest young man on The Third Saturday in October in 1974?

That one is easy to choose.

"It's a great feeling to beat Tennessee in Knoxville," Fraley said just after he rushed for 26 yards and completed three of five pass attempts for 41 yards. "Now, maybe I can go home without hearing all that static from the Tennessee people."

Alabama got the scoring under way in the second quarter. Willie Shelby ran 13 yards for a touchdown, and Danny Ridgeway kicked the extra point.

Tennessee cut the lead to 7-6 at halftime. Stanley Morgan made a dramatic 64-yard run for a touchdown. He was hit near the line of scrimmage by a Crimson Tide defensive halfback, bounced back from the collision, and outran the opposition to the end zone. The extra point kick failed.

Alabama began to dominate the game in the third quarter, with Shelby running 19 yards for a touchdown and Calvin Culliver running 30 yards for another. Ridgeway kicked the extra points.

In the fourth quarter Culliver scored the last touchdown, running six yards. Ridgeway kicked the extra point.

Alabama produced 375 yards rushing as a show of dominance.

The onslaught by Alabama was described by Marvin West in the *Knoxville News-Sentinel.* He wrote:

> If the horse is good enough, it doesn't matter who's riding.
>
> Aggressive Alabama, with subs at the throttle, leaped on Tennessee errors and slashed out with the deadly wishbone in an overwhelming triumph at Neyland Stadium.
>
> A record crowd of 74,286 on an otherwise perfect football day saw the unbeaten Tide tear up the Vols' meager offense and cash in turnovers for their sixth victory, fourth in a row over the Orangemen.
>
> Willie Shelby and Calvin Culliver, big-play running backs, got two touchdowns each for Alabama. The wishbone whipped out 425 yards. Tennessee totaled 182.
>
> It wasn't much of a contest after halftime. It wouldn't have been much before except Stanley Morgan, on a bounce-off play, fled 64 yards to score for the Vols. They made one other first down before intermission. They made five in the second half.

The tone was set in the early moments. After Alabama fumbled on its first possession, Tennessee had a first down at the Crimson Tide 15-yard line. Four plays netted three yards.

"It really didn't matter who played quarterback for Alabama," said Fraley, now an attorney in Orlando, Florida. "The way the defense was hitting and the line was blocking, anybody could have played and graded a winner in this one."

Still, after all these years, Fraley cherishes precious memories associated with Alabama scoring 21 points in the second half.

"There are a lot of things that made that game fun for me," said Fraley. "It was special, for sure, because the rivalry against Tennessee was a whole lot more important to me than was our rivalry against Auburn.

"It was a perfect setting. What a great stadium in which to play. The changing of the season from summer to fall. The excitement of the fans, who annually get ready for the game, and the respect each program has for the other, even during and after hard-fought games.

"And, I'd been recruited by Tennessee at a time when the Volunteers were in command in the series. One of their assistant coaches had told me I'd never win over them if I went to Alabama. We never lost. It wasn't a spite thing, because I respected Tennessee so much, but I got a lot of pleasure out of beating them so much.

"I've got one other treasured memory. Coach Bryant came back to visit with me on the bus ride to the airport in Knoxville after the game. He said, 'I guess this makes all those shoulder injuries worth it?' I don't remember my exact response, but I can tell you now that victory sure made all that pain much easier to take."

Fraley had hoped to start the game. Bryant had decided on O'Rear. For a while it looked like Pete Cavan, a halfback who had never played quarterback in a college game, would get the opportunity to open against Tennessee.

"Coach Bryant said later that he didn't start me because he wanted to ease some of the pressure," Fraley said. "I was pretty disappointed, actually, and then he had the gall to put me in there the first time on a third-down-and-three-yards-to-go play. Now, that's pressure.

"But my teammates rallied around me, probably because they knew how much the game meant to me, and we got a nice win."

It was an impressive Alabama show, as remembered by Rutledge and by Sylvester Croom, who started at center for the Crimson Tide that afternoon.

"We showed Tennessee the value of team offense and team defense," said Rutledge, who watched from the Alabama sideline.

"We just blew them out," said Croom. "We went straight at them. We walked down their gut."

What Alabama players did, as much as anything, was create grief for a former Crimson Tide player. It was the Monday afternoon after that game that Eugenia Battle, wife of the Tennessee coach, discovered that irate Big Orange fans had sent a moving van to their house.

"The thing I hated about that was the way a few sick people bothered Eugenia when she was eight months pregnant," Battle said. "I found out that day how tough she is.

"Wayne Stiles, one of our staff members, eased up to me at the office and said, 'Bill, did somebody send a moving van to your house?' He'd heard about it on the radio, of all places.

"I telephoned Eugenia. I asked her, 'How are you doing, honey?'

"'Has anything unusual happened today?'

"'No, everything is fine.'

"'Tell me, did somebody send a moving van to the house?

"'Yeah, but I just went out there and told them to leave, that it was a bad mistake.'"

There are no scars.

"That's life," Battle said. "We've forgotten it now. We both loved living in Knoxville. And, of course, I loved coaching at Tennessee."

49

1975
Alabama 30, Tennessee 17

THE TENNESSEE GAME PLAN was simple enough when the Volunteers went to Birmingham to play the University of Alabama on October 18, 1975: Make Richard Todd run the football.

Todd did—for 90 yards and three touchdowns! And the Crimson Tide made it five victories in a row over the Big Orange, 30-17, in front of an appreciative audience at Legion Field.

John Ward, radio voice of the Big Orange Network, noticed Todd's skill while sitting in the press box high above the playing field. "I always thought Coach Paul 'Bear' Bryant had a quarterback who was in control as an extension of him. To him, in the wishbone offense the quarterback was like the tailback in the single wing Tennessee used to run, the key man. He always had a great quarterback at his disposal.

"Bryant had a fabulous quarterback in Todd in 1975. He was another in a long list of great quarterbacks from Alabama.

"Todd was an extension of Bryant as a coach. You could see the coach in the quarterback. He was in charge. He was a splendid athlete. He got the job done against Tennessee.

"Of course, Alabama was doing a good job against everybody in the 1970s. What the Crimson Tide did under Bryant over a ten-year period was a greater dynasty than the New York Yankees.

"I kept up with it because people here were saying there was no way we could beat Alabama. They were saying Battle could not do it. I reminded them that nobody could beat them.

"They lost four conference games in ten years. Two of them were flukes. Look at the scores of those games from 1971 through 1980. Auburn blocked two punts in an unbelievable game to win 17-16. Ole Miss shocked them, 10-7, after intercepting a lateral and running it for a touchdown. Georgia beat them, 21-0, after the fans in Athens were so rowdy the Alabama players could not sleep the night before the game.

"Then, after Alabama won twenty-eight straight games, Mississippi State ended the streak with a 6-3 win in Jackson.

"That was the most unbelievable conference record in history. There were a lot of good teams then, including Tennessee, and Alabama kept winning.

"They had great players, wonderful talent, but not that much better than everybody else they played through a decade. It was a case of Bryant controlling the tempo of every game they played.

"Alabama definitely had control over Tennessee in 1975."

The Crimson Tide wishbone was rolling along in fine fashion. But it was the Tennessee defense "Sir Richard" recalled during the summer of 1986 at his home in Florence, Alabama.

"That defense took the pressure off our offense," Todd said about a unit that in 1975 limited Tennessee to 117 yards, an incredible 12 yards on 39 rushing attempts. "It was the best defense in the nation. They gave our offense the opportunity to put points on the scoreboard.

"They were terrific. Our offense literally wore people out, beat them down with a persistent attack, but our defense set us up."

The Alabama defense recorded ten sacks on Tennessee quarterbacks, four by end Leroy Cook, three by tackle Charley Hannah, and three by tackle Bob Baumhower. Because he won that statistical war, other members of the Crimson Tide defense had to buy Coca-Colas for Cook the week after the game.

"If you looked closely at those defensive guys now, you'd wonder if you're big enough to play today," said Robert Fraley, a senior quarterback at Alabama in 1975. "But, boy, they got after Tennessee that day. They knew how to play team defense. It was a classic Crimson Tide defensive performance."

Cook left Big Orange quarterback Randy Wallace with a memory after the final sack on the last play of the game. "You're a great athlete. You've got a great arm. It's a shame you didn't have time to use it."

Todd, meanwhile, used all of his skills.

"Richard Todd was a great athlete, even then, and he disrupted our game plan totally," said Bill Battle. "We did a good job making him keep the football on their triple option plays. But he did a better job deciding what to do with it after we forced him to run."

With Todd at the controls, Alabama was rolling toward another major bowl game. The Crimson Tide, 11-1 that season, capped its merriment with a 13-6 victory over Penn State in the Sugar Bowl, the first played in the Louisiana Superdome. He was the most valuable player in the game.

Tennessee was slipping badly, posting a 7-5 record for the season. Losing the fifth time in a row to Alabama did not help spirits much.

Marvin West wrote in the *Knoxville News-Sentinel* about the frustration among Big Orange people in 1975.

> Perhaps in time Tennessee will grow accustomed to losing to Alabama.
>
> It's now five in a row, and this one wasn't close.
>
> The Tide had a terrific performance, marred only by four fumbles, and smashed the Volunteers at windswept Legion Field. There seemed to be no question about it—just how much.
>
> Richard Todd, on his finest day, scored three touchdowns and offered up a scoring pass to tight end Jerry Brown. Bucky Berrey kicked a 44-yard field goal.
>
> Randy Wallace and Larry Seivers teamed up on the high jump play for Tennessee's score. It was a 29-yarder that looked like an interception until Larry transformed it into a touchdown.
>
> "That one hacked us off," said Tide linebacker Conley Duncan. "That's why we laid it on them there at the end. We've got this thing about no giving up touchdowns. They really shouldn't have done that."
>
> Alabama toyed with Tennessee in other departments. Rushing statistics tell one grim tale—318 yards for the Tide, 12 net yards for the Vols.

It was a beating, to say the least, and Battle remembers it as being hard to stomach.

"That was the year our team got off to a great start against a murderous schedule, then got banged up badly before we played Alabama," Battle said at his office in Atlanta. "We beat a great Maryland team opening up. We lost by a touchdown to a great UCLA team in a game that came down to who had the football last. We beat Auburn with a stirring comeback in the fourth quarter. We beat LSU by a couple of touchdowns.

"But during the open week after the Auburn game and in the LSU game, which is always hard-fought, we got five of our best players hurt.

"We'd been pointing at Alabama, getting ready for them in advance, which is the only time I ever did that. I called all of our people together, after programming our coaches, and told them that LSU was struggling, that I'd heard rumors they might be going to the wishbone offense as a last resort and that we might oughta work against it in preparation for them. In reality, I was getting a jump on preparations for a fine Alabama team.

"We were ready, too, at least mentally. Physically, we were crippled beyond belief. We had people hurt, [split end] Larry Seivers, [halfback] Stanley Morgan, [quarterback] Randy Wallace, [linebacker] Andy Spiva, and several others.

"We'd played well. But against Alabama we weren't playing with a full deck, not even close.

"And we know what happened. They just beat the hell out of us.

"That's when the press got rough on us. They were saying we wouldn't ever beat Alabama again, that the season was lost, that the good times were over. It was like somebody stuck a pin in a full balloon. All the air was out after that loss. No matter what I tried to do, I couldn't pump it back in."

50

1976
Alabama 20, Tennessee 13

Dᴵᴅ ᴀɴ ɪɴᴀʙɪʟɪᴛʏ ᴛᴏ defeat Alabama lead to Bill Battle's forced resignation as head coach at Tennessee following the 1976 season?

Most people think so.

Battle contemplated the question during the summer of 1986 at his sports licensing office in Atlanta. His conclusion?

"The biggest thing was not being able to beat Alabama and Auburn regularly enough, that's for sure," Battle said about the events that led to his resignation. "We were in those games almost every year, fighting both of them into the fourth quarter, but the folks in Knoxville didn't care that Alabama was wearing out almost everybody it played then. Close didn't count among Tennessee fans, which I won't fault.

"But, yeah, that's where the problem rested. We weren't winning over Alabama. In fact, we were losing several games in a row to them.

"Actually, the situation in Knoxville started swinging out of control after we lost to Alabama in 1974. Everybody started moaning and groaning. They were talking down our team while sitting in the stands at games. They were even telling our prospects visiting campus that we'd never win over Alabama.

"But we fought back that time.

"It got beyond my control in 1975, after Alabama beat us one week and North Texas State beat us the next week.

"And it didn't help that the next coach was standing in the wings. I understand how everybody always screams for the athletic director to fire the coach when things go badly. But there aren't many places where they already have the next coach picked like they did at Tennessee.

"As early as 1975, the local press was writing more about what John Majors and Pittsburgh were doing than what we were doing at Tennessee. It got worse in 1976."

Battle's last game against his alma mater came on October 16, 1976.

Alabama won, 20-13, in Knoxville. It was painful for all Tennessee fans because it marked the sixth straight loss for their team on The Third Saturday in October. The game seemed typical of the way the Big Orange was not quite good enough to win over the Crimson Tide.

Having a punt blocked to set up the second Crimson Tide touchdown added to the misery, or utter despair, the Volunteers felt.

Mike Kramer blocked Craig Colquitt's punt on the first possession of the third quarter with the score tied, 6-6. He had a broken wrist.

Kramer removed a cast from his left wrist just before Alabama went onto the field for pregame warmups. He had another cast put on his left wrist in the dressing room after the game.

That bit of doctoring was done under the supervision of Crimson Tide trainer Jim Goostree, a Tennessee graduate, who added much to the celebration Alabama players had by dancing for them "the hustle, the bustle, the twist, and the wrist," as he named them.

It was quiet in the Big Orange dressing room.

"I wish we were winners," said David Brady, a Tennessee tackle. "We want to be winners so badly. We hit with Alabama. I promise you we did.

"I did want to beat Alabama before I left this place. I got to get something else to tell my children about."

"I guess we embarrassed ourselves on national television," said Andy Spiva, a Tennessee linebacker.

Neither team flew particularly high that season.

Alabama had lost two games before it arrived in Knoxville. It finished with a.9-3 record. Tennessee posted a 6-5 record.

But Crimson Tide coach Paul "Bear" Bryant was pleased with his team's accomplishment in Neyland Stadium against Tennessee. He was so happy with the outcome, in fact, he announced he planned to give his players the following Sunday morning off from practice. He had worked his struggling team on Sunday several times earlier in the season.

Alabama did not secure its sixth straight win over Tennessee until the fourth quarter, when the Crimson Tide got the decisive touchdown after the game had been tied, 13-13, after three quarters. The winning touchdown came on a six-yard run by Calvin Culliver, with Bucky Berrey kicking the extra point.

The Crimson Tide went 79 yards for its final touchdown, solidifying its dominance in the series and making quarterback Jack O'Rear the man to remember. He gained 119 yards running the outside option in the wishbone offense.

"I think we turned the corner," Bryant said. "I think this one might turn us around."

The game certainly left Battle in a bad predicament. You can tell that by reading what Marvin West wrote in the *Knoxville News-Sentinel* about the game:

> Tennessee's Vols used to end up at the crossroads each year when they'd lose to Alabama. This time it's worse. They ran all the way to the depot and caught the wrong train.
>
> The 20-13 setback was especially bad because:
> 1. Tennessee fought hard and didn't have enough clout.
> 2. The Vols lost a tailback, Kelsey Finch.
> 3. Alabama isn't outstanding, just crusty.
> 4. There are tougher games to come.
>
> Bill Battle's up-and-down Orangemen were up enough, but giant errors led to their sixth straight loss to the Tide. A blocked punt cost a touchdown and motion penalties disrupted two drives.
>
> Almost as serious was the endless leak on defense. Tide quarterback Jack O'Rear ran keepers for 119 yards and one touchdown. The Vols had three plans for stopping O'Rear, but they didn't develop.
>
> The struggle of this unpredictable season is now at 3-3. Tennessee has not won a Southeastern Conference game, nor come very close.
>
> Before 82,417 on-hand observers and a national TV audience, the Vols offered Frank Foxx and Greg Jones as home-team heroes. Frank gained 131 yards and almost scored. Jones, middle linebacker, was in on 25 tackles.

Jimmy Gaylor kicked two field goals and topped off Bobby Emmons' two-yard touchdown rush. Tony Nathan broke for 11 yards and Alabama's first score. O'Rear flanked right and ran left for 15 and a touchdown. Calvin Culliver, switched from halfback to fullback, crashed seven yards for the final score with 5:39 left in the fight.

Alabama definitely intends to do some moving. Coach Paul (Bear) Bryant spoke of this victory giving his team direction. He said the Tide improved a lot in one week. He was really proud of the second half show of strength. And, he had deep feelings for one of his boys.

"I think Bill Battle is a great coach and class gentleman," said "Bear," in response to questions about the future.

The future was already taking place, it seems. A movement was under way to lure John Majors, who in 1976 was coaching a national champion Pittsburgh team, to Tennessee.

"He was already making speeches in East Tennessee," said the personable Battle, who, as successful as he was, had fought his last round against his alma mater.

Alabama was just too powerful, particularly on defense, which saved the winning streak for the Crimson Tide in 1976.

"Tennessee was always tough against us, particularly in Knoxville, but we sort of had the feeling that nobody would be good enough to beat us during that time at Alabama," said Bob Baumhower, a Crimson Tide senior defensive tackle in 1976, who was with the Miami Dolphins of the National Football League. "With the exception of the Auburn game, which was always it for Alabama players, the rivalry with Tennessee was top-of-the-line with us.

"It was obvious back then that they'd rather beat us than anybody else they played. In turn, that helped us prepare for them. We didn't take anything less than seriously when we got ready for Tennessee.

"I think the edges we had over them rested in talent and attitude. We had a lot of awesome players on defense. Tennessee was having trouble, in that regard, although they had good players. It's just that we went into every game thinking of it as a sin if people scored on us.

"We didn't blow away Tennessee in 1976, obviously, but we were good enough to win when it counted."

Battle remembers how that loss to Alabama prompted him to do something that made him feel good.

"The wolves were circling us the week after that loss," Battle said. "There were a lot of Tennessee people who'd quit on our program, when we were still fighting to save the season. I didn't appreciate that. I'd been attracted by Tennessee spirit. I didn't like prospects coming into my office after games and saying things like, 'Coach Battle, I can't come to Tennessee because your fans are pulling for you to lose games, not to win them.'

"So, the week after the Alabama game, I called a press gathering and blasted everybody. I told them I didn't think we should quit in the middle of the season, that it wasn't the Tennessee way. I told them I wanted them to quit being so negative, when the team was trying to remain positive.

"It came straight from the heart. I felt good about it."

So the change in coaches at Tennessee at the end of the 1976 season was not a surprise.

"I've never seen a more unrelenting demand for a change among fans," said Col. Tom Elam. "It's the people who get rid of coaches. The people were extremely demanding that year. They wanted Majors back on the Hill.

"Battle was a victim of circumstances. Majors had won a national championship at Pittsburgh in 1976. The demand was understandable. It was as strong as I can remember."

So was the urge among Tennessee fans for a victory over Alabama. They would be left wanting again the following season.

51

1977
Alabama 24, Tennessee 10

THEY WERE AFTER HIS hide in September.

They loved him in October.

Leading a University of Alabama football victory over Tennessee can help a Crimson Tide player like that.

Alabama quarterback Jeff Rutledge discovered as much in 1977, when he threw five interceptions in a loss to Nebraska, 31-24, and scored three times in a 24-10 win over Tennessee on October 15 in Birmingham.

"Our fans wanted to shoot me after that performance against Nebraska," Rutledge said at his house in Los Angeles. "They felt much better about me after we beat Tennessee.

"I did, too, because Alabama players could always count on Tennessee getting after us in an enthusiastic way."

Rutledge ran for two touchdowns and a two-point conversion against the Big Orange, which was playing for the first time under Coach John Majors. He added a touchdown pass to split end Ozzie Newsome.

The Crimson Tide led, 24-3, before Tennessee scored a field goal in the third quarter.

The touchdowns of four and nine yards by Rutledge, plus an extra point kick by Roger Chapman, enabled Alabama to secure a 16-3 halftime lead.

Chapman and Tennessee place-kicker Jim Gaylor had swapped field goals in the first quarter.

Rutledge padded the lead with a 30-yard touchdown pass to Newsome in the third quarter. He capped his scoring by running for the two-point conversion.

Tennessee scored its only touchdown in the third quarter, with Kelsey Finch catching a 13-yard pass from Joe Hough. Gaylor kicked the extra point.

The Crimson Tide running attack gained 347 yards. It was the seventh consecutive victory for Alabama over the Volunteers.

For Majors, who had led Pittsburgh to a national championship the previous season, it was a step to a new level on The Third Saturday in October. He had played admirably in the game as a tailback at Tennessee from 1954 through 1956. He was excited about coaching the Big Orange against the Crimson Tide.

"To think I was on the field with a Tennessee team coaching in the fabulous series, well, that was exciting to me," Majors said at his office at Stokely Athletics Center in Knoxville. "I was out there in an arena where great people had played, where some of the most memorable games in history had been staged, where championship teams had been molded, where All-Americans had been made, and where colorful stories had been developed. It was extremely special being a part of The Third Saturday in October again in 1977.

"We weren't winning or competing like we should have been when we got to that game that season, but there was always excitement when it came to playing against Alabama. I told our players how that game annually brings out the best in people, about the excitement of wearing the orange and white with the pride it should be worn with, how I didn't remember a year when a Tennessee team didn't give its best against the Crimson Tide.

"In 1977 we were trying to get back in step with Alabama. They had more talent than us. They had that confidence. They had great coaching, of course, with Paul "Bear" Bryant and his staff.

"Winning definitely breeds winning. They had it all going for them when I returned to Tennessee."

Rutledge agrees. The National Football League quarterback remembers Alabama being better in 1977 than voters in national polls thought.

JOHNNY MAJORS

Gᴀᴍᴇ 1: Tᴇɴɴᴇssᴇᴇ ᴄᴀᴍᴇ from behind late in the fourth quarter on Alabama and won, 14-9, in Knoxville.

Game 2: Tennessee dominated Alabama and won, 27-13, in Birmingham.

Game 3: Tennessee was outclassed by Alabama and lost, 20-0, in Knoxville.

Those were the first three Tennessee football games watched by John Majors. It is important to him that Alabama was the opponent.

So began the love affair Majors has for The Third Saturday in October, the day put aside each season for the playing of *the* game.

A lot of ,people admire the series.

Few people, if any, get as emotional about it as the Tennessee coach, who played tailback for the Big Orange from 1954 through 1956 and began leading the Volunteers against the Crimson Tide in 1977.

"I'd challenge anybody to show me a better series," Majors said. "Texas-Arkansas. Ohio State-Michigan. Nebraska-Oklahoma. Oklahoma-Texas. Notre Dame-Southern Cal. They're all great rivalries. But they're not any better than Tennessee-Alabama.

"The Third Saturday in October will always be special. I doubt we'll ever change the game to early or late in the season for the sake of football. There's just too much reverence involved in the series.

"The Tennessee-Alabama series has been treated with utmost respect for a long time, as it should be, because it's a classic rivalry that has it all. It's had great coaches. It's had great players. It's had great championship teams. It's had great games. It's had great significance.

"I've been involved with the series actively since I arrived at Tennessee as a freshman in 1953. I've played in games. I've coached in games. I'm certain of one thing: The rewards of being a part of the excitement of The Third Saturday in October— being there in the arena—are much greater than

the agony both programs have experienced from time to time.

"To this day, it's a thrill to play and coach in that game. It's always intense. It's been that way since the days of Bob Neyland coaching Tennessee and Wade Wallace coaching Alabama, maybe before then, because the general always said it was the most important game of the year for his teams.

"I'm sure of this: You've got to beat Alabama to have a chance to win the conference championship. You tell what kind of team you have when you play Alabama. Whether you are 11-0 or 2-9, the Alabama game will bring out the best and, maybe, the worst. But it always finds out who the men are.

"The great thing about that, one of the significant things about the Tennessee-Alabama rivalry, is I've seen teams that weren't very good rise up and play a little bit better than they were capable of playing, if there is such a thing, because of who they were playing against.

"Tennessee people feel that way.

"Alabama people feel that way.

"Even though young men are from New York and California, much less from Tennessee and Alabama, they get the feeling rather quickly.

"The color. The drama. The quality rivalry, which has never been known for its bad-mouthing, excuse-making, brawling, dirty play, and the like, has been, is at present, and will be in the future a special thing.

"Through the years I've encountered a lot of people who've played on The Third Saturday in October. And, to the man, they all say the same thing, that it's a great rivalry conducted with class and respect."

The introduction for Majors came when he was a child in Lynchburg, Tennessee. His father, Shirley Majors, the famous coach from the high school ranks

continued on next page

and Sewanee, told him about Tennessee and Alabama football.

By 1944 the future star tailback and coach had developed an appreciation, putting Tennessee and Alabama on par with a famous Army program that he was infatuated with.

"One of the first things I remember my dad talking about was seeing Beattie Feathers play for Tennessee in the 1930s," Majors said. "He used to talk about Beattie Feathers and John Cain of Alabama in the great kicking duel in Birmingham in the rain in 1932.

"I followed Vanderbilt early, because that was the closest program to Lynchburg, but the first teams I remember anything about were Army, my favorite, Tennessee, and Alabama in 1944. That was the first time Tennessee and Alabama made strong impressions on me. I followed them both.

"Dad came up [to Knoxville] from Lynchburg to watch Tennessee and Alabama on two occasions. I remember him coming back talking about the games.

"Then, during my sophomore year of high school, I got to come to Knoxville and watch Tennessee and Alabama play. That was in 1950. We drove up early the morning of the game with two adults, one of them a big Alabama fan, and I sat in the Tennessee student section.

"It was ,fantastic. I was overwhelmed. I'd heard about these great teams. I'd listened to them on the radio. And there I was, sitting in the stadium, as gratified as I could be.

"One of the more impressive things I remember about it was that beautiful Tennessee orange and that good-looking, deep Alabama red, which I have learned to get ready for and to dislike when we play them.

"To this day, it's always been a thrilling game to me. It's so significant to me, has been since 1950, when I saw the two spectacular teams play in Knoxville.

"I saw them play in 1951. I saw them play in 1952. I saw them on a snowy television set back home in 1953, when I was a Tennessee freshman, play to a scoreless tie in Birmingham.

"I've heard my dad talk about it. I've read about it. I've listened to it on the radio. I've seen it on television. I've played in it. I've coached in it.

"What a great thing The Third Saturday in October is for so many people, including me, and I'd still love to sit back and watch a game in which Alabama wears its crimson jerseys and Tennessee wears its orange jerseys."

That is a beautiful sight, one that has since been abolished by rules that mandate that one team be outfitted in white jerseys. But the color scheme—crimson clashing with orange—is implanted in the mind of a Tennessee man who has special respect and admiration for Alabama.

"We had a fine team that season," Rutledge said, "one deserving of the national championship. By the time we got around to whipping Ohio State in the Sugar Bowl, 35-6, we were polished.

"Tennessee, on the other hand, was not up to its usual standards. We caught them in a down cycle.

"But I remember how excited we got after that victory. Our dressing room was joyous. Coach [trainer Jim] Goostree and Coach [Ken] Donahue were particularly happy we beat them, being Tennessee graduates, and seeing them dance around the dressing room was always a highlight for us.

"We all loved beating the Volunteers. It never was like beating Auburn for me, since I was raised in Birmingham, but it was close. The series has always been a great one. I loved playing against Tennessee. I loved going to Alabama games against them when I was in high school.

"In fact, there was one year when I was being recruited, 1974, when I scheduled my official visit to Tennessee so I could be in Knoxville when Alabama played up there. I was happy when we won, too, although I was up there as their guest."

Rutledge conned Tennessee again in 1977. The passing quarterback became the running quarterback.

"I wasn't afraid to run with the football," Rutledge said, "and I'd had more experience doing that than people thought. But, honestly, it was a pretty rare happening when I did run. I'm sure Tennessee was surprised."

So was the Alabama coach, in a different way. He was surprised his team was streaking against an old rival.

"I never dreamed I'd see one team win seven straight games in this series," Paul "Bear" Bryant said in the dressing room after the game. "Frankly, they were tougher than I expected them to be. I am glad to get rid of them for another year."

His team steamrolled through the remainder of its schedule. Alabama, with an 11-1 record, finished second to national champion Notre Dame, which leaped from fifth place past the second-ranked Crimson Tide with a bowl game victory.

But nothing came cheaply for the men in crimson against the Big Orange.

"Our defense fought its tail off," said Majors. "I admired our defense. It never quit."

His team stumbled and finished with a 4-7 record in 1977. But the new coach in the series, who had played so well on The Third Saturday in October, cherished being part of the series again.

"This is a colorful series," Majors said after losing to Alabama in 1977. "Our people think it's the greatest of all the rivalries."

THAT OPINION considered, it seems incredible that Majors asked a favor of Bryant after Alabama defeated his first Tennessee team. But he did, requesting an opportunity to observe the Crimson Tide during practice three days after the game.

"Every time I got a chance I visited with people who had worked with Coach Bryant ," Majors said. "I wanted to pick their minds, like he'd done, I'm told, with people who had worked with Coach Bob Neyland. I even went to Tuscaloosa in 1964, when I was an assistant coach at Arkansas, to observe a few of his practices.

"So after we played in 1977, with an open date the next weekend, I called Coach Bryant and told him I'd like to come back to Tuscaloosa and watch his team work. I had to make a speech to the Tuscaloosa Quarterback Club that Tuesday night, so it was convenient for me.

"Coach Bryant said, 'Ah, Johnny, you won't learn anything watching us at practice.'

"I told him I just wanted to watch the tempo. I told him I knew we'd be coaching against each other some more, but that our game had already been played that season.

"He kept saying, 'Ah, you won't learn anything.'

"It was always hard to debate Coach Bryant, but I tried one more time.

"Finally, he said, 'Ah, okay, just come on down.'

"When I walked out on the practice field, he came down from his tower and greeted me. Then he took me up to his tower. We stood there for about two hours talking about everything, how he liked going home and cooking a steak with Mary Harmon, his wife, and, of course, about our series with them.

"Coach Bryant said Tennessee-Alabama is one of the best rivalries, that some of his best friends were Volunteers, Bob Neyland, Bowden Wyatt, Gus Manning, and others. We talked and talked about that. I didn't have the chance to observe much of his practice.

"Later, one of his top assistant coaches, Bill 'Brother' Oliver told me, 'Dadblame you, Johnny, Coach Bryant wouldn't let us use but one offense and one defense that day you came to practice. He limited us when we were out there trying to get ready for our next opponent.'

"Coach Bryant and I had what I considered a warm relationship. We visited a lot at coaching conventions. About a month before he died, I visited with him in his hotel suite in San Francisco. He started talking about Alabama-Tennessee games, as well as other games at other places, and he went on for more than two hours. He even had dinner sent up to his suite. It was one of the more enjoyable occasions in my life."

52

1978
Alabama 30, Tennessee 17

HO HUM. WAS IT just another University of Alabama football victory?

Nope. That was not the case on October 21, 1978, when the Crimson Tide went to Knoxville to claim a 30-17 win over Tennessee at Neyland Stadium.

On the field Alabama rolled up its sleeves and zapped the Volunteers in a contest that served as a launching pad for Crimson Tide aspirations for a national championship, eventually realized after a Sugar Bowl victory over Penn State.

Off the field in their dressing room, Alabama players behaved like children, showing that an eighth consecutive win over Tennessee meant more to them than students of the grand series had reason to believe.

It was an *Animal House* scene.

There was linebacker Barry Krauss, defensive tackle Byron Braggs, defensive end E. J. Junior, defensive halfback Don McNeal, and linebacker Rich Wingo throwing themselves onto the floor while singing disco-like music: "Shout, take it a little higher . . . Shout, take it a little lower . . . Shout. . . ." At one point in the display of happiness, their heads formed a star-like cluster on the floor.

"We picked up the routine watching the *Animal House* movie," said Wingo, who became a linebacker for the Green Bay Packers of the National Football League. On the The Third Saturday in October in 1978, he led his group of singers while wearing a pair of sunglasses.

"Most of us saw that movie at least five times. We loved it. And we loved beating Tennessee. So what better way was there to celebrate?"

"Do the dead bug, Rich," Braggs suggested to Wingo in the dressing room. Wingo responded by falling to the floor, rolling over onto his back, and frantically kicking his legs and waving his arms.

The cigars also were present, the result of the continuation of an Alabama tradition after wins over its bitter rival.

"Coach Bryant gave everybody a cigar," said Wingo. "I recall him walking around the dressing room and telling us it was time to smoke a stogie, that victories in Knoxville deserved such reward."

Victory was particularly sweet for Alabama that day because the Crimson Tide was struggling as it moved toward Knoxville. While the record was outstanding, 6-1 after early season games with Washington, Missouri, Nebraska, and triumphant Southern Cal, the team had developed a lifeless demeanor.

"We were dead, but now we are alive," Steadman Shealy shouted after quarterbacking Alabama, after Jeff Rutledge had started. "God has blessed this team today. He has granted us the chance to live."

After Wingo, the most energetic man in the Alabama dressing room was trainer Jim Goostree. A Tennessee graduate, he did his "UT fast-step" dance to the cheers of Crimson Tide players.

"You couldn't very well call it the 'Tennessee Waltz,' because it was too fast and the music wasn't right," Goostree said when describing his performance. "It was just my way of celebrating another wonderful victory over the Vols.

"This is the most excited I've ever been after a win over Tennessee up here. The rivalry is traditional. An Alabama man knows he is expected to be at his best against Tennessee. Today our players accomplished that, all of them."

Tim Travis, a tight end who scored two touchdowns on reverse runs, said, "Beating Tennessee in Knoxville is probably the greatest thrill I'll have as a player. I'm proud to have contributed so much, because I've heard for a long time the importance of us coming up here and winning."

Tennessee, which dropped to 1-3-1 with the defeat, had its fans at a feverish pitch for the game. The night before the game, during a wild pep rally on Cumberland Avenue, Volunteers became riotous to the point that several turned over a University of Alabama van that ventured into the business district. On game day, 85,436 fans, then the second largest in Neyland Stadium history, watched in horror as the Crimson Tide established a 30-3 lead in the third quarter and waltzed to victory.

Bryant remembered the game in 1982. "Before the game started, I was very much concerned about crowd noise," he said. "I'd heard all week how their fans were going to make a lot of noise when we had the ball. And they did until we took control of matters.

"I think we beat them convincingly that day, but it was still exciting, as all Alabama-Tennessee games are to me. I recall being relieved getting out of that place. The setting was typical for our games with them."

The Crimson Tide quieted the throng.

Alabama gained control for keeps with 17 points in the third quarter. Tennessee saved some face with 14 points in the fourth quarter.

Travis got it started for Alabama with a four-yard touchdown run in the first quarter. Alan McElroy kicked the extra point. Shealy made it 13-0 with a 15-yard run for another Crimson Tide touchdown in the second quarter.

Tennessee fans developed some hope in the second quarter when Alan Duncan kicked a 27-yard field goal. But Big Orange hope was fleeting.

Alabama put the game out of reach in the third quarter with an awesome display. McElroy kicked a 41-yard field goal. Steve Whitman ran six yards for a touchdown, and Travis ran nine yards for another. McElroy kicked both extra points.

Two touchdown passes by David Rudder provided Tennessee fans with something to cheer about in the fourth quarter. The first went for six yards to Hubert Simpson. The second went for nine yards to Reggie Harper. Duncan kicked both extra points. But the Big Orange rally did nothing to subdue a Crimson Tide that was suddenly living up to expectations.

Alabama had opened the 1978 season ranked number one in both national polls. The Crimson Tide had also started play with a somewhat boastful disposition, but its pride was shattered when Southern Cal arrived in Birmingham to claim a 24-14 victory. The victory over Tennessee lifted the Crimson Tide to a number three national ranking and set the stage for a fruitful conclusion to a national championship season.

"We'd done a lot of talking early that season," Wingo said, "when we should have been playing football. We had some tough games early, and the loss to Southern Cal was painful. But that loss also opened our eyes. We bounced back. When we went to Knoxville to play Tennessee, we knew it was time to either put up or shut up.

"We answered our critics that day. I'll remember the Tennessee game as the time we shut our mouths and went to work. We just rolled up our sleeves and slugged it out with them. It was that day that the national championship chase really started for us."

The game with Tennessee was ideal tonic for Alabama, which posted an 11-1 record.

"There's something psychological about playing Tennessee," said Murray Legg, an Alabama safety in 1978. "There's something about Tennessee orange that makes Alabama turn mean. It was that way for us in 1978. I honestly think it'll always be that way."

That viewpoint is shared by people at Tennessee.

"So we lost another one to Alabama," said Craig Puki, a Tennessee linebacker as the Volunteers posted a 5-5-1 record in 1978. "Our turn will come soon. I'll never quit thinking that Tennessee can beat Alabama. Someday that's gonna happen again."

It was not to be that year.

But Marvin West, in the *Knoxville News-Sentinel,* found consolation in Tennessee winning the final quarter. His game story reflected as much.

> It was really just another Tennessee loss to Alabama, a record eighth in an unholy row, but there were some little diamonds in the wreckage.
>
> It doesn't help the won-loss record, but the gutty Orangemen won the fourth quarter, 14-0, a stinging blow to Tide pride.
>
> Alabama did win the game, before 85,436, on sunswept Shields-Watkins Field, first leaves of autumn swirling, pageantry and tradition on a peak.
>
> Tennessee coach John Majors thought the best team won, but he spotted "positive points" in Tennessee effort.
>
> "We had more fight from start to finish than at any time this year," said John.
>
> Alabama had a host of heroes.

Goostree, now an Alabama assistant athletic director, said a picture is worth a thousand words when describing what happened on

The Third Saturday in October in 1978. "All you have to do is look at the cover of this press guide to understand how Alabama beat Tennessee in 1978. Here is Marty Lyons. Here is Jeff Rutledge. Here is Rich Wingo. Here is Barry Krauss. Here is Tony Nathan. All of these guys were good enough to make it to the NFL.

"And, of course, that was a strange blend of talent. We had some zany characters, like Wingo and Krauss, and we had some straight guys, like Rutledge and Nathan. Some were carefree. But all of them worked hard.

"The 1978 team, I suppose, pointed out more than any of the others that you could work hard to win and have fun at the same time."

53

1979
Alabama 27, Tennessee 17

STEVE WHITMAN SAYS HE was worried Paul "Bear" Bryant had lost his sanity on October 20, 1979.

It was that day Alabama, with Whitman playing fullback, defeated Tennessee, 27-17, in one of the strangest games ever played between the Crimson Tide and the Volunteers.

Tennessee, which was attempting to avoid its ninth consecutive loss to Alabama, led the Crimson Tide, 17-7, at halftime. At one point it had been 17-0.

"Coach Bryant came into the dressing room at halftime that day clapping his hands," Whitman said. "And he said, 'Men, we've got Tennessee right where we want them.' I thought he had lost it. I honestly thought Coach Bryant thought we had 17 points and they had 7. But he added, 'If you come back and win this game, nobody in the country will doubt that you deserve to be number one. If you come back and win today, I'll believe that you have what it takes to win a national championship this season:

"We tore down the door to get back onto the field for the second half. Coach Bryant had challenged us."

Instead of becoming unraveled in the face of adversity, after being whipped in the first half, Alabama held together like glue, made a few vows, said a prayer, and went back into battle. The result was a stirring victory that propelled the Crimson Tide to an unbeaten season capped by a second consecutive national championship.

"I've never seen a team make a comeback like that against Tennessee," Bryant said, reflecting in 1982 on a victory treasured by Alabama fans. "It has happened many times against other teams, but not against Tennessee.

"Do I recall halftime that day? Sure, and I remember that our players didn't seem rattled. That was a good sign. They knew what had to be done. I think they realized they were about to be tested. I think they passed that test with flying colors. It set the tone for the rest of the year."

The star for Alabama was junior quarterback Don Jacobs, who spelled starting quarterback Steadman Shealy.

"The first half had been terrible," said Jacobs. "We were struggling for anything to build momentum on, a first down, a fumble recovery, anything. Coach Bryant was real cool at halftime. He put a challenge before us. We challenged ourselves, then as everybody knows, we went out and whipped their butts."

Statistics tell the story of The Third Saturday in October in 1979 as well as the scoreboard that flashed the unbelievable at Legion Field in Birmingham. Alabama had 235 yards in offense during the second half, after getting 161 yards during the first half. Tennessee, meanwhile, gained only 81 of its 220 yards during the final two quarters, and had only three yards running.

"At halftime, [defensive halfback] Don McNeal jumped up and told everybody not to quit," said E. J. Junior, an Alabama defensive end. "And I was sitting there thinking there is no way any of us would quit, that Alabama players aren't raised that way."

Then Alabama players bowed their heads.

"Just before we went onto the field for the second half, E. J. Junior, [middle guard] Warren Lyles and I got together and prayed," said David Hannah, an Alabama defensive, tackle. "The Lord was good enough to help us win. It was not by us that we won, but by Him."

For whatever reasons Alabama won, 77,665 fans saw a brutal show, a battle reflected by the comments of Jacobs, who took many licks from Tennessee linebacker Craig Puki.

"Craig Puki showed a lot of class that day," Jacobs said. "He was a great player, who made life miserable for me much of the game. I think the relationship we had that day kind of reflects what Alabama-Tennessee games are about.

"When Puki hit me the first time, he like to have killed me. My chin strap was on my nose, my teeth were rattling. So what did he do? He reached down, took my hand, lifted me to my feet and patted me on the fanny. On the way back to the huddle, I thought, 'Man, is this what I have to go through all afternoon?' It was never easy against Tennessee, although we beat them every time we played them, but it was always classy."

It was understandable in 1979 that Tennessee players and coaches wondered if maybe they deserved to win.

"We should have won," said Brad White, a Tennessee defensive tackle. "What happened, I'll never know."

Perhaps John Majors, the Tennessee coach, did know.

"Alabama won the ball game, but we won the effort," Majors said. "We played shoe-to-shoe with the best football team in the nation. We played with a lot of confidence, which is great.

"I've never been prouder of a football team's effort than I was today. I'm very disappointed because of the loss, but I'm also proud.

"We had our chances to win. It's a tribute to Alabama that they came back on us like they did.

"Gosh dog, this is a classic rivalry, this Alabama-Tennessee thing, and I'm hoping our people saw something today that'll make them want to fight until the end in future games against them. That's little consolation right now, but I'm proud of our kids, and I'm encouraged about the future."

Alf Van Hoose, sports editor of the *Birmingham News,* was left to ponder two questions when writing about the Crimson Tide victory:

> Going into that famous third Saturday in golden October, the popular question was "how much?"
>
> Twenty-one minutes into Dixie's greatest football series, the question became "how?"
>
> Both mysteries involved Alabama, No. 1 team in the land, defending king of the college game.
>
> Paul Bryant's poised Crimson Tide found the second answer. The first one became academic, of no importance.
>
> Blanked, behind by 17 points to a Tennessee team reaching beyond itself toward a shocking drama, Alabama dug deeper into pride and performance and relentlessly cut the heart from the never-quitting Vols.

Alabama won 27-17.
It was closer than that.

It was, as Tennessee fans boasted, the only real scare Alabama had while marching toward a national championship.

Junior, now a linebacker With the St. Louis Cardinals of the National Football League, remembered there was reason for prayer in the Alabama dressing room. On The Third Saturday in October in 1979, he was concerned that the Crimson Tide was losing its mastery.

"Tennessee was definitely getting better," Junior said. "They were going too fast to suit me. They were closing the gap on us. From then on, I knew it'd take Alabama sixty minutes of football to beat the Volunteers. I thought we'd be in for a bloodletting the next year in Knoxville."

That stood to reason.

It was also apparent by then that Alabama would add salt to the Tennessee wound two weeks after it defeated the Volunteers. On that day, with a clubbing of Mississippi State, the Crimson Tide claimed its twenty-first consecutive Southeastern Conference victory.

That was a record.

The previous record had been established by Tennessee teams from 1937 through 1940. Interestingly, that Big Orange streak came to an end when Alabama defeated the Volunteers, 9-2, on October 18, 1941.

But that streak took place a long time ago.

Nine straight defeats at the hand of Alabama were more troublesome to Tennessee people.

"I remember our loss to them in 1979 significantly," Majors said. "We jumped out front. We had chances to put them away.

"Leading 17-7 just before halftime, we passed to Anthony Hancock over the middle. Jimmy Streater hit him right in the hands with the ball. He was behind the secondary. But he dropped the ball.

"That would've put the final nail in their coffin.

"Then they got a fumble recovery right after we got an interception on the first series of the second half. They got the ball back just like that. That was probably the biggest play in the game.

"The remainder of the second half, with Don Jacobs at quarterback, they ran their big fullback, Steve Whitman, right at us. We were down to our fifth-best nose man. They just hammered it out, busted up our confidence. They wore us down. They got away from their fancy stuff and went back to their bread and butter. We couldn't slow them down.

"They had superior talent. Their depth, confidence, and talent wore us down. They just took over."

The scoring indicates that.

Tennessee got two touchdowns in the first quarter. Jimmy Streater passed 11 yards to Phil Ingram for the first and ran three yards for the second. Alan Duncan kicked both extra points. Duncan kicked a 45-yard field goal to give Tennessee a 17-0 lead in the second quarter.

Shealy passed 33 yards to Tim Travis for a touchdown late in the second quarter. Alan McElroy kicked the extra point.

Major Ogilvie ran one yard for an Alabama touchdown early in the third quarter, with McElroy kicking the extra point. Then Ogilvie ran six yards for a touchdown, with McElroy kicking the extra point that gave the Crimson Tide a stunning 21-17 lead entering the last quarter.

Jacobs iced the victory with a 13-yard touchdown run.

A pro-Crimson Tide crowd breathed a sigh of relief.

Alabama made its rousing comeback against a Tennessee team that posted a 7-5 record en route to an invitation to the Bluebonnet Bowl.

They had a great team," Majors said. "We didn't have the stuff. It was very disappointing, but we had the weaker team, no doubt about that. It would've been a great upset. It almost went our way, but you don't win Tennessee-Alabama games with almost."

John Ward recalls the dramatic comeback by Alabama after Tennessee should have taken a 17-point lead into the dressing room for the halftime break.

"It should have been 24-7 at halftime," Ward said. "We had Anthony Hancock wide open behind the Alabama defensive secondary for a touchdown pass from Jimmy Streater just before halftime. He had the football in his hands. He was going to score. He was absolutely gone. It was gonna be six points. He dropped the football.

"I always thought we would have won had we gone up by 24-7. It probably would have been impossible for Alabama to come back.

"But with Bryant at the controls, Alabama had a chance to come back. As I have said many times, he almost always had something up his sleeve. As it was, Jacobs had a great second half. We floundered from there on."

That helped along what is remembered as the Great Comeback.

54

1980
Alabama 27, Tennessee 0

WHAT IF TENNESSEE'S SPLIT end Anthony Hancock had been able to hold on to a long pass from quarterback Steve Alatorre in the end zone during the early moments of the first quarter?

At Neyland Stadium in Knoxville in front of 96,748 fans and a national television audience, Alabama defeated Tennessee, 27-0. The victory on October 19 was the tenth straight for the Crimson Tide over its bitter Southeastern Conference rival.

With television cameras running and about ten thousand Alabama fans cheering, the Crimson Tide built a 17-0 halftime lead and played terrific rain-aided defense to escape a trap many Tennessee faithful thought too sure to fail.

The Tennessee spirit during pregame hours in 1980 was remembered by John Ward, the television and radio voice of the Big Orange. "They had a pep rally in a large parking lot down by the river on campus," Ward said. "I went to it with Coach John Majors. We got up on a flatbed truck. It was unbelievable. Everybody was up, definitely, and it was a loud and large pep rally.

"Tennessee people really thought we would win that year. We had drilled Auburn after losing close games to Georgia and Southern Cal. They thought we really had a shot that year.

"We were never in it once play got under way.

"When the Hancock pass floundered, the high was gone, with Alabama taking control. We got drilled. It was wishful thinking."

All that happened on Saturday.

"I honestly think this game was won Wednesday night, when Coach Bryant made an inspiring talk to our team," said Don Jacobs, an Alabama senior quarterback, who a few minutes earlier had led his nationally number one-ranked team to victory on a puddled artificial surface. "He told us the difference between winners and losers, how they react in all situations. He told us that winners always find a way to reach their goals, no matter how tough the challenge, and he told us that he considered us winners."

To which E. J. Junior, an Alabama senior defensive end that season, said, "Coach Bryant really got to us with that talk. He was so emotional that we all understood how much he wanted to win over Tennessee. I honestly think we would have won the game 40-0 had it been played Wednesday night."

To which Byron Braggs, an Alabama senior defensive tackle that season, said, "When we arrived here and saw all this orange, I honestly thought we were in for a blood-letting. It was, after all, Alabama and Tennessee, and that feeling runs deep. But, you know, I honestly think Coach Bryant took away any home advantage they had with his pep talk Wednesday night. It was as if it was our stadium, our show, our game to win."

The victory was the twenty-seventh straight for Alabama, which raised its season record to 6-0. It was not, said Bryant, the result of his motivational magic.

"We had a little meeting Wednesday night, sure, but we always have a little meeting that night," Bryant said in 1982. "Yes, the meeting was a little longer than usual. No, I'll never tell you what I said to the team, because that's private. You don't tell people what you tell your wife when you go to bed with her, do you? Give credit to our players. They won themselves a terrific victory.

"You never can tell what might happen in an Alabama-Tennessee game, particularly one played in Knoxville, where their fans help them so much, but I had a gut feeling about this one. I could tell all week that we were anxious to play this game."

Hence, Alabama totally dominated the game, as expressed by Wayne Hester, a former sports editor for the *Anniston* (Ala.) *Star:*

Great football teams are made in Knoxville on The Third Saturday in October.

If Alabama wasn't a great one when it rolled into Neyland Stadium here Saturday, it was a great one when it rolled out, and a record crowd of 96,748, plus millions more who watched on ABC-TV, couldn't deny it.

The Crimson Tide played its best game since last year's Sugar Bowl rout of Arkansas, and thoroughly beat and embarrassed the Tennessee Vols, 27-0.

"Bear" Bryant's coaching made the game seem slightly unfair.

Alabama's offense, normally dull but effective, showed a few new wrinkles Saturday because Bryant believed a little more was needed to knock off the fired-up Volunteers. The result was a game plan that included the shotgun formation, halfback pass, the old flea-flicker [pass] and a shuffling of Alabama quarterbacks to execute the game plan. •

"Alabama did it all, and did it with uncharacteristic flair on offense. Meanwhile, its defense reemphasized its might by holding the Vols' highly regarded offense to a mere 22 yards rushing, 37 yards passing and 59 yards total. Bryant said it was the best defensive performance he'd ever seen.

Even the singing in the Alabama dressing room was good.

"We don't give a damn about the whole state of Tennessee," sang the players, and then, "Defense! Offense!" And, finally, "Ten in-a-row!"

But never have so many Tennessee fans been so quiet.

Alabama got four field goals from Korean-born Peter Kim, a school record for one game, touchdowns from halfback Major Ogilvie and quarterback Ken Coley, and a two-point conversion pass from Jacobs and Ogilvie.

Tennessee got nothing except bruises.

"It's the most disappointing and humiliating loss of my career," said Alatorre. "Alabama just whipped us, physically pounded us. What else can be said?"

Reggie Harper, a Tennessee tight end in 1980, tried to add something, "Alabama's been a winner for so long that I guess they just know what to do. That was definitely the case today. We honestly thought we could beat them. They obviously had other ideas about that."

Alabama was a winner, as ordered by its coach in a speech that had wisdom and a lot of clout.

"That talk Coach Bryant made," said Braggs, "was about as subtle as a nail going through your head."

The Crimson Tide was likewise while marching through Knoxville.

Marvin West of the *Knoxville News-Sentinel* noticed Alabama power. The day before the game he had suggested that Tennessee might be ready to end its drought. His account of the action the day after the game read to the contrary:

> Stop the music. Pour out the punch. The party is over.
>
> Alabama took all the fun out of football. The Tide tore up Tennessee. It was a terrible whipping. The Vols went a half without a first down, got five after intermission. They rushed and they rushed for a stirring total of 22 yards. Passing was dangerous,.
>
> Since the romp over Auburn, waiting for this opportunity was fun. The Vols were improving. Enthusiasm bobbled. Maybe this was going to be the time and the place.
>
> When it finally got here, the day was a disaster. Tennessee fans, most of the record 96,748 at tradition-rich Neyland Stadium, trudged away wet and wounded. Some cursed. This once-great rivalry is ridiculous, a broken record.

Ten straight. Unbelievable.

"This is where I came in," said a Tennessee fan as he left the stadium that rainy afternoon in 1980.

"We'll get them," said his friend. "We'll build more seats."

"That's all we've got," said the disgruntled fan, "a bunch of seats."

Kirk McNair, an Alabama assistant sports information director in 1980, recalled hearing another Tennessee fan say something significant that afternoon in the rain.

"The guy screamed at Coach Bryant as the teams left the field," McNair said. "He said, 'Just two more years, Bear.' He knew Coach Bryant was nearing mandatory retirement age."

It was a time of frustration at Tennessee. That was expressed during the summer of 1986 by Tim Irwin, a Big Orange senior tackle in 1980 who went on to a stellar career with the Minnesota Vikings of the National Football League. "It was a frustrating series for me," said Irwin, "because we never beat them in my five years at Tennessee. If there is one thing I would change about my college days, it would be to beat them. Undoubtedly, it was the biggest game we played each year.

"I think we might have developed a mental block against them. They had great teams, first, and I think them having Coach Bryant and Coach Ken Donahue had something to do with it. Our confidence level was down."

But Tennessee coach John Majors, who lost for the fourth time in as many tries against Alabama in 1980, said during the summer of 1986 that he saw the Big Orange coming back that season.

The Crimson Tide finished with a 10-2 record.

Tennessee finished with a 5-6 record.

"That was a season that could have been for us," Majors said. "I definitely could see an upturn in our program, although the record wasn't good, because we had some talent.

"That Alabama team was one of the best defensively that I've ever had a team face. It was one of the finest defensive teams I've ever seen.

"So I'm not stupid enough to say we would've beaten them had Anthony Hancock scored on our first possession. That's the kind of thing you can't predict, although one play can make a difference.

"But I remember them scoring twice in the span of three or four minutes just before halftime to turn a tight game into something different.

"In the second half, their defense dominated us. I don't think we made a first down until either late in the third quarter or the first series of the fourth quarter. Their defense was that good.

"The only other thing I remember is it was raining like cats and dogs, which prompted Coach Bryant to say something I thought was humorous. He said, 'When I came out for the second half and it was pouring down rain, I sort of felt sorry for ol' Johnny.'

"Dadblame his time. 'Felt sorry for ol' Johnny.' That was his diplomatic way of saying they were more than happy to whip our butts."

55

1981
Alabama 38, Tennessee 19

ALAN GRAY LEARNED DURING his University of Alabama football playing career to take words spoken by Coach Paul "Bear" Bryant to heart.

So, said Gray, that is why he became the unsuspected star of a 38-19 Crimson Tide victory over Tennessee on October 18, 1981.

"On Tuesday night before that game, on Saturday afternoon, Coach Bryant told us that we had to beat Tennessee, Gray said, recalling his most treasured performance as a Crimson Tide player. "He told us that we needed to win over Tennessee for our children, our grandchildren, our parents, our grandparents, and for everybody else remotely interested in the Alabama program. He said it has always been important to beat Tennessee, and he said that since Alabama had won ten straight games in the series, nobody really realized the significance of our battles with them.

"I think Coach Bryant was right about everything he said. I even sensed before the game that some of our younger players failed to realize the significance of the game. But, somehow, it all fell into place for us. We got off to a fast start in the game and made it number eleven in a row against them.

"And, as you might suspect, I remember thinking after the game that Coach Bryant was the happiest man in the stadium."

That, of course, was a dressing room point of view. Outside the Crimson Tide dressing quarters at Legion Field in Birmingham that day stood a man, a happy dad, wearing a smile as broad as the Alabama margin of victory.

Win one for the Buff?

"This is the second time Alan has given me a great birthday present on the football field," Buff Gray said as he stood among a multitude of Alabama fans. "Once in high school in Tampa he quarterbacked his team to a victory over a powerhouse. But this is the one I like the best. All of my prayers have been answered. This is one proud moment for Alan and the rest of us."

As Alabama fans rejoiced, Tennessee fans might have left Birmingham wondering what shining star would come to the rescue of the Crimson Tide in the 1982 game at Knoxville. They knew that many times during a decade of losing to Alabama, an unexpected hero, many times a quarterback, had emerged to haunt them.

In 1981 it was Gray, whose angelic looks and willingness to quote passages from the Bible must have seemed terribly deceiving to Big Orange supporters.

Two weeks before the game, Gray was considered a fourth-team quarterback, a young man who seemed destined to play out his uneventful five-year career as a holder for placement kicks. But on a beautiful Third Saturday in October, he became the second coming of Robert Fraley, the quarterback who had come seemingly from nowhere to help Alabama beat Tennessee in 1974 at Knoxville.

"Yes, I remember that game," Gray said to reporters after he led Alabama to its most splendid offensive first half of what had otherwise been an uneventful season. "I watched it on television. I remember hearing how all of the Alabama quarterbacks were hurt except him, that he had to do the job against Tennessee.

"And I also remember how we got behind Tennessee, 0-17, two years ago [in 1979] before Don Jacobs came in to save the day for us [in another victory].

"Well, let me tell you that I am not sure how this game ranks with those other two, but I know I had more fun playing today than I ever have.'

Gray had only 25 yards rushing on seven carries, and he completed only five of eight passes for 90 yards. But he was outstanding directing the Alabama triple-option offense to the point that his first collegiate touchdown pass, an 8-yard completion to split end Jesse

Bendross 21 seconds before halftime, lifted the Crimson Tide to an astonishing 28-0 lead.

Alabama scored 13 points in the first quarter. Peter Kim kicked a 31-yard field goal. Jeff Fagan ran one yard for a touchdown. Kim kicked the extra point. Kim kicked a 32-yard field goal. The Crimson Tide added 15 points in the second quarter. Linnie Patrick ran 10 yards for a touchdown, and Joe Carter ran for the two-point conversion. Gray passed to Bendross for a touchdown, and Kim kicked the extra point.

Tennessee scored first in the second half. Willie Gault caught a 75-yard touchdown pass from Steve Alatorre. Fuad Reveiz kicked the extra point. Kim kicked a 29-yard field goal for Alabama. Bart Krout caught a 16-yard touchdown pass from Paul Carruth for another Crimson Tide touchdown. Kim; kicked the extra point.

Tennessee got two touchdowns in the fourth quarter to end the scoring. Doug Furnass ran 28 yards for the first. Alatorre ran 18 yards for the second. The Big Orange managed only 85 yards rushing.

"Alan Gray played extremely well," Bryant said. "I was proud of him. Throughout his career, he had been a man in waiting. His chance came. He made the best of it. He had a tough game placed in his lap for the first time and he did beautifully."

Thus, the power of the written word comes into play.

"My fiancée and I were reading the Bible a few nights ago," Gray said while reflecting on the victory. "She pointed out a verse to me that said, 'God blesses us if we fear him: It took a while for that to sink in, but I found strength in it. I know there are quarterbacks with stronger arms, more speed, and faster mechanics than me. I know I have a lot of shortcomings. God helped me overcome them.'"

The victory was especially pleasing to anybody associated with the Alabama program, because it lessened the pain associated with an agonizing season. Oh, the Crimson Tide did well enough in the record department, 9-2-1 after a loss to Texas in the Cotton Bowl, but a rash of disciplinary problems dimmed the glory associated with Bryant becoming the winningest coach in collegiate history.

Bryant accomplished that feat with a victory over Auburn in the final game of the regular season, his 315th win, dropping Amos Alonzo Stagg to second place.

Tennessee posted an 8-4 record including a win over Wisconsin in the Garden State Bowl, which was improvement. The Volunteers spent the summer thinking about another loss to Alabama, as well as remembering their proud tradition.

"This game, this loss, hurts a lot," said Reggie White, a Tennessee defensive tackle in 1981. "But we love each other on this team. This is still Tennessee."

The frustrations were growing, as were Alabama victories over the Volunteers.

"It hurts me to lose to anybody, but especially Alabama," said Steve Knight, a Tennessee offensive guard in 1981. "When I was in high school in Virginia, I always compared our teams to Tennessee teams, and I always dreamed about us beating Alabama. We even had a high school rival that played like Alabama, and they had a coach with about two hundred wins. I always made the comparison. I had Tennessee blood in me even back then."

That lament had many verses as the Tennessee faithful again licked their wounds.

Bryant, who raised his Alabama coaching record against Tennessee to 16-6-2 with the victory, after it was 5-6-2 in late October 1970, basked in the glory of another triumph and warned his legion of fans about the future.

"This is truly incredible," Bryant said the day after his team had defeated the Volunteers. "I didn't think the day would come when Alabama would win eleven in a row over Tennessee. But I know, and everybody else knows, that this streak can't go on forever.

"I just hope these players understand what they've accomplished winning this many in a row.".

Gray answered that. "It never gets old beating Tennessee, not for an Alabama player, not for Crimson Tide fans."

Halfback Jeff Fagan offered an echo. "It's an Alabama tradition to beat Tennessee. It's like an old daddy with a new baby. It's happiness year after year after year. It'll never get old."

That depends on one's perspective. In Knoxville, Tennessee, Coach John Majors was tired of losing, as well as of having to come up with fresh things to say nice about Alabama.

"All I remember is they were better than we, and they beat us again," Majors said.

The bomb, Tennessee style, was developing a short fuse. The explosion was imminent.

56

1982
Tennessee 35, Alabama 28

Damn, we've got our spirit back! We're going to raise hell tonight!"
As University of Tennessee student Tim Evans said that, pandemo-
nium was already present in Knoxville late on the evening of October
16, 1982. The Volunteers had just done what had begun to seem
impossible, defeating Alabama in football.

The score was 35-28, ending an eleven-game losing streak at the
hands of the Crimson Tide. A score of 3-2 would have been good
enough.

"I can't believe it! I just can't believe it! It's a shock, just unreal!"
Yes, Tennessee student Susan Nadolsky was correct, because Alabama
was a 13-point favorite to defeat the Volunteers at Neyland Stadium.

And as the goal posts tumbled under the weight of delirious Tennessee fans, who sat with about ten thousand Alabama fans in a crowd
of more than ninety-five thousand, the comments went on and on . . .

"It feels good! It just feels so good after being kicked by Alabama
for eleven years. Go to hell, 'Bear.'"

As strangers kissed strangers, the Pride of the Southland Band
played "Rocky Top" and anything else near and dear to the hearts of
Tennessee faithful. The Tennessee team, prompted by its fans who
would not leave the field and go home, came out of the dressing room
for another bow, adding fuel to the cheering throng.

"We Beat Bama!" bumper stickers appeared on automobiles less
than thirty minutes after the end of the game, and drivers steered

their way toward Cumberland Avenue and Neyland Drive, creating a mass that was slow to thin.

Caught in the middle of all this was a couple from Alabama.

"Oh, what the hell, have a good party," the male Alabama fan said.

Tennessee fans did that, whether they were in malls located in Knoxville, where many had listened to the game on radios and chanted down the final seconds—"10, 9, 8, 7, 6, . . ."—or whether they were in other towns or states.

In Albertville, an Alabama town on Sand Mountain, Larry Parker, a devout Tennessee fan listened to the game on the radio. When it was over, he rushed downtown and bought orange Christmas tree lights for the windows of his home, orange sherbet for his refrigerator, orange sugar-coated candy for a bowl in his dining room, orange crepe paper to decorate his den, and enough chicken to prepare a postgame feast for a multitude. And he went to the local radio station and secured a recorded version of "Rocky Top" to play for anybody who would listen.

The *Knoxville News-Sentinel*, which printed the above quotes in a front-page story the morning after the Tennessee victory, received an interesting telephone call the night after the game. The caller was Dale Drinnon, who graduated from Tennessee in 1975, and who now lives in Baltimore.

"I'd been working all day, came home, turned on the television, and saw the score," Drinnon said to *Knoxville News-Sentinel* reporter Lisa Hood. "Is it really true? I've been waiting for this day for a long time. This is the greatest day of my life. God, I wish I was going to be on the Strip [on campus] tonight. We beat the 'Bear.'"

Yes, and Alabama Coach Paul "Bear" Bryant was aware of what was happening among Tennessee faithful.

"The folks in Knoxville are happy," Bryant said. "The folks who graduated from Tennessee are happy. The folks who live in Tennessee are happy. And all of those folks have every right to be happy. They lined up and beat us."

While the world was shaking out of control around him, as the final sounds ticked off the scoreboard clocks on The Third Saturday in October, Tennessee coach John Majors had a quiet thought. "I stood on the sideline and said, 'I wish my dad could be here to see this,'" Majors said.

His late father was a former football coach at Sewanee. Shirley Majors had introduced John Majors to the sport.

Tennessee fans, meanwhile, let him know in no uncertain terms that a victory over Alabama was needed in 1982.

"The World's Fair was in Knoxville that year," Majors said while reflecting on his happiness. "A couple of our friends from Pittsburgh came down for a visit, including Eddie Ifft, a German. So did Gordon White of the *New York Times*.

"I took them to the Straus House on the fair site, so Eddie could hear some German music and all of them could see some Tennessee clogging. The place was packed. There were people from all over the country in there, but mostly they were from Tennessee. They'd noticed us being there.

"At some point, the band broke out in 'Rocky Top' and everybody went crazy, dancing inside and outside, standing on tables and singing. Then, they started screaming, 'Alabama! Alabama! Alabama!' It got to be a crescendo, and Eddie Ifft said, 'John, if I were you, I think I'd try to beat Alabama real soon!'

"It got louder and louder and louder. This was in July. Those people were hungry. It was eleven years of frustration all built up."

How did Majors recall the game?

"It was a game in which we had a chance to get blown out," he said. "We were down 10 points twice, I think, and we kept coming back on them.

"It was a game of big plays.

"We were expanding our passing game. We got more out of it than ever before. We grew offensively.

"It was fate and timing for us. Their good fortune ran out.

"I recall Coach Bryant after the game. He was a great winner. Also, he was a champion when it came to losing, although he detested it. He told me after the game, 'Johnny, you had a great game plan.' That was quite a compliment coming from him. It was his way of telling me he understood it was one of the happiest days of my life.

"I appreciated that. I'm sure it went through his head how significant it was to beat a team he coached. Knowing him, knowing how smart he was dealing with human beings, the feeling for life he had, I bet it went through his mind that it was a great day for John Majors. He wasn't gonna take it away."

What was said by the people who did defeat unbeaten, nationally number two-ranked Alabama?

"It's a dream come true," said Tennessee defensive end Mike Terry, whose pass interception with seventeen seconds remaining sealed the victory in an end zone being attacked by gallant Alabama. "I saw the ball pop loose. It was just hanging there for somebody to catch. Why not me? Glory to God. It was a precious apple."

The football popped loose because Tennessee defensive halfback Lee Jenkins made his second consecutive big, possibly game-saving, play. He hit Alabama split end Darryl White in the end zone, just as the Crimson Tide pass receiver put his hands on a football passed by quarterback Walter Lewis from the 17-yard line. He had his breath knocked out of him by the collision, and he lay on the ground in pain as his teammates celebrated.

"I didn't know who had come up with the ball, the Alabama player or us," said Jenkins, who on the previous play had knocked away a passed football intended for Alabama split end Jesse Bendross in the end zone. "I just wanted life to come back into my body. When one of my teammates hollered that we had won, I felt a whole lot better about my condition.

"On those last two plays, I was just trying to give everything I had. The game is something I'll remember the rest of my life. It was well worth the bumps and bruises it took to get it."

Bill Bates, another Tennessee defensive halfback, also hit White on the play that sealed the victory.

"I've wanted to beat Alabama for so long, since I was young, ever since their winning streak started," said Bates. "Before the game, Coach Majors told us that the clock eventually strikes twelve on everybody. Today, it definitely struck twelve on them."

As its seemingly Cinderella story ended, Alabama had a great deal to do with it ending so tragically. The Crimson Tide had eight penalties for 60 yards in the game, while Tennessee was penalized only four times for 26 yards. Alabama fumbled four times, with two resulting in turnovers, while the Volunteers did not fumble.

John Ward called the plays for the Big Orange Network in 1982. During the 1986 season, he and his business associates had the tape of that radio broadcast on their telephone line, with people on hold listening to it.

It was a dramatic broadcast.

"It was a great day for Tennessee," Ward said.

"I have to reflect back on Bill Anderson in the press box with me that afternoon. He is a genius when it comes to knowing what is going on down on the field. He has such a feel for it.

"I can recall how disappointed he was with the way Alabama played defensively. He was for Tennessee winning, obviously, but he could not understand why a Coach Bryant team had lost control of the game defensively.

"It never looked right. It never really felt right.

"Anderson called it in the first quarter. He knew Alabama was not right that day. He knew something had gone wrong with their program.

"We beat them. But I never thought that was the real Alabama. I went to Chattanooga to make a speech on the Monday after the game. I predicted that Georgia Tech would win over Tennessee the following week. They drilled us.

"It was a great win for Tennessee. But Alabama did not play well. Alabama did not look like Alabama. I was reading Bill Anderson all the way through it. His face told me something was wrong out there."

Tennessee scored first on a 22-yard field goal by Fuad Reveiz, a Colombian-born place-kicker who had four field goals in the game.

Alabama scored next on a 4-yard run by halfback Joe Carter, with Peter Kim kicking the extra point for a 7-3 lead.

Alabama raised its lead to 14-3, when Lewis passed 35 yards to Bendross for a touchdown and Kim kicked the extra point.

Tennessee answered that score with a 52-yard pass from quarterback Alan Cockrell to split end Willie Gault for a touchdown, followed by an extra point kick by Reveiz. Reveiz kicked a 32-yard field goal to cut the Alabama lead to 14-13.

Lewis passed 38 yards to split end Joey Jones for an Alabama touchdown, and Kim kicked the extra point to leave the halftime score 21-13.

Tennessee got a 45-yard field goal from Reveiz, 21-16.

Cockrell passed 39 yards to flanker Mike Miller for a Tennessee touchdown, which was followed by a two-point conversion pass from Cockrell to tight end Kenny Jones, giving the Volunteers a 24-21 lead.

Reveiz kicked a 40-yard field goal to up the lead to 27-21.

Fullback Chuck Coleman ran 34 yards for a Tennessee touchdown, which was followed by a two-point conversion pass from Cockrell to Jones, and the Big Orange had a 35-21 lead with 7:21 remaining in the game.

Then up sprung Alabama.

With 5:04 remaining, halfback Linnie Patrick, who took a pitch from Lewis at the 5-yard line, was credited with a 14-yard touchdown run. Kim kicked the extra point to cut the final margin of victory.

In the final minute, Lewis attempted three passes into the end zone from the Tennessee 17-yard line, Jenkins was there to break them up, and the unthinkable became reality.

"I'm not sure how long eternity is, but the ending was pretty long," said Majors. "The last six minutes seemed like eternity. There was no way we deserved to lose. We chased the ball so well. This game was played to the hilt, to the fullest of our potential. I've had more talented teams, but never one that played harder. I still don't know how good this team can be, but it was mighty fine today."

Tennessee's victory over Alabama came on the last visit Bryant made to Neyland Stadium, as well as his last game against the Volunteers.

"It's the last time I saw Bryant," said Col. Tom Elam. "I went out to the Alabama team bus after the game. A police officer stopped me, but Bryant, who was sitting in the front right seat of the motor coach, threw up his hand and motioned for the cop to stay out of it.

I told him I was delighted to end that streak. But I told him I hated for anything bad to happen to him. He said it had to end sometime. I concurred, or else we were gonna take a few classroom buildings and throw them in the river.

"Bryant was most gracious in defeat. That was a Bryant trademark. He always had nice things to say after our games against them, compliments for Tennessee. I had a high regard for him. Bryant was a person who displayed class, in victory and in defeat."

From Marvin West in the *Knoxville News-Sentinel:*

Of course they can . . . and they did . . . and it was wonderful.

In the beauty of mid-October, in the perfect setting, Neyland Stadium, before the multitudes that never give up, Tennessee finally turned terrific. The gutty Volunteers slapped down Alabama, 35-28, and put behind them all the awful things the Tide has done.

This was the end of 11 years of frustration.

This was the end of thinking Alabama always finds a way.

This was the end of Tide talk about another national title.

Hopefully, this was the beginning of better times for Tennessee. Alabama was favored by two touchdowns, but it could not contain the intelligent Tennessee offense . . . .

However great the orange offense was, the burden of winning came down on defensive heads . . . and hearts. Alabama amassed 486 yards, but when it went for the big one, for the chance to win, Tennessee turned back the Tide . . . .

Alabama lost with dignity, considering how little practice it has had. This was only the fifth Southeastern Conference defeat in 83 games.

In another story, West drew an analogy between a Tennessee victory over Notre Dame a few season earlier and the win over Alabama:

If the win over the Irish was heady wine, this was red meat and potatoes, a thick, juicy filet. Earn one, eat one, savor it . . . and it is hard to go back to hotdogs and baked beans.

Tennessee, 6-5-1 that season, lost to Georgia Tech the week after it beat Alabama. Alabama, 8-4 that season, defeated Cincinnati the week after it lost to Tennessee. And everybody was left waiting for The Third Saturday in October in 1983, when nothing from the past mattered, only the war at hand.

57

1983
Tennessee 41, Alabama 34

A<small>LMOST A YEAR HAD</small> passed since University of Tennessee running back Johnnie Jones had made a long touchdown run against Alabama.

This was during the summer of 1984, nine months after The Third Saturday in October in 1983, when Jones looked at a picture hanging on the wall in his room at Gibbs Hall on the Tennessee campus.

The picture showed him moving down the sideline at Legion Field in Birmingham, all alone, racing toward the fame that waited for him in the end zone.

"I don't know what I'll do in future games," Jones said on this afternoon in the athletic dorm. "But I doubt anything I do will top that, as far as Tennessee fans are concerned. It's the most memorable thing that's ever happened to me.

"It's the run that helped us beat Alabama, which makes it the run I'll be remembered the most for.

"The Alabama game is special for Tennessee people, all of us: fans, coaches, and players. That's why that touchdown will always mean so much to me, even when I get old and tell my grandchildren about it."

The Run covered 66 yards. The Run came in the fourth quarter, with 77,237 fans watching. The Run won the game for Tennessee over Alabama, 41-34, on October 15, 1983.

John Ward saw the decisive touchdown coming.

"I absolutely had the play called cold," Ward said. "I saw it coming. I knew it would work when the play started and I could see the defense Alabama was utilizing against it.

"Jones ran left, right toward us in the press box, then cut right. It was a perfect play. It was exciting. It was a thing of beauty.

"The game was a dandy. It looked grim for Tennessee. We looked out of it. It went back and forth. There was so much excitement. One team was up, then the other team was up. Then Jones made the great run to end a great game."

For the second year in a row, after the dreadful eleven losses in a row, the Big Orange defeated the Crimson Tide in dramatic fashion.

The Volunteers, 13-point underdogs, rallied from deficit after deficit to win. They were behind midway through the third quarter, 27-17, and they were behind, 34-24, when the mood of the afternoon got tense.

"I was concerned," said Alan Cockrell, the former Tennessee quarterback who made an audible call to send Jones winging toward the decisive touchdown.

"We won with TENN-icity," said Jones.

All Tennessee coach John Majors knew when the game was over was his squad had won, as it had in 1982 in Knoxville, after a lot of grief.

"I couldn't measure the two wins," Majors said to Thomas O'Toole, who was a sportswriter at the *Knoxville News-Sentinel*. "This one wasn't sweeter than the last one, because one of the hardest things a program has to do is break the ice against an opponent that has been on a long winning streak. But this had to be one of the greatest, most exciting games ever played."

It was that.

The scoring, as well as when it came, indicates as much.

It was 14-14 after one quarter.

Alabama led, 24-17, when the offenses took a needed halftime rest.

The Crimson Tide led, 34-31, after three quarters.

The points came this way:

Alabama got a 31-yard touchdown pass from quarterback Walter Lewis to split end Joey Jones, with Van Tiffin kicking the extra point. Tennessee got an 80-yard touchdown pass from Cockrell to flanker Lenny Taylor, with Fuad Reveiz kicking the extra point. Alabama got a three-yard touchdown run from fullback Ricky Moore, with Tiffin kicking the extra point.

RAY PERKINS

IT WAS THE MOST beautiful sight in college football."

Former University of Alabama football coach Ray Perkins was not talking about a Crimson Tide touchdown or a Southeastern Conference championship trophy. "The Perk," as he was called in Tuscaloosa, was talking about a lost work of art.

"I always thought seeing Alabama in red jerseys and Tennessee in orange jerseys, the two teams on the field at the same time, particularly at Legion Field in Birmingham, was one of the more beautiful things in the world," Perkins said about a scene that was washed away in the 1970s by a National Collegiate Athletic Association rule that mandates the visiting team must wear white jerseys for games. "It was one of the best things about the series."

Perkins played split end for Alabama (1964–66) when The Third Saturday in October was more colorful, in that regard. He starred on Crimson Tide teams that won two national championships and posted a 2-0-1 record against Tennessee. He appreciated the series then. He thinks just as much about it now that he has coached four games in it.

But he contends it is not, nor will it be, as special to him as it is, and will remain, to Tennessee coach John Majors. That became more the case for Perkins after he resigned as Alabama coach after the 1986 season to become coach of the Tampa Bay Bucs of the National Football League.

"I can't say it's as special to me as it was to Coach Paul "Bear" Bryant [his coach] or to John Majors," Perkins said before he left Alabama, "because we've got Auburn to contend with each year. But our series with Tennessee is only a little of half-a-notch under our series with Auburn, as far as importance goes each year. I think it's like that for all Alabama people.

"We're *the* big game for Tennessee. I think that's true because they don't have that intrastate rival like we do with Auburn. Their people look at our game with them in a much bigger sense than our people do.

"But that doesn't mean it isn't important to Alabama people. It's natural that there are certain teams on your schedule that you get more motivated for. Tennessee is one for Alabama. It's always there, that game, always on The Third Saturday in October.

"It's a class rivalry. It's based on intensity, fair play, mutual respect, and loads of tradition. It'll always be conducted that way."

Perkins is proof of the ups and downs prevalent in the aged series. He had success as a player. He lost his first three games to Tennessee as a coach, all of them close and decided in the fourth quarter: seven points in 1983, one point in 1984, and two points in 1985.

"They hit us with gobs of big plays in those games," Perkins said. "They beat us in the fourth quarter. I've come to realize that Tennessee can be a nemesis for Alabama."

But on The Third Saturday in October in 1986, in Knoxville, Perkins stood in a postgame press conference and reflected on a Crimson Tide victory over Tennessee that should have soothed some of the ache experienced from 1983 through 1985.

Alabama won, 56-28, in as convincing a victory as any in the series.

It was Perkins-type football personified.

"It was just old-fashioned, simple, tough football," Perkins said. "Nothing more. It was blocking and running. Just that.

"We wanted to seize control of it early, on our first possession, hopefully running on Tennessee. We did that with a nice touchdown drive of 74 yards.

"I think our team touched on greatness with the victory. The players on this team are the greatest young men I have been around."

Then Perkins said, almost as an afterthought, "This is one of the sweetest victories of my career as a coach."

His predecessor, Bryant, felt the same way about The Third Saturday in October.

continued on next page

"Coach Bryant made it a big game for us as players," Perkins said. "He made it important to us because of the lack of success he had coaching against Tennessee when he was at Kentucky. I can remember how excited he would get the week we played the Big Orange, even to this day, because it was so obvious.

"Other than that, I remember only a couple of things. First, in 1964, I remember how their players came out of the dressing room and ran right through our bench. That can have an intimidating effect, if you let it, which is why they did it, because that damn T they ran through was right there in front of us.

"We always had to stand and wait for them, because we were the visiting team, but we were good enough to beat them twice up there.

"Second, I remember our game up there in 1966 was the birth of another chapter in the legend of Coach Bryant. It rained hard before the game. When we came out on the field for warmups, the rain got lighter.

"That happened a lot with Coach Bryant, which made people talk a lot about how he could control the weather. We sort of thought so."

Victories by Tennessee over Alabama from 1982 through 1985 gave the Big Orange a four-game winning streak in the series, matching the longest in history for the Volunteers.

"That's in my craw a little bit," Perkins said during the summer of 1986, months before his Crimson Tide broke the streak. "I'd be lying if I said otherwise. But, to me, the losing streak is only at three games. I wasn't around here in 1982.

"And, correct me if I'm wrong, but I'm sure Alabama has managed to win four in a row over Tennessee somewhere along the way."

Perkins smiled when he made that last statement. The number 11 was dancing in his head. His obvious Alabama pride was shining. Maybe he was thinking about leaving the series as a winner even then.

Tennessee got a six-yard touchdown run from Cockrell, with Reveiz kicking the extra point.

That ended the first quarter. Fans were already dizzy.

Then came some more offense.

Tennessee got a 28-yard field goal from Reveiz. Alabama got a six-yard touchdown run from Lewis, with Tiffin kicking the extra point. Alabama got a 25-yard field goal from Tiffin.

That ended the first half. Sportswriters in the press box were talking about the game being the most exciting of the century.

Then came some explosive scoring.

Alabama got a 26-yard field goal from Tiffin. Tennessee got an 80-yard touchdown pass from Cockrell to split end Clyde Duncan, with Reveiz kicking the extra point. Alabama got a six-yard touchdown run from Moore, with Tiffin kicking the extra point. Tennessee got a 57-yard touchdown pass from Cockrell to Duncan, with Reveiz kicking the extra point.

That ended the third quarter.

The outcome of the game was still hanging in the balance. The Volunteers had heroes in waiting.

Tennessee got a 37-yard field goal from Reveiz. Alabama was still ahead. But Tennessee got the memorable 66-yard touchdown run from Jones, with Reveiz kicking the point, and it was over.

Incredibly, with all the emotion and drama present, the game went sort of like Ed Murphey, a Memphis businessman and devoted Tennessee fan, had predicted it would.

"Mr. Murphey recruited me out of Munford," Jones said. "His big pitch was, 'Someday, Johnnie, you're going to score the winning touchdown against Alabama.'

"I thought he was just saying that to get me to sign a Tennessee scholarship. It was a strong pitch.

"After all these years, it looks like he knew what he was talking about. At least that's how it happened that day in Birmingham."

The play Jones scored on, 49 Option, was called at the discretion of Cockrell, who noticed the Alabama defense was set to stop it. So he changed the direction from right to left.

"I can still see that play in my mind," Majors said during the summer of 1986. "Cockrell made a fake, stepped down the line of scrimmage, read the defense, and pitched the football to Jones. It'll always be imbedded in my mind. Three of our pass receivers blocked three of their defensive players, put them on the ground, and Jones weaved his way toward the end zone.

"I'll always remember Jones running into the corner of the end zone, right into the heart of our fans, who were shaking those orange and white pompons and going nuts."

That left Ken Donahue feeling bad. "Nobody else is at fault for that loss except me," Donahue said in retrospect. "It was my fault. But Alan Cockrell made a great audible that afternoon. He made a great play for Tennessee."

It was a game for offense.

"Actually, Alabama dominated the game," Majors said. "They moved on us all day long. But when they'd hit a big play, we'd counter with a big play. Our big plays kept us in it.

"It went together to form one of the more dramatic games in our history, as well as one of the classic games played on The Third Saturday in October. We fell behind. We came back. We held on for dear life."

Tennessee picked up 232 yards rushing and 292 yards passing.

Alabama picked up 208 yards rushing and 245 yards passing.

"We called ourselves the No-Name Defense," said Randy Edwards, who played defensive tackle for Alabama in 1983 and for the Seattle Seahawks of the National Football League. "After what Tennessee did to us, I was glad we had that name. I didn't want anybody to know me."

Both of the rival coaches—Majors and Ray Perkins of Alabama—recall a lot of emotion during the game.

"That was sort of a wild game," said Perkins, who was making his debut in the series in 1983. "There was a lot of excitement up until the time Johnnie Jones made that long touchdown run for them. We got caught in the wrong defense, they made a solid play, a smart audible at the line of scrimmage, and that was that."

Some people thought it was more exciting than just that.

It was so thrilling a strange visitor made her way to the Tennessee dressing room. Elizabeth Majors, mother of the happy coach, celebrated among the joyous Volunteers.

"It's the first time I've done anything like that, even though my husband coached and my sons played and coached," Elizabeth Majors said. "I've always considered the dressing room hallowed ground. I suppose I got carried away with the excitement of that game."

Majors remembers seeing his mother in the dressing room. "It wasn't my idea, but I'm glad she came by to visit with our players and coaches. Heck, everybody seemed to be in there that day, our minister and several of our friends included."

Could such a game be matched?

Yes.

Tennessee and Alabama, old rivals, were just warming up.

58

1984
Tennessee 28, Alabama 27

THE EXPRESSIONS OF THE rival coaches told the story.

Ray Perkins, normally undaunted, with a boyish grin on his face, sported a scowl on the Alabama sideline. He knew the football game was slipping from his grasp.

John Majors, forever enthusiastic, with the smile of a young child, sported eyes that glowed on the University of Tennessee sideline.

Andre Creamer had caused these reflections at Neyland Stadium on October 20, 1984. The Big Orange defensive halfback, then a freshman, had just returned a punt from his 45-yard line to the Alabama 11-yard line. It was getting late in the fourth quarter. Tennessee trailed the Crimson Tide by seven points.

Let us not forget Big Orange fans. There were 95,422 people in the stadium at Knoxville. They had been quiet. Many had left for home after it appeared dominating Alabama had matters in hand.

But at that moment, after Creamer had returned the punt, as Tennessee made its move, the fans who had stayed were roaring.

"I really think their fans won the game for them that day," Perkins said. "They got loud. We didn't handle it well."

They got louder.

Four plays after Creamer made his punt return, halfback Johnnie Jones dived into the end zone from one yard out, moving the Volunteers to within one point of Alabama. This was with 2:09 remaining in the game.

Majors called a time-out. He huddled with quarterback Tony Robinson, then called a play for a two-point conversion.

No sooner had the roar of the crowd subsided, than Robinson took the ball, ran to his right on a favorite Tennessee play—48 Option— faked a pitchout to Jones, and dived into the end zone.

A third consecutive Tennessee victory over Alabama was complete, 28-27, and the treasured series had done an about face.

It matters not that the two teams were winless in the Southeastern Conference before that meeting.

It matters not that Alabama stumbled forward to a 5-6 record, its first losing season since 1957.

It matters not that Tennessee went on to a 7-4-1 record.

All that mattered at that moment was *the* game.

The goal posts were brought to the ground.

"It was then that I started thinking about using wooden goal posts for our home games with Alabama," said Bob Woodruff, the retired Tennessee athletic director. "They're cheaper than aluminum.

"But, as I felt in 1982, dangerous or not, let the hungry fans have their fun after beating Alabama."

The victory was stunning, sort of like an old gray mare winning the Kentucky Derby, sort of like a blind man regaining his sight.

As Majors remembered the game, "We weren't in it much of the game. It was our pride and determination that won it for us. That was a game in which we barely escaped, which was becoming normal in Alabama-Tennessee games. We were on the verge of being knocked out. We never gave up. We played with pride. And, of course, we had a certain amount of good fortune."

As said defensive halfback Tommy Sims, who was a junior in 1984, "It looked bad for us in the fourth quarter. We were down 14 points. The stadium was quiet.

"But we thought we could win. We talked about pride and determination. That was our theme for the week. We talked about fighting to the finish. We knew fighters could win in the end.

"So it was three-and-zero against Alabama for me.

"Beating them was becoming a Tennessee tradition."

Majors was beaming in the dressing room after the game, naturally so, and he was struggling for the proper words to use while placing the third consecutive dramatic victory over Alabama into perspective.

"Anybody who plays in this game—Tennessee against Alabama—will put his courage on the line, no matter the stakes," Majors said. "A lot of players wearing orange and red did that today. We did. They did.

"We almost waited too late, but we stuck it in there when we had to. Everything had to click in the final seven or eight minutes for us to win. We made it happen. We maintained our poise. We showed character. It was a dogfight between two hungry teams.

"This game brings out the best in both teams. I can remember us playing against two of their national championship teams. They had the upper hand then. They were better. But we did some things those years against them that seemed impossible.

"I know why. Everybody I talk to says if there is one game they could play again for Tennessee, it would be one against Alabama."

It was the Crimson Tide that wanted to play again this time.

"It could've been different if we had handled their crowd better," said Mike Dubose, who during the summer of 1986 still coached under Perkins at Alabama. "But that's what you have to expect in Knoxville. I learned that a long time ago.

"When I was in any first year as an Alabama player in 1970, we went to Knoxville to play, a meaningless freshman game. They must have had thirty-five thousand people there for a meaningless game. And they were loud, even when nothing much mattered except pride. After that, I always dreaded going to Knoxville to play, not because Tennessee always got after us like crazy, but because their fans always help them so much.

"I thought about that again after the 1984 game. We had them beat, but they came back on us. Their fans helped them.

"The Tennessee team we had beaten for three quarters was not the same in the fourth quarter, not after their fans got into the game, because they sort of came alive and got the job done."

While doing that, Tennessee rewrote an old song, "When Johnnie Comes Marching Home Again," because Jones had run 66 yards for the decisive touchdown against Alabama in 1983. His dive into the end zone in 1984 merely gave the Volunteers a chance to win again. It helped the Big Orange along the way to a Sun Bowl berth dampened by a loss to Maryland.

Mike Strange, a sportswriter at the *Knoxville News-Sentinel*, talked to Jones after the victory over the Crimson Tide. He wrote:

He had a rough day, a bloody nose and a red eye, but Johnnie Jones got in the last word on Alabama.

Again.

"Three in a row. It's been a long time since that happened," Tennessee's splendid tailback said after the Vols' 28-27 victory.

Three wins in a row over the Crimson Tide, and the last two have been made possible when Jones crossed the goal line late in the fourth quarter.

"I knew they were looking for me," Jones said. "They always key on me, whether I get the ball or not."

And, that's what happened when the Vols went for the two-point conversion and the victory. Quarterback Tony Robinson dived into the end zone, when an Alabama defender hesitated, expecting a pitch to Jones on the option.

"He had to get me or Tony, and he took me," Jones said.

Jones missed several plays in the second half after an Alabama forearm crushed his helmet down into his nose and one eye.

"They had to stop the bleeding," Jones said. "It was kind of hard for me to breathe."

Asked whether he would have had sufficient oxygen intake to motor 66 yards at full tilt if the situation required it, Jones flashed a grin. "I would have spit out my mouthpiece," he said, as if he had already considered the possibility.

Such is the manner in which *the* game is played on The Third Saturday in October—blood here and blood there, determination always, happiness for one team, and gloom for one team.

Alabama started off early, striking for the first 10 points. Van Tiffin kicked a 36-yard field goal in the first quarter. Paul Ott Carruth ran four yards for a touchdown, and Tiffin kicked the extra point.

Tennessee came alive in the second quarter. Robinson passed eight yards for a touchdown to Joey Clinkscales. Fuad Reveiz kicked the extra point. Reveiz kicked a 27-yard field goal to tie the score at 10-10.

Greg Richardson caught a 68-yard touchdown pass from Vince Sutton late in the second quarter, with Tiffin kicking the extra point, and the Crimson Tide took a 17-10 lead at halftime.

Carruth ran 12 yards for an Alabama touchdown in the third quarter, with Tiffin kicking the extra point. It looked like Tennessee was whipped, and thousands of Big Orange fans left the stadium.

They missed some drama.

Reveiz kicked a 29-yard field goal; Tiffin answered with a 21-yard field goal. Tim McGee caught a 17-yard touchdown pass from Robinson, and Reveiz kicked the extra point. Tennessee was within 27-20. Then Creamer made his punt return, and Jones made his touchdown run.

Finally, Robinson dived into the end zone on the two-point conversion that made the probable loss an exciting victory for Tennessee.

Three losses in a row to Tennessee hurt Alabama players, as remembered by former Crimson Tide defensive end Emanuel King, who missed stopping Jones and Robinson on the decisive two-point conversion.

"I can't believe it happened," King said about the two-point conversion and three straight losses to the Volunteers. "It was my fault, pure and simple, because I could have made sure we won by one point. I was slow playing the quarterback on the two-point conversion. Instead of attacking him, I laid back and waited, thinking I could stop the running back.

"Either one of them would have scored."

Now Tennessee was on a roll, and Alabama was in a stall.

Curt Jarvis was a sophomore middle guard for the Crimson Tide in 1984. "In the last three minutes, all I saw was Tennessee," Jarvis said, pointing out the Big Orange intensity during that time span.

Perkins saw a lot of the same. He was so upset when it was over that he did not show up for his postgame radio program.

"I was disappointed, very much so," Perkins said. "All we had to do was play the final three minutes to get out of there with a win. We had it won. We should have won.

"Two things really disturbed me. The first was the punt return they made to get in position to win. All we had to do was make one tackle, and the game was ours. We missed at least three chances to do that on that play. The second was the fact we lost our composure in the final minutes of the game. That really bothered me a lot."

John Ward recalls Tennessee being "out of it" before it won in 1984. He also remembers a crucial measurement on a close first down call that angered Perkins. It was important to the outcome.

The call came on a fourth-down play, a Tennessee run at left guard, as the Big Orange was forced to gamble to get back in contention.

"I remember how upset Perkins was," Ward said. "He was right, too, because it was not close. There was no way we got the first down. But they gave us one, and we went on to score the first touchdown in the fourth quarter.

"I could not believe they would consider it a first down. I thought we lost yardage on the play. I remember saying on the broadcast that something was wrong on the field.

"We got the call, and the crowd got into the game.

"We won it. Alabama was in shock."

59

1985
Tennessee 16, Alabama 14

Maybe University of Tennessee linebacker Dale Jones should have been writing movie scripts instead of playing for the Volunteers between 1983 and 1986. His creative abilities—he calls them "dreams and visions" could excite a mass audience.

On The Third Saturday in October in 1985, at Legion Field in Birmingham, he dazzled 78,848 football fans with a play—a pass interception—that will forever remain a part of Tennessee folklore.

His heroics, which came with about eight minutes remaining in the game, helped the Big Orange to a 16-14 victory over Alabama, the fourth consecutive triumph for Tennessee over its most bitter rival.

"I had thought it out," Jones told sportswriter Mike Strange. "I felt I was going to do it.

"I can picture things happening. I can sit down the night before the game and play the whole game in my head. I put myself in every situation I can. Then when we play and I get up from making a tackle, sometimes I'm shocked. It happened just the way I visualized it would."

The way it happened against Alabama in 1985 boggles the mind. He made a nice catch on a pass, batting the football into the air and holding on to it as he fell to the ground, in the process stopping one of many Crimson Tide assaults against the Tennessee defense.

Strange was there to record the action for the *Knoxville News-Sentinel*. He described the game, as well as the importance of the heated series, in a story the next morning. He wrote:

For a Tennessee football player, there is no better time to be a hero than The Third Saturday in October. That is a day reserved for Alabama.

Two years ago there was Johnnie Jones' run. Last year it was Andre Creamer's punt return.

Saturday, if one play stood out in the dramatic panorama, Tennessee's 16-14 win over Alabama, its fourth consecutive victory over the Tide, it was Dale Jones and his interception.

"We all remember the things we do in the Alabama game," said Tennessee coach John Majors. "That play will be one of the great plays, in my opinion."

Majors was holding court in a bus parked outside Legion Field, not far from where fans had watched Alabama's Van Tiffin's game-ending, 61-yard field goal attempt fall short.

The play that thrust the junior linebacker into a cherished spot among Alabama-Tennessee lore happened very quickly.

With 7:43 to play, Alabama was driving into Vol territory, needing only to get within range for Tiffin to win the game.

Tennessee was clinging to a two-point lead and not likely to add to it. Quarterback Tony Robinson was already in the dressing room, his right knee wrapped in ice.

"When T Rob went out," said Jones, "we knew that if we were going to win, the defense was going to have to do it!"

Alabama quarterback Mike Shula took the snap from center Wes Neighbors on first down at the Vols' 37-yard line. He straightened up and threw a short pass to his left in the direction of fullback Craig Turner.

Almost as soon as the ball left Shula's hand, it was in Jones's hands. He leaped into the air from his outside linebacker spot, batted the ball, snatched it to his chest, and fell to the ground.

"That's probably my favorite play ever," said Jones, trying to accommodate a mob of reporters and dozens of elated Vol fans milling around outside the locker room dispensing hugs and backslaps.

Doubt not that it was a joyous day for Tennessee fans, who would watch their team post a 9-1-2 record en route to a first Southeastern Conference championship since 1969, capped by a stunning victory over favored Miami in the Sugar Bowl.

Doubt not that it was an agonizing day for Alabama fans, who would watch their team post a 9-2-1 record, including an impressive victory over Southern Cal in the Aloha Bowl.

Things looked grim for Tennessee when Robinson was injured. But John Ward recalls how good fortune smiled on substitute quarterback Daryl Dickey and the Volunteers on the first play after the starter went down with a knee injury.

"I could see the Alabama defense getting a little aggressive, maybe too aggressive," Ward said, "maybe because it was trying to get the crowd into the game. Alabama was in deep trouble.

"Anyway, Robinson went down and Dickey came in.

"The one play I recall was his first pass. He threw it into the hands of an Alabama linebacker. The linebacker dropped it. That was the game. Had he intercepted that pass, he was gone, on his way for a touchdown.

"Doug Dickey [father of the quarterback and during 1985 the new Tennessee athletic director] was in the radio booth with us. I looked at him, for some reason, after that pass. He showed no emotion, but that play, the interception that got away, had to relieve him more than anything that happened the remainder of the season.

"That was the play that saved the game, saved the season, saved the conference championship, and saved the Sugar Bowl appearance.

"The interception by Dale Jones was important, obviously, but the dropped interception was the play I remember the most."

Choose to doubt, if you wish, that Jones knew it would unfold in the dramatic way it did, including Daryl Dickey playing quarterback for the Big Orange after the talented Robinson was injured on a tackle.

Who would have believed it? There was Robinson, the superstar, lying on the ground after two Alabama players sandwiched him. It looked like the Crimson Tide had taken control of the game with a hard, but clean, tackle. But by all means doubt not that playing against and defeating Alabama are of supreme importance to a Tennessee player.

"This is why a football player goes to Tennessee, to beat Alabama," Keith Davis said as he walked from the playing field.

Davis, a freshman running back, was walking slowly. Sweat was pouring from his face. His white jersey with an orange 28 on the front and back was drenched by the perspiration and decorated by a few streaks of blood.

The crimson stuff was as appropriate as the salty stuff.

Rarely does anything come easy for either team when they go to war. The victory by Tennessee in 1985 was true to form.

"I'm tired," said Davis, who was making his first start for the Volunteers, which he handled by rushing for 141 yards on 27 carries. "I'm sort of bruised up, too. But my happiness overcomes my fatigue and soreness. I'm sure I'll be able to feel those more tomorrow.

"I was nervous before the game. Starting against Alabama is a heart-attack thing. I actually felt pains in my chest in the dressing room.

"But it's over now. We put it on the line, just like Coach Majors said we'd have to do. We talked about doing that all week. We gave all we had for a sweet victory."

Happiness was apparent in the Tennessee dressing room.

Said Majors, "It's no different when we win over Alabama. They're all the same to anybody from Tennessee. This one was as courageous as our victories in 1982, 1983, and 1984, maybe more because we wrapped it up without our quarterback."

Said Tennessee defensive halfback Charles Davis, "Yes it is! Yes it is! This is what it's all about."

Said Jones, "I've never been prouder after a victory in all my life. It's an unbelievable feeling. I've got a wonderful feeling in my heart."

And usually subdued Ken Donahue wore a smile. The Tennessee defensive coordinator, a former Big Orange player in his first season coaching in Knoxville, had served as defensive coordinator for twenty-one years at Alabama. He was clutching the game football as he mingled with Volunteers.

"I'm proud to have this game ball," Donahue said. "I'm proud of our offense and our defense for winning a tough game. I did a little jig in the dressing room after the game."

Majors was too drained to dance. He had paced up and down the Tennessee sideline during the final dramatic minutes.

"People tell me that was a game of drama on every play, from the first to the last, that there was more intrigue from start to finish than any other game they have sat through," Majors said at his office. "I agree with them. It was like that.

"There were great plays. Dale Jones made one of them. Daryl Dickey held us together after Tony Robinson got hurt.

"From that point, we felt our way, held on for dear life, tried to hold off Alabama.

"It was like fencing—touching and feeling. The last field goal was great drama. A great series, Tennessee and Alabama, on The Third Saturday in October every year."

At his office in Tuscaloosa, Perkins scoffed at talk about the game being a thriller. "Maybe it was exciting for fans," Perkins said. "But I never have viewed games through the eyes of fans. Nothing about it was too damn exciting to me."

That made The Third Saturday in October in 1986 all the more pleasing for the Alabama coach.

60

1986
Alabama 56, Tennessee 28

OTHER THAN UNIVERSITY OF Alabama supporters, who stayed until the end, the only people smiling at Neyland Stadium in Knoxville on The Third Saturday in October in 1986 were doomsayers.

The messengers of doom were large in number before the Crimson Tide and Tennessee played in front of 95,116 fans and a national television audience. They thought unbeaten Alabama would romp past the thrice-beaten Volunteers.

They were correct.

The Crimson Tide, hellbent on ending a four-game losing streak at the hands of the Big Orange, ran and ran and ran and ran to a 56-28 victory that left no doubt that Alabama was far superior to the struggling Volunteers.

On a magnificently beautiful fall afternoon—cool and sunny—another young man placed his name squarely and firmly in the series folklore that since 1901 has been built to massive proportions.

The Bobby Humphrey show was awesome. The Crimson Tide sophomore tailback ran for three touchdowns and 217 yards on 27 attempts. He was only 16 yards short of the school record for rushing in a game, 233 by Bobby Marlow in 1951 against Auburn. He was powerful enough to run over a few poorly tackling Volunteers along the way, with his determination reflecting both the muscle and the manner of a team on a mission.

"Tennessee is usually a good, fired-up defensive team," Humphrey said while answering questions from news media representatives outside the Alabama dressing room. "The hitting was the same, for the most part, but I could tell by looking into their eyes that something was different out there.

"But that could have been the result of what we did in the first quarter, the first time we had the football. We were challenged to try to dominate them early. We drove for the first score [going 74 yards in nine plays]. That let us know we could beat them in Knoxville.

"After that, we just kept driving and driving, moving and moving, going after them."

In the aftermath rested some startling numbers.

It was the most points scored against Tennessee since Duke won, 70-0 in 1893. It was the most points either team had surrendered on The Third Saturday in October since Alabama won, 51-0, in 1906. The 21 points Alabama scored in the first quarter were the most produced that quickly in the history of the series.

"I had no idea we could score like that on them," Humphrey said. "Either their defense is weak, or our offense is strong."

The Crimson Tide had 457 yards rushing. Most of the yards came on one play, Toss Sweep 28, which was a basic power run around right end by a tailback after a pitch from the quarterback. Alabama ran the play twenty-seven times.

"Twenty-seven times for one play?" asked Ray Perkins, the winning coach who secured his first victory over Tennessee after three losses. "That has to be a record for one of my teams, a first. But we ran it early with success. Why stop? Tennessee never solved it."

Alabama had the football ten times and scored eight touchdowns. The Crimson Tide had drives of 74, 43, 12, 74, 62, 48, 80, and 56 yards. Tennessee, which overcame the 21-0 deficit to cut the lead to 21-14 in the second quarter, had 309 yard's passing as quarterback Jeff Francis completed 23 of 30 attempts.

"The Tennessee defense never showed up," said John Majors, the coach of the Volunteers.

"Our offense was super. Our kicking game was super. Our defense did not play with a winning style," said Perkins.

In retrospect, the numbers game can be summed up by the respective records the teams had after the game. Alabama, the favorite for the Southeastern Conference championship, was 7-0. Tennessee, the defending champion, was 2-4.

For Alabama, the dreadful losing streak to Tennessee was over. "Beating them is good," said Crimson Tide center Wes Neighbors. "All of us seniors feel that way. Beating them the way we did, with muscle, is great. I can look at myself again and feel good."

For Tennessee, the humiliation was hard to swallow. "They did what they wanted to do to us today," said Big Orange safety Charles Davis.

That left Alabama players to smoke victory cigars in their dressing room, a The Third Saturday in October tradition started by the late coach Paul "Bear" Bryant, and to reflect on a pleasing afternoon.

In the aftermath, Col. Tom Elam, the seventy-seven-year-old chairman of the Tennessee Athletics Board, and Doug Layton, the color analyst on the Alabama Radio Network, were left to look like prophets. On Saturday morning, mere hours before the opening kick-off, they had predicted doom for the Big Orange.

"I'd rather see a swarm of locusts come through Knoxville today than those fierce birds from Alabama," said Elam.

"We're gonna drill Tennessee like an enraged wild boar," said Layton.

That was the pregame mood.

That was the postgame verdict.

Alabama got touchdowns from (in order) fullback Bo Wright on a 13-yard run up the middle, split end Clay Whitehurst on a 34-yard pass from quarterback Mike Shula, Shula on a one-yard run around left end, tailback Gene Jelks on a four-yard run around right end, Humphrey on a 27-yard run up the middle, tight end Angelo Stafford on a 31-yard pass from Shula, Humphrey on a one-yard run up the middle, and Humphrey on a seven-yard run up the middle.

Van Tiffin kicked all eight extra points. That left him with 124 consecutive attempts without a miss, one short of the national record.

Alabama led, 21-7, after the first quarter, 42-14 at halftime, 49-21 after three quarters, and by the final margin.

"Humphrey was great running," said Perkins. "Shula did a great job running our offense. Wright had to have done a good job blocking for our tailbacks. Jelks ran extremely well. The offensive line knocked Tennessee out of there to give us some room to operate."

Tennessee got touchdowns from (in order) tailback Keith Davis on a 2-yard run around left end, split end Anthony Miller on a 70-yard pass from Francis, split end Terrance Cleveland on an 11-yard pass from Francis, and Cleveland on a 6-yard pass from quarterback Moses Collins.

Carlos Reveiz kicked all four extra points.

"Our offense played better than it has all year," said Francis.

"We don't have the feeling of attack, attack, attack on defense," said Terry Brown, a Tennessee safety. "We're not as hungry as a defending conference champion should be."

Two postgame scenes outside the Alabama dressing room told the story of the massacre adequately enough.

So excited was Wright that he ran down under the goal post, down a tunnel, through a gate, and having missed a turn to the Alabama dressing room, out of the stadium. Maybe he was so used to running north and south that the detour to a shower was strange to him.

So classy was Tennessee defensive halfback Andre Creamer that he ran down the same tunnel to catch up with Alabama split end Greg Richardson. They shared a handshake, symbolic of the treasured series, and a story or two before going to their respective dressing rooms.

"It was embarrassing," said Creamer. "Never have I been beaten so badly."

The old rivals entered the game from contrasting directions and exited it the same way. Tennessee was floundering. The loss was its fourth in five games. Alabama, working its way toward one of the more demanding schedules in history, was soaring in an effort to secure a berth in the Sugar Bowl as conference champion.

So after the game, with contrasting moods, Majors and Perkins talked about the present states of their programs.

From Majors: "We've got miles and miles and miles of work to do in an effort to come back from this. We've been solidly defeated by a team that has no weaknesses. We're at a low point in terms of confidence."

From Perkins: "This just means we are 7-0 with a tough schedule still in front of us. Our players will be allowed to savor it for a couple of hours. I plan to savor it for ten minutes. When we get on the bus to ride to the airport, maybe before then, I plan to start working on our game plan for our battle next weekend with Penn State."

Alabama lost the next weekend, 23-3, to a Penn State team that was also entertaining national championship hopes. The Crimson Tide lost two more times, to LSU and Auburn, to finish at 10-3, including a victory over Washington in the Sun Bowl.

Tennessee was in dire straits. Georgia Tech defeated the Big Orange the following weekend, 14-13, and fans were up in arms. But the Volunteers rallied, winning their last five games to finish at 7-5, including a victory over Minnesota in the Liberty Bowl.

The prevailing question after The Third Saturday in October: Is Alabama ready to make another long run against Tennessee?

Crimson Tide fans think so. Big Orange fans think not. Such was the enthusiasm when only the future knew the answer.

YES. THINGS have changed at Alabama and Tennessee since 1901.

One of the more recent things that changed, for the second time in four years, is that the Alabama coach, Perkins, resigned at the end of the 1986 season to become coach of the Tampa Bay Bucs of the National Football League. Former Georgia Tech center and coach Bill Curry was named as his replacement. Curry will learn to appreciate the wonderful day.

The reason is obvious. The Third Saturday in October has not changed that much at all. It remains *the* day for an old and treasured series that sparkles anew each fall in brilliant crimson and impressive orange.

61

1987
Alabama 41, Tennessee 22

FORMER UNIVERSITY OF TENNESSEE coach Johnny Majors was correct. From the Volunteers' standpoint, what happened on October 17, 1987, was "a horror show" that does not need extensive rehashing.

Of course, Alabama folks look back on a 41-22 victory at Legion Field in Birmingham as something more pleasant, like the continuation of a nightmare the Crimson Tide produced for Tennessee a year earlier.

Alabama won, 56-28, in 1986. The Crimson Tide scored the first 24 points, including 21 in the first quarter, as it romped past the Volunteers in 1987.

The 1987 game was the first staged at night in the history of the series, thanks to the Southeastern Conference giving in to the wishes of a television network, and Tennessee faithful remember it as dark indeed.

"I saw the game live and have no desire to dwell on it," Majors said about the lopsided decision. "I am not all that enthusiastic about reliving the gory details, but to summarize matters, I don't see how a team can play better than Alabama did in that game.

"The kicking game, so important historically in the Tennessee-Alabama rivalry, belonged to the Crimson Tide, starting with their punt return for a touchdown in the first quarter.

"Alabama's rushing defense took away our running game, making us a one-dimensional offensive team through most of the game.

"They won the battle of turnovers, getting six, and that had been one of our advantages in recent history.

325

"A redshirt freshman quarterback with no appreciable experience took command and gave Alabama tremendous leadership and execution. We knew Jeff Dunn was a talented player. What we didn't know was he would be good enough to win ESPN player of the game honors.

"Coach Bill Curry and his staff did an excellent job in bringing their team back from a shattering loss the week before. Alabama was thoroughly prepared and highly motivated."

Majors was on the money, point by point, while describing how an Alabama team with a 4-2 record, including an aforementioned 13-10 loss to Memphis State a week earlier, defeated a Tennessee team with a 4-0-1 record, including a 20-20 tie with Auburn as the only blemish.

Alabama scored three touchdowns in the first quarter, driving 80 yards in 14 plays for the first, getting a 63-yard punt return for the second and striking for a 90-yard pass for the third. Bo Wright scored the first on a one-yard run, Gene Jelks scored the second and Pierre Goode scored the third on a pass from Jeff Dunn. Three extra point kicks by Phillip Doyle gave the Crimson Tide a 21-0 lead.

When Doyle made a 47-yard field goal in the first five minutes of the second quarter, pushing the advantage to 24-0, a crowd of 75,808 was stunned by the fact Alabama had produced 80 points in a little more than six quarters of game action against its longtime rival.

"I was a little nervous at the start," Dunn said. "I think the entire team was a little tight. Then we got that big lead, 21-zip, and had a confidence boost. I don't think there's any doubt we played four quarters of Alabama football."

"It isn't easy getting up after getting steamrolled like that," Majors said about the punishing effects of three touchdowns surrendered so quickly.

Thus enters his second and third points.

The Alabama defense limited Tennessee to 51 yards rushing and the Crimson Tide recovered two fumbles and intercepted four passes. To his credit, the Volunteers' quarterback, Jeff Francis, completed 26 of 44 pass attempts for 358 yards. But he was a sitting duck most of the evening, having been sacked twice and run out of the pocket numerous times.

Meanwhile, Dunn was spectacular leading the Alabama offense. The third quarterback to start for the Crimson Tide during the season, he completed 10 of 17 passes for 229 yards and was almost flawless executing the game plan. Of course, having running back Bobby Humphrey in the offensive backfield was pivotal because he rushed 23 times for 127 yards, including touchdown runs of 4 and 17 yards. That came after he rushed for 217 yards and three touchdowns a year earlier in Knoxville, Tennessee.

The Alabama scoring was rounded out by Doyle, who added a 40-yard field goal and two more extra point kicks.

Tennessee got touchdowns from William Howard, a two-yard run, and John Rollins, a 33-yard pass reception, two two-point conversions from Thomas Woods on passes from Francis and two field goals from Phil Reich, 20 yards and 36 yards. The Volunteers saved some face with 16 points in the final quarter after the Crimson Tide led 34-6.

"We learned a lot about the Alabama pride factor," said Curry, who needed the win more than anybody else after his team faltered against Memphis State. "The chips were down and our players got it done against a good Tennessee team."

Curry was making his debut on The Third Saturday in October after replacing Ray Perkins as Alabama's coach. His hiring created an uproar in many circles because he is a former Georgia Tech player and coach, in fact a center when the Yellow Jackets and Crimson Tide were rivals of the highest order.

The heat on Curry picked up after the victory over Tennessee. After two more victories, Alabama lost its last two regular season games, to Notre Dame and Auburn, and a Hall of Fame Bowl game to Michigan. That fixed the record for his first year in Tuscaloosa at 7-5, which was not satisfactory given the fact Perkins had 9-2-1 and 10-3 records his last two years.

On the flip side, Tennessee regained its step and finished the season with a 10-2-1 record.

But the first loss of the season was a stinger for Tennessee, which was ranked eighth in the nation when it arrived in Birmingham and was dazed when it left.

"This was Tennessee's time to die," said Russ Bebb, a veteran columnist at the *Knoxville Journal.* "No matter how you slice it, nothing the Vols did caused Big Orange chests to swell. Alabama, on the other hand, was as brilliant as Tennessee was lackluster."

62

1988
Alabama 28, Tennessee 20

ANYBODY WHO SAW DERRICK Thomas play football, at the collegiate level with Alabama or at the professional level with the Kansas City Chiefs, realizes what the Tennessee offense faced on October 15, 1988, at Neyland Stadium in Knoxville.

Although the Volunteers neutralized his presence by attempting to run the football the other way, Thomas epitomized a Crimson Tide defense that helped Alabama to a 28-20 victory over Tennessee in front of 93,025 highly supportive fans

The matchup was strange because Tennessee entered with a shocking 0-5 record after losses to Georgia, Duke, LSU, Auburn, and Washington State, and Alabama entered with a relatively unimpressive 3-1 record after a loss to Ole Miss.

So dismayed were some Tennessee fans they put sacks over their heads before, during, and after the game, as if they were afraid to watch or to be seen themselves. A Nashville radio personality continued a lengthy stay on a billboard platform. He vowed to complete the vigil of sorts only after the Big Orange won a game.

Tennessee responded by playing its best game of the season, at least to that point, but Alabama established a 14-0 lead at the end of the first quarter and used its defense to stymie the home team. When the Volunteers clawed their way back into contention, trailing only 14-12 at the end of the third quarter, the Crimson Tide responded with 14 unanswered points. The Big Orange scored its final eight points with 13 seconds remaining in the game.

It was the seventy-first game between Alabama and Tennessee. The Crimson Tide won for the third consecutive year and claimed a 37-27-7 advantage in the series.

The prevailing topic of conversation in the dressing rooms after the game was Alabama's power and speed on defense.

"We pride ourselves on stopping the run and we believe we can do that at any place on the field," said Thomas. "We did that today against a Tennessee team with a lot of offensive weapons that came out with a lot of spark. We just go out every week and win on defense."

Or, as Tennessee coach Johnny Majors said, "We had our best overall effort of the season and I'm proud of the hustle I saw out there. But we lost to a good team that has an outstanding defensive unit. That Alabama defense can throw you out of kilter in a hurry with its speed, its power, and its quickness."

The statistical leaders for the Alabama defense were linebacker Greg Gilbert, nine tackles; linebacker Keith McCants, eight; and defensive halfback John Mangum, six, plus a touchdown on a pass interception he returned 60 yards during the final minute of the first quarter.

"The pass interception for a touchdown was critical, a real blow in a heartbreaking loss," Majors said.

Alabama definitely made some important plays, but the top performance in the game was produced by Tennessee linebacker Keith DeLong. He had 19 unassisted tackles, a pass interception, a broken-up pass, and a quarterback sack. Even in an old series it is difficult to remember a finer defensive effort.

"Before the game our defensive coaches said our linebackers needed to be reckless," DeLong said. "They said we shouldn't be cautious at all because we needed to make something happen to end our losing streak. I took some chances and it paid off.

"But it was a loss, just the same, another one to Alabama."

Tennessee entered the game with an enormous amount of enthusiasm, as if the aged rival was what it needed to right a wayward ship, and it is appropriate to wonder what might have happened had Alabama gotten off to a slower start.

As it was, the Crimson Tide drove 97 yards in six plays for its first touchdown. Wayne Shaw, a fullback, scored on an eight-yard run and Phillip Doyle kicked the extra point with 3:50 remaining in the first quarter.

With twelve seconds remaining in the first quarter, Mangum intercepted a Jeff Francis pass intended for Thomas Woods and returned it for a touchdown. Doyle kicked the extra point.

A heavy pall settled in Neyland Stadium, except for the noise being made by ten thousand or so Alabama fans.

Then Tennessee bounced back, quickly, with Francis and Woods teaming on an 11-yard touchdown pass with 13:00 remaining in the second quarter. Chip McCallum kicked the extra point, cutting the lead to 14-7.

With 1:24 remaining before halftime, Preston Warren of Tennessee blocked a punt for a safety and the Crimson Tide led 14-9 when the teams took a break.

Suddenly, it looked like Tennessee was the team with momentum. That became more apparent when McCallum kicked a 23-yard field with 9:16 remaining in the third quarter. The Big Orange was within two points, 14-12, and its defense was stuffing a hot and cold Crimson Tide offense that ended up gaining only 299 yards.

But the Volunteers could not score any more points until the final seconds of the game. That futility surfaced although the Big Orange had possession of the football for ten minutes in the third quarter and the Tennessee 40-yard line was the average starting position for drives throughout the game.

That says something for Alabama's defense that afternoon.

The Crimson Tide, which averaged starting drives at its 28-yard line, had two nice marches to touchdown in the fourth quarter to lock up the victory.

Alabama went 52 yards in 10 plays, with David Casteal scoring on a seven-yard run with 7:33 remaining in the game. Doyle kicked the extra point.

The Crimson Tide went 68 yards in five plays, with Murry Hill scoring on a 55-yard run with 1:38 remaining. Doyle kicked the extra point.

Hill, a giant in the game even at 5-foot-7 and 170 pounds, rushed for 86 yards on 14 carries. The Crimson Tide gained only 130 yards on the ground.

Strangely, the victory over Tennessee on its home field got Alabama players a Sunday afternoon of practice. Coach Bill Curry was livid after seeing his kicking game come apart—a blocked field goal, a blocked punt, and a fair catch at the one-yard line.

"We won that game with a flat-out gut effort by the defense," said Curry, who raised his record against Tennessee as Alabama's coach to 2-0 and evened his overall record at 4-4-1. "We might have won it when they intercepted a pass and had a first down inside our 15-yard line with us leading 14-9. Our defenders gave them a field goal, nothing more, and that was pivotal. You don't want to trail Tennessee in Knoxville, particularly after you've been ahead 14-0, so that 14-12 score looked mighty good at that time.

"As for our offense that day, well, it did hang in there and kept pecking until something worked."

Alabama lost only two more games that season, by a point at LSU and by five points to Auburn.

So what did Tennessee do?

The Volunteers, 0-6 after the loss to the Crimson Tide, won their remaining five games.

63

1989
Alabama 47, Tennessee 30

UNIVERSITY OF ALABAMA FOOTBALL fans never will forgive Tennessee linebacker Darryl Hardy for an honest mistake.

More neutral observers will be more indulgent.

Hardy had just seen Alabama running back Siran Stacy account for 317 yards, in the process scoring four touchdowns, when he was asked about the performance.

"Oh, that Danley guy," Hardy said after the game, a memorable and explosive 47-30 victory by Alabama over Tennessee on October 21, 1989.

Excuse me, but Stacy Danley was an Auburn running back at the time.

However, dizzying afternoons can do that to memories on occasion—and Alabama and Tennessee certainly produced one for CBS Sports on the football field.

During a game that brought together the old rivals as unbeaten and united teams for the first time since 1973, both 5-0, Alabama won because it had a sledgehammer and a rifle at its disposal.

First up, Stacy, a junior who had recently transferred from junior college. He had 125 yards rushing on 33 attempts and three touchdowns.

Second up, Alabama quarterback Gary Hollingsworth, a former benchwarmer. He completed 32 of 46 pass attempts for 379 yards, three touchdowns, and one shot from the rifle went for 75 yards to the sledgehammer.

The nationally sixth-ranked Volunteers were considered an even match for the nationally tenth-ranked Crimson Tide. But the fourth consecutive Alabama victory in the series started much like the previous three, with the victors rolling early on and with Tennessee left to chase the lead.

How does 10-0 Alabama sound after one quarter?

Familiar, for sure.

How does 19-14 Alabama sound at halftime?

Familiar, for sure.

Then came the second half avalanche, with Stacy running and Hollingsworth passing, and Alabama was home free again—on its home field, Legion Field in Birmingham, with 75,962 fans watching.

Alabama had 183 yards rushing and 379 yards passing. That totals a bewildering 562.

For its part, Tennessee had 373 yards, an adequate total but not enough to keep pace.

For the third consecutive year, an Alabama coach few people favored had defeated Tennessee. Of course, a third straight loss to Auburn (with Stacy Danley included) was waiting in the wings to signal the demise of embattled Bill Curry.

Obviously, the Alabama victory, or the Tennessee defeat, helped along the creative juices of newspaper sports columnists, such as John Adams of the *Knoxville News-Sentinel.*

Adams observed:

The schedule said the Vols were returning to Legion Field. It said nothing about 1988.

But the statistics and the record did. So did the scoreboard.

Alabama quarterback Gary Hollingsworth, who moves like an old Y. A. Tittle and passes like a healthy Joe Montana, completed a school record 32 passes for 379 yards and three touchdowns.

None was intercepted. A couple were rumored to have been deflected.

Tailback Siran Stacy set a school record with 317 yards and tied his own single game record by scoring four touchdowns. He rushed for 125 yards, gained 158 yards on nine passes and turned a two-yard shovel pass into a 75-yard touchdown.

The defense obviously remembered how bad it played in 1988. How else could it have given such a convincing portrayal of that defense?

If [Tennessee graduate and actor] David Keith had been as convincing in his halftime impersonation of Elvis, half of the female audience would have swooned.

Hear this from Phillip Marshall, who was writing for the *Montgomery Advertiser:*

Gary Hollingsworth is the boy next door, the type guy you would be delighted to see your daughter bring home for dinner. He is softspoken, quick to smile and slow to boast. He seems almost embarrassed to talk about the incredible story his right arm is writing at Alabama.

Hollingsworth was all but unknown before the season, a redshirt junior from Hamilton [Alabama] who had never seen a game. Doomsayers moaned when Jeff Dunn was injured and he was forced into the breach at quarterback.

What Hollingsworth is today is the best quarterback in the Southeastern Conference. He proved it for the entire nation to see while leading the Crimson Tide to a 47-30 smashing of Tennessee at Legion Field. His 32 pass completions is an Alabama record that will stand beside the record five touchdown passes he threw against Ole Miss.

The Alabama victory over Tennessee allowed Hollingsworth to become one of the more ballyhooed players in Crimson Tide history. He was starting only his fourth game. He was tall and thin, six-feet-four-inches tall and 180 pounds. He had passed for five touchdowns against Ole Miss two weeks earlier.

Also, the points total against the Volunteers added to the fame of Alabama offensive coordinator Homer Smith, the intellectual man who took Hollingsworth under wing after quarterback Jeff Dunn was injured.

"When Gary sits down to eat, he is the kind of person who crosses his legs and starts a conversation," Smith said about the personable and thin quarterback. "He needs to eat more."

Alabama and its quarterback feasted on Tennessee on The Third Saturday in October. The Volunteers helped along matters with four turnovers to none for the victors.

Alabama led 10-0 at the end of the first quarter. Hollingsworth passed four yards to Kevin Turner for a touchdown and Phillip Doyle kicked the extra point. The scoring drive covered 67 yards in 13 plays. Doyle kicked a 22-yard field goal after the Crimson Tide drove 61 yards in 10 plays.

Tennessee cut the lead to 10-7 midway through the second quarter. Greg Amsler scored on a one-yard run and Greg Burke kicked the extra point.

But two plays later, Alabama extended the lead. Hollingsworth made a shovel pass to Stacy, who ran 75 yards for a touchdown. The extra point kick was blocked, leaving the Crimson Tide with a 16-7 advantage.

Quarterback Andy Kelly passed 33 yards to Anthony Morgan for a touchdown with about three minutes remaining in the second quarter. Burke kicked the extra point, cutting the Alabama lead to 16-14.

But the Crimson Tide answered again, quickly, and Doyle kicked a 19-yard field goal with five seconds remaining in the first half.

The score was 19-14.

Fans in the stadium had been thoroughly entertained.

Television viewers were having fun, too.

Then Alabama established a sense of dominance with two quick touchdowns and two extra point kicks in the third quarter. Hollingsworth passed 11 yards to Lamonde Russell for the first score and Stacy ran five yards for the second score, which was set up by a Tennessee turnover at the Volunteers' 19-yard line.

"That was a devastating turn of events," said Johnny Majors, the Tennessee coach. "Bam, two touchdowns in less than two minutes. We tried to fight back, but we couldn't catch them. We couldn't slow down their offense.

"It was simply two great teams on the field and the better team that day won the game."

Burke kicked a 43-yard field goal to cut the Alabama lead to 33-17. Chuck Webb scored a touchdown on a one-yard run and Burke kicked the extra point to cut the Crimson Tide lead to 33-24 with 1:30 remaining in the third quarter.

Again, Alabama answered the challenge. Stacy scored on a six-yard run and Doyle kicked the extra point. That came at the end of an 83-yard, 12-play drive that consumed more than four minutes.

Carl Pickens scored a touchdown on a three-yard pass from Kelly with 3:59 remaining in the game, giving Tennessee scant hope.

However, with a 40-30 lead Alabama drove for another touchdown and extra point. Stacy ran 15 yards into the end zone and Doyle kicked the extra point. The final margin was fixed.

It was the first loss for Tennessee after ten consecutive victories, dating to the loss to Alabama in 1988. The Volunteers went on to produce an 11-1 record, including a 31-27 victory over Arkansas in the Cotton Bowl.

Alabama lost its last two games of the season, 30-20 at Auburn, and 33-25 to Miami in the Sugar Bowl. After producing a 10-2 record, Crimson Tide coach Bill Curry decided to resign. He moved to Kentucky, where he did not have the type success against Tennessee that he had while in Tuscaloosa.

However, Curry did get a nice forty-seventh birthday present that season, on The Third Saturday in October. He was given the game football. "It's the best I've ever received," he said.

64

1990
Alabama 9, Tennessee 6

ALABAMA AND TENNESSEE DUSTED off an old script, with a few revisions made, when they played on October 20, 1990, at Neyland Stadium in Knoxville.

As Beattie Feathers of Tennessee and John Cain of Alabama had a punting dual in 1932, when the Volunteers won 7-3 in Birmingham, place-kickers Phillip Doyle of the Crimson Tide and Greg Burke of the Big Orange produced all of the scoring.

Alabama won, 9-6, in improbable fashion, too. The Crimson Tide blocked a field goal attempt by Burke to set up a field goal by Doyle that determined the outcome.

The scoring summary is shallow.

Burke kicked a 20-yard field goal in the first quarter.

Doyle kicked a 30-yard field goal in the second quarter.

The score: 3-3.

Doyle kicked a 26-yard field goal in the third quarter.

Burke kicked a 51-yard field goal in the fourth quarter.

The score: 6-6.

Doyle kicked a 47-yard field goal on the final play of the game, after Stacy Harrison of Alabama blocked a 50-yard field goal attempt by Burke with 1:35 remaining.

The score: 9-6.

The drama was deep.

"The snap was good and the hold was good," Burke said about the blocked field goal. "But I heard the second thump awfully quick after I kicked the football. You hate to hear that sound."

Adding insult to injury for the Big Orange, the football bounced off of Harrison's facemask and rolled 23 yards toward the Tennessee goal line before it was recovered by the Volunteers' Jason Julian at the 37-yard line.

"I got a seam and nobody touched me on the blocked field goal," said Harrison, who dubbed himself "the Assassin" while playing for the Crimson Tide. "I went all out for it, sort of just ran through the football.

"When I saw the football rolling backward, past the 50-yard line, I said, 'Wow, victory is on the way.' I don't think anybody on our side thought Phillip Doyle would miss a field goal to win it."

Alabama passed on first down, incomplete. Kevin Turner ran the football on the next two plays, gaining seven yards. With four seconds on the scoreboard clocks, Doyle kicked the field goal, easily clearing the crossbar, although he did not see that.

Doyle was knocked to the ground after the kicking the football by a frustrated Tennessee player. "I hit it well," he said about the field goal attempt. "I just wish I had been able to see it."

The Volunteers had good reason to be upset. It was the fifth consecutive victory by Alabama over Tennessee. It marked only the third time in twenty-five games the Big Orange had lost, with all of them coming to the Crimson Tide. The home team, ranked third nationally with a 4-0-2 record, was an 11-point favorite, one of the larger betting lines in the history of the series. The visiting team had a 2-3 record with the wins coming over Vanderbilt and Southwestern Louisiana.

"I'm sure our players and our staff were the only people who thought we had a chance to win over Tennessee," said Gene Stallings, the Alabama coach who was in his first season with the Crimson Tide. "It was a great victory and an unbelievably great finish—the blocked field goal and the made field goal.

"We sort of won against all odds because we didn't have much go right for us on offense. We had terrible field position all day, but our defense refused to give in. We played the fourth quarter backed up against our end zone, clinging to a field goal lead or a 6-6 tie.

"It was simply a throwback to the old days more than anything else, when defense and kicking won games."

The loss was particularly disheartening for Tennessee coach Johnny Majors, as well as damaging to his job security. His program was winning at an impressive clip, but the five losses in a row to Alabama were troublesome to Big Orange fans.

"It was a strange and unusual game, hard to sum up," Majors said. "There were some outstanding defensive plays from both teams. Our defense played as well as it could play. We had our share of ample opportunities on offense, but we couldn't cash in on them.

"We tried a little bit of everything from an offensive standpoint, but we couldn't manufacture any continuity. We ran, we passed, we ran the reverse, and we tried special plays. Alabama's defense simply did a terrific job throughout the game."

Evidence of that rests in numbers. Tennessee had averaged 42 points per game, then got 6. The Volunteers gained 175 yards, averaging 2.92 per play.

Alabama did not do much better on offense, gaining only 222 yards, averaging 3.13 per play.

Thus comes to mind a reflection from Ben Byrd, the highly respected former sports columnist at the *Knoxville Journal*.

"On the sidelines two minutes before the game ended I was talking with Scott Hunter, Alabama's great quarterback in the late 1960s," Byrd said. "He said, 'The only people enjoying this game are General Neyland and Coach Bryant.'

"That was before the blocked field goal try, which trimmed that number in half. I'm pretty sure the general left after that."

It is safe to assume a lot of Tennessee fans also departed disheartened, given Ray Melick's column in the *Birmingham Post-Herald*:

Signs started just past Chattanooga, hanging off the overpasses on the road to Knoxville.

"Beat Bama—Everybody Else Has."

"Dig, Bama, Dig."

"Bear Is Dead—And So Is Bama."

Sure it was rude. Sure it was cocky. Sure it made Alabama fans headed toward the game see red. But there didn't seem to be much hope for the Alabama fans, no reason to think this Alabama team could do much to avoid the tail whipping the Vols had planned.

Except for one thing both sides might have forgotten on the way to The third Saturday in October—history.

"We should have to pay property taxes on this place because we own it," a jubilant Alabama center, Roger Shultz, said only moments after the Crimson Tide celebrated its way off the floor of Neyland Stadium after a stunning 9-6 victory.

The first lesson of history is that those who forget the past are doomed to repeat it—and history knew no member of this Alabama football team had lost to Tennessee.

History repeated itself in another way. Harrison foiled the Tennessee field goal in the fourth quarter while Alabama was in a "desperation block" defensive formation. It was the same alignment the Crimson Tide used on October 18, 1989, to block an extra point at Penn State to preserve a dramatic 17-16 victory over the Nittany Lions.

Doyle kicked a field goal in that game, too, but the one he kicked against Tennessee came at a more opportune time—to the delight of Danny McWilliams, an Alabama sophomore. He caught the football after it cleared the crossbar and landed in the grandstand.

"Alabama got a great victory, unbelievably, and I got something to keep for a lifetime," McWilliams said.

65

1991
Alabama 24, Tennessee 19

WHEN A STATE RECORD crowd for a sporting event, 86,293, gathered on October 19, 1991, to watch Tennessee and Alabama play football, nobody had to explain the meaning of the banner in an end zone at Legion Field in Birmingham.

The banner read: "86, 87, 88, 89, 90"—and Tennessee wide receiver J. J. McCleskey reacted to it after the Crimson Tide won the game, 24-19, with a flurry in the fourth quarter.

"It's humiliating," said McCleskey, a Knoxville, Tennessee, native. "You work hard to prepare yourself to play Alabama every year and they beat you every year. I grew up supporting Tennessee and Alabama beat us. I come to Tennessee and they beat us. They just keep on beating us.

"It's frustrating."

The victory was the sixth in a row for Alabama over Tennessee. It was the seventeenth in the most recent twenty-one meetings. The Crimson Tide raised its advantage in the storied series to a much more dominating 40-27-7.

As it had in recent years, Alabama won over a team that was ranked higher in national polls. The Crimson Tide entered the game with a 5-1 record. Tennessee entered the game with a 4-1 record. Both teams had suffered a loss to Florida.

The story of the game was told skillfully enough by talented sportswriter Jimmy Bryan of the *Birmingham News* in an article he wrote just after it ended:

Alabama and Tennessee, those two longtime October antagonists, teased the multitudes packed into Legion Field for three quarters and then sent Crimson and Orange hearts racing with a flaming windup that placed the outcome in doubt until the final play.

Alabama sent the majority of an announced crowed of 86,293 into the lovely autumn mid-afternoon celebrating a 24-19 victory that undoubtedly won a prominent place in this storied series.

The 14th-ranked Crimson Tide and eighth-ranked Volunteers plodded through three quarters with the Vols fiercely protecting a 6-3 lead. Then Alabama delivered three shocking fourth-quarter touchdowns in a row under the steady hand of backup quarterback Jay Barker to apparently put the Vols away.

The lead was 24-6 with 6:21 left.

But Tennessee rose from its grave. The Vols scored one touchdown, outfought the Crimson Tide for an onsides kick and scored another. Now it was 24-19 with 2:25 to go.

When Alabama's Kevin Turner smothered the next onsides kick effort under his red shirt, it looked like a no-sweat win had been secured.

Then sure-handed Siran Stacy fumbled on third down at the Tennessee 35-yard line and the Vols had one final opportunity to fling at the Crimson Tide. With 1:29 remaining, there was time.

The Crimson Tide defense didn't let it happen. When end John Copeland chased scrambling quarterback Andy Kelly down with the clock ticking inside 10 seconds, Alabama happily counted out Tennessee.

Alabama played the final three and a half quarters without big play wizard David Palmer, who went out with an ankle injury. It played the final quarter and a half without starting quarterback Danny Woodson, out with a hamstring injury.

Rushed into the glaring vacancies, Barker, subbing for Woodson, led three touchdown drives at quarterback and Chris Anderson, subbing on the special teams for Palmer, delivered a 56-yard punt return to set up a crucial touchdown.

Alabama played that afternoon under the direction of Coach Gene Stallings, who saw his record for two seasons improve to 13-6, after losses in his first three games. He remembers a shorthanded team that won in the fourth quarter against a talented team that could not hold onto the lead.

"The thing I was pleased about most is we lost some key people and the people who went in off the bench did an outstanding job," Stallings said. "We had a number of big plays, which is always the case in games like that, but you have to give Tennessee credit. It looked like we had the game sort of in hand, up 24-6, and they went down and scored, got an onsides kick, and carried on down the field again.

"I thought Jay Barker did an outstanding job in the second half that day. He took us on a long drive for a touchdown in the fourth quarter, when we needed one in a bad way, and then we got that great punt return from Chris Anderson to set us up for another touchdown.

"In the first half, we had nothing going for us on offense. But the defense kept us in the game until we could find a way to move the football.

"I don't think there's any question about whether that win helped us get ready for the big run we had in 1992. Any time Alabama gets a win over Tennessee, it's a big one and always has been."

In the losing dressing room that afternoon sat a beleaguered coach, Johnny Majors of Tennessee. It was his fifteenth game against Alabama as leader of the Volunteers and his record had dropped to 4-11. His inability to defeat the Crimson Tide with even scant regularity had critics howling, even though the Big Orange was winning at an impressive pace other than on The Third Saturday in October. Normally kind, or at least understanding, sportswriters took sensible enough shots at his game plan.

Said Russ Bebb in the *Knoxville Journal*:

Let's face it: Tennessee's 24-19 loss to Alabama was not due to a lack of execution or effort on the Vols' part. It was more likely a lack of derring-do.

The people at Tennessee headquarters chose to be conservative and paid the price.

The people in the stands left the game wondering how would the Vols have fared had they chosen to be a bit bolder, to use a little pizazz, to let it all hang out once in a while.

Tennessee elected to play it cozy in the second half and hope the defense could keep on keeping on, as Coach John Majors likes to say.

Into the third quarter of this high noon duel before the ABC cameras they went, a battle of evenly matched teams. For almost three quarters, Alabama-Tennessee was everything Tennessee fans are always hoping it will be, but rarely is.

If Tennessee had held on to win, it would have been a great bit of strategy. But, as it turned out, Tennessee wouldn't hold on to win.

Said Randy Moore of the *Knoxville Journal,* who was a bit more to the point:

> When a horse loses the Kentucky Derby because its jockey kept the reigns too tight for too long, you can't blame the horse.
>
> Likewise, when a football team loses because the coaching staff kept the offensive reins too tight for too long, you can't blame the team.
>
> Essentially, that's what happened at Legion Field, where Alabama edged Tennessee by a nose. Like the aforementioned jockey, the Vols' coaching staff waited until its horse was 18 lengths back entering the home stretch [down 24-6 with six minutes left] before easing up on the reins. By then, the race was already lost, despite a gallant closing kick.

Actually, to continue that theme, both offenses looked as if they were carrying added weight.

Alabama took a 3-0 lead with 9:36 remaining in the first quarter when Hamp Greene kicked a 21-yard field goal.

Tennessee tied the game, 3-3, with 3:32 remaining in the second quarter when John Becksvoort kicked a 33-yard field goal.

Tennessee took a 6-3 lead with 20 seconds remaining the first half when Becksvoort kicked a 43-yard field goal.

Then Alabama took control—or seemed to.

Stacy scored on a one-yard run and Greene kicked the extra point with 11:46 remaining in the game. The 70-yard touchdown drive spanned eleven plays.

Derrick Lassic scored on a one-yard run and Greene kicked the extra point with 7:54 remaining. That touchdown came after the punt return by Anderson.

Stacy scored on a two-yard run and Greene kicked the extra point with 6:21 remaining.

The score was 24-6 and somebody might have been trying to paint "91" on the aforementioned banner in an end zone.

Then Tennessee rallied.

Aaron Hayden scored on a one-yard run, and a two-point conversion run was stopped with 4:25 remaining.

Hayden scored on an eight-yard run and Becksvoort kicked the extra point with 2:25 remaining.

Alabama fumbled and Tennessee recovered.

The Volunteers had hope, albeit false in variety.

66

1992
Alabama 17, Tennessee 10

IT WAS A WEEK of highly charged and severely strained emotions, to say the least, as Alabama and Tennessee moved toward their seventy-fifth meeting on the football field, played the game, and to the surprise of many observers, went in strikingly different directions.

Antonio Langham, an Alabama defensive halfback, looked at the recent success the Crimson Tide had experienced against its bitter rival and said, "We own Tennessee." That statement made bulletin boards in Knoxville.

Heath Shuler, a Tennessee quarterback, was asked about a strong Alabama defense and said, "We've got a great offensive line. They won't put a hand on me." That statement made bulletin boards in Tuscaloosa.

Alabama Coach Gene Stallings was so mad about the statement attributed to Langham—"It was taken out of context," he said—he banned Tennessee newspaper reporters from the Crimson Tide's practice the day before the game.

Shuler was mad, too, about the statement attributed to him. "I didn't say it exactly like that," he said.

From this mess Alabama and Tennessee emerged to play on October 17, 1992.

The Crimson Tide won, 17-10, to remain unbeaten and to rise in the national polls from a number four ranking. Alabama went on to win a national championship.

After the game, Langham apologized for his remark, then said an unidentified Tennessee player came up to him and said, "You're exactly right about you guys owning us."

It was the seventh win in a row for Alabama over Tennessee.

Crimson Tide players sang "Rocky Top" and "Sweet Home, Alabama" as they celebrated.

Shuler was sacked four times for 21 yards in losses. That helped Alabama limit Tennessee to 78 yards rushing. Then things got uglier.

As Tennessee Coach Johnny Majors was walking off of the playing field after the game, an angry Big Orange fan threw a cup of ice at him and struck him in the head.

That drew an angry response from Tennessee center Brian Spivey, who said, "For fans to dog Coach Majors like that, it's ridiculous. I know it's easy when you're sitting there looking down on the field to say, 'Why doesn't Coach Majors do this and why does Coach Majors do that?' Well, Coach Majors is doing all he can. He's coaching his butt off."

As it worked out, Majors did not complete the season. He was forced out of the position of coach and replaced by Phillip Fulmer, a former Tennessee offensive lineman and longtime assistant coach. The Volunteers completed the season with a 9-3 record, suffering only one more defeat, but the house was divided as The Third Saturday in October said farewell to one of its more honored combatants.

All of this came to pass after Alabama and Tennessee put on an entertaining show at Neyland Stadium, with both offenses pulling out all stops in a game with a low score.

Alabama raced to a 17-0 lead with about eight minutes remaining in the second quarter. Derrick Lassic, a running back who gained 142 yards on 33 carries, scored two touchdowns, both on one-yard runs. Michael Proctor kicked a 33-yard field goal in between and added two extra point kicks.

John Becksvoort kicked a 44-yard field goal for Tennessee with 4:20 remaining in the second quarter to cut the Crimson Tide lead to 17-3.

However, few fans watching thought the Volunteers had much of a chance of winning, even halfway through the game. The Crimson Tide had rushed for 214 yards and gained 229 yards in the first two quarters. Tennessee had gained 113.

Tennessee clawed back into serious contention early in the fourth quarter, when Shuler passed three yards to tight end David Horn for a touchdown and Becksvoort kicked the extra point. But the 17-10 score held up because Alabama played crushing defense and controlled the football with a rushing offense. The Crimson Tide had possession for almost 14 minutes more than Tennessee.

"They put the wood to us," said Todd Kelly, a Tennessee defensive end. "It surprised me. They ran it at us, hit us in the mouth, and knocked us off the ball."

Alabama managed to do that through the use of some nicely calculated deception.

Tennessee feared Crimson Tide wide receiver and kick returner David Palmer most. The Volunteers knew he often ran the football on reverses. They kept an eye on him.

Alabama countered by faking reverses, with Palmer in motion, running Lassic at the heart of the defense and, on occasion, giving Palmer the football on reverses. It was apparent the Crimson Tide had a strong arsenal with which to work.

"We knew they were good, but we didn't expect them to move the football up and down the field like that," said James Wilson, a Tennessee defensive end. "They executed better than we did, did more things right."

Palmer got his numbers on an afternoon when Lassic was the focal point of the Alabama offense. He had 157 yards on two rushes, three pass receptions, four punt returns, and two kickoff returns. That means he averaged more than 14 yards per touch.

Meanwhile, Tennessee opened up its offense to an extreme after being criticized a year earlier for a conservative attack against Alabama. The Volunteers passed from deep in their territory, often on first down and sometimes on all three downs, ran reverses, rolled out the quarterback on option runs and passes, and incredulously, attempted a scrum of sorts on the second half kickoff, an ultimate hidden ball trick that involved everybody on the receiving team.

For all of that, Tennessee got one touchdown and gained 194 yards—and the hidden ball trick on the kickoff return resulted in a Volunteer being tackled well inside the 20-yard line.

"We shot our best guns and lost," Fulmer said after the game.

As for Majors in his last postgame press conference after a Tennessee-Alabama game, he said, "I've been involved in a lot of brilliant, hardfought, tenacious football games and many Tennessee and Alabama games. But I don't know when I've seen the two teams play with more intensity, effort, mental application, and contact in my entire life.

"I congratulate Alabama. But I'm proud of our Tennessee team, too, for its effort."

67

1993
Tennessee 17, Alabama 17

COACH PHILLIP FULMER OFFERED an indication a college football rivalry between Alabama and Tennessee would be postured differently in the future with a pair of statements he made just before and a pair of statements he made just after the Crimson Tide and Volunteers played a game on October 16, 1993.

The new Tennessee leader was asked about the impact of seven consecutive losses to Alabama.

"This is a new season," Fulmer said. "What happened last year or for the previous six years before that shouldn't have any effect on this game, just as what happens this time won't affect next year's game."

Fulmer was asked about the tradition surrounding the grand old series.

"A victory over Alabama would mean a lot to us anytime," he said. "It would keep people in Tennessee happy, including those on our campus."

Fulmer led Tennessee for the first time in a game the Volunteers seemed destined to win. However, the result was a stunning 17-17 tie in front of 83,091 fans at Legion Field in Birmingham.

Trailing 17-9 and looking defeated, Alabama drove 82 yards in eleven plays for a touchdown, scoring with twenty-three seconds remaining in the game. The Crimson Tide made a two-point conversion to secure the deadlock.

"We played toe to toe with the defending national champions on their home field and they tied us," Fulmer said after the game. The emphasis was on "they tied us"—and that did not sound like something a man from a program that had not won in the rivalry since 1985 might say.

Then Fulmer said, "We'd welcome the opportunity to play Alabama again." He meant in the Southeastern Conference championship game at the end of that season, with the same players in action.

It was an inspiring game and few in-person observers or those watching by way of regional television believed Alabama would win over Tennessee or secure a tie.

Alabama led 3-0. Tennessee led 7-3 at the end of the first quarter.

The Crimson Tide cut the lead 7-6, then led 9-7 at halftime.

Tennessee led 10-9 after three quarters.

The Volunteers extended the lead to 17-9 in the first minute of the fourth quarter.

Then came the Alabama heroics.

Statistically, it was about as close as a tie. Tennessee gained 406 yards and Alabama gained 370 yards, although that is a bit skewed because the Crimson Tide had possession of the football about seven minutes more. The Volunteers had five turnovers, three lost fumbles, and two pass interceptions, and the Crimson Tide had two, one of each.

Both teams got some good breaks. One of the Tennessee lost fumbles was unforced and came at the Alabama one-yard line. The Crimson Tide missed two field goals. The Volunteers made a field goal after intercepting a pass at the Alabama 19-yard line.

All of that considered, it was far easier to see Alabama losing for the first time after twenty-eight consecutive wins, a sight not lost on numerous fans dressed in crimson who were in the parking lot when the Crimson Tide rallied to tie.

When he got in the huddle with the football at the Alabama 18-yard line, quarterback Jay Barker told his teammates, "I've got confidence in you. Have confidence in me. Give me some time to pass and we'll take it the length of the field for a touchdown."

Barker completed passes for 12, 15, 22, and 7 yards. Alabama was at the Tennessee 34-yard line.

On third down and four yards to go at the Tennessee 27-yard line, Barker passed to Kevin Lee for nine yards and a first down at the 18.

On fourth down and 10 yards to go, with 30 seconds remaining, Barker passed to Lee at the four-yard line. He lunged forward to within six inches of the goal line.

On the next play, Barker sneaked into the end zone. The score was 17-15.

Alabama inserted wide receiver David Palmer at quarterback, utilizing the wishbone formation, and Tennessee called a time-out. The Volunteers expected a pass attempt on the two-point conversion try.

But Palmer streaked around end and got into the end zone untouched to tie the game.

When Tennessee defensive end Horace Morris saw Palmer in the end zone, on his feet, he said, "Oh, my God, not again."

When asked to reflect a little more, Morris said, "They kept hitting us with quick passes. Next thing you know, they were upfield. I was saying, 'We gotta stop 'em . . . We gotta stop 'em.' But we didn't stop 'em."

When the game ended, neither team knew how to react, although there was more jubilance on the Alabama side of the playing field.

Tennessee had just lost the chance to end a dreadful streak of not winning against Alabama.

"We can't be happy about this," said Kelvin Moss, a Tennessee offensive guard. "It's hard to accept. We played the defending national champion and they were happy to get out with a tie."

Alabama had just lost the chance to established a Southeastern Conference record for consecutive wins.

"We had to score, so we did score—the touchdown and the two-point conversion," Palmer said. "We dug down and got something deep inside us. But, no, it's not like a victory. It's just a little better than a loss."

Nobody felt good.

Said Fulmer: "It was a great game with great plays. There were two outstanding teams going at each other's throats. This isn't a victory for Tennessee, rather a tie, because the scoreboard said we didn't win. I don't think any of my players feel like they won the game the way it turned out at the end."

But that was merely the end of one game played on one day. The National Collegiate Athletic Association changed the outcome when it placed Alabama on probation for rules violations. Part of the sanctions was the forfeiture of eight regular season victories and one regular season tie.

So, in retrospect, with the forfeiture that came much later figured in, Alabama went to Knoxville the following season with a 41-28-7 record in a series that had its last official tie on October 16, 1965. The score that year was 7-7 at Legion Field in Birmingham.

Unless another rules change is enacted, that will be the last tie in the series because overtime now determines the winner in games.

68

1994
Alabama 17, Tennessee 13

THE ROARING GREW MORE deafening with every play as Tennessee moved up the field late in the fourth quarter of a football game with Alabama at Neyland Stadium on October 15, 1994.

Most of the crowd of 96,856, a packed arena, sensed the dramatic end to a long-time drought, victory at last, even as the visitors were clinging to a small lead.

Alabama had scored a touchdown and extra point with 3:04 remaining in the game. The four-yard run by Sherman Williams and the extra point kick by Michael Proctor had given the Crimson Tide a 17-13 lead after Tennessee had led 13-10, thanks to a 22-yard field goal by John Becksvoort about four minutes earlier.

Suddenly, what had been a defensive struggle, 3-3 at halftime and 10-10 after three quarters, had become a wild affair.

Up the field came Tennessee, starting at its 21-yard line. Alabama had just marched 80 yards to score and the Volunteers were trying to answer.

Quarterback Peyton Manning was at the controls of the offense, a freshman on a mission. He passed for 17 yards, ran for nothing, ran for three yards and, on third down, passed for 17 yards. Joey Kent made both pass receptions, obviously the man of choice for the drive.

It was first down at the Alabama 42-yard line.

Manning was sacked for a six-yard loss and Tennessee took a time-out with 2:09 remaining.

Manning passed for 18 yards to Kent, Aaron Hayden ran for 16 yards and Manning passed for five yards to Kent. It was second down at the Alabama five-yard line and Big Orange fans were riotous.

James Stewart ran for two yards, Tennessee was penalized five yards for illegal procedure, and a Manning pass intended for Kent was knocked down by Alabama linebacker Michael Rogers.

Tennessee took a time-out with 1:07 remaining. The football was at the Alabama 12-yard line, fourth down, and Crimson Tide fans were chanting, too, ten thousand strong, in an effort to soften the roar of their rivals.

Manning was intercepted on a pass. But there was a yellow flag on the playing field. Alabama was offsides. Tennessee had one more chance.

With Alabama closely guarding Kent, Manning passed to Nilo Silvan. The football sailed out of his reach and, again, the Crimson Tide had won.

It was the fifth consecutive game between Alabama and Tennessee that had been decided by seven or fewer points, including the on the field tie a year earlier.

The Volunteers were getting closer. After all, they were inside the Alabama 10-yard line five times, with only 13 points to show for the effort.

But it still seemed as if they had a long way to go, especially after losing again on their home turf. A team with a 3-3 record, this time the underdog, had almost mastered a team with a 6-0 record.

This is how Mike Strange saw the game for the *Knoxville News-Sentinel:*

> Tennessee remains under Alabama's big crimson thumb for at least another year, maybe forever.
>
> Once again the Vols inched up to the brink of their most agonizing threshold, only to fall back for the ninth year in a row.
>
> The 10th-ranked Crimson Tide rallied in the fourth quarter for a 17-13 victory and the Tennessee partisans in a crowd of 96,856 filed out wondering when it will end.

Hayden would have told those questioners the pain and agony would be over in short order. After he had rushed for 145 yards and had caught two passes for 49 yards, in a losing cause, he said, "We showed we were the better team and they still won the game. It seems like that's the case every year. People can say what they want and Alabama knows it—we lost the game ourselves. They didn't beat us."

But that was a familiar refrain Alabama players, coaches, and fans found amusing. After all, the Crimson Tide had its stars, too, like quarterback Jay Barker, who played after an arm had been in a sling all week; Williams, who rushed for 142 yards on 26 carries; defensive halfback Tommy Johnson, who intercepted two passes; defensive halfback Cedric Samuel, who made 12 tackles; and defensive tackle Dameian Jeffries, who had three quarterback sacks.

Then there was the Crimson Tide's coach, Gene Stallings, who improved his overall record at Alabama to an astounding 37-9-1. His program was being scrutinized by the National Collegiate Athletic Association, creating distractions, and his quarterback was injured, but he kept his team focused.

"It was a tough, physical game in which we made defensive plays when we had to," Stallings said, looking back. "It was a game any football fan would enjoy, and it was the kind players remember. Our players handled the tough environment, the big and loud crowd, and a talented and inspired Tennessee team.

"Obviously, it was a game either team could have won. But we did win—at least that's what the scoreboard said."

Tennessee coach Phillip Fulmer told his players something just after the game that set the stage for the future of the series. He said, "I told our players to hold their heads high, to not make any excuses, to congratulate Alabama, and to go back to work. I told them I don't believe in jinxes."

Still, talk of hexes and the like continued in East Tennessee. Consider these words written by John Adams, sports columnist at the *Knoxville News-Sentinel:*

> When does a streak become something else? When does it become an era or a dynasty?
>
> Is nine winless seasons enough? Or must Alabama's dominance reach double figures before you refer to this as the Dark Orange Ages of UT football?
>
> Whatever you call it—streak, era or dynasty—you know it will end next year. Next year is always UT's year against Alabama.

After the loss in 1994, Kent was more troubled than most of the Volunteers. He was reared in Huntsville, Alabama. He said, "Losing to the Crimson Tide is harder on me than most people. I'm from down there. I have to live with this all year. I'm ready for this humiliation to end."

69

1995
Tennessee 41, Alabama 14

THE SMILE JOEY KENT flashed in the Tennessee dressing room after the game was as absolutely beautiful as the pass he caught on the first play had been breathtakingly pivotal to a much-needed win over Alabama.

Kent, a Huntsville, Alabama, native, picked up where he had left off about one year earlier, by feeling humiliation and doing something about it. The wide receiver caught a pass thrown by Peyton Manning on the first play, 14 yards up the field, and turned it into an 80-yard touchdown that set the tempo for a 41-14 victory by Tennessee over the Crimson Tide.

"It has been a long time coming," Kent said between grins about the first Tennessee victory over Alabama since 1985. "I can't tell you what it means to me and everybody else associated with our program."

Kent did not have to explain. Just after the game, Tennessee Governor Don Sundquist contacted the Volunteers' coach, Phillip Fulmer, to let him know the following Monday had been proclaimed Tennessee Football Day in the state. In a statement the politician said, "This is a class team and a class coach and they deserve all of the credit for this win." To the victorious coach he said, "I want you to know just how proud we all are of you."

Fulmer was as surprised as Sundquist and crew were gratified, although not because his team had won. He had planned to let his offense throw the football a lot, but he had not counted on three touchdowns, three extra point kicks and a 21-0 lead after the first quarter, nor a 28-7 lead at halftime. He liked his players, thought they were improving each week, but he did not anticipate such dominance of Alabama at Legion Field in Birmingham in front of 83,091 fans, all except about 10,000 wearing crimson apparel.

"Coming out early and setting the tempo was important, but I hadn't anticipated it would happen like it did," Fulmer said, reflecting on the convincing victory. "I never looked at our winless streak against Alabama as a jinx or anything like that. But there was a lot of frustration lifted by the win."

Manning, then a sophomore, said it was customary for Kent to come up to him during a game and say, "Hey, Peyton, let's hook up." But he recalled the wide receiver telling him that just before the opening kickoff.

Kent caught the football and broke clear in the middle of the field. He ran untouched into the end zone. After Jeff Hall kicked the extra point, Tennessee led 7-0 with only fourteen seconds elapsed.

"That was huge," Manning said about the first touchdown.

"We wanted to strike fast, to go to the lead like they had so many times against Tennessee in recent years," said Kent, who caught five passes for 117 yards. "When I saw their defense at the line of scrimmage on the first play, I knew it was there for a big gain. I wasn't counting on 80 yards and six points."

Six points became seven, seven became fourteen, and fourteen became twenty-one, all within the first ten minutes, and the romp was on. Tennessee scored on its second possession, with Manning passing for 25 yards to Marcus Nash, and, after an Alabama fumble, on its third possession, with Manning running one yard.

The Volunteers had gained 197 yards on a vaunted Crimson Tide defense in less than a quarter of The Third Saturday in October installment that, because of television, was played for the first time since 1928 on the second weekend of that month.

An honored tradition died because the Southeastern Conference sold it for television money.

Alabama dominance took a heavy jolt because Tennessee had a far superior team.

The score matched that from a Tennessee victory over Alabama in 1969. It was only the fourteenth time the Crimson Tide had surrendered forty or more points in a game. Interestingly, the last time that had happened was when the Volunteers scored forty-one to win by seven points in 1983 at Legion Field.

The victory was particularly pleasing to David Cutcliffe, the offensive coordinator at Tennessee. He was a Birmingham native who signed to play football at Alabama, but never did because of an injury. He had seen the Volunteers come close to victory many times.

"This is my seventh trip to Birmingham for a game against Alabama," Cutcliffe said. "It was getting old.

"I played this game over a hundred times in my mind, sorting through strategy, but I never envisioned us leading Alabama 21-0 after one quarter.

"Peyton Manning got it done. He sees the field better in presnap situations than anybody I've seen."

Manning had a big night. He completed 20 of 29 passes for 329 yards as Tennessee piled up 496 yards in offense against the Crimson Tide.

"I knew the importance of Tennessee winning," Manning said. "I probably watched a little too much film of Alabama."

There was a mission.

The mission was accomplished.

The ten-year itch was scratched, or so said Mike Strange while writing in the *Knoxville News-Sentinel*:

Imagine that. After all these years, beating Alabama wasn't so hard after all.

Sixth-ranked Tennessee ended a nine-year winless streak against its greatest rival and nemesis, not with a whimper, but with a resounding bang.

The final count was 41-14 and the Vols were in control from the opening snap until the last chorus of 'Rocky Top' reverberated through Legion Field.

In the end the 10,000 or so Big Orange fans didn't want to leave. They cheered Coach Phillip Fulmer, who gained the most important victory of his career. They saluted sophomore quarterback Peyton Manning, who was never better.

"From my vantage point, we got what we deserved," said Alabama Coach Gene Stallings. "We didn't seem to know what we were doing out there."

Manning did. He was 20-of-29 passing for 329 yards as Tennessee mashed the Southeastern Conference's top-ranked defense for 496 yards and scored the most points Alabama has surrendered since Tennessee's 41-34 win in 1983.

The points came in this manner.

After the Volunteers bolted to their 21-0 advantage, Alabama scored to cut the lead to 21-7 with 6:10 remaining in the second quarter. Chad Key scored on a two-yard pass from Freddie Kitchens, who was substituting at quarterback for Brian Burgdorf. Michael Proctor kicked the extra point.

Then Tennessee scored a crowning blow, albeit lethal, when Manning passed 30 yards to Nash for a touchdown 43 seconds before halftime. The extra point was kicked by Hall and the Volunteers were cruising.

After a defensive struggle through most of the third quarter, Alabama scored when Montoya Madden ran 15 yards and Proctor kicked the extra point. The score was 28-14 and Crimson Tide fans hoped for a miracle.

Boom.

On the first play after the kickoff, Jay Graham ran 75 yards for a touchdown, untouched, and Hall kicked the extra point to give Tennessee a 35-14 lead with 1:43 remaining in the third quarter.

Hall kicked two field goals in the fourth quarter, from 25 and 37 yards, and the final margin was fixed.

John Adams wrote in the *Knoxville News-Sentinel*:

It was a Manning against boys.

Tennessee quarterback Peyton Manning established his dominance on the first snap. After that, it was child's play.

It was one pass after another that Alabama couldn't defend. It was one play after another that Alabama couldn't stop.

There was no Alabama quarterback running off the bench into the headlines. There was no fourth-quarter magic. There wasn't a hint of Alabama dominance.

Instead, there was relief among Tennessee players, to go with joy after the demon had finally been silenced.

"This is an incredible feeling," said Scott Galyon, a Tennessee linebacker. "I was surprised at how we were able to put them away."

70

1996
Tennessee 20, Alabama 13

THROUGHOUT ITS HISTORY THE football series between Alabama and Tennessee has been filled with memories of seemingly meaningless plays that have proved to be the difference in victory and defeat— action that did not directly impact the scoreboard, like a blocked field goal, a missed field goal, a goal-line stand, or a poorly thrown pass.

Alabama fans had a few of those to ponder after Tennessee defeated the Crimson Tide, 20-13, on October 26, 1996, the fourth Saturday of the month. Similarly, Big Orange fans had an explosive touchdown run on which to smile.

The first example is what happened to the Alabama defense and offense during the second quarter, with the Crimson Tide leading 3-0 after outplaying the Volunteers from the opening kickoff. To fully understand the impact, a person must know the visitors went on to a 13-0 lead in the third quarter before the Big Orange mustered a mighty rally to win.

With 6:23 remaining in the second quarter, with the Alabama defense having its way, Tennessee quarterback Peyton Manning attempted to pass from the Volunteers' 20-yard line. He was sacked hard by Alabama linebacker Ralph Staten, causing him to fumble. The football was picked up at the six-yard line by defensive end Chris Hood, who could have walked into the end zone. Instead, he stumbled and fell to the ground at the three-yard line. Later, he said he thought he had crossed the goal line.

On first down Alabama halfback Dennis Riddle was tackled by Jonathan Brown for a two-yard loss. One second down, Riddle was tackled by Billy Ratcliff for a one-yard loss. On third down, a Freddie Kitchens pass was incomplete, broken up by Raymond Austin. On fourth down, a 19-yard field goal attempt by Brian Cunningham was missed, deflected by Leonard Little.

It does not take a math major to figure the significance of that minute and a half. In other words, Tennessee would have been hard-pressed to come from behind if the Alabama advantage had been 20-0 instead of 13-0 in the latter stages of the third quarter.

But Tennessee did rally in incredible fashion in front of 106,700 fans. With 4:26 remaining in the third quarter, Manning completed a 54-yard touchdown pass to Joey Kent. The extra point kick was missed. The score was 13-6.

With 9:41 remaining in the fourth quarter, Jay Graham ran five yards for a touchdown and Jeff Hall kicked the extra point to tie the game. That opportunity came after Terry Fair intercepted a pass at the Tennessee one-yard line and returned it to the end zone. A penalty, however, nullified the score and made the official return 56 yards to the Alabama 43.

With 2:17 remaining in the fourth quarter, Graham created an explosion in Neyland Stadium when he ran 79 yards for a touchdown. The extra point by Hall gave Tennessee its only lead of the game, by the final margin.

By that point on a rainy afternoon, Alabama had felt like it had suffered through enough misery. But the Crimson Tide was moved to add to it.

On its final possession, Alabama started at its 22-yard line and drove to a first down at the Tennessee 11. Kitchens was incomplete on three consecutive passes, two that sailed over the heads of open receivers in the end zone. He fumbled on fourth down when he was belted by Little, with the football recovered by Brown.

"I've never made a play like that," Little said. "It was the greatest feeling in my life, ending a victory over Alabama in that way."

As Alabama had on numerous occasions in the past, Tennessee won against long odds. The Volunteers, 4-1 entering the game, finished the season with a 10-2 record. Alabama, 7-0 entering the game, finished the season with a 10-3 record.

For Graham the victory marked the second consecutive year he had burned Alabama with a long touchdown run. He considered the second more meaningful than the first.

"The Alabama defense was bunched in the middle," Graham said, reflecting on the play that gave Tennessee the victory and kept the first overtime in the history of the series from materializing. "We had the right play called at the right time, after the Alabama defense had played great the entire game.

"I saw a big hole, a massive hole, which is a credit to our offensive linemen. I just got through there and set my sights on the checkerboard [painted end zone].

"After I scored, I thanked the Lord for giving me the strength and ability to get to the end zone.

"It was the biggest run of my career."

Tennessee rallied after Coach Phillip Fulmer made a simple statement at halftime that proved prophetic. He told his players, "There are one or two crucial plays out there to be made. Let's make them."

After the game, Fulmer was ecstatic, although softspoken. He said, "This win is special because it is Alabama. It was a great win. It was two evenly matched teams. It was a classic defensive battle. It ranks right up there with a lot of big games. It was the best defensive effort I've seen in all my years at Tennessee."

Manning said the Alabama defense was the best he had faced during his three years at Tennessee. "It was a tough game throughout," he said. "We won because our defense held on for four quarters."

Although nobody knew it at the time, the Alabama-Tennessee game in 1996 was the last for Crimson Tide coach Gene Stallings. He announced his impending resignation just before the final game of the regular season, a 24-23 victory over Auburn. He led the team during a 45-30 loss to Florida in the Southeastern Conference championship game and during a 17-14 win over Michigan in the Florida Citrus Bowl.

Counting the forfeit ordered by the National Collegiate Athletic Association after the tie in 1993, Stallings had a 4-3 record against Tennessee. Counting only the outcomes of games as they were settled on the playing field, he had a 70-16-1 record while leading the Crimson Tide.

71

1997
Tennessee 38, Alabama 21

THE PEYTON MANNING FOR the Heisman Trophy campaign was in place and was picking up momentum. The quarterback had just led Tennessee to a 38-21 victory over Alabama on October 18, 1997, the third win in a row for the Big Orange over the Crimson Tide. Fans wearing orange did not want to leave Legion Field in Birmingham. The Pride of the Southland Band kept playing "Rocky Top" for maybe the one thousandth time.

To get the picture up close, let us turn to Gary Lundy, a sportswriter at the *Knoxville News-Sentinel*. He was covering Manning like a blanket that evening. He wrote:

> His place assured in Tennessee football history as the only quarterback to defeat Alabama three times, Peyton Manning climbed to the fourth step of a ladder in front of the UT band and played maestro.
>
> As the band played "Rocky Top" at Legion Field, Manning grinned and directed the musicians to cap the wildest postgame celebration of his career after leading the Vols to a 38-21 victory. In completing 23 of 37 passes for 304 yards, his seventh consecutive 300-yard game, he took a giant step toward winning the Heisman Trophy.
>
> "I need to work on my band directing," he joked. "I knew the words and the rhythm of the song. I've heard it a few times. It was a little off beat, though. I heard a guy in the back was off key and it was my fault. I'm not as good at directing as I should be."

365

Manning said he wanted to salute the UT section of fans and show how much he appreciated their support during his career.

"Obviously, I'm prejudiced, but our fans are the greatest in the world," he said. "To have a great section of orange in a stadium of crimson is special and it was important to go over there and give thanks to them. Legion Field is what college football is all about. There have been so many great games and great players here. This is huge for our seniors.

"For me personally, it's special because I grew up around SEC football. It's a great night for Tennessee. To beat Alabama three times and to win twice here in Birmingham is something I'll always remember."

Manning headed for the locker room once, but turned back to salute the UT fans again and tossed his cap into the stands.

"It's just a great feeling to be a part of a program to beat Alabama three years in a row," a beaming Manning said after giving his dad, Archie, a big hug.

Manning showed up in the interview room wearing a "Waitin' on Peyton" shirt he said "just showed up in my locker."

"It's the only dry shirt I had," Manning said with a laugh.

"I know Alabama has lost a couple of games, but Alabama will be back. It's a great football state. This is one of those games you'll always remember you played in. It's fun. But it's more fun to say you won."

The fact is Alabama was snoring as Tennessee was roaring. The loss was the third consecutive within the Southeastern Conference, the first time that had happened since 1984. For the first time in six seasons the Crimson Tide was not ranked in the national top twenty-five.

It was obvious to people who watched the game that Tennessee was coming on, getting better by the year, as Alabama was fading.

More proof could be found in the echoes coming out the dressing rooms after the game, including those of two coaches who were familiar with the series.

Alabama was in its first season under Coach Mike DuBose, who had played defensive end for the Crimson Tide in victories over Tennessee in 1972, 1973, and 1974. His team was 3-2 entering the game. The record at the end of the season was 4-7.

"My hat's off to Tennessee for winning like it did," DuBose said. "Obviously, we have a long way to go before we're in that category again, in that class again.

"We're hurting right now, as we should be after a loss to Tennessee."

A few minutes earlier, Alabama defensive halfback Fernando Bryant said, "Tennessee is the better team now. I'll admit that."

Tennessee was in its fifth full season under Coach Phillip Fulmer, who had played offensive guard for the Volunteers when they defeated Alabama in 1969 and 1970 and lost to the Crimson Tide in 1971. His team was 4-1 entering the game. The record at the end of the season was 11-2. The only major disappointment was Manning not winning the Heisman Trophy.

"We've got a great senior class, as well as some outstanding underclassmen," Fulmer said. "It's a senior class that can say it won three times over Alabama. There aren't many players in Tennessee history who can say that. That should be enough said about those players."

The victory by Tennessee cut the Alabama advantage in the series to 42-31-7. It was complete domination.

Alabama led 6-0 early on, but Tennessee took a 7-6 lead at the end of the first quarter, a 21-6 lead at halftime, and a 31-14 lead at the end of the third quarter.

Tennessee gained 393 yards and averaged 5.7 per play. Alabama gained 225 yards, only 72 rushing, and the first ten runs gained six yards.

The Volunteers were talented and they were ready to play.

That goes back to the Fulmer influence because there was a time when Tennessee players got too worked up for games against Alabama and played tight. His approach to the long-running rivalry was to prepare well and perform well—leave the hoopla to others.

Of course, that does not mean a famous quarterback cannot direct a band after his labor is complete.

72

1998
Tennessee 35, Alabama 18

TENNESSEE FOUND A SUPERB answer for every perplexing question that surfaced during the 1998 college football season.

The Volunteers turned every proposed crisis into a conquest, a 12-0 record that led to the first consensus national championship for Tennessee since 1951.

Peyton Manning had graduated. But Tee Martin was still in the fold at quarterback.

The defensive unit was too slow and too weak. At one point, opponents went eleven quarters without scoring a touchdown.

The special teams were not talented enough to turn in big plays. Yes, but only for a while.

The running game was in trouble because Jamal Lewis was injured. Enter Travis Henry and Travis Stephens to pick up the load, plus a lot more.

The team as a whole was not seasoned enough to handle the rigors of tight games decided in the fourth quarter. That notion was put to rest quickly, when the Volunteers won in the fourth quarter at Syracuse in the first game, 34-33; in overtime against Florida in the second game, 20-17; and in the fourth quarter at Auburn in the fourth game, 17-9; and the dramatics continued in a victory over Arkansas in the ninth game and a victory over Florida State in the Fiesta Bowl.

Oh, let us not forget Tennessee defeated Alabama, 35-18, on October 24, 1998. That was an afternoon when all of the above came into play as the Volunteers won over the Crimson Tide for the fourth time in a row, matching their longest streak of dominance in a series that started in 1901.

There was not as much hype as usual surrounding the game with Alabama at Neyland Stadium, because the visitors were 4-2 and had not impressed anybody and the home team was 6-0 and was ranked third in the nation. But it was the Crimson Tide the Volunteers had to face, which had Coach Phillip Fulmer fuming a little not long before the opening kickoff.

Fulmer thought his players were being too passive in their approach to The Third Saturday in October, which was being staged on the fourth for the sake of television money. He cleared the dressing room of bystanders and let them know they would have to play harder than they appeared ready to.

Fulmer had an attentive audience, no doubt, as he should have after leading Tennessee to 10-2, 8-4, 11-1, 10-2, and 11-2 records during his first five full seasons as leader of the program.

Had that not been the case, Alabama might have recorded a major upset. After all, with shifts in momentum considered, as has always been important in the hotly contested series, the Crimson Tide was much closer to doing that than the final score indicates.

Tennessee started fast, about as expected, driving 76 yards in seven plays for a touchdown and extra point on its first possession. Martin scored on a one-yard run and Jeff Hall kicked the Volunteers to a 7-0 lead with 14:48 remaining in the first quarter.

Alabama got a 41-yard field goal from Ryan Pflugner with 4:48 remaining in the first quarter.

Martin ran five yards for a touchdown with 4:43 remaining in the second quarter, at the end of a 77-yard, 12-play drive. Hall kicked the extra point and Tennessee led, 14-3, at halftime.

The Volunteers amassed 200 yards during the first half and limited the Crimson Tide to 119. But there was a bit of an uneasy feeling among 107,289 fans because Alabama seemed to be hanging around in sneaky fashion.

Then with 5:11 remaining in the third quarter, uneasiness grew when Shaun Alexander of Alabama ran 44 yards for a touchdown and

Andrew Zow passed to Quincy Jackson for a two-point conversion. The Tennessee lead was three points, 14-11, and the Volunteers were appearing a bit sluggish on both offense and defense.

Meanwhile, confidence was growing on the Alabama side of the playing field. The Crimson Tide had missed a field goal on its first possession of the second half, after driving 41 yards, as had Tennessee, and the two rivals had played almost two and two-thirds quarters and the total yardage gained was about even.

Enter Tennessee wide receiver and kick returner Peerless Price— after a conference on the sideline during which Fulmer told the kick-off return team, "Let's get a big one."

Price took the kickoff at the goal line, broke through a wedge, got to the sideline and ran into the end zone. He spent most of the 100 yards in front of the Alabama bench, which added to the stabbing effect. The extra point kick gave Tennessee a 21-11 lead twenty seconds after the Crimson Tide seemed to have seized control.

"I knew momentum was shifting their way," Price said about his thoughts just before the kickoff return.

"The blocking was great in the wedge. It gave me just enough room to break clear in the middle and then get to the sideline. I hit the seam hard, like our coaches tell us to on a kickoff return. After that it was just a matter of outracing everybody to the end zone.

"Then after getting mobbed and knocked down in the end zone, I saw a yellow flag on the field. The officials were having a conference. My heart sank. Then I saw them call Alabama for an illegal block.

"Thank God that flag was on them because the game was sort of hanging in the balance, at least I thought.

"That's how it is against Alabama. You never can count them out, not totally, until all the time is gone."

After that turn of events, a huge momentum swing, Tennessee put down the sword and went to the hammer.

With 12:56 remaining in the fourth quarter, Henry scored on a one-yard run and Hall kicked an extra point to extend the lead to 28-11. The Volunteers drove 84 yards in eleven plays to score.

Zow ran two yards for a touchdown and Pflugner kicked the extra point with 6:14 remaining in the fourth quarter to cut the lead to 28-18.

Henry scored on a five-yard run and Hall kicked the extra point with 54 seconds remaining to fix the final margin.

By that point it was merely a question of whether Tennessee would try to score another touchdown or run out the clock. Fulmer considered the options and, rightfully so, concluded power ratings are important to a team chasing a national championship.

After the game, Fulmer said, "We're trying to win a championship any way we can. This game hasn't lost any luster. This wasn't just another football game because you can never underestimate Alabama.

"I thought Alabama played extremely hard. There weren't any turnovers on either side and that made for a hard-hitting game. Our team kept its focus after we had a heart-to-heart talk before the game. Our players did a great job.

"The biggest play in the game was Peerless Price's kickoff return. There was a big momentum change just before that and a big momentum change just after we got that touchdown."

Price exited The Third Saturday in October rivalry with a perfect record against the Crimson Tide, four wins in four tries.

"I'm 4-0 against Alabama, but I'm glad I don't have to play them any more," Price said in the dressing room after the game. "We've been a little more talented than them in recent years, but they've given us some great games."

73

1999
Tennessee 21, Alabama 7

THE SETTING WAS FRESH and breathtakingly beautiful when Tennessee and Alabama got together for their annual college football game on October 23, 1999. The only problem was the date, the fourth Saturday in the month, and that was more troubling to traditionalists because of the historic nature of the contest about be played.

For the first time in almost seven decades Tennessee was visiting Tuscaloosa, Alabama. The Crimson Tide won on October 18, 1930, 18-6, in that meeting. That was two years after the Volunteers had won, 15-13, on the Alabama campus on October 20, 1928, in the first of a multitude of consecutive games between the rivals that were played on The Third Saturday in October.

No longer would Alabama host Tennessee at Legion Field in Birmingham, the old stadium that was once known as the football capital of the South because of the many great games it hosted.

The new venue was aged Bryant-Denny Stadium, a spectacular facility that had been remodeled to make it one of the more attractive arenas in the nation.

The change to Tuscaloosa was welcomed by almost everybody, including Tennessee players, coaches, and fans, because Legion Field was worn out and the atmosphere there was not as crisp as that found in a campus environment.

The weather was almost ideal, 62 degrees with skies crystal clear. There was a wind factor, with gusts between ten and twenty miles per hour, and that would become important as the game progressed.

After several years in which Tennessee seemed to have the more talented team—some observers thought that was the case for an entire decade—Alabama appeared to be on equal footing with the Volunteers. The Big Orange had a 4-1 record, after a 23-21 loss to Florida, and the Crimson Tide had a 5-1 record, after a 29-28 loss to Louisiana Tech.

Thousands of fans from both sides arrived early, about four and a half hours before the opening kickoff, and they mingled on the campus quadrangle. They listened to music. They shared food. They swapped a million memories from games between Alabama and Tennessee.

Big Orange supporters talked about the most recent four, all victories. Crimson Tide supporters talked about two more dominant streaks, eleven straight victories between 1971 and 1981, and nine games without defeat on the playing field between 1986 and 1994. The tie in 1993 that was forfeited was considered official by some fans and not official by some fans.

Therein lies the beauty of the Tennessee-Alabama series. The fans normally squabble hard for about three hours a year, as games are being played, then shake hands and move on. Streaks are joyous and painful, no doubt, depending on the points of view, but mutual respect normally prevails.

That was what looked so wholesome in Tuscaloosa before the game was played and during it, when normally subdued Alabama fans found their voices magnified by the moment at hand. They were not quieted in total until about midway through the fourth quarter when Tennessee scored a touchdown and extra point to take a 21-7 lead, which was the final score.

After a scoreless first quarter, Alabama took a 7-0 lead with 13:55 remaining in the second quarter. Shaun Alexander scored on a 26-yard pass from Andrew Zow and Ryan Pflugner kicked the extra point. The Crimson Tide drove 99 yards in fourteen plays, an impressive march that delighted most of the crowd of 86,689, the largest ever assembled for a sports event in the state.

Tennessee bounced back. With 5:14 remaining in the second quarter, quarterback Tee Martin ran six yards for a touchdown and

Alex Walls kicked the extra point. The Volunteers drove 60 yards in eleven plays. The Big Orange made a first down on fourth down at the Crimson Tide nine-yard line, with Jamal Lewis diving over the line of scrimmage for two yards.

The Tennessee drive got a jump start because of a 30-yard punt, the first evidence of the wind as it related to an impact on the game.

The score at halftime was 7-7. Alabama had gained 146 yards. Tennessee had gained 102 yards.

The first half had been made more interesting because of injuries sustained by the starting quarterbacks. Zow was on the sideline and Martin was on the sideline. It looked like both teams might have to play the remainder of the game with substitutes, Joey Mathews for Tennessee and Tyler Watts for Alabama.

Martin came back and starred.

Zow sat awhile, came back and struggled.

Tennessee took a 14-7 lead with 11:13 remaining in the third quarter when Martin passed 43 yards to David Martin, and Walls kicked the extra point. The drive covered 57 yards and took only four plays.

Again, the drive got a jump start when an Alabama punt traveled only 28 yards.

Alabama missed a golden opportunity, actually a cinch chance to tie the game late in the third quarter. On third down at the Crimson Tide 46-yard line, Zow passed to a wide open Alexander at about the Tennessee 20. He juggled the football and dropped it. He would have trotted into the end zone.

As it had often in recent years, Tennessee hammered it way to the touchdown that locked up the game. The Volunteers marched 84 yards in eleven plays, a convincing drive, and Martin scored on a 21-yard run and Walls kicked the extra point with 8:26 remaining in the game.

Alabama had time.

But the Crimson Tide was shorthanded because Zow was too immobile to make an impact passing the football, and Tennessee was too tough to run against with any degree of consistency.

The star of the game was Martin, a Mobile, Alabama, native who raised his record as the starting quarterback at Tennessee to 18-1. He had directed the Volunteers to a national championship one year earlier. Later, he would have a street named for him on campus. On this afternoon he rushed nine times for 49 yards, crucial plays, and he completed 11 of 18 passes for 143 yards.

"Tee Martin is a warrior," said Tennessee coach Phillip Fulmer. "He's a winner. There was a question as to whether he'd come back into the game in the second half. But he came right back. He's a good worker and the good Lord shone down on him in a big way."

Fulmer said his team was in a good mood the evening before the game and adopted a "why not us" attitude in the national championship chase.

That did not happen. The Volunteers had some slippage and completed the season with a 9-3 record.

In fact, it was Alabama that finished strong. The Crimson Tide won the Southeastern Conference championship with a victory over Florida, 34-7, and advanced to the Orange Bowl, where it lost to Michigan in overtime, 35-34, to complete a 10-3 record.

But while reflecting on a solid season, Alabama was left to contemplate five consecutive losses to Tennessee, the first time that had happened.

"I think the news media makes more of that than we do," Fulmer said. "Each game is a different challenge. It doesn't matter from year to year."

That was from the victors' point of view.

"This was another disappointing loss to an outstanding football program," said Mike DuBose, the Alabama coach.

DuBose knew his team had squandered a terrific opportunity to end the losing streak. He knew he and his players would have an entire year to think about that.

74

2000
Tennessee 20, Alabama 10

Perhaps what happened in a dressing room at Neyland Stadium was a fitting conclusion to the sixth consecutive Tennessee victory over Alabama in a college rivalry that has been as streaky as it has been dramatic.

After the Volunteers won over the Crimson Tide, 20-10, on October 21, 2000, Coach Phillip Fulmer rewarded his seniors by giving them game footballs. His logic, it could be said, was if Alabama can smoke cigars for more than a decade, from 1971 through 1981, then our players should be able to collect something larger and more long-lasting as keepsakes.

So the footballs disappeared quickly, stuffed in duffle bags, stuck under coats, and put inside travel bags, after Tennessee stole three on the playing field by intercepting two passes and recovering one fumble.

Come to think of it, one pass interception came at the Tennessee 33-yard line, with Tad Golden doing the honors, one pass interception came at the Volunteers' 32-yard line, with Teddy Gaines doing the honors, and the fumble recovery came at the Big Orange's 10-yard line, with Willie Miles doing the hitting and Kevin Burnett doing the fetching of the loose football.

No wonder Alabama appeared so ready to go home with 3:35 remaining in the game that it punted the football to Tennessee despite being behind by the final margin.

Two frustrated teams clashed, Tennessee with an uncustomary 2-3 record and Alabama with a 3-3 record, and the losers went home bewildered after having a decent chance to become the winners. In fact, the Crimson Tide did not win another game, finishing 3-8, which was the end of the line for coach Mike DuBose. The Volunteers finished 8-4, which included a loss to Kansas State in the Cotton Bowl.

Tennessee went to the lead quickly. Casey Clausen passed 23 yards to Cedrick Wilson and Alex Walls kicked the extra point with 4:26 remaining in the first quarter.

Walls kicked a 31-yard field goal with 4:52 remaining in the second quarter to extend the lead to 10-0.

After one half, Alabama had gained 71 yards, including 5 on 14 rushes. Tennessee had gained 139 yards, 96 on the 11-for-17 passing of Clausen, who was making his first start at quarterback.

Ultimately, the statistical war tightened as Alabama seemed to have the better of things in the second half, although the scoreboard called it even. Also, it was pivotal that the Crimson Tide finished with 44 yards rushing after entering the contest as the Southeastern Conference leader in that category.

Both teams scored 10 points in the third quarter.

Alabama got its points on a 50-yard field goal by Neal Thomas, a 17-yard touchdown pass from Andrew Zow to Jason McAddley, and a Thomas extra point kick.

Tennessee got its points on a three-yard touchdown pass from Clausen to Wilson, an extra point kick by Walls, and a 28-yard field goal by Walls.

Only a hint of an Alabama rally in the second half, when misfortune plagued the Crimson Tide, kept it from being the most uninspiring Third Saturday in October in recent memory.

But there are some important facts to ponder.

Tennessee cut the Alabama lead in the series to 42-34-7. The Crimson Tide left the fray with a 19-18-1 record in Knoxville, a 21-14-6 record in Birmingham, and a 2-2 record in Tuscaloosa.

The teams left Neyland Stadium with Tennessee having produced an 11-9 record against Alabama in the most recent two decades. That includes a forfeit after a tie.

Tennessee became only the second team to defeat Alabama six consecutive times. Sewanee did that between 1896 and 1911.

So Alabama and Tennessee completed the millennium, the official version, and are about to embark on a new one.

The last quarter of a century has seen the programs change, the Crimson Tide more drastically than the Volunteers.

Tennessee has had two coaches since 1977, Johnny Majors and Phillip Fulmer.

Alabama has had six during that same time period, Paul "Bear" Bryant, Ray Perkins, Bill Curry, Gene Stallings, Mike DuBose, and now Dennis Franchione.

Fulmer enters the next round against the Crimson Tide with an 84-18 record at Tennessee. He is 7-1 against Alabama.

Frachione enters the next round against the Volunteers as a new man on the block, albeit a serious enough student of Deep South football to know what the treasured series means to players, coaches, and fans on both sides.